JSP™ and Tag Libraries for Web Development

Contents at a Glance

JSP™ and Tag Libraries for Web Development

Wellington L.S. da Silva

New Riders

www.newriders.com

201 West 103rd Street, Indianapolis, Indiana 46290
An Imprint of Pearson Education
Boston • Indianapolis • London • Munich • New York • San Francisco

JSP™ and Tag Libraries for Web Development

International Standard Book Number: 0-7357-1095-3

Library of Congress Catalog Card Number: *00-111217*

05 04 03 02 01   7 6 5 4 3 2 1

Interpretation of the printing code: The rightmost double-digit number is the year of the book's printing; the rightmost single-digit number is the number of the book's printing. For example, the printing code 02-1 shows that the first printing of the book occurred in 2002.

Printed in the United States of America

Trademarks

Warning and Disclaimer

Publisher
David Dwyer

Associate Publisher
Stephanie Wall

Managing Editor
Kristy Knoop

Acquisitions Editor
Ann Quinn

Development Editor
Laura Loveall

Product Marketing Manager
Stephanie Layton

Publicity Manager
Susan Nixon

Project Editors
John Rahm
Stacia Mellinger

Copy Editor
Krista Hansing

Senior Indexer
Cheryl Lenser

Manufacturing Coordinator
Jim Conway

Book Designer
Louisa Klucznik

Cover Designer
Brainstorm Design, Inc.

Cover Production
Aren Howell

Proofreaders
Debbie Williams
Katherine Shull

Composition
Deborah Hudson

To Ana Paula, my most beloved daughter.

TABLE OF CONTENTS

About the Author

Wellington L. S. da Silva has been working in application development for the last 12 years, mostly with client/server applications in a diversity of environments from mainframe computers to local area networks. He has always been involved in prospecting and discussing new technologies. Since 1998, he has been developing Servlet API–based applications and has been working with the Apache Software Foundation Java Open Source projects.

About the Technical Reviewers

These reviewers contributed their considerable hands-on expertise to the entire development process for *JSP and Tag Libraries for Web Development*. As the book was being written, these dedicated professionals reviewed all the material for technical content, organization, and flow. Their feedback was critical to ensuring that *JSP and Tag Libraries for Web Development* fits our reader's need for the highest-quality technical information.

Jim Michael has more than 10 years of experience in information technology as a developer, analyst, and architect. He has developed applications for Internet e-commerce, competitive intelligence, data mining, repair tracking, and automatic identification technologies. He has been a longtime researcher in artificial intelligence and holds a master's degree from Georgia State University. His current work is in the area of speech-recognition technologies and voice-data convergence.

Piroz Mohseni is the president of Bita Technologies, focusing on business improvement through specialized training and effective usage of technology. His areas of interest include enterprise Java, XML, and mobile applications.

Acknowledgments

This book benefits greatly from the comments, corrections, and criticisms provided by the technical reviewers: Piroz Mohseni and Jim Michael, who reviewed the manuscripts during the course of writing this book. Naturally, any errors that remain are my own.

The staff at New Riders is responsible for turning my scribblings into the finished work you hold in your hands. Stephanie Wall is my Associate Publisher, first Karen Wachs and then Ann Quinn were my Acquisition Editors, and they all helped me get under way and took lava-hot heat when I missed deadlines. Laura Loveall, my Development Editor, helped me with the thousands of details that separate free writing from serious writing. For them and all the others, my deepest thanks.

Most of all, I want to express my appreciation to my wife, Ita, for putting up with this dream come true, and for her understanding and patience on everything.

Tell Us What You Think

As the reader of this book, you are the most important critic and commentator. We value your opinion and want to know what we're doing right, what we could do better, what areas you'd like to see us publish in, and any other words of wisdom you're willing to pass our way.

As the Associate Publisher for New Riders Publishing, I welcome your comments. You can fax, email, or write me directly to let me know what you did or didn't like about this book—as well as what we can do to make our books stronger.

Please note that I cannot help you with technical problems related to the topic of this book, and that due to the high volume of mail I receive, I might not be able to reply to every message.

When you write, please be sure to include this book's title and author as well as your name and phone or fax number. I will carefully review your comments and share them with the author and editors who worked on the book.

Fax: 317-581-4663
Email: stephanie.wall@newriders.com
Mail: Stephanie Wall
          Associate Publisher
          New Riders Publishing
          201 West 103rd Street
          Indianapolis, IN 46290 USA

Introduction

Tag libraries are a recent technology built on top of the Servlet/JSP APIs, aimed to provide modularization and reuse of processes to the JSP design arena. The capability to handle custom tags is considered a key advantage of the JSP over competing technologies because tags introduce modular composition of content generation. This affects the overall web application and content creation process, resulting in the establishment of a new role of the tag library designer, who will relieve the content designer of the responsibility of writing scriptlets. The traditional way pages are designed will also be affected. Tag libraries are defined in the portion of the Servlet API, which is generally referred to as the Tag Library Extension API.

A tag, in the sense of the Tag Library Extension API, is a module of Java language code with roots in Java Beans objects, which implements some or part of some process called an *action*. This is represented in the JSP page with XML notation. Technically, the Java object that implements the action is called a *tag handler*. The XML notation of the invocation of a tag handler in a JSP is called tag. Tags and their respective handlers can be used either individually or collectively, depending on the process they implement and how they were designed.

Who Should Read This Book

This book is intended to be read by anyone involved in web application and web content design. Content designers will find invaluable information about tag libraries already available from a number of sources and ready to use.

Experienced web development professionals as well as newcomers will benefit by understanding this new API and ways to create custom tags and tag libraries to encapsulate reoccurring processes. One of the main concerns that was kept in mind when writing this book was to keep the concepts clear and the language simple and straightforward.

Who This Book Is Not For

This book is not about XML development. Although JSP pages can be composed as XML documents, this book is more focused on Java mechanisms and tag libraries available for processing XML documents. New Riders has published a number of titles on the subject of XML development, including *Inside XML* and *Inside XSLT*, by Steven Holzner, and *XML, XSLT, Java, and JSP: A Case Study in Developing a Web Application*, by Westy Rockwell.

Other technologies use the term *tag* to refer to encapsulation of code for reuse. Although there are obvious parallels, this book refers to tag libraries developed with the Java language under the JSP API. New Riders offers a number of books on Flash, Python, C++, PHP, HTML and XHTML, and others.

Overview

This book is organized in four parts. The idea was to provide an evolutionary pathway to the technology from the core programming concepts to the several ways of usage, discussing the way tag libraries interact with the rest of the world to provide a powerful and complete solution to the Java web arena.

Part I, "Understanding the Tag Library Extension API," presents the Tag Library Extension API, starting in Chapter 1, "Introduction to Servlets and JavaServer Pages," which explains what the Servlet API is, describes its components, and discusses the JSP API inside it. Emphasis also is placed on the syntax of the JSP scriptlet and the objects that make a JSP page runtime environment. In addition, this chapter introduces the JSP standard actions and describes each of these elements with examples.

Chapter 2, "Introduction to Tag Libraries," introduces the concepts behind the Tag Library Extension API. It shows what a tag looks like, tells what it is, and tells what it is not. Chapter 2 shows how to configure a JSP page to use a tag library. It answers these questions: What are the relationships between the several configuration files? What is the Tag Library Descriptor file?

Chapter 3, "Writing Custom Tags," goes deep into the programming and describes how to create a custom tag, tells what the interfaces and base classes on the API are, describes the main concepts involved, and details the most useful design patterns that emerged so far. This is done with a lot of code examples.

Chapter 4, "Cooperating Tags and Scripting Variables," continues along those lines, introducing the concept of a tag handler regarding the Java J2EE API. It also discusses the Servlet API, explains the techniques involved to create cooperating tags, shows groups of tags developed to implement some complex task acting together, and explains validation and the classes and processes to validate the most complex cases of tag structuring.

Chapter 5, "Design Considerations," closes Part I by presenting design recommendations and techniques for creating a tag library. It explores the main ideas behind the API from the software process perspective. It also addresses the issue of planning and effectively designing a tag library that implements a custom process and an API, and it explores how the decision of which architecture and design pattern to use will influence the choice of which actions the tag library will implement.

Part II, "The Struts Framework," presents the Struts framework as an eloquent example of an Open Source M-V-C framework, consistently based on a number of tag libraries that give it a foundation for web development. It comprises Chapters 6, 7, and 8. Chapter 6, "Jakarta Struts," presents the main concepts found in Struts, details the core objects, and discusses the way it works.

Chapter 7, "Struts Tag Libraries," presents the Struts tag libraries in detail, with examples on usage and the commented source code of some of its most important tags. It presents in great detail how such concepts are integrated.

Chapter 8, "Anatomy of a Struts Application," covers a Struts application and shows all the concepts presented so far in action. It also explores how the tags integrate with the application objects.

Part III, "The Jakarta Taglibs and Other Resources," presents what is beyond the M-V-C world. Chapter 9, "The Jakarta Taglibs Project," introduces the Jakarta Taglibs project, which is a repository for tag libraries developed in Open Source mode, from SOAP RPC to XSLT. The libraries available at the time of this writing are discussed and are presented in detail with examples.

Chapter 10, "Commercial Tag Libraries," covers a number of tag libraries supported by application servers and deployed commercially. Three examples are discussed: the JRun tag library, bundled with the JRun server; the Orion tags, which are not bundled but can be downloaded for independent use; and the Bluestone tag library, available across the product line of Bluestone.

Chapter 11, "Other Resources," refers to external resources with a number of interesting links and pointers.

Part IV, "Appendixes," includes the appendixes and provides foundation information on the servers referred to in the text, the database material (which was MySQL), and a cross-reference on concepts from the servlet world to the JSP world.

Conventions

This book follows a few typographical conventions:

- A new term is set in *italics* the first time it is introduced.
- Program text, functions, variables, and other "computer language" are set in a fixed-pitch font—for example, `<taglib>` tag.

I

Understanding the Tag Library
Extension API

1

Introduction to Servlets and JavaServer Pages

THIS CHAPTER PRESENTS THE BUILDING BLOCKS for Java-based web application programming, the Servlet and JavaServer Pages (JSP) APIs. Together, these two APIs provide the components necessary to build the sophisticated web applications needed by the e-business–driven world today. Because the subject of this book is JSP tag libraries, this chapter introduces servlets and the core components in the Servlet API, and it examines JSP structure and syntax in greater detail.

The first part of the chapter presents a historical perspective on the evolution of web applications and the application models used. Then the chapter shows the Servlet API, discusses the core concepts that it defines, including the web container or web application context, and explores the actual Java components in the API that implement those core concepts.

The second part of the chapter covers the JSP API and the structure of a JavaServer Page. Each element of a JSP is presented with examples.

The Need for Web Applications

The network society is just beginning. The economy reflects these transition times in waves, such as the e-business, e-economy, and e-procurement waves. You are now constantly challenged to understand and support those business models and to maintain the company in the market—no matter what the market becomes.

In the network society, the market is not right around the corner. The market is the network around the world; it is the Internet. Companies must offer products and support sales on the Internet. The whole production chain tends to be online, and that chain must be supported by applications capable of dealing with this market. A new class of applications, called web applications, is being built to support the production chain processes in this digital network economy.

A web application is no different from a conventional computer application, such as a client/server order-entry application at some sales point, because it automates some process needed by some client in some node of a process chain. The difference lies in the technologies used to implement and support it. Web applications use the web to support both the application runtime cycle and the presentation technology.

The application runtime cycle is built on the web protocol HTTP request-response cycle, with some mechanism to provide coherence to the interaction. Because the HTTP protocol is stateless, a mechanism called the session mechanism is needed to track which set of requests was issued by the same client in the server side. This is usually managed by the application protocol in conventional client/server applications.

Web applications also use web presentation technologies such as HTML pages, XML documents, and Flash routines on the client side. XML has been gaining a lot of momentum lately because it promotes a uniform way to interchange information, provided that a standard XML vocabulary is agreed upon. In fact, you can think of XML in a broader way, as you will in this book.

The concept of the web application evolved as the concept and the role of the web itself evolved. Its social and economic impacts are being better understood, and technology itself has evolved to provide the new classes of services and devices needed to implement them. They were introduced as a response to the demand for an interactive World Wide Web. Today they are the pillars for the e-society.

A Dynamic Internet

Before defining JavaServer Pages and other core notions such as containers and contexts, it's important to understand the process that led to this state of things—the ultimate players that defined the way this millionaire game is played today.

When we talk about the Internet today, we are implicitly talking about a dynamic Internet that provides more than information. It also provides an overwhelming set of services. The Internet is there to serve you. It's there to enable your businesses to enact transactions more efficiently and effectively than your competitors in less time. A commerce site designed to be a CD shop, for instance, cannot succeed if it doesn't provide an online catalog where the client chooses desired CDs. The site must also enable a customer to make payments without fear of electronic fraud, and it must provide quick delivery of the product.

This kind of service-intensive site is so common that it has been named an *e-shop*. A web site that limits itself to providing static images of CD covers and inviting the client to visit the physical store or to call or fax to place an order won't be a match for a well-structured e-shop. Businesspeople soon realized this, and it ultimately led to the frenetic e-business world emerging today. Of course, the basis for all this is a capable information systems infrastructure. You can think of the web, web-based business processes, and e-commerce as the infrastructure of a worldwide information system that is emerging to provide a more efficient service network to satisfy your needs.

The Challenges to Meet

To build such an information systems infrastructure, systems must be created and maintained. Achieving programming productivity to build web applications is quite problematic, and many challenges must be met. The main issues are as follows:

- There's no such thing as a "simple web page." Many technologies and languages are involved in the design of a professional-level web page, including Flash, DHTML, JavaScript, and Java and ActiveX objects. These technologies sometimes have few points of contact with each other. A simple but very important example is browser compatibility, because the typical client for a web application is the web browser.

  Any programmer or designer who has tried to write a piece of dynamic HTML for a fancy page knows that he can end up with completely different results depending on the browser he uses, if he doesn't design that page carefully. For instance, these are issues to consider:

  - **Font rendering**—Font rendering in Internet Explorer is done differently than in Netscape. If you have a page designed to depend on some font aspect, you will be surprised by the difference in the results.

  - **JavaScript implementation**—Programming in JavaScript to create dynamic HTML involves a lot of pitfalls. You must detect which browser you are using to circumvent the many different aspects of the implementation. The means of detecting a browser version differ from browser to browser.

  - **More on JavaScript**—Many functions and events are implemented differently in several browser versions. It's not only a matter of JavaScript level; the way events can be trapped and fired also differs. (Try to perform an `onChange` event in a `Select` object in IE and Netscape, and you will understand this.)

  A great deal of effort is expended in writing code that will run in mainstream browsers and, for each browser, across releases. Even so, extensive—and thus, time-consuming and difficult—testing is necessary to guarantee a seamless result.

- The protocol for web processing is the Hypertext Transfer Protocol (HTTP). It's an RPC protocol designed for resource retrieval upon requests, and it is the protocol that browsers use to communicate with web servers. HTTP is not designed to transfer data to information systems; instead, it transfers resources to hypertext-oriented web pages. The major problem with using HTTP as an information systems data-transfer protocol is its lack of state. Each request is served, and the connection with the server is closed. That's it. There's no way to associate a request with another one. There's no concept of session, as a group of requests logically correlated. On corporate systems, built on top of conventional client/server local area networks or mainframe systems, control is tight regarding the state of a client. This is crucial for the maintenance of coherent data and process flows. Thus, this level of control must be implemented and maintained on a per-case basis.

- There's the need to cope with several distinct components and their specific protocols to build a complete web service. There's the data-management component, the web request processing and presentation component. Business rules are implemented in a business processes component. These are commonly planned to serve the entire organization and are usually implemented in a distributed server configuration. To provide information services to clients, the web server itself must communicate with other servers in the organization, such as database servers, message queues, directory services, or even some kind of middleware, such as TP monitors. The communication must be set up and maintained, and resource access must be tightly controlled. Connections must also be efficiently managed to avoid the overhead of connection establishment that affects the remote client. As is the case with session control, server configuration must be implemented and managed as well.

- Security is another permanent challenge for web application designers. In an enterprise environment, the customer is identifiable in most cases. On the Internet, the client is anonymous, and this anonymity is a threat even behind a firewall. There's no invulnerable product or "bulletproof vest" on the web. There are safe processes, however, in which the security component is introduced at very early stages and is maintained throughout the processes execution. There's also early detection, warning, and reaction. This is an overhead commonly avoided by the adoption of ultimate technology, and a mistake, in the sense that tonight's top security products tend to be obsolete by tomorrow morning. (Top security products become obsolete when a hacker finds a vulnerability during the night, so they are already obsolete the next morning.) All components in a process must be considered based on their threat to security: They must be tested to track vulnerabilities, and they must be stressed to avoid stress breaches. There's no point in sending a password over the SSL protocol if it will be stored on the HTML source on the client's browser in plain text. Again, this process tends to be time-consuming and tedious.

CGI Programming and Other Approaches

The Common Gateway Interface (CGI) was the first protocol used to design and implement web applications. It was not originally developed for the web or the HTTP protocol, which explains some of its shortcomings:

- CGI has a lousy life cycle. In a CGI application, each request requires the creation of a heavyweight process. On CGI-Perl, for instance, each request involves starting the Perl interpreter on a different process. This is a serious overload for the server because it consumes time and resources.

- CGI applications tend to have complex scalability problems. This is partly a result of the previous issue and partly a result of lousy integration with the web server environment.

- There's no mechanism for session management in the CGI protocol. The typical mechanism that CGI programmers use to provide session tracking to CGI applications is HTML hidden fields.

- CGI is not portable. The protocol is not uniformly implemented in web servers from distinct vendors.

Despite these shortcomings, CGI scripts established the first generation of web applications. Protocol alternatives appeared, including FastCGI and mod_perl, but these are not available to a number of platforms or servers, and none has completely addressed the many issues affecting the original protocol.

The web server extensions were a tentative approach to providing web server-side functionality useful for web application development. Two commercial mainstream players, Netscape and Microsoft, provided a mechanism to extend their servers with in-process plug-ins. Netscape's protocol was called NSAPI, and MS-IIS's counterpart was called ISAPI. Despite the advantages compared to CGI applications, the server extension approach was heavily bounded to the original servers. Applications designed on the first didn't run on the second, and vice versa. Many languages originally designed for the RAD world implemented these protocols as an attempt to succeed in the Internet arena. An example is Inprise's Delphi language. Server-side extensions faded with the appearance of Java; today they're limited to server-side plug-in, filter-level applications.

Java was released in 1995. Shortly afterward, it introduced Java applets, which became quite popular on the web. Applets were initially intended to provide an alternative to browser plug-ins. The idea was that the plug-ins wouldn't need to be installed statically in the browser, which was supposedly a risky and space-consuming process. Applets, on the other hand, could be downloaded on demand, executed safely, and discarded when finished. Soon the programming community started to note that applets offered a way to decentralize the application processes to alleviate the server load, and this resulted in a new dimension of dynamism and creativity in the already interactive Internet.

Unfortunately, it soon became clear that those promises would prove to be very difficult to accomplish. The early versions of the Java Virtual Machine (JVM) performed poorly and presented a number of security breaches. Complex processes based on applets were error-prone because of the diversity of implementations of browser JVMs. The introduction of the Swing components made the need for a revised applet model even more urgent. Systems deployed over the enterprises' intranets suffered from disparate browser distributions because update processes on large corporations tended to be planned in yearly bases. Later, Sun introduced the Java plug-in as a way to alleviate the impact of browser JVM implementations over applet-based applications.

Applets implement an application model called a thick client application, in which the client contains all the logic needed to provide a response to the client, such as database connection and access, business rules, and so on. In the end, the download times for sophisticated applets, which tend to be large, were very discouraging. Applets are used today for applications with very specific requirements, such as 3D graphics manipulation.

The many issues with applet programming led to the concept of thin client web application. Since the times of CGI, web applications residing in a web server could process requests, generate a response page, and send the page to the browser, just for rendering. What was lacking was a more efficient way to do this. Sun introduced the servlet technology as a Java alternative for that.

Servlets, the J2EE, and Web Application Design

In 1997, Sun introduced another API for the Internet. Initially intended as a server-side extension API, the Servlet API soon gained attention and today is the preferred Java way to create web applications. Servlets started to gain market acceptance with the Servlet API 2.0.

Servlets at a Glance

Servlets offer a number of innovations over CGI applications, server extensions, and other technologies:

- **Portability**—Because the Servlet API is written in the Java language, it will run in any platform for which there is a JVM. This is the write once, run anywhere (WORA) premise. The only additional prerequisite is a servlet container, which is an environment where servlets can run. Because the Servlet API is designed for the web, there must also be a web server capable of hosting the container. Servlets can also be ported from container to container without recompilation.

- **Simplicity**—Servlets are Java classes, so they benefit from the extensive JAVA API seamlessly. They can use any Java protocol to access enterprise resources, such as the JDBC for databases and the JNDI for lookup and directory services.

- **Extensibility**—Servlets can build upon other servlets via inheritance and can implement Java interfaces to provide specific services.

- **Performance**—Servlets present a much better life cycle compared with CGI applications. They use a lightweight thread to process requests, saving server resources and allowing for a more elastic scalability.

- **Session management**—The Servlet API offers a set of classes and interfaces to implement a rich session-maintenance mechanism, which improves security at several levels.

- **Better design**—Because a servlet runs as a single instance and has multiple threads, it can maintain object pools to save and reuse connections with enterprise resource servers such as message queues and databases.

- **Better integration with the Web server environment**—The Servlet API provides a number of generic interfaces for request/response wrapping, resulting in easier access to request parameters and resources in the server's environment.

However, the early servlets were designed much like CGI applications were, sometimes generating complete sets of HTML and JavaScript code in many possible responses for a given request. Given their programmatic nature, servlets soon became too difficult to maintain, and weaknesses started to become more clear. Then Sun released its JavaServer Pages API (JSP API), built on top of the Servlet API, as a declarative way to handle web page generation. The roles of these APIs were not clearly defined, so they seemed to collide with each other.

Things became clearer with the release of the Java 2 Enterprise Edition (J2EE). In the J2EE blueprints, several concepts were drawn to support a complete redefinition of the roles of servlets and JSP as complementary technologies.

J2EE Application Model and the Web

J2EE introduced a programming model for web applications called Model 2, or Model-View-Control–based model. To better understand its architecture, it's necessary to briefly examine the Model 1 architecture.

In the Model 1 architecture, created in the early days of servlet programming, each web component is responsible for the complete processing of a request. The component receives a request from the client, extracts its parameters, processes them and generates its response, and renders the response to a format that the client's browser can accept (see Figure 1.1).

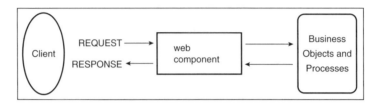

Figure 1.1   The Model 1 architecture for servlet- and JSP-based web applications.
The model in Figure 1.1 presents many issues:

- If each component (JSP or servlet) supports a complete request-response cycle, how redundant does the control structure of the overall system become? How complex is it to tune such a system when it grows in size?

- What kind of policies may be implemented to optimize resource and performance, such as response caching, resource pooling, and so on? How can we implement them in a distributed structure in which each component is independent and unaware of the others?

- How can we provide an effective separation of presentation, control, and core logic with a single component to manage them all? Which components address each transaction? If transactions are interrelated, how can we stack them so that they can be easily maintained afterward?

The Model-View-Control (MVC) design pattern offers some answers to these questions by promoting a rigorous separation of roles from control, core or business logic, and the user view. It was introduced in the Smalltalk language as a way to cope with GUI component implementation issues. The whole idea behind this design pattern is presented here.

Every process has three components, which are orthogonal:

- **CONTROL**—The CONTROL component is responsible for selecting what should be done to sustain the process execution. That's all. In this case, the CONTROL component is responsible for attaching requests received from the client machine to a certain business process/object, and that to a view (most likely a JSP).

- **MODEL**—The MODEL component, on the other hand, is responsible for providing the request with a response according to the business rules and data available. You place a request for it, and it returns coherent response data. It doesn't care how the request arrived or where the response should be sent (at least, theoretically). That's the CONTROL component's concern. The MODEL component also doesn't care how it will display to the user. That's the VIEW component's responsibility.

- **VIEW**—The VIEW component gets whatever comes from the control and renders it adequately to the user, no matter what.

On conventional applications, these three components are mixed at a certain level, which is undesirable because it makes maintenance and extension difficult. On so-called MVC systems, on the other hand, these components are well-defined and separate, done by different pieces of code. Figure 1.2 depicts this design pattern.

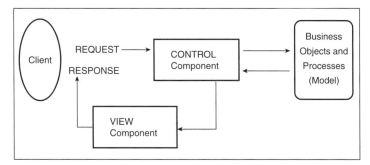

Figure 1.2   The MVC structure. Note that each component in the design pattern is implemented by a distinct software component.

A transaction submitted to the system is directed to an execution structure selected by the control mechanism that will activate the adequate core logic components and execute the specific business processes. The data objects retrieved from these processes are redirected to the adequate presentation component that will render them to the client.

The sole purpose of the control structure is to decide which business processes must be executed in response to a specific request and which presentation object the response should be redirected to. It can implement several control policies because control is materialized there; it's not replicated in each JSP or servlet, potentially with different implementation details. It can implement several layers of caching (row sets, response bean caching, result Hashtable caching, and so on), resource pooling (JDBC data sources and connection pools, control structure object pooling, connectors, and so on), and security mechanisms (selected SSL transport, single-point-of-login, and so on), for a start. The control structure itself is more likely to be distributed in several components, such as request processors, resource controllers, and transaction controllers in a number of decision-making policies.

The core logic represents enterprise-level business processes implemented with distributed object architectures (EJBs, Corba objects, and so on) or document structures (such as XML trees) that will be activated and executed to respond to specific requests. Response data is created, likely in the form of JavaBeans or CachedRowsets, and redirected to the corresponding presentation component, where it is rendered to data rows, tables, graphics, or whatever presentation strategy is more adequate.

The presentation layer becomes well defined. Much of the questioning about JSP technology (and ASP as well) is related to the need to put as much Java code in a page to fulfill a request as the HTML that was put on a equivalent servlet to present the results for the same request. Taking the control structures off the presentation JSPs (or taking the presentation off the servlets) greatly simplified them, making their code more accessible to nonprogrammers and making the maintenance reasonable.

In this scenario, the only missing part is the data access component in the presentation JSPs, the objects that will build the presentation from the data objects received from the control structure. Using Java scriptlets brings back the complexity problem, although at a lower level. Another issue is maintaining and tuning those scriptlets, not to mention the capability to take advantage of newer composition tools. That's where custom tag libraries and standard actions come in.

Even if you provide a good control structure, separate the roles of presentation, and provide a coherent data object flow from the business processes out, you still need to implement the logic to access the information encapsulated in those data objects. And that logic still is a programmatic component at the presentation level. To cope with that, JSP technology offers standard actions and custom tag libraries. Standard actions and custom tags have the same form, borrowed from XML namespaces. Standard actions are like HTML tags, but they provide actions to deal with JavaBeans, page inclusion, and redirection. Custom tags are tags that you can supply to provide some specific behavior, as well as to encapsulate and reuse a specific process.

The scenario presented in the rest of the book puts a servlet at the center of the control structure. JSPs are used at the presentation layer and are supported by standard actions and custom tags. A flexible infrastructure is used backstage, supplying core business processes. For such a scenario, the overview of servlets and JSP in the remainder of this chapter is necessary.

The Servlet API

A servlet provides a programmatic way of processing a request and generating a response to the issuer of the request. It can generate dynamic content in the form of character data, binary data, or HTML code, for example. A servlet can be designed to trigger behavior; for instance, it can be designed to start a process in the server upon parameters sent in a request. In doing so, a servlet extends the behavior of the server as an accessory service.

Servlets are essential. Every JSP is translated into a servlet before becoming byte-code. Therefore, every JSP is actually a servlet. Keeping this in mind will help to solve some odd problems in JSP programming.

Containers and Web Containers

Since the release of J2EE and the Servlet API version 2.2 specification, several concepts were introduced—mainly to facilitate the deployment of servlet- and JSP-based web applications to a wide variety of web servers without needing reconfiguration. This was meant to make the web layers on the J2EE platform uniform. Even in heterogeneous distributed environments, the EJB and web layers would be capable of being integrated regardless of the vendors of the respective containers.

What Is a Web Container?

A web container, also called a servlet container, is a runtime environment in which servlets, JavaServer Pages, and tags reside and are run in response to a client's request. It is called a *container* because it *contains* the web components that will provide the services desired. Vendors may implement their containers with a variety of supplemental services, but they must offer a unified directory structure at some level and a common set of services to the web application.

Directory Structure

Because web applications are essentially resource-oriented, with their pages, graphics files, and so on, they must be deployed in a web container under some directory structure. On the TOMCAT web container, the root directory for web applications is the /webapps directory. Each web application has its own uniquely named root directory under that, which is also called the context root of the application. Under the context root, an application can implement its own particular directory structure, but an operational directory called WEB-INF is needed.

The WEB-INF directory holds the web application deployment descriptor file, called web.xml, which contains the configuration data for the web application. It contains a classes directory, which is the preferred directory to hold the application's servlets and other classes. It contains a /lib directory to hold jam-packed libraries needed by the application's processes.

The WEB-INF directory is a protected directory with no visibility from the outside, other than through the container itself. This means that a text file requested by a client, located inside the WEB-INF directory, is off-limits. It can be reached only if a servlet gets it and serves it back to the client. So, any configuration data that a web application needs must be placed inside the WEB-INF directory, to keep it safe from external access. Figure 1.3 shows a typical directory structure for the Apache Software Foundation's TOMCAT web container.

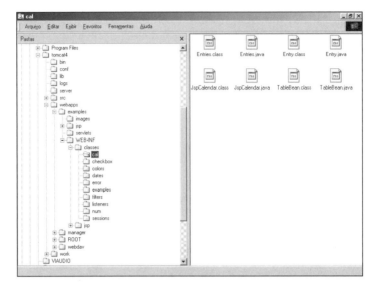

Figure 1.3   TOMCAT directory structure.

Web Applications and Contexts

A web application is like any other application. The distinction relies on the technology that implements it. Physically speaking, a web application is a collection of static and dynamic resources (such as servlets, HTML files, XML documents, graphics files, JSPs, class files and beans, custom tag libraries, and archive files such as .zip or .tar files) that provide a number of services to the client who requests them via the HTTP request-response protocol. It can be deployed as a single archive file, called the *web application archive file*, with the extension ★.war. Each vendor can implement a specific way to access resources inside a .war file, but this must be transparent to the web developer.

Web Application and Context

Each web application component must have a view of the resources that are part of the application. This view is important because a component might need to access some method or redirect a request to another more appropriate component, or might need to access some static resource, such as a data file. The Servlet API defines such view, called *context*. Physically, the context is the repository in the web container that will contain the web application.

After it is deployed, a web application is made into a directory structure inside the web container's /webapps directory called *context's root*. The web application's name is the name of the context. The context's root is the basic reference inside the web application. Paths inside the application are referenced to the context's root. A servlet can redirect requests only inside some context under the container.

A container provides a special context called default context, represented by the / path. Servlets and JSPs without a context must be placed under the default context.

A context has a logic representation defined by the Servlet API, which is the `ServletContext` interface.

The Web Application Deployment Descriptor

A web application deployment descriptor file is an XML file described in the Servlet API specification that controls the deployment of a web application in the container environment. It describes a number of services that a container offers to the web components and holds configuration information on security, interoperability with EJB containers, and so on.

Tag libraries are to be described in the deployment descriptor with the `<taglib>` tag. Listing 1.1 shows a small application deployment descriptor.

Listing 1.1   **Small Application Deployment Descriptor**

```xml
<?xml version="1.0" encoding="ISO-8859-1"?>

<!DOCTYPE web-app
  PUBLIC "-//Sun Microsystems, Inc.//DTD Web Application 2.2//EN"
  "http://java.sun.com/j2ee/dtds/web-app_2.2.dtd">

<web-app>
  <Servlet>
    <Servlet-name>Init</Servlet-name>
    <Servlet-class>com.wlss.cac.WLSSInitServlet</Servlet-class>
    <load-on-startup>1</load-on-startup>
  </Servlet>
  <Servlet>
    <Servlet-name>Main</Servlet-name>
    <Servlet-class>com.wlss.cac.WLSSMainServlet</Servlet-class>
  </Servlet>
  <Servlet>
    <Servlet-name>Login</Servlet-name>
    <Servlet-class>com.wlss.cac.WLSSLoginServlet</Servlet-class>
  </Servlet>

  <Servlet-mapping>
    <Servlet-name>Main</Servlet-name>
    <url-pattern>/dispatch.htm</url-pattern>
  </Servlet-mapping>
  <Servlet-mapping>
    <Servlet-name>Login</Servlet-name>
    <url-pattern>/login.htm</url-pattern>
```

continues

Listing 1.1 **Continued**

```
</Servlet-mapping>

<!-- A Tag Library Descriptor -->
<taglib>
  <taglib-uri>/WEB-INF/tlds/wlss.tld</taglib-uri>
  <taglib-location>/WEB-INF/tlds/wlss.tld</taglib-location>
</taglib>

</web-app>
```

Listing 1.1 shows a small yet complete web application deployment descriptor file. It defines the web application components and configuration (parameters, policies, and so). Here you can see defined a number of servlets (Init, Main, and Login) and a number of mapping rules used to associate a servlet call to a resource name. In this case, for instance, the Main servlet is mapped to the dispatch.htm resource name. Requesting dispatch.htm will call the Main servlet. The last section defines a tag library needed by some JSPs. Many other parameters can be defined in the web application deployment descriptor. For a complete description of the elements in the file, check the Servlet API specification document from Sun.

Servlet API Components

The Servlet API is the foundation for all the web layers of the J2EE platform. Servlets themselves are highly flexible web components; they are the building blocks for the JavaServer Pages technology. On TOMCAT, the reference web container, the JSP translator, JASPER, is a servlet that intercepts all *.jsp resource requests. In fact, TOMCAT offers a nice example of how you can use servlets to supply a number of web services to the web container and, ultimately, to the web server.

The Servlet Interface

The main component of the Servlet API is the servlet interface. It presents three methods that form the structure of the servlet life cycle: `init`, `service`, and `destroy`. Servlets implement the servlet interface either directly or (more likely) indirectly, subclassing the HTTP protocol-bound `HttpServlet` class, which subclasses the `GenericServlet` class, which implements the servlet interface.

The servlet container reinforces the servlet life cycle as follows:

1. The container loads and instantiates the servlet, either on startup or when the first request to that servlet arrives. If the deployment descriptor contains a `<load-on-startup>` tag, the servlet is loaded in the order specified. After loading and instantiating the servlet, the container calls the init method, to allow the servlet to initialize specific resources. The container passes information on the environment to the servlet through the ServletConfig parameter of the init method.

2. After completion of the `init` method, the servlet is ready to receive requests. It does so through the `service` method. The `service` method has two arguments: the request and response objects. The request object implements the `HttpServletRequest` and wraps the request information sent by the web server (then an `HttpServletResponse`) to the servlet. The response object holds the information to be sent to the client in response to a request, such as the requested HTML page generated by the servlet or an error code. Multiple requests are passed via multiple threads, so the servlet must be made thread-safe if resources don't support it.

3. Eventually the servlet must be released, either because the servlet container itself is unloading or because it has already fulfilled its role and must terminate. In that case, the container calls the `destroy` method. The `destroy` method is used to release all resources that can't be garbage-collected or that need a specific release routine, such as connection pools.

The `HttpServlet` class offers a number of methods to deal with each of the HTTP protocol's methods. These are named `doXXX()` where `XXX` is the name of the method desired, as in `doGet` for the `GET` method and `doPost` for the `POST` method. The difference with the `service` method is that a `doXXX` method is invoked by the servlet container only if the corresponding HTTP method is used on the client's transaction. If you need the client to use only the `POST` method, you should override `doPost()` accordingly, ignoring the other methods.

Listing 1.2 shows a simple servlet that accesses a database via the JDBC protocol, performs some query, and returns the result to the client as an HTML page. Note the `init` method that creates the connection with the database, how the `service` method uses the connection established, and the `destroy` method that closes the connection before the release of the servlet.

Listing 1.2 presents a servlet that implements the full life cycle. It initializes a database connection pool with MySQL connections, submits a query in the `service` method, and releases the pool in the `destroy` method.

Listing 1.2   **An Example of a Simple Servlet**

```
import java.sql.*;
import java.io.*;
import javax.Servlet.*;
import javax.Servlet.http.*;
import java.util.*;
import com.javaexchange.dbConnectionBroker.*;

public class DataBasedServlet extends HttpServlet
{
  DbConnectionBroker conPool;

  public void init (ServletConfig config) throws ServletException
```

continues

Listing 1.2 **Continued**

```
  {
    super.init(config);
    String logPath = config.getServletContext().getRealPath("/WEB-
INF/tmp/bahiana.log");
    try
    {
      conPool = new DbConnectionBroker("org.gjt.mm.mysql.Driver",
                   "jdbc:mysql://localhost/EXAMPLE",
                   "admin","",2,6,logPath,0.01);
    }
    catch (IOException e5)
    {
      config.getServletContext().log("init of example",e);
    }
  }

  public void service (HttpServletRequest request, HttpServletResponse response)
  throws ServletException, IOException
  {
    PrintWriter out = response.getWriter();
    Connection conn = null;
    Statement stm = null;
    response.setContentType ("text/html");
    try
    {
      conn = conPool.getConnection();

      out.println("<h3>Databased Model 1 Servlet</h3>");

      stm = conn.createStatement();
      ResultSet rs = stm.executeQuery("select * from alunos");

      while (rset.next())
      {
        out.println("Name: " + rs.getString(1)+"<br>");
        out.println("Age: " + rs.getString(2)+"<br>");
        out.println("Course: " + rs.getString(3)+"<br>");
        out.println("Year: " + rs.getString(4)+"<br>");
      }
    }
    catch (SQLException e)
    {
      getServletContext().log("database error",e);
    }
    finally
    {
      try{if(stm != null) stm.close();}
      catch(SQLException e){};
      conPool.freeConnection(conn);
    }
```

```
    out.close();
    response.getOutputStream().close();
  }

  public void destroy ()
  {
    conPool.destroy();
    super.destroy();
  }
}
```

Request and Response

The container supplies the information about the client's request, as well as an object to help with the construction of a response wrapped on the `request` and `response` arguments of the `service` method (or `doGet`, `doPost`, and so on). The request object has four main purposes:

1. Provides access to the client's parameters. This is essential for form processing.

2. Carries information about the requester and the requested page, such as whether HTTPS was used instead of HTTP, whether the client has been authenticated, the client's SSL attributes, the request headers, cookies, and so on.

3. Provides access to the session object. A servlet must join a session before having access to it, and the request object provides access through the `createSession` method.

4. Provides request attributes. The container uses them to hold extra information about the request. For instance, if a request was redirected to a page, there will be an attribute there to indicate this. The developer can define request attributes also. You will see this in more detail in Chapter 2, "Introduction to Tag Libraries."

Request attributes are a fine way to provide transport to data objects. Because the scope of the objects returned by a transaction are the requests that created them, returning them in request attributes saves the trouble of controlling session objects' mutual interference when data generated by a previous transaction is considered valid for the next one, causing a series of Byzantine errors.

The following snippet illustrates how to use request attributes:

```
// return a product item for a product code
String code = request.getParameter("CODE");
if (code != null && code.length() > 0)
{
  PrdItem item = new PrdItem(code);
  request.setAttribute("item", item);
}
```

Because most of the functionality of the response object is provided automatically by the JSP processing, it isn't of much interest for a JSP developer. Response objects control the way the response is created and returned to the client. The response's main function lies in its utilitarian methods for redirecting the request and defining response headers.

In the JSP page that receives this request object, the `PrdItem` object can be retrieved with the `request.getAttribute` method or the `jsp:useBean` tag with request scope (more on that in the following section "`<jsp:useBean>`").

ServletContext and *RequestDispatcher*

The `ServletContext` object provides a servlet with information about its web application. This object is obtained from `ServletConfig`, passed as an argument by the container to the `init` method, using the `getServletContext` method. The context provides access to the web application's resources to the servlet.

Context's attributes are a mechanism to define general control objects or general access resources that must be available to all servlets on the application. For instance, a mapping application can make available a big shape file handler, saving the mapping servlets the trouble of loading and initializing it themselves. Another web application can make available a connection pool manager through a context attribute so that all data-oriented servlets and JSPs can access a connection directly from the connection pool. Every resource made available in a context attribute must be thread-safe. A servlet could have initialized the `conPool` and put it on a context attribute so that it will be available to all the other web components, as shown in the following example:

```
// 1. Initialize connection pool
try
{
  conPool = new DbConnectionBroker("org.gjt.mm.mysql.Driver",
              "jdbc:mysql://localhost/EXAMPLE",
              "admin","",2,6,logPath,0.01);

  context.setAttribute("POOL",conPool);
  context.log("SET CONPOOL");
}
catch (Exception e) {context.log(this.getClass().getName()+": ",e);}


}
```

`RequestDispatcher` is an interface that allows a servlet to transfer the responsibility of returning a response to a client's request to another servlet, JSP, or resource in general. It is the responsibility of the `ServletContext` object to wrap a resource in `RequestDispatcher`. It has two methods: `include` and `forward`.

The `include` method is used when the result of processing a servlet, JSP, or HTML page must be included as part of another servlet or JSP. The included resource can't change the response settings. A page can include as many resources as needed, as shown in the following code snippet:

```
ServletContext sc = getServletConfig().getServletContext();
RequestDispatcher rd = sc.getRequestDispatcher("/header.jsp");
rd.include(request,response);

out.println("<ul>");
for (int i=0;i<dataVector.size();i++)
{
  ItemBean ib = (ItemBean)dataVector.elementAt(i);
  out.print("<li>"+ib.getItemCode()+":");
  out.println(ib.getItemQty());
}
out.println("</ul>");
rd = sc.getRequestDispatcher("/footer.jsp");
rd.include(request,response);
```

The forward method must be used when the target resource must provide the full response. The control is transferred to the target and doesn't return. This method can be used only if the response wasn't already committed and nothing was sent back to the client's browser. Otherwise, the forward method will raise an exception. The next snippet creates the vector dataVector, as shown in the following code snippet:

```
Vector dataVector = new Vector();

while (rSet.next())
{
  ItemBean ib =  new ItemBean(rSet.getString(1),rSet.getString(2));
  dataVector.addElement(ib);
}

request.setAttribute("dataVector",dataVector);
ServletContext sc = getServletConfig().getServletContext();
RequestDispatcher rd = sc.getRequestDispatcher("/showItems.jsp");
rd.forward(request,response);
```

The maximum scope a RequestDispatcher is the container. If the servlet needs to redirect the processing of a page to an URL outside the container, the response.sendRedirect method should be used instead.

RequestDispatcher objects must be obtained from a ServletContext object, either the actual context or some context obtained in the container via the getContext method of ServletContext. A RequestDispatcher object can be named when it has a name declared in the web application deployment (web.xml). The code snippet that follows shows how to obtain a named dispatcher for a servlet.

```
ServletContext sc = getServletConfig().getServletContext();
RequestDispatcher rd = sc.getNamedDispatcher("LoginServlet");
rd.forward(request,response);
```

Sessions and Session Management

The need for session-management mechanisms becomes very clear on web applications. It's necessary to track who the user is and which rights are granted to him, to determine whether this request is built on top of some previous transaction results, and so on. Together, the HttpSession and HttpSessionBindingListener interfaces and the HttpSessionBindingEvent class form the session-tracking mechanism of the Servlet API.

A session is first created through the getSession method of the request object when none exists. The container associates a unique ID with the newly created session and provides it with a storage area where session objects can reside. When a request arrives, if a session was already created, a second call to the getSession method makes the session-stored objects available. Any servlet within the container can access the client's session. This process is called *joining the session*. Objects can be stored on the session. Objects implementing the HttpSessionBindingListener interface get notified by receiving a HttpSessionBindingEvent when they are bound and unbound to the session.

There are many patterns of usage for the session-tracking mechanism. The most obvious is to ensure that data transcends their request, when needed. An example of this is a shopping cart, in which the items selected are saved for further computing. Another typical scenario is user identification. The user rights must be reinforced throughout the application, but as soon as the session expires or is invalidated, the user control servlet must be notified.

Listing 1.3 shows how to use the session inside a JSP. A special object, called application, is defined in every JSP and contains the ServletContext object. This object will be explained better in the upcoming section "Implicit Objects."

Listing 1.3   **Using the Session Mechanism**

```
<%--first page is the session setter--%>
<%

Vector dataVector = new Vector();

while (rSet.next())
{
  ItemBean ib =  new ItemBean(rSet.getString(1),rSet.getString(2));
  dataVector.addElement(ib);
}

session.setAttribute("dataVector",dataVector);
RequestDispatcher rd = application.getRequestDispatcher("/showItems.jsp");
rd.forward(request,response);

%>

<%--Second Page--%>
```

```
<%
    // This is the page getter

    Vector dataVector = (Vector)session.getAttribute("dataVector");
%>
```

JavaServer Pages

After Microsoft's introduction of Active Server Pages (ASP), a great deal of criticism arose against the servlet approach. It is difficult to maintain by nonprogrammers, and it is difficult to design even for programmers because all the code must deal with HTML and potentially client-side scripting and DHTML. To provide a capable competitor and an alternative for web developers without sophisticated programming skills, Sun introduced the JavaServer Pages (JSP) technology and API.

Conceptually, this expresses a declarative way to process a request and generate a response to the issuer of the request. Physically, a JSP is a text file made of template static data and Java code specifications for dynamic data that is processed by a JSP translator into an executable Java class file when it is first requested.

Using JSP

Because of its declarative nature, JSPs have a natural role as a front end in web applications. The idea is that the static HTML code inside a JSP is easily maintained by a nonprogrammer because the JSP API specification establishes the use of special tags to mark the Java code, providing a clear separation between Java code and HTML.

JSP technology is not specifically bound to the Java programming language. In theory, a JSP can use any language as a scripting language, including JavaScript or even Perl. So far, however, the only language supported is Java. To simplify the discussion of topics ahead, this book assumes that the scripting language is always Java.

The Life Cycle

The JSP life cycle is defined as follows:

1. The client requests a file with the .jsp extension.

2. The container looks for a servlet loaded with the name convention according to the container's standard. Each container has the freedom to implement a specific name convention to derive the translated servlet from the JSP source.

3. If such a servlet is loaded and initialized, it threads on the `service` method of that servlet.

4. If no such servlet is found, it calls the JSP processor (for instance, TOMCAT's JASPER) that will parse the .jsp file, execute custom tags and standard actions, derive the translated servlet out of it, and compile it into bytecode that the container will load and run.

Some differences exist in the execution path from servlets and JSPs. Servlets get loaded and instantiated, and then the container executes its init method. The very first action that the servlet programmer needs to remember is to call super.init when it is passing the ServletConfig object received by the container. After you are inside the init method, you won't have access to any of the service method's typical objects, such as request or session objects.

JSPs cannot overload the init method. You must overload the jspInit() method instead, which doesn't need to call super.init and doesn't receive a config object. Also, all your implicit objects are already available (which doesn't happen in a servlet) within jspInit—for instance, you can use the request object inside the jspInit method.

You never overload the jspService method, which is entirely generated by the translation process.

If you need some finalization, you can overload the jspDestroy method, as was done for jspInit.

The Translated Servlet

The result processing the JSP translator is to generate a servlet from a JSP static file. In that process, all static text is output by out.println member functions inside the service method of the generated servlet. Expressions are converted into Java expressions output by out.println. Declarations are generated as instance variables, member functions, or whatever is declared. Scriptlets are generated in position, as statements of the service method of the generated servlet. Listing 1.4 shows a typical JSP translated by TOMCAT.

Listing 1.4   **A Typical JSP Translated by TOMCAT**

```
import javax.Servlet.*;
import javax.Servlet.http.*;
import javax.Servlet.jsp.*;
import javax.Servlet.jsp.tagext.*;
import java.io.PrintWriter;
import java.io.IOException;
import java.io.FileInputStream;
import java.io.ObjectInputStream;
import java.util.Vector;
import org.apache.jasper.runtime.*;
import java.beans.*;
import org.apache.jasper.JasperException;


public class _0002frealPath_0002ejsprealPath_jsp_0 extends HttpJspBase {

// basic initialization stuff was removed here for the sake
// of simplicity
```

```
public final void _jspx_init() throws JasperException {}

public void _jspService(HttpServletRequest request,
HttpServletResponse  response)
throws IOException, ServletException {

 JspFactory _jspxFactory = null;
 PageContext pageContext = null;
 HttpSession session = null;
 ServletContext application = null;
 ServletConfig config = null;
 JspWriter out = null;
 Object page = this;
 String  _value = null;
 try {

    if (_jspx_inited == false) {
       _jspx_init();
       _jspx_inited = true;
    }

    _jspxFactory = JspFactory.getDefaultFactory();

    response.setContentType("text/html;charset=8859_1");

    // Check how the page context object will initialize all
    // other implicit objects of this Jsp

    pageContext = _jspxFactory.getPageContext(this, request,
                  response,"", true, 8192, true);

    application = pageContext.getServletContext();
    config = pageContext.getServletConfig();
    session = pageContext.getSession();
    out = pageContext.getOut();

    String vPath = request.getRequestURI();
    String rPath = getServletConfig().getServletContext().getRealPath(vPath);
    out.print(vPath);
    out.write("</p>\r\n<p>The real path is ");
    out.print(rPath);
    out.write("</p>\r\n<p>The real path is ");
    out.print( getServletConfig().getServletContext().getRealPath("/realPath.jsp")
};

    out.write("</p>\r\n</body>\r\n</html>");
  } catch (Exception ex) {
     if (out.getBufferSize() != 0)
        out.clearBuffer();
        pageContext.handlePageException(ex);
  } finally {
```

continues

Listing 1.4 **Continued**

```
        out.flush();
        _jspxFactory.releasePageContext(pageContext);
    }
  }
}
```

Implicit Objects

To provide an easy way to access the core Servlet API components, every JSP has implicitly created and declared objects. This avoids complex object declarations being embedded in the code, making it easier to read and providing a standard way to access standard objects.

These implicit objects are the `pageContext`, request, response, application, config, out, exception, and session objects. The `pageContext` object has a number of responsibilities, such as to provide a way to access all the page-level information, to initialize the other implicit objects, to provide a way to manage and access the various scoped namespaces (page scope, request scope, session scope, and context scope), and to provide a number of methods that access the other implicit objects from the page and from any accessory component that needs to access that page's objects. The application object wraps upon the `ServletContext`.

Check the JavaServer Pages API specification document for further information on implicit objects and the `pageContext` object itself.

Syntax Explained

JSP syntax is based on five JSP tags and six standard actions:

- Tags are JSP comments, directives, declarations, expressions, and scriptlets.

- Standard actions are `useBean`, `getProperty`, `setProperty`, `include`, `forward`, and `plug-in`.

<%-- Comments

The JSP comment tags (also called hidden comments) `<%--` and `--%>` enable you to place information that won't be translated into content. The JSP translator will ignore this material. JSP comments are nice to use in passing instructions along the page design pipeline. Because the JSP programming model reinforces a strong separation of roles between class builders and content builders, sometimes one in the pipeline must pass a remark to the next. With such comments, this can be done without leaks to the client layer. Listing 1.5 shows an example of a JSP comment tag.

Listing 1.5   **Example of a JSP Comment Tag**

```
<%--
Directions of use:

1. Replace the XXX fields with the style sheet filenames you want to use
2. You  MUST implement the .P class !!
3. NEVER alter the order of the fields! This page gets scanned from another
application, and changing the order of the fields will break that one.

Thx,

The Developer Team --%>

...The rest of your JSP here...
```

In Listing 1.5, whatever is in the rest of the JSP gets translated into content and will display at the client side either as active content (live data) or as static template. The "Directions of use," on the other hand, won't be displayed this way. The designer dealing with the JSP source directly will have access to it.

It's important to remember that JSP comments and HTML comments are completely different things. HTML comments are considered part of the static template and are generated as HTML comments in the resulting page. Any JSP elements inside HTML comments are evaluated as if they're in a noncommented part of the page—for instance:

```
<%-- This is a hidden comment. The next expression won't ever show: <%=3*30%> --%>

<!-- This is an HTML comment. This expression is HOT DATA : <%=3*30%> -->

NOTHING IN THE PAGE
```

The expression inside the HTML comment gets evaluated to **90** and is replaced with the result.

<%@ Directives

Directives instruct the JSP translator into special procedures regarding the code. There are three directives: `include`, `page`, and `taglib`. The `include` directive provides a mechanism for static inclusion similar to the `#include` of the C language. The page directive is very rich, with many parameters and many purposes. The `taglib` directive is used to declare that the page uses custom tags, and it will be extensively explored throughout the rest of the book. They are coded within the directive tags `<%@ and %>`.

The <%@ include directive

The `include` directive is used to include statically the contents of a text file into the current JSP at the point where it was declared. Statically means that the included file is included and is not the result of its processing. The syntax for the `include` directive is as follows:

```
<%@ include file="relativeURL">
```

If `relativeURL` starts with `/`, the path is relative to the JSP's web application root directory. If it starts with a directory name instead, the path is relative to the JSP location.

The process of inclusion is roughly as follows:

1. The JSP translator starts translating a page.

2. The translator finds an `include` directive in the middle of the page.

3. The translator locates the file to include according to its relative URL.

4. If the file to include is a static text file such as HTML or text, it is simply added to the page's static template at that point.

5. If the file to include is a JSP file, it is parsed. If it is valid, it is included and then processing of the page continues on the next element after the directive.

The next example shows two `include` directives; one is valid and loads the testo.txt file. The other is invalid, trying to include oops.txt that doesn't exist. Uncomment the invalid directive and try it:

```
this is a valid include: <%@ include file="testo.txt"%> <br><br>

this is an invalid include commented: <%-- <%@ include file="oops.jsp"%> --%>
```

The `include` directive is very useful to improve the clarity of the code because repetitive patterns inside pages may be put on an external file and included by them, which saves effort in writing and understanding. Listing 1.6 shows a simple template mechanism that places a standard logo on all pages of the application.

Listing 1.6   **The *include* Directive**

```
the included logo.htm:

<table width="90%">
<tr>
 <td width="20%"><img src="logo.gif"></td>
 <td width="80%"><h1>The Example Company</h1></td>
</tr>
</table>

first page:

<html>
<body>
<center>
<%-- here comes the logo --%>
<%@ include file="logo.htm"%>
```

```
</center>
<table>
<tr><td> first line of the page 1.</td>
<tr><td> second line of the page 1.</td>
</table>
</body>
</html>

second page:

<html>
<body>
<center>
<%-- here comes the logo again --%>
<%@ include file="logo.htm"%>
</center>
<table>
<tr><td> first line of the page 2.</td>
<tr><td> second line of the page 2.</td>
</table>
</body>
</html>
```

Because the logo page is included, it must be assumed that elements such as <html>, <body>, and <form> can cause conflict with similar tags in the including page.

Together, the static template and the included files form what is called a *translation unit*. A translation unit is the whole JSP template and code that will be translated in a single translation operation by the JSP translator during the processing of a page. The translation unit is a valid scope to a number of elements, such as the JSP declaration. This means, for example, that a method declared in the page is known in all files included after it with the include directive, and a method declared in an included file is known to the page after the inclusion point.

The page *Directive*

The page directive is used to set several attributes of a page and to import classes needed to execute the page code. It is an example of a tag that applies to a translation unit; for instance, an imported package is known in the page where declared and all JSPs included with the include directive.

The syntax of the page directive is as follows:

```
<%@ page parameter="value"%>
```

Some of the most used parameters of the page directive are listed here:

- **import="packageDescription"**—A package or fully qualified class name to import. The same rules for common package/class imports apply here.

- **session="true|false"**—An indication that this page must join the session. The default value is true and/or the page joins a session, or it creates a new one if it doesn't exist. If `false`, this parameter indicates that no session will be accessible and that trying to access it will cause an error. The default is `true`.

Check the JSP API documentation for a complete description of all page parameters.

The taglib *Directive*

The `taglib` directive is used to declare that the page uses a specific tag library. It takes two parameters: a universal resource identifier (an URI) and a prefix. The URI is a name that uniquely identifies the tags of the declared tag library. The prefix associates each tag with its URI. The tags must be preceded by this prefix, similar to XML namespaces (see Section 2.2.1, "Tags and Actions," in Chapter 2).

The syntax of the `taglib` directive is as follows:

```
<%@ taglib uri="someUri" prefix="somePrefix"%>
```

When the tag library is declared with a `taglib` directive, its tags can be used in the page. Each of the tags must be prefixed like `<somePrefix:tagName attributes.../>`. For instance, consider this code:

```
<prefix1:myFirstTag anAttribute="value">.

<%@ taglib uri="XYZWCompanyInc-LayoutTags-v.1.0" prefix="xyzw"/>
<%@ taglib uri="XYZWCompanyInc-MenuTags-v.1.0" prefix="menu"/>

<xyzw:placeLogo type="wide" title="Module One"/>

<menu:placeToolbar>
 <menu:toolbarItem name="operations">
  <menu:menuItem name="new article" action="insert.op"/>
  <menu:menuItem name="edit article" action="edit.op"/>
 </menu:toolbarItem name="operations">
 <menu:toolbarItem name="admin">
  <menu:menuItem name="new user" action="insertUsr.op"/>
  <menu:menuItem name="statistics" action="stats.op"/>
 </menu:toolbarItem name="admin">
</menu:placeToolbar>
This is an example page for the XYZW Company.

Select an operation or Admin to perform administrative routines.

<xyzw:placeFooter type="SimpleAddr"/>
```

The last page shows a top header with the company's logo and then a drop-down menu with two operations. The `XYZWCompanyInc-LayoutTags-v.1.0` URI identifies the tags. For this specific page, the prefix chosen is `xyzw`. This can be a specific prefix assigned enterprise-wide to the common tag libraries, or it can be assigned only locally, as a means of differentiating tags with the same name from different tag libraries.

You can use as many `taglib` directives as necessary to declare the `taglibs` you need, but the prefixes must be all distinct. A tag library can be declared with a different prefix from page to page, but a better practice is to have a standard prefix for each tag library and reinforce it throughout the organization.

<%= Expressions

In computer language, expressions are the ultimate way to express meaning. JavaServer Pages provide a mechanism to write Java expressions that get evaluated and replaced by the string conversion of their respective values. JSP expression tags `<%=` and `%>` can contain any valid Java expression and can be comprised of any variable declared previously in the JSP.

Expressions cannot have semicolon separators, so they are lone statements. You can declare only one expression at a time. The translation of such expression is a JSPWriter `out.print()` statement as follows: An expression such as

```
<%=a+1%>
```

is translated in the translated servlet into

```
out.print(a+1);
```

At the execution phase, that evaluates to a+1, translates the result to a string value, and prints the result in the JSPWriter output. The next example prints a well-formatted date in the result page:

```
<%@ page import="java.text.SimpleDateFormat"%>
<%@ page import="java.util.Date"%>

<%!
  // declares a SimpleDateFormat formatter
  SimpleDateFormat sdf = new SimpleDateFormat("YYYY-MM-DD HH:MM:SS");
%>

This page was last accessed at <%=sdf.format(new Date)%>
```

<%! Declarations

A JSP can be thought of as a servlet (in fact, you can write scriptlets as pure JSPs, and some authors differentiate such JSPs from content-generation JSPs). It is the servlet that is generated by the translation process, and its semantics follow the servlet semantics over which it is built. Sometimes you must specify subsidiary data attributes or functions to help in the execution of the process that the JSP implements. To declare such attributes and member functions, or to declare some specific initialization routine using `jspInit()`, you use JSP declarations.

The declaration is a fragment of Java code that declares variables or methods in the scope of the translation unit being considered. The translation unit comprises your page and all static that your page does with the `include` directive. It must be a valid Java declaration, according to the Java Language Specification document. Your declarations must be enclosed in <%! and %> tags.

You can use as many declaration snippets as you need, provided that the following rules are followed:

1. Each variable declaration must end with a semicolon.

2. Each block declaration must be enclosed within curly braces ({ and }).

3. Whatever the item declared is, it must be declared before being used.

Listing 1.7 provides a variety of declarations: scalar elements, objects, and methods that will be rendered to the translated servlet's methods.

Listing 1.7 **Using Declarations**

```
<%!
   int a = 0; // an int declaration
   String message = "This is a message"; // a String

   public String clip (int b) // this is a method declaration
   {
     if (b < message.length())
       return message.substring(a, b);
     else return message;
   }
%>

This page presents a truncated message: <%=clip(10) %>.<br>

<%! boolean d = true; %>

And has a boolean value, true ? <%=d%>.
```

Listing 1.8 gets more complex with the declaration of an inner class. Although it's not recommended as clean MVC style, this is possible and will work smoothly.

Listing 1.8 **An Inner Class Inside a Declaration**

```
<%!
   protected class StringPair
   {
       String item;
       String code;

       public StringPair(String c, String t)
       { code = c; item = t; }
   }
%>

Here we have an inner class :<br>
```

```
<%
   StringPair sp = new StringPair("1.1","Socks");
%>

The string pair values are <%=(sp.code+"="+sp.item)%>
```

Of course, pages can get far more complex than the examples showed in Listings 1.7 and 1.8. This can be hard to maintain and difficult for designers with lesser Java programming skills. To avoid this, the JSP counts with two fundamental mechanisms: standard actions and custom tags.

<% Scriptlets

Scriptlets are code fragments that provide the core functionality for the JSP. After it's translated, scriptlet code is placed in an orderly manner on the `jspService` method of the translated servlet. (*Orderly* here means the order of appearance.)

Scriptlets contain Java statements separated by semicolons. Declarations inside a scriptlet are considered local to the `jspService` method. Expressions are treated like ordinary Java expressions. Files included with the `include` directive are inserted after parsing when JSP files.

You can mix block statements scriptlets, such as `while()`and `if()` with the static template, to create conditional content. (See Listing 1.9.)

Listing 1.9   **Using Scriptlets**

```
<%
  // first scriptlet
  // example of conditional generation with scriptlets
  if (x > 10)
  {
%>
<!-- This is the static template INSIDE an IF statement -->
<h1> x is BIGGER than 10 </h1>
<%
  }
  // second scriptlet
  else
  {
%>
<h1> x is SMALLER OR EQUALS to 10 </h1>
<%
  }
%>
```

Standard Actions

Standard actions are predefined tag-like actions that are available to the JSP developer by default with the JSP API. Six standard actions exist: useBean, getProperty, setProperty, include, forward, and plug-in. They use tag-like syntax with the namespace prefix jsp, as explained in the following sections.

<jsp:useBean>

The jsp:useBean standard action loads a bean from the given scope with the given identifier and instantiates it from the given class or type, if it couldn't be found in the scope:

```
<jsp:useBean id="employee" class="com.xyzw.Employee" scope="session"/>
```

This action tries to instantiate a variable employee from a bean stored in the session. If it found no employee on the session, it creates it and instantiates it from the class com.xyzw.Employee. Keep in mind that <jsp:useBean> gets translated into code that comes before all scriptlets.

<jsp:getProperty>

The jsp:getProperty standard action gets the named property from the bean using the appropriate getter method, as shown in the following example:

```
<!-- this instantiates a bean from the session -->
<jsp:useBean id="employee" class="com.xyzw.Employee" scope="session"/>

<!-- these get the value of the employee's properties -->
name: <jsp:getProperty name="employee" property="name"/>
social security: <jsp:getProperty name="employee" property="socSecNum"/>
```

<jsp:setProperty>

The <jsp:setProperty> action is analogous to <jsp:getProperty>, except that it sets the property using the respective setter method.

```
<!-- this instantiates a bean from the session -->
<jsp:useBean id="employee" class="com.xyzw.Employee" scope="session"/>

<!-- these set the value of the employee's properties -->
<jsp:setProperty name="employee" property="name" value="<%=currentName%>"/>
<jsp:getProperty name="employee" property="salary"
value="<%=baseSalary+additionals-(discounts+taxes)%>"/>
```

<jsp:include>

The <jsp:include> action includes the page from the relative address. If the page is static, it merely includes the static content in the current page. If the page is dynamic (a servlet or a JSP), it includes the response from that page's execution.

Listing 1.10 presents the first approach to a simple link-based menu. In Chapter 3, "Writing Custom Tags," you will see an enhanced version of this menu based on tags:

Listing 1.10   **The Menu Example**

```
<!-- first page: filter menu -->
<%
    String serviceName = request.getServletPath().substring(1);
    String qs = request.getQueryString();
    String newQs = "";
    String pre = "";
    String pos = "";
    String filter = request.getParameter("FILTER");
    if (filter == null) filter = "G";

    if (qs.indexOf("FILTER") > -1)
    {
        pre = serviceName+"?"+qs.substring(0,qs.indexOf("FILTER"));
        pos =
qs.substring(qs.indexOf("FILTER")).substring(qs.substring(qs.indexOf("FILTER")).in
dexOf("&"));
        newQs = pre+"FILTER="+filter+pos;
    }
    else
    {
        pre = serviceName+"?";
        pos = "&"+qs;
    }
%>

<%  if (!filter.equals("A"))
    {
%>
    <a href="<%=pre+"FILTER=A"+pos%>">All</a>
<%
    }
    else
    {
%>
    <B>ALL</B>
<%
    }
%>
    ¦
    ¦
<%  if (!filter.equals("P"))
    {
%>
    <a href="<%=pre+"FILTER=P"+pos%>">Specific</a>
<%
    }
```

continues

Listing 1.10 **Continued**

```
    else
    {
%>
    <B>Specific</B>
<%
    }
%>

<!-- end of first page -->

<!-- second page -->

<h1> test of status menu </h1>

<div align="right"><jsp:include page="stmenu.jsp" flush="true"/>

Click on the above links to change the status of this page !

<!-- end of second page -->
```

You can have as many includes in your page as needed.

<jsp:forward>

The <jsp:forward> action forwards the request to the target page. The main difference between this action and RequestDispatcher forward and response.sendRedirect is that both of these complete the execution of the current method after the request is forwarded, whereas the <jsp:forward> action doesn't (see the following example).

```
<!-- emitter -->

<jsp:useBean id="employee" class="com.xyzw.Employee" scope="session"/>

<%
  if (employee.getNovice())
  {
%>
<jsp:forward page="rulesOfConduct.jsp">
<%
  }
%>

If you see this page, you are NOT a rooker!

<!-- end of emitter -->
```

Although you can have more than a single `include` in a page, you can't have more than one `forward`. This is because the `forward` action that requires the page buffer hasn't been committed before it, and the target page actually commits the page buffer at some point. This is also because it doesn't return the control to the originating page. Therefore, the second `forward` would never been reached anyway.

Summary

In this chapter, you learned about the idea of a web application, got a historical perspective on the evolution of the technologies involved, and saw what the Java API has to offer on the subject. You also learned about how the Servlet API is a better alternative to CGI, and you discovered JavaServer Pages, the scripting technology.

This chapter showed you that a web application is not that different from any other class of application. The difference resides in the technologies used to implement the application runtime cycle, based on the HTTP protocol. Web applications also rely on web pages as a presentation mechanism. In addition, you learned that web applications need a session-tracking mechanism to circumvent the lack of state in the HTTP protocol.

These main concepts of the Servlet API also were presented as well:

- **Container**—A web or servlet container contains web components, such as servlets and JSPs. It provides them the runtime environment needed to execute. TOMCAT is the web container from the Apache Software Foundation and is considered the reference implementation for a servlet container. Web applications are deployed to a container in a context.

- **Context**—The context is the repository where the elements that comprise a web application are deployed. It has a logical representation in the Servlet API, which is the `ServletContext`. The `ServletContext` is the view that a web component has of its context and the web application itself.

- **Servlet**—A servlet implements the servlet interface. The `HttpServlet` is a subclass of a servlet that is compatible with the HTTP protocol's request-response cycle. The `HttpServlet` interface has three methods: `init`, `service` and `destroy`.

- **Request**—The request contains information about the client's request, attributes set by the container or by the application itself, the session, and request parameters.

- **Response**—The response holds the information to generate the output to the client. It can contain response headers or HTTP return codes. The `sendRedirect` method is the way to redirect a request outside the container.

- **RequestDispatcher**—This wraps a resource to accept the request sent by some web component. The `RequestDispatcher` is factored by the context and can be named, if a name is defined in the web application deployment descriptor for it.

The JSP API is an extension of the Servlet API and implements web page scripting. The main components in the JSP API are as follows:

- **Page**—The page is a text file that contains code that a JSP processor can compile. The code in a JSP specifies how to compute a response from a request. It is not compiled directly into bytecode. The JSP processor translates the JSP into an intermediary servlet and compiles that servlet into bytecode.

- **PageContext**—The PageContext object has a number of responsibilities, including to provide a way to access all the page-level information, to initialize the other implicit objects, to provide a way to manage and access the various scoped namespaces (page scope, request scope, session scope, and context scope), and to provide a number of methods that access the other implicit objects from the page and from any accessory component that needs to access that page's objects.

- **Implicit objects**—Every JSP has defined a number of implicit objects to ease the access to the underlying mechanisms without needing too much Java code in the page. These are application, config, request, response, pageContext (in the sense that it exposes the page scope and environment), out, exception, and session objects.

- **Standard actions**—Standard actions encapsulate standard behavior useful in diverse situations. They have a syntax derived from XML, within the JSP namespace prefix, and are the include, forward, useBean, getProperty, setProperty, and plugin actions.

- **Tag libraries**—Besides standard actions, JSPs can make use of tag libraries. Tags are as standard actions but are defined by the developer. They are the focus of the rest of this book.

2

Introduction to Tag Libraries

GRASPING THE CONCEPT OF TAG LIBRARIES is very important. With this knowledge, you can better comprehend the complex mechanisms behind frameworks such as Struts, as will see in Chapter 6, "The Jakarta Struts Project," and the MVC design pattern.

Actions

Actions are a fundamental concept of JSP programming. They represent the processes embedded in the page that will be executed to generate a response from the client's request parameters. However, unlike scriptlets, actions are encapsulated in an XML-like representation. They can be seen as program devices instead of program fragments.

There are standard actions and custom actions. As you learned in the previous chapter, standard actions must be implemented in all JSP 1.1–compatible web containers. Custom actions are created using the Tag Library Extension API in the form of custom tag libraries. It is important for you to understand standard actions so that you can understand how tag libraries can be used and become familiar with many of the mechanisms common to both.

What Is an Action?

Actions are programmatic devices that are used in a JSP to provide some pluggable functionality. According to the JSP spec, actions may do the following:

- **Use, modify, and create objects**—Actions can access the several namespaces defined in the web container—namely, context, session, request, and page—to retrieve objects or to post objects that they've created or modified. These will be available for further use by other components in the page, such as other JSPs or servlets.

- **Affect the out stream**—Actions can interfere in the way the output is created, interrupt the evaluation of the page, or generate specific output.

Actions are encapsulated within an action element, whose syntax is based on XML prefixes conforming to the XML Namespaces recommendation.

Standard Actions in Detail

The JSP specification defines six standard actions that all conforming web containers must implement, as you learned in the previous chapter: useBean, getProperty, setProperty, include, forward, and plugin. They are all prefixed with the *jsp* prefix. In the TOMCAT web container, standard tags are implemented as part of the JASPER JSP processor.

Getting Data from the Scope

A bean or other common object can be bound to a number of namespaces—context, session, request, and page. These can be used by any web application component, such as servlets, via the interfaces on the Servlet API; by JSPs, via the pageContext or implicit objects; and by actions, also via the pageContext action. These namespaces define distinct scopes for the object or bean, and each scope has a role that can be associated with it. From the most general to the most strict, these are as follows:

1. **The context scope**—The context scope is defined by the context namespace and is implemented as a context-level attribute. The ServletContext interface has methods to define and access attributes in the context scope. Beans and objects put in the context scope will be available to all components in the web application until they are removed by an application's process or the web container gets shut down. This means that the context scope is more bound to store general objects and parameters.

   For instance, in a government-oriented application, the representation of state-level entities (such as state-level financial institutions or a table of financial account codes in a financial-oriented application) can be useful if bound generally throughout the application. Thus, it is a good candidate for a context scope attribute. This saves time and increases responsiveness for the client because the page that will display them will get it from the context alive instead of generating it from an EJB transaction.

2. **The session scope**—The session scope brings structure to the sequence of requests that a client submits to the application. For instance, the client can connect to the system and submit a new entry, edit the attributes of another, and delete a third one. It's useful to have the client's identification for login and activities tracking.

    Objects bound to the session will be available to all web components that join the session until they are removed or the session becomes invalidated by a call to the session's `invalidate` method. Thus, it is not as general as the context scope, in which web components access attributes unconditionally while the container is running. Joining the session means having access to session data when the component receives a request from that client and a session was already created, or creating a session for that client. Hence, the session scope is more bound to store cross-transaction–level information.

    The classical example of cross-transaction–level information is a shopping cart in e-commerce applications. This is where many kinds of attributes, such as consumer identification, consumer categorization, items bought, and payment preferences, are needed to be available throughout the pages in the application. However, they must not be available to all pages. Generally, they shouldn't be available in places that a specific consumer hasn't visited. Even more crucial, they must not be visible by other consumers. Thus, this kind of data is best stored at the session scope.

3. **The request scope**—The request scope is more bound to store information specific to a request-response transaction. The request scope is also used by the container to store request-level control information. Objects are bound to the request scope through request attributes. A request attribute lasts until a response is returned to the client. This means that, once stored at request scope, such objects won't be available in a next request unless specific action is taken to ensure that. For instance, back to the e-commerce application, the consumer accesses data regarding an item to buy. The information, description, pointers to resources, pricing information, and so on are best stored at the request scope.

    Sometimes the criteria to decide whether information must be stored as session attributes or request attributes might seem blurred. In fact, there are no rules of thumb. But there are some hints. In the previous example, the e-commerce application clearly will be dealing with two levels of information scope: session data that must be available subsequently and request data that will be discarded after the response is committed and requires that something be returned to the client. Which one is it? In this case, you must ask, what is the minimum needed to be available to enable the next transaction to run?

    You can see that item information will be presented to consumer appreciation, and it is clearly in request scope because this information changes for a different item. But some pieces survive if certain conditions are met. If the consumer decides to buy the item, the item identification must be saved for pricing in a later stage. So, the item codes migrate from the request to some shopping cart structure on the session. It transcends its original scope and is scoped at a higher level. Where to store such information is sometimes much harder to decide.

Another point to consider is request attribute mobility. The request scope usage is not restricted to a single page, but it can be moved throughout the path to generate the appropriate response. A request can be forwarded from page to page; on each, some attributes can be read and some new ones can be added to the request. Then the request can be forwarded or included again until some page returns a response to the client. A common example is in the MVC pattern, the communication between the servlet in the role of the controller, some bean in the role of request resolver and the view JSP page. The request will be carried through all of them until a response is generated. Figure 2.1 illustrates this situation.

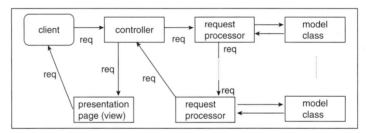

Figure 2.1   This figure shows how a request can migrate through a number of pages, either via request dispatching or as a parameter in a method invocation, until a final response is sent back to the client.

4. **The page scope**—The page scope is the most restrained of the scopes discussed. It is more bound to store information needed during the JSP processing and then discarded afterward. Page-level information is stored as `pageContext` attributes, and it is available to the translation unit (the collection of elements present in the page and all statically included fragments). An example of usage for the page scope is parameter passing between custom tags. If tag A requires a value that will be generated by tag B, then tag B can pass that to tag A by storing it as a page-level attribute. Then tag A can access the attribute and retrieve the value. This is useful when more complex types must be passed.

Figure 2.2 summarizes the different scopes and their respective usage.

Figure 2.2 shows the several namespaces available and their respective scope. Attribute A is at context scope. It's available to all pages all the time, until it gets removed. Attribute B is at session scope. It will be available to page 1 and servlet 1 only, no matter how many times the user accesses these pages, until the session is invalidated. Attribute C is available to page 2 at request scope. Then the request is forwarded to page 3, where a response is generated. On a subsequent request to page 2 or page 3, attribute C won't be there anymore. Attribute D is at page scope in page 3. It will be available to the translation unit encompassing page 3 during the unit's processing, but it won't be available to any other page or servlet.

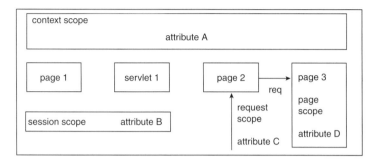

Figure 2.2   The different scopes created by the different namespaces inside the Servlet/JSP API.

To use these namespaces and respective scopes, objects can be stored as attributes on the respective scope, as you've seen. These attributes are used as communication pipelines by the components in the web application. This is not exclusive to the MVC design pattern; any application developed under any model can use them. The next section explains how to use standard actions to instantiate and retrieve objects bound to each of these scopes, and it discusses how to organize standard actions in a page to provide the desired functionality.

An important thing to keep in mind is that these namespaces have distinct scopes and also distinct duration. The context scope will be available to all web components inside the web application while the container is running—that is, most of the time. Overloading the context scope with attributes that don't necessarily need to be there will impact the container (consuming disk and memory space) for a rather long time. The session scope, the second more persistent namespace, suffers from the same problem. Despite the fact that you can determine how long the session will be maintained, this time is always an approximation. The idea is to put your objects in a namespace where they will be discarded as soon as they fulfill their purpose, so that you have tight control on where each object was placed and when and how it will be trashed.

An Article Database

Consider an example article database, to illustrate the use of standard actions to access data beans on the several scopes.

A MySQL database on articles and statistics about Brazilian soccer (which is actually called football) must be available to students on history and sports. This database is organized as shown in Table 2.1.

Table 2.1 **MySQL Database Example**

Articles	Authors	Journals
Article_Id integer	author_Id char(2)	journal_Id char(4)
year char(4)	name char(45)	name char(45)
MAIN_author char(2)	nationality char(2)	origin char(2)
pages integer		publisher char(45)
category char(1)		area char(20)
number integer		
volume integer		
country char(2)		
abstr char(250)		
journal char(4)		
title char(80)		

A search page must be implemented that will retrieve articles by title, author, year, and keywords on the abstract. A page must be implemented with summaries of the results and a detailed table with all information available on a certain article.

The data on these tables will be represented as three JavaBeans: `ArticleBean`, `AuthorBean`, and `JournalBean`. The focus will always be on the article, however. The application will be centered on a servlet, the `ArticleDBServlet`, which will have to do the following:

1. Initialize the connection with the database on the `init` method. (You learned how to do this in Chapter 1, "Introduction to Servlets and JavaServer Pages.")

2. Receive a request that can demand to search the database or retrieve detail data on a specific article in the search result set.

3. If the request demands a search on the database, search the database and store a list of found articles on the section. If successful, return the result set as a vector of found articles to a summary page. If not successful, return to a failure report page.

4. If the request demands detail on a certain article, then retrieve the result and return to an article detail page.

5. Disconnect the database with the `destroy` method, to ensure a controlled disconnection.

This application implements the MVC design pattern: The beans implement the model. `ArticleDBServlet` implements the control, and a number of JSP pages implement the view. In the following chapters, you will be working with this kind of design.

Listing 2.1 is the code for the `ArticleDBServlet`.

Listing 2.1   *ArticleDBServlet*[1]

```
import java.sql.*;
import java.io.*;
import javax.Servlet.*;
import javax.Servlet.http.*;
import java.util.*;
import com.javaexchange.dbConnectionBroker.*;

public class ArticleDBServlet extends HttpServlet
{
  DbConnectionBroker conPool;

  public void init (ServletConfig config) throws ServletException
  {
    super.init(config);
    String logPath = config.getServletContext().getRealPath("/WEB-
INF/tmp/bahiana.log");
    try
    {
      conPool = new DbConnectionBroker("org.gjt.mm.mysql.Driver",
                  "jdbc:mysql://localhost/ARTICLE_DB",
                  "admin","",2,6,logPath,0.01);
    }
    catch (IOException e5)
    {
      config.getServletContext().log("init of article db servlet",e);
    }
  }

  public void service (HttpServletRequest request, HttpServletResponse response)
  throws ServletException, IOException
  {

    Connection conn = null;
    Statement stm = null;
    try
    {
      conn = conPool.getConnection();
      String type = request.getParameter("REQ_TYPE");

      // this is a rudimentary request processor
      if (type.equals("SEARCH"))
         searchDatabase(conn, request);
      else if (type.equals("DETAIL"))
         retrieveArticle(conn, request);
```

continues

1. The examples presented throughout the book, as well as the instructions on how to run them, are available on the book's web site. Refer to the inside back cover, "About the Web Site," for more information on how to download and install the examples.

Listing 2.1   **Continued**

```
      else
         invalidRequest(request, response);

   }
   catch (Exception e)
   {
     getServletContext().log("Error during retrieve",e);
   }
   finally
   {
     try{if(stm != null) stm.close();}
     catch(SQLException e){};
     conPool.freeConnection(conn);
   }

}

public void destroy ()
{
  conPool.destroy();
  super.destroy();
}
}
```

In Listing 2.1, the `init` method just initializes the connection pool that will manage the database connections. It uses the same structure that you saw in the previous chapter. This connects the database ARTICLE_DB on the localhost system (which yours will be, if you install the example code). If you have another database server configuration, then modify the appropriate lines of the `init` method to ensure that the example will find your server. More details on the MySQL database, the mm.mysql jdbc driver, and the poolman connection pool, can be found in Appendix D, "MySQL."

The `service` method basically defines a rudimentary request processor that will decide what to do with a request parameter. In the discussion on Struts, you will learn a much more sophisticated way to decide how to respond to a client's request. This simple example is based on an if-else construct that tests the type parameter, a parameter that tells the request processor which kind of transaction the client is trying to submit. When a match is found for a certain type, the associated method is called and the request is fulfilled.

The `searchDatabase` method retrieves the criteria parameters from the request, binds them to a prepared statement, and calls `executeQuery`. If there are results, it wraps them with `summaryBean` objects and puts the `summaryBeans` in a vector. Then it stores the vector in the session and redirects to the summary JSP.

Why store the summaries vector in the session? Because the natural flow of processing is designed with the user performing a query and navigating through the solutions retrieved after that. So, the same set of results will possibly be used many times while the user navigates back and forward for his target article. Using the request scope will force you to implement a way to preserve the results vector between requests, which is a pointless additional effort. Using the context scope is also inadequate because each user will submit his own criteria parameters—thus, overlapping might occur, causing a bizantine fault. The page scope is completely out of the question, for obvious reasons (servlets don't have a page namespace). Hence, the results vector will be stored in the session.

The `retrieveArticle` method retrieves an article's data and wraps it within the adequate beans. Then it stores the beans in the request scope and forwards the request to the detail JSP. Again, because an article's data is retrieved upon a specific request and will vary in subsequent requests, it's pointless to store it in the session. Its life cycle coincides with the request scope attribute's life cycle. After that, the request is forwarded to the detail page.

The index page for the database, index.html, provides some background information and the search parameters.

The JSP pages that make the view of this web application are summary.jsp and detail.jsp. The first presents a simple table of contents type of view that contains the article's title, the author, the year of publication, and the abstract. The second presents a view like a database record, showing all the data about the article itself, the publisher, and the author. On each JSP page, there are a number of objects to be rendered. The summary page must present the contents of the summary beans. The detail page, on the other hand, must render the article, author, and publisher beans.

Because both mechanisms are deployed differently in both pages, you will have to understand both of them.

The summary page gets a vector of `SummaryBeans` from the session, and spans the vector's `summaryBeans` to fill the summary JSP page. Check the Listing 2.2 that follows.

Listing 2.2   **The Summary Page**

```
Vector summary = (Vector) session.getAttribute("SUMMARY");

....

<%
  // spans the vector's beans
  for(int i=0;i<summary.size();i++)
  {
    // get an article summary
    SummaryBean aSummary = (SummaryBean) summary.elementAt(i);
%>
    <tr>
    <td><%=aSummary.getYear()%></td>
    <td><a
href="article.htm?ACTION=DETAIL&ID=aSummary.getId()"><%=aSummary.getTitle()%></a><
{/td>
    <td><%=aSummary.getMainAuthor()%></td>
```

continues

Listing 2.2   **Continued**

```
<td><%=aSummary.getAbstr()%></td>
</tr>

<%} // end for %>
```

Even though Listing 2.2 is not that complex, you can easily see that Java code structures are used all over the place. There's a main loop, the for structure, which will generate the summary's data page.

Listing 2.3 shows a completely different style of page. Here standard actions will be used whenever possible, to try to reduce dependency on Java coding and possibly to allow page designers to work on this without needing constant help from a Java programmer.

Listing 2.3   **The Article Detail Page**

```
<jsp:useBean id="article" scope="request" class="examples.jspBook.ArticleBean">
<jsp:useBean id="author" scope="request" class="examples.jspBook.AuthorBean">
<jsp:useBean id="journal" scope="request" class="examples.jspBook.JournalBean">

<tr>
  <td>
    Article ID:
    <jsp:getProperty name="article" property="articleId"/>
  </td>
  <td>
    Title:
    <jsp:getProperty name="article" property="title"/>
  </td>
</tr>
<tr>
  <td>
    Author:
    <jsp:getProperty name="author" property="name"/>
  </td>
  <td>
    Journal:
    <jsp:getProperty name="journal" property="name"/>
  </td>
</tr>

...
```

Compare Listing 2.3 with the summary page in Listing 2.2, and see the difference. Here, you are practically writing plain old HTML—better said, XML—which is in every designers' basic skill set. In the summary page, on the other hand, there are scriptlets. In fact, it's much more reasonable to think that the designer will work these funny tags prefixed with jsp: more easily than learning enough Java server-side programming to produce those pages.

But it's not all roses over there. Despite the fact that standard actions are widely available in every JSP 1.1–compliant web container and are quite simple to use, they are not flexible at all. It's impossible to represent processes other than what is shown here. Not even the more sophisticated bean structures are covered—for instance, indexed bean properties are not covered, nor are complex properties implemented with other beans. These can seem quite far from day-to-day programming, but they actually are not. That's where custom tags enter the stage. The idea is to deploy custom tags, specifically designed for your needs, in this XML-like way.

Custom Tags

Custom tags are a mechanism defined in the JSP 1.1 API to implement custom actions in the web container for use by page designers. Custom tags are web components, part of the J2EE web layer. They are run in the web container runtime environment within a JSP processor.

Custom tags provide the JSP framework a simple, yet powerful mechanism to encapsulate and reuse custom standardized processes. A process—for example, sending an email message to a system administrator when a certain condition is reached—can be encapsulated in a tag that takes the target email and uses the Javamail API to send the notification email. A tag such as this one can represent this situation:

```
<ex:notifyAdmin email="ADB-Admin@wlss.com " text="A message"/>
```

A page designer can place such tag in a JSP error page in such a way that, when the page gets automatically called by the container, the tag sends the notification message when an error condition is detected. In fact, the custom tags mechanism introduces a separation of roles in the web application design pipeline between typical page designers (possibly with a limited knowledge of Java programming and focus on the visual design of a page) and tag designers (who must have a strong background in JSP and Java programming and a focus in programming).

Custom tags are delivered in the form of tag libraries. They can be designed to provide some general standardized process to the market. A JSP page can use as many tag libraries as needed, declaring each of them with a `taglib` directive (as seen in Chapter 1).

Tags and Actions

Custom tags are used to enable web application developers to implement actions that are specific to some context, whether it is oriented to the market or to the organization's internal effort. Custom tags represent custom processes. They can encapsulate some recurrent process that repeats throughout the pages in some web application, or they can be defined to supply some packaged functionality to a specific market.

Custom tags provide abstraction reuse, process encapsulation, improved code maintainability, and easier application manageability. They are easily redistributable, can be integrated with sophisticated page-composition tools, and support a better division of roles on the web application design pipeline.

What Is a Custom Tag?

Custom tags are analogous, in the web application arena, to software components in the RAD arena. Tags can generate web content (or not), can be aggregated in composites working cooperatively, and can represent data or data structures. Such flexibility in usage is a consequence of its structure.

Custom tags are implemented as JavaBeans that implement the `Tag` or `BodyTag` interfaces. Such beans are called tag handlers. The attributes of a tag are implemented as properties of the tag handler, and they are made accessible to the runtime environment via its associated `get` and `set` methods. Attributes in a custom tag can be of any valid Java type.

The process that the tag encapsulates is implemented as logic in the tag handler, possibly within specific methods. For instance, an email tag must parse the destination address and invoke the Javamail objects that will send the email. These can be implemented as some parse and `sendMail` methods in the tag handler.

The tag handler must pass some predefined responses to the JSP processor to allow the JSP processing to continue. A tag can allow the rest of the JSP be evaluated and processed. If the tag contains a body, it can allow the body be evaluated and processed. This way, a tag developer has a good deal of control on the interaction between the tag and the page and between the tag and its body, whether this includes a number of tags or data.

Tags as JSP Elements

After it is placed in a JSP, a tag can access all the JSP elements. They access the `pageContext` object and, through it, the several implicit objects available in the JSP, such as the session and the application (the context). A tag can access request parameters and attributes placed in all predefined scopes (context, session, request, and page). Tags can also define, remove, and set attributes in any predefined scope.

In addition, tags can define scripting variables and make them available to other page elements even after the processing of the tag. There are two mechanisms for that. The variables can be described in the tag definition file, called Tag Library Descriptor (TLD), or it can use another class, called `TagExtraInfo` (TEI class), to do that. You will learn more on the TLD in the next sections. The TEI class will be discussed in Chapter 4, "Cooperating Tags and Validation."

What a Tag Is Not

It now should be obvious that a tag is a programmatic structure. Nevertheless, the syntax of custom tags is heavily based on XML, which is declarative metalanguage, and this can confuse newcomers.

Custom Tags Are Not XML Elements

XML elements are entities that represent abstractions in XML documents. They have a declarative nature rather than a programmatic one. This establishes a profound distinction between custom tags and XML elements.

Furthermore, the process chain for JSP processing is very well defined and implemented in the JSP processor. The whole life cycle of a tag is entirely contained in that process chain. XML elements, on the other hand, don't have a predefined life cycle. It can be generated as a result of an e-commerce process, it can be used as input of a process, and it can be parsed for data extraction, rendered by an XSL processor, and processed by the server and the client seamlessly.

Nevertheless, because JSP pages can be used to create XML, in some situations both tags and XML elements can be put on the same page. In that case, the tag prefix will be the determining factor in the process. If an XML fragment uses the same namespace prefix that a tag is using, the JSP processor will be misled to process it as a custom tag, and the process will fail. Be careful about selecting prefixes.

XSP, ColdFusion, and Other Technologies

The idea of having processes encapsulated in HTML/XML–like syntax in some dynamic page is not exclusive to JSP custom tags. Other mechanisms and languages for dynamic web content generation and applications exist beyond the Java language.

The Cocoon project (`http://xml.apache.org/cocoon`), from the Apache Software Foundation (ASF), is an example of such an application. Its primary goal is to serve as an open-source web publishing system, based entirely on XML. Cocoon can be considered an umbrella project with a number of technologies and subprojects developed under it.

Technologies involved in the Cocoon pipeline are Xerces, the ASF's XML parser, which evolved from IBM's XML4J; and the Xalan XSL processor, which evolved from Lotus's LotusXSL processor, among others. Examples of Cocoon's subprojects are the several Cocoon generators and XML Server Pages, XSP, a technology inspired partially by JSPs but with complete emphasis on XML generation.

XSP has a mechanism for creating user-defined tags to reuse XML generation logic. Although the concept is the same, such tags can be created with Java (currently JavaScript is also supported), and the resulting tags can be put in a library also called a tag library. These are not compatible with JSP tag libraries.

The same is valid with ColdFusion custom tags. ColdFusion is a web development language created by Allaire (`http://www.allaire.com/coldfusion`) whose syntax is based on XML. ColdFusion also has a logic-reuse mechanism called custom tags. In fact, it offers two different kinds of custom tags.

The concept repeats here again. ColdFusion Markup Language (CFML) custom tags enable the CFML programmer to reuse tags defined in CFML. But ColdFusion allows for another kind of tags, called ColdFusion API tags (CFX tags). CFX tags can be written in Java. Again, although the jargon and the concepts are the same, these are a completely different kind of tags.

It is important to understand that the concepts being discussed here, such as using HTML/XML markup to represent process encapsulation and reuse devices, are not unique to Java and JSP. Newcomers might believe that such implementations are inter-changeable—and soon find out that they are not.

Custom Tags and XML Namespaces

To correctly locate the definition of each tag in a document and to avoid naming conflicts when using more than one tag library simultaneously, the `taglib` directive demands a prefix that will be used to differentiate tag libraries in the style of XML namespaces. XML namespaces are an XML technology used to differentiate entities with similar names within XML documents.

In XML, abstractions are represented by XML documents and entities inside a document. The set of entities defined by an organization or standardization body to describe a context can be thought of as the vocabulary for the context. Vocabularies on a specific context are described by a Document Type Definition (DTD) document and can be designed by more than one organization. Because they describe the same abstractions, naming conflicts can occur. They use the same name for entities defined in distinct DTDs. When using these entities in the same document, you must deal with a collision of those definitions. Figure 2.3 illustrates this.

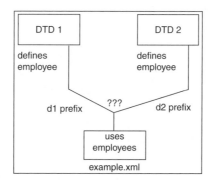

Figure 2.3   Collision between DTDs:
The same name denotes entities with distinct definitions.

To solve this problem, the World Wide Web Consortium (W3C) released an XML technology specification called *XML Namespaces*. This technology gives the document designer the capability to attach a prefix to entities defined in a DTD. This then differ-entiates them from the entities defined in another DTD, enabling entities defined in both DTDs to be used in the very same XML document. Figure 2.4 illustrates this new situation.

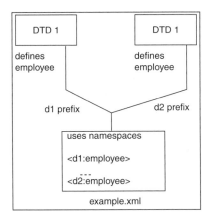

Figure 2.4 Distinct namespaces for distinct definitions: The same name but with distinct prefixes denotes entities with distinct definitions without the problem of a collision.

It is fairly simple to use namespaces in a document. You declare a prefix and a universal resource identifier (URI) that will uniquely identify the entity source. A URI is just a naming convention; it's a unique name for a resource. You can specify the resource as a universal resource locator (URL) as well. In that case, the resource will be designated by a path containing a protocol, some server location, and a resource path inside that server. URLs are pretty well known in the WWW world. URI also can be simply a common name, without an associated location. In that case, it is called a universal resource name (URN). The namespace is defined when you associate that URI to a prefix inside a document.

Listing 2.4 shows an XML fragment with two distinct namespaces associated: healthcare and human_resources. Note that the entity called employee is defined in both, but with completely different meanings.

Listing 2.4   **XML Namespaces Example**

```
<report
    xmlns:org="http://oemserver:8080/defs/HC001.dtd"
    xmlns:healthcare="http://healthserver:8080/defs/HC001.dtd"
    xmlns:human_recs="http://hrserver:8080/defs/HR314.dtd">

  <operation type="reimbursement">
   <amount>1200</amount>
   <beneficiary>
    <healthcare:employee HCNumber="100312"/>
   </beneficiary>
   <transaction>
    <healthcare:operation>
     <healthcare:type>100312</healthcare:type>
     <healthcare:date_op>2000-03-12</healthcare:date_op>
```

continues

Listing 2.4   **Continued**

```
  </healthcare:operation>
 </transaction>
 <approval>
  <human_recs:employee index="314234">
   <human_recs:position>DeptHead</human_recs:position>
   <org:deptcode>Production</org:deptcode>
  </human_recs:employee>
 </approval>
 </operation>
 ...
</report>
```

Listing 2.4 shows how namespaces can be used in a document. The employee used in the beneficiary element must be described in terms of which rights are granted to him to claim this reimbursement. This is based in a healthcare operation. To the healthcare department, an employee must be identified with a healthcare number (that is, his medical profile). The transaction element defines the operation that generated the benefit. Note that there are no ambiguities about the operation—because that can be any operation in the organization, namespaces are being used to define the origin of the operation instead. In the approval, there is the second definition of employee. The healthcare number of the approver doesn't matter, but its organization index and position will identify him as an authorized approver. So, instead of focusing on the rights claimed, this second usage of employee focus on the credentials of the approver.

Custom tags might present the very same problems, but with different reasons. If you use a tag library, you must inform the JSP processor where to find the definition of the tags; in that document, the processor will find the definition of each of them. Tag libraries coming from distinct vendors can still be named the same, but that poses another problem: The JSP processor must still be informed where to collect the tag definitions for each library.

To solve this, the `taglib` directive must be declared with a distinct prefix for each library, in the very same spirit of the XML Namespaces specification. Furthermore, its URI must point to the location of the document that defines that library. Listing 2.5 shows a JSP fragment with the definition of two `taglibs`: one from the Apache `taglibs` project (the subject of Chapter 9, "The Jakarta Taglibs Project") and one from the human recs division of the company.

Listing 2.5   **Using JSP Tags**

```
<html>
<body>
<%@ taglib uri="http://java.apache.org/tomcat/examples-taglib" prefix="eg" %>
<%@ taglib uri="http://hrserver:8080/libraries/hr-taglib" prefix="hr" %>

...

<ul>
```

```
<eg:foo att1="98.5" att2="92.3" att3="107.7">
<li><%= member %></li>
</eg:foo>
</ul>

<hr:showEmplProfile index="<%=emp.getIndex()%>"/>

...

</body>
</html>
```

In Listing 2.5, the initial portion of the JSP shows two `taglib` directives. The first declares Apache.org TagLib project's session `taglib`, which contains tags that deal with the session in a page. This is basically a utilitarian `taglib` that can be used in many pages. The second `taglib` directive declares an in-house library, which deals with employee application operations. In this case, there is a tag called `showEmplProfile` that will display, in that position, some sort of well-defined HTML design to show an employee's profile's data.

You can see that there's no ambiguity here, but the prefixes are still needed to advise the JSP processor that the definition of the session tag should be collected in a document residing at `http://jakarta.apache.org/tomcat/examples-taglib` on the Internet, and that the definition of `showEmplProfile` should be collected from an internal server at `http://hrserver:8080/libraries/hr-taglib`.

Even if the tags were named the same, the JSP processor would have no problems associating the correct definition with each.

Basic Structure of a Tag

A tag is represented in a JSP page in an XML/HTML–like element with the following structure:

```
<tagPrefix:tagName [list-of-attribute-value-pairs]>

A Body. The body can contain raw text, JSP syntax, custom tags, etc.

</tagPrefix:tagName>
```

The first part contains the attribute list, as a set of a name-value pairs; it is generically called the tag head element. This is the opening part of the tag. The tag body follows the tag head.

You attach an attribute to a tag to parameterize the underlying process. Whether you should use more attributes or cooperating tags in the body is always a delicate decision because it can have a dramatic influence in the complexity of the underlying implementation of the tag and its usage afterward.

In this case, it is important to pay attention to the number or the complexity of the attributes and to determine whether they require pre- or post-processing before they're processed by the tag itself.

If the process parameters won't require specific processing and will be used directly by the underlying implementation, then it makes more sense to define them as tag attributes. Attributes can have many different types:

- **Scalar `String` converted attributes**—In this case, the attribute has type `String` or can be converted to a type according to the rules of conversion of the type with a `valueOf(String)` method:

```
<example:displayLogo posx="30" posy="225" extrude="0.25"/>
```

In this example, the parameters will position the logo on the resulting page and will extrude the image up to 25 percent.

- **Request-time attributes**—Request-time attributes are attributes that can be computed on the fly with JSP expressions. These are often the result of some existing method or else are not scalar. The next examples show both cases of request-time attributes:

```
<example:displayExchange
    currency="<%= country.getCurrency()%>"
    rate="<%= country.getRate()%>"/>

<example:displayEmployee impl="<%= employee%>"/>
```

The first example here shows a tag in which the attributes are calculated at runtime using the methods of the country bean. The second example shows a tag that receives the employee bean and processes it internally.

The body of a custom tag is a template that will be processed by the JSP processor according to what was specified in the Tag Library Descriptor file. You will see it in the section ahead; it may contain raw text, HTML, JSP syntax, or custom tags.

The closure element of the tag is the tag tail. This structure can vary in form and function. In fact, some tags can have no body. In this case, the tag tail collapses into the tag head, following the XML syntax:

```
<tagPrefix:noBodyTag [attr-list] />
```

Note the closure bar. If this is not included, it will cause a number of exceptions processing the JSP page.

Structural View of Custom Tags

Tags can be understood by the way they were implemented in the JSP Tag Extension API, which is defined in the body of the JSP API 1.2. Tags under that perspective can have three possible structures:

- **Simple tags**—Simple tags implement the `Tag` interface and represent tag components that don't have a body or, if they do have one, don't iterate the body template or manipulate its content. The template, if specified, is processed in appearance order and is processed only once.

- **Iterative tags**—Iterative tags implement the `IterateTag` interface, built upon the `Tag` interface by the addition of a capability to loop through the body template, generating the loop until some condition is satisfied. These tags must have a body, but they don't manipulate the body content.

- **Body tags**—The most sophisticated of the three, body tags implement the `BodyTag` interface. They have the capability to read their body template content and modify it, reassign it, and inspect it at will.

Simple tags are the most common of these. Despite their name, simple tags are the most important element in the API because they are the most generic. Also, the fact that a tag doesn't generate a body template doesn't mean that the tag cannot interact with it. Simple tags can implement sophisticated cooperation schemas with other tags that will complement their complex processes. Tags with no body can't have cooperate tags to complement their processes, but they can participate in other tag's bodies. Simple tags can also generate and access attributes in the several scopes available and can generate and access scripting variables.

Listing 2.6 shows a number of simple tags that cooperate to produce a complex action.

Listing 2.6   **Tags Used to Produce a Map**

```
<example:drawMap setViewport="500X500">
  <example:setRegionBaseMap region=<%=country.getRegion()%>/>
  <example:setRegionRoadMap region=<%=country.getRegion().getRoads()%>/>
  <example:setRegionHydroMap region=<%=country.getRegion().getHydrology()%>/>
  <example:setSQLMap region=<%=country.getInstituteSQL()%>/>
  <example:setLegend range=<%=targetMap.calculateRange()%>/>
  <example:setHTMLMap region=<%=country.getInstituteSQL()%>/>
</example:drawMap>
```

The `drawmap` example tag is a simple tag. It neither inspects nor generates body content, but each of the tags in its body performs some task in the process of map generation. It doesn't iterate through the body tags because the process is meant to generate a single map.

The `IterateTag` interface represents a tag that will hold an iterative process. The tag will signal each time that it completes a loop through the body. Having a tag that naturally controls iteration is very important in a number of typical situations, such as when generating content from databases or Java collections. The `IterateTag` interface was introduced as a response to this need in the JSP Tag Extension API version 1.2.

Iterative tags don't need to inspect or generate body content, either. Listing 2.7 shows a tag that receives an enumeration holding a list of customer numbers that will be used to build a table with the latest orders placed by each customer in the list.

Listing 2.7   **Using an Enumeration in an Iterative Tag**

```
<example:showOrders customerList="<%=customerHash.keys()%>">
  <example:showOrder order=<%=customerHash.get(aCustomer)%>/>
</example:showOrders>
```

In Listing 2.7, the `showOrders` tag has an attribute that will hold an enumeration. The inner tag, `showOrder`, will present the `Order` object for each customer in the list. Chapter 3, "Writing Custom Tags," shows how this is done inside `IterateTag`.

Body tags manipulate their content. They inspect it, generate it, or both. This is essential when the process generates the template itself or the body contains pieces of code in an external language or raw data. The tag inspects the body to collect the data to process or the statement to be transferred to the external compiler or interpreter. The classic example of a body tag is the SQL tag, in which the body holds an SQL statement:

```
<example:sqlQuery connect="conparams.xml">
    Select Name, Phone, Age, Count(OrderNumber)
    From Customers, Orders
    Where Orders.customer = Customers.Number
    Group by Name, Phone, Age
</example:sqlQuery>
```

This tag is supposed to present the result of processing the SQL statement in the body, using the attribute `connect` to find the connection parameters. The body tag `sqlQuery` has access to its body content, extracts the SQL statement from that content, and sends it to the SQL processor reached by the connection parameters. In fact, many tag libraries in the market have some sort of SQL tag set. The Jakarta Taglib project and the JRun Tag Library are two examples.

Functional View

Tags can be categorized by the way they work and the role they fulfill in a JSP page. Although this doesn't imply adding any kind of new interface or class to the API, this will help a lot when understanding or designing cooperative tags or determining the adequacy of a tag library for a certain task. You can have four kinds of tags:

- **Bodyless tags**—Bodyless tags play the role of a self-contained process. They can be hosted by a parent tag that will need that process to complete some higher-level process in turn.

- **Body as data**—These are body tags in which the body contains raw data or pieces of code in an external language, for instance. No subprocess is involved. The template will have to be scanned, processed, and generated. In the classic body tag case, the body contains either raw data in some specific format or the text of a procedure written in some external language.

The next example shows a body tag that manipulates its body. It's part of the Jrun Tag Library:

```
<%@ taglib uri="jruntags" prefix="jrun" %>

<jrun:sendmail host="mail.myserver.com"
               sender="jsp-expert@myserver.com"
               recipient="designer@mysever.com"
               subject="tag usage">
Note:

Using tag libraries will ease the way our company can embed its own processes
in the Web layer. Of course, this is an example statement.

Signed: The jsp guy.

</jrun:sendmail>
```

This is a real-life example of a body tag. In this case, the tag will send an email message. The attributes define the email parameters, as the mailhost, the sender, the recipient, and the message's subject. The body contains the message itself. Note that the message could be generated dynamically by embedded scriptlets or embedded tags.

- **Body as data structure**—In this case, the body will contain JSP code or other tags that will build upon some data structure that the parent tag needs to fulfill its process. The `drawMap` tag that you saw before falls into this category. It's not that the subtags don't contain processes—instead, they aim to fill in blanks in some data structure, to provide plug-in functionality.

- **Body as process**—In this case, the body is made of tags that provide some plug-in functionality and fulfill the parent tag's own process. This is common when the process to represent is too large or too complex to fit in a single tag. The difference from the previous point is that this concentrates on the plug-in's functionality instead of filling in blanks in some data structure. The collaboration component here can be as strong as in the former case, but the approach is clearly different, both in designing these tags and in using them.

These categories help in deciding which is the best approach to design a tag library. Chapter 5, "Design Considerations," returns to this subject by investigating in much more detail what design and use scenarios and decisions are involved.

Tag Life Cycle

You have just seen that several kinds of tags exist: tags that are plain and simple, tags that have a number of attributes, tags that have a body but don't interact with it, tags that iterate through their body, and tags that interact with their body. A number of interfaces represent these kinds—one for each. Depending on how the tag is defined, that tag will obey a different life cycle.

A Simple Tag's Life Cycle

A simple tag is a tag that doesn't interact with its body. Either it doesn't have body content at all, or it just passes whatever is defined between its head and tail to the JSP processor. Simple tags implement the `Tag` interface of the Tag Extension API.

This is the simplest case for a tag. All that is needed is signaling the tag and the availability of a body (if any). The life cycle of a simple tag reflects this need, as illustrated in Figure 2.5 and described here:

1. **Create**—A tag is created with the `new()` operator, and the tag's properties get their default values.

2. **Initialize**—Properties get custom initialization, the `pageContext` gets evaluated, and the tag's attributes are scanned and validated against the TLD and a set of `TagAttributeInfo` objects, one for each attribute declared in the TLD.

3. **Process head**—After initialization, for each reference to this tag in the page, the JSP processor will call the `doStartTag()` method of the `Tag` interface. The `doStartTag()` method returns a flag that signals the JSP processor to process the body, generating the output on the out stream, or to ignore it. Bodyless tags must return the value to ignore the body. (More detail on these methods will come in Chapter 3.)

4. **Process tail**—After the `doStartTag()` method, the JSP processor calls the `doEndTag()` method. The `doEndTag()` method should return a flag to the JSP processor to signal whether everything was okay in processing of that tag and the page evaluation is clear to resume, or whether something went wrong and the page must be abandoned.

5. **Release**—The tag gets released. The `method release()` is called to ensure proper finalization.

Steps 3 and 4 are repeated while such tags are found in the page. Figure 2.5 represents the dynamics of this life cycle.

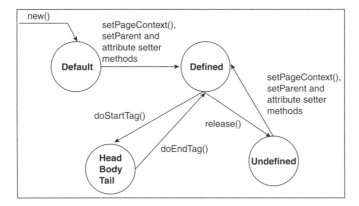

Figure 2.5   Simple tags life cycle.

The tag designer has both the doStartTag and the doEndTag methods to define the process that the tag is supposed to implement. Either it is processed before body evaluation (when doStartTag hosts the process implementation), after body evaluation (when doEndTag hosts the process), or both (when part of the process decides what to do with the body and the other part decides what to do with the rest of the page).

The doStartTag and doEndTag methods are used by all three kinds of tags in exactly the same way.

IterateTag's Life Cycle

The IterateTag builds upon the simple tag, adding the capability to iterate through the body content and generating the body as many times as needed. This is especially useful when generating data from database query results, from tabular data sheets, or from Java collections and enumerations.

A new step is added to signal the looping through the body. The initialization and finalization parts of the life cycle are the same.

1. **Create**.
2. **Initialize**.
3. **Process head**—The doStartTag method is called. It will return the same flag as before, but this time it will optionally enable the iteration.
4. **Loop through**—In this step, the doAfterBody method of the IterateTag interface is called whenever the body has been looped through. This method enables the tag designer to implement any kind of iterative process on the body. The doAfterBody method returns a flag indicating whether the tag must loop through the body again.

5. **Process tail**—The doEndTag method follows at least one call to the previous doAfterBody method if the body is allowed to be evaluated.

6. **Release**.

Figure 2.6 presents the dynamics of the IterateTags life cycle.

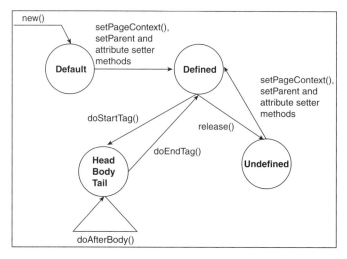

Figure 2.6 IterateTags life cycle.

Body Tag Life Cycle

A body tag is a tag that has access to the contents of its body. It is aware of that content via a BodyContent object. It can modify the body via the setBodyContent method of the BodyTag interface. This affects the life cycle, which must accommodate a phase to initialize the BodyContent object and a phase to signal the beginning of body processing.

A number of steps are added to signal introspection through the body, as shown in the following list. The body tag can also loop through the body. The initialization and finalization parts of the life cycle are the same.

1. **Create**.

2. **Initialize**.

3. **Process head**.

4. **setBodyContent**—The body content is captured in a BodyContent object.

5. **Process the body**—Body content is processed via the doInitBody method of the BodyTag interface. The tag designer can use this method to specify behavior necessary to implement the core process that the tag is supposed to represent.

6. **Loop through**—In this step, the `doAfterBody` method of the `IterateTag` interface is called whenever the body has been looped through. This method enables the tag designer to implement any kind of iterative process on the body. The `doAfterBody` method returns a flag indicating whether the tag must loop through the body again.

7. **Process tail**.

8. **Release**.

Figure 2.7 presents the dynamics of the life cycle.

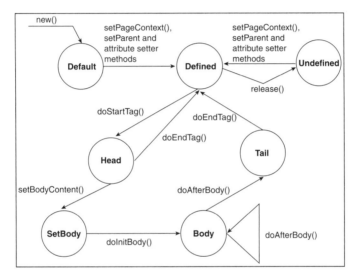

Figure 2.7 Body tag life cycle.

The Tag Library Descriptor File

Now that you have a good idea of what a custom tag is and how it can be used, you need to understand how it is linked to a JSP and how it is located and processed by the web container.

Four components are involved in this equation:

- **The JSP**—The JSP contains a `taglib` directive and uses a tag.
- **The application's web deployment descriptor**—The web.xml file contains a tag library element that associates the `taglib` directive with a Tag Library Descriptor.

- **The tag library descriptor file**—A tag library descriptor (TLD) file is an XML file that describes the several components that make a tag library: tags, their helper classes, validator classes, and application-level event listeners.
- **The tag handler class**—The tag handler is the bean that implements some tag interface, optionally extending one of the support classes altogether. This class file implements the desired functionality.

Figure 2.8 illustrates these four components.

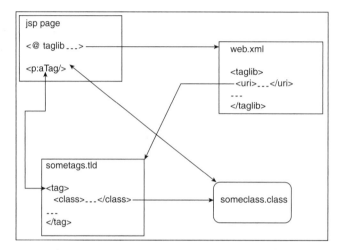

Figure 2.8   The four components involved in custom tag processing.

Deployment

A tag library is a collection of tags that implement a set of services and their accessory classes. Eventually, contextual classes, classes needed to implement the desired functionality, are also included.

This collection can be deployed in an ad-hoc manner as a set of files. This is more often the case with in-house tag libraries.

It can also be deployed as a jar file, as with commercial tag libraries that must be prepackaged for out-of-the-box functionality. In this case, the tag library descriptor, the tags, and the helper and contextual classes are packaged in a jar file. When packaged this way, the TLD file is placed in the META-INF subdirectory. All the resources that are needed are also packaged in.

The next section describes the TLD file.

The Tag Library Descriptor File

The tag library descriptor file is an XML file that describes all the elements in a tag library. These include the `taglib` description parameters, validators, application-level event listeners, tags, and accessories. The idea behind the TLD is that it does the following:

- **Serves the JSP processor**—The TLD file provides a way for the JSP processor to identify the necessary arguments to run the library's tags. In that sense, using XML, defined by the Tag Library Descriptor DTD, is a suitable way to provide configuration information in a platform- and container-independent manner.

- **Is manageable by the tag designer**—XML can be composed by hand with almost any kind of text editor and with sophisticated XML editing tools. A GUI composition tool can generate it automatically. This flexibility makes it trivial for the JSP tag programmer to provide the essential information needed by the taglib users.

- **Is easily digested by GUI composition tools**—In the same way that a JSP processor will easily access configuration information in a tag library to process its tags, a composition tool will find configuration information to present and compose tags, validate usage of tags in JSP pages, and feed information in for newly created tags.

Currently, the TLD implements the DTD JSP Tag Library version 1.2. It defines two levels of elements: tag library–level elements and tag-level elements.

The tag library description parameters are designed to provide information to document the tag library. This allows both the JSP processor and the GUI composition tools to identify information such as versioning, iconic representation, name, description, validation, and resource control.

The second part of the tag library descriptor concerns the definition of tag elements. These elements provide such information as which tags are in the library, how they are defined, what the defined attributes are, whether the tag has a body, whether the tag defines scripting variables, and so on.

The *taglib* Element

The `taglib` element is the higher-scope element—the root element, in XML jargon—present in a TLD. It encompasses all the other tag definitions. Here's the description of that element:

```
<!ELEMENT taglib (tlib-version, jsp-version?, short-name, uri?,
                  display-name?, small-icon?, large-icon?, description?,
                  validator?, listener*, tag+) >
```

You can see here all the information that you can specify about a tag library. The JSP API 1.2 introduced a number of elements to the `taglib` element regarding the previous version of the TLD DTD. These are `display-name`, `large-icon`, `small-icon`, `validator`, and `listener`. The `description` element replaced the former `info`.

The `taglib` element has an implied fixed attribute called `id` that identifies the default namespace where the elements in the `taglib` descriptor are defined:

```
<!ATTLIST taglib id ID #IMPLIED xmlns CDATA #FIXED
  "http://java.sun.com/dtd/web-jsptaglibrary_1_2.dtd">
```

The elements defined under the `taglib` element describe the several components in the tag library.

Descriptive and Version-Control Elements

The descriptive elements and version-control elements provide information required to document the library. Developers can use this information when choosing a library for a specific application, when using graphic composition tools in displaying the tag library icons and description, or when using the JSP processor to verify version coherence. The descriptive elements are listed here:

- **tlib-version**—Holds the tag library implementation version. The tag library developers may use this element both as an internal version number and as a public version number. It's a Dewey Decimal number.

- **jsp-version**—Holds the JSP version required by this tag library. A developer can create a commercial tag library upon a certain JSP API version and document this dependency. For instance, if you want to use `TryCatchFinally` in a tag, you must ensure that the JSP API is version 1.2; otherwise, that interface won't be available. Its value is a Dewey Decimal number. The default value is 1.2.

- **short-name**—Is a name that can be used both by composition tools and programmers, to create variables and temporary objects, or to serve as the prefix in the `taglib` directive in a page. Whitespace cannot be used. This name can't start with digits or an underscore.

- **uri**—Is an URI that identifies this tag library uniquely. This is used by vendors of commercial tag libraries to attach their brand to the library.

- **display-name**—Designates a name that will appear in composition tools descriptors and configuration. The difference from `short-name` is that this is intended to be a descriptive name, while `short-name` is intended to be used as a variable name prefix or seed.

- **small-icon and large-icon**—Also are mainly intended to provide the library with additional graphic style when loaded in composition tools. These elements contain a name of a graphic file that must be 32 × 32 pixels (large) and 32 × 32 pixels for the small image. The images must be JPEG or GIF images.

- **description**—Replaces the `info` element, from the previous version of the TLD. It's a short text.

Listing 2.8 is an example of a tag library descriptor fragment that illustrates how to use the description elements.

Listing 2.8   **Tag Library Descriptor Fragment**

```
<!ATTLIST taglib id ID #IMPLIED xmlns CDATA #FIXED
  "http://java.sun.com/dtd/web-jsptaglibrary_1_2.dtd">

<taglib>

  <tlib-version>1.1.0</tlib-version>

  <!-- this is optional since 1.2 is the default -->
  <jsp-version>1.2</jsp-version>

  <short-name>exampleTags</short-name>

  <!-- this is also optional -->
  <uri>urn:jspBook.exampleTags</uri>

  <display-name>JSP/TagLib Book Example Tags</display-name>

  <small-icon>/icons/example.gif</small-icon>

  <large-icon>/icons/examplel.gif</large-icon>

  <description>
This fragment illustrates the use of descriptive elements in the TLD. You can
see that its purpose is twofold: to be used by designers when creating
or using the tag library, and to be used by automatic or composition tools to
integrate and acknowledge the presence of the tag library in the environment.
  </description>

...

</taglib>
```

Validator

The JSP Tag Extension API comprises two kinds of Java classes: translation-time classes, which help the JSP processor in the translation process, and runtime classes, which actually are responsible for the desired processing. Translation-time classes can be thought of as only internal and user-defined classes. Internal-only classes are classes that the JSP processor always creates or instantiates as part of the core translation process and to which the tag designer has no active role in defining. Examples of these are `TagInfo` and `TagLibraryInfo`.

User-defined translation-time classes are the ones that the designer has an active role in defining. This means that the designer will have to provide a Java class that implements a required interface or extend a base class that helps in the translation process. That class will provide the JSP processor additional information that will be needed when translating the JSP that uses the tag library into the target servlet, as you saw in Chapter 1.

A tag library sometimes defines objects that provide a context for the process being implemented. There's no way for the JSP processor to know that this particular condition must be met by the page—in other words, that the context must be present or at a certain state—to use the tag library. So, the JSP processor will need some external information.

The validator class is used for that. This is a user-defined translation-time class that will be used to test the conformance of the actual JSP page to use this tag library. This also ensures that these contextual objects are present and at an adequate state, allowing the tags to be used without further problems. If the validation succeeds, the translation process continues and the tag library can be used in that page. If the page validation fails, a `JspTagException` is raised and the translation process stops.

The `validator` element of the TLD defines a class that extends the `TagLibraryValidator` abstract class. Data about the page is passed to the validator class via the `PageData` object that holds an XML representation of the page. Data about the tag library is passed via a `TagLibraryInfo` object. The syntax for the validator is as follows:

```
<!ELEMENT validator (validator-class, init-param*) >

<!ELEMENT validator-class (#PCDATA) >

<!ELEMENT init-param (param-name, param-value, description?)>

<!ELEMENT param-name (#PCDATA)>

<!ELEMENT param-value (#PCDATA)>
```

This `validator` element defines two subelements: `validator-class` holds the fully qualified class name for the validator, and `init-param` defines name-value pairs for parameters necessary for the validation. It can hold more than one name-value pair. The name-value pairs are defined through the subelements `param-name` and `param-value` (see Listing 2.9).

Listing 2.9   **Describing a Validator in the TLD**

```
...

<validator>

  <validator-class>
    jsp.book.examples.XMPValidator
  </validator-class>

  <init-param>

    <param-name>
      exampleHelperPath
    </param-name>
```

```
    <param-value>
      /WEB-INF/examplesHelpers
    </param-value>

    <param-name>
      exampleHelperDefaultValue
    </param-name>

    <param-value>
      true
    </param-value>

  </init-param>

</validator>
```

Listener

As you saw in Chapter 1, one important addition to the Servlet API 2.3 is the application-level event listeners. These provide a finer-grained means of managing resources allocated by the application components that must be orderly deallocated to prevent problems in the application environment.

The `listener` element allows application-level event listeners to manage resources allocated by tag library components—for example:

- **Detecting container startup**—A JDBC-based database access tag library can register a `listener` that will monitor container startup events to allocate JDBC data sources and pools.

- **Detecting container shutdown**—The same library can register a `listener` that will monitor container shutdown events to deallocate JDBC data sources and pools.

- **Detecting session data binding**—A tag library can be notified when one of its contextual classes is bound or unbound to the session.

The syntax for the `listener` element is as follows:

```
<!ELEMENT listener (listener-class) >

<!ELEMENT listener-class (#PCDATA) >
```

There's only a subelement with the fully qualified class name to be registered as an event listener. This registration process is implemented at the container. When an event such as a context shutdown arrives, the `listener` is called by the container and can perform its action in proper time. The following example illustrates a fragment of a TLD that declares a `listener` for a tag library:

```
...
<listener>
  <listener-class>
    jsp.book.examples.AContextStartupListener
  </listener-class>
</listener>
```

Check the Servlet 2.3 specification for more information on application-level event listeners.

Tags

Tag elements are the main elements in a tag library descriptor. They describe the tag and the associated translation-time helper classes needed by the JSP processor to translate the tag definitions to runtime structures. At a certain level, the tag element resembles the `taglib` element because it also has descriptive and nondescriptive elements. Translation-time and runtime elements are also there. Here's the syntax of the tag element:

```
<!ELEMENT tag (name, tag-class, tei-class?, body-content?, display-name?,small-
icon?, large-icon?, description?, variable*, attribute*) >
```

You can see some subelements that have already been defined. You can see here the same `display-name`, `small-icon`, `large-icon`, and `description` subelements that were defined for the `taglib` element. The difference is that here they describe the tag instead of the library. These elements will be used inside a tag element to enable an automatic tool—for example, to show an iconic representation of a certain tag through its small icon or to display the short name through the `short-name` subelement.

DTD Declarations and the TLD

You must remember that XML DTDs have no scoped declarations. Because of that, any element is declared at the same level as the others, and element names cannot be duplicated. The same applies to Tag Library Descriptor files because they are XML files as well.

You'll now examine the tag element's subelements and see some comprehensive examples on tag definition.

The `name` element holds the name that this tag will have inside a JSP page. This element is mandatory and must be unique through the tag library. As you learned in the previous discussion on namespaces, you don't need to create exotic names, such as using GUID numbers as tag names, because the `taglib` directive enables the user to designate a prefix that clarifies the name. However, it must be unique inside the library that is being defined.

The `tag-class` element holds the fully qualified name of the class that implements this tag. Its syntax is analogous to that of the `validator-class` element.

If a tag defines a scripting variable, which is a variable visible to the page, then it might have an associated `TagExtraInfo` (TEI) class. The `TagExtraInfo` class is used to provide information about the scripting variables that the tag defines and to validate the tag attributes. It is a translation-time class. The `tei-class` element changed from mandatory to optional in this version of the API. The `variable` subelement (discussed shortly) was introduced to supply that information. You can use either to provide this information.

Tags can have body. The content of the body, as you learned in the previous section, can vary greatly. To give the JSP processor a hint to what it will find in a tag's body, there's the `body-content` element. It can have one of three possible values:

- **empty**—The body will be empty. This is the case for simple tags.

- **tagdependent**—This indicates that the tag itself will interpret the content. The classic example is with SQL processing, but you can consider other options as well, such as XML fragments or raw data. The JSP processor will ignore the body content, eventually passing it to the tag via a `BodyContent` object.

- **JSP**—The body tag contains a JSP. It can be either content, custom tags, or JSP elements, such as scriptlets, expressions, and so on.

So far, you have seen the simple tag subelements. These have quite a simple syntax:

```
<!ELEMENT name (#PCDATA) >

<!ELEMENT tag-class (#PCDATA) >

<!ELEMENT tei-class (#PCDATA) >

<!ELEMENT body-content (#PCDATA) >

<!-- and for the body-content element -->

#PCDATA ::=  tagdependent | JSP | empty
```

Here's a fragment of tag declaration:

```
<tag>

  <name>defineHREmplRecord</name>
  <tag-class>hr.defineHREmplRecord</tag-class>
  <body-content>empty</body-content>

  ...
</tag>
```

The remaining subelements are `variable` and `attribute`. They describe the scripting variables that this tag is defining and the attributes that this tag may have.

The `variable` subelement was introduced by version 1.2 of the Tag Extension API to ease the task of declaring tag-defined scripting variables or the variables that the tag uses. This subelement makes optional the use of the TEI and `VariableInfo` classes to

describe scripting variables. Tags that introduce such variables must have either the
`tei-class` or the `variable` subelements specified. Using both causes a translation-time
error. The syntax for the `variable` subelement is as follows:

```
<!ELEMENT variable ( (name-given | name-from-attribute), variable-class?,
declare?, scope?) >
```

You can see that this is quite a rich element.

The `name-given` element holds the name of the variable, if it is constant and predefined by the tag designer. This is mostly the case for variables used internally only, such
as those that provide communications inside the tag library only.

The `name-from-attribute` element holds the name of the attribute that, at translation-time, will define the name of the variable. An example of such a mechanism is
the id attribute of the `jsp:useBean` standard action. It defines the name under which
the bean to be instantiated will be known. This is the case when the tag is designed to
interact with external resources or possibly external tags. In this case, it is better to
leave the decision about the naming of variables to the tag library customer.

These two elements are mutually exclusive. Either a variable name is constant
(`name-given`) or it is customer-defined (`name-from-attribute`). However, at least one
of them must be provided.

The `variable class` element holds the fully qualified name of the Java class
that the variable implements. This is an optional element. The default class is
`java.lang.String`.

If the tag is declaring this variable to the page, the declare element must be valued
`true`; this is also its default value. If it is just using the variable declared previously, then
it must be valued `false`. This element is optional.

The scope element defines the scope of the scripting element. A variable can have
either of these:

- **NESTED scope**—With variables available only inside the body of this tag.
  Utilitarian variables that will provide communication among the tag and its
  body fall in this scope. NESTED is the default scope.

- **AT_BEGIN scope**—With variables that are defined in the processing of the
  `doStartTag()` member function. You can think of this as taking place when the
  head, the opening part of the tag, is processed. The variable will be available to
  the body and will remain available to the rest of the page afterward.

- **AT_END scope**—With variables that are generated after the tag is processed,
  upon processing of the `doEndTag()` member function. You can think of this as
  taking place at the tail, the closing part of the tag. These variables aren't available
  to the body. They are available only to the remainder of the page.

Now that you have seen the structure of the `variable` subelement, you can take a look at its syntax:

```
<!ELEMENT name-given (#PCDATA) >

<!ELEMENT name-from-attribute (#PCDATA) >

<!ELEMENT variable-class (#PCDATA) >

<!ELEMENT declare (#PCDATA) >

<!ELEMENT scope (#PCDATA) >
```

Chapter 4 extensively explores the subject of cooperating tags and the role of scripting variables in providing communication among the tags. The following are some examples of how to describe variables in the TLD.

Listing 2.10 shows two string variables that will hold some parameter inside the body of a tag.

Listing 2.10   **Declaring Variables**

```
<variable>
  <name-given>firstExample</name-given>
</variable>

<variable>
  <name-from-attribute>secondExample</name-from-attribute>
</variable>
```

The first variable will be called `firstExample`. The second variable will be named by the attribute called `secondExample`. By specifying that attribute, the customer can assign any name to it.

Listing 2.11 defines a bean that holds complex information to be built inside the body that must be available to the rest of the page.

Listing 2.11   **The AT-BEGIN Scope**

```
<variable>
  <name-from-attribute>thirdExample</name-from-attribute>
  <variable-class>
    jsp.book.examples.ThirdVarExample
  </variable-class>
  <scope>AT_BEGIN</scope>
</variable>
```

Listing 2.12 shows a variable that is used but not defined by the tag.

Listing 2.12 **Using a Predeclared Variable**

```
<variable>
  <name-from-attribute>fourthExample</name-from-attribute>
  <variable-class>
    jsp.book.examples.FourthVarExample
  </variable-class>
  <declare>false</declare>
</variable>
```

The `attribute` element defines a tag's attribute. Attributes hold information needed to parameterize the core process that the tag implements. This defines the attribute's name, if it is required, tells whether it is dynamically calculated, and gives the attribute's type. The syntax for the attribute element is as follows:

```
<!ELEMENT attribute (name, required? , rtexprvalue?, type?) >
```

The `name` subelement is the only one required, and it holds the name of the attribute.

If the attribute is mandatory, then the value of the required subelement must be `true` or `yes`. If the attribute is not mandatory, the value must be `false` or `not`. The default value is `false`. This is a per-attribute configuration. For instance, suppose that you have a tag such as `checkSecurityRule` (see the example in Chapter 3) that takes two attributes: `GROUP` and `ROLE`. You want to reinforce *at least* one of them. There's no way to specify this *at least one* condition. You must set all of them as optional attributes, making `required` equal to `false` and putting code in the tag to make sure that at least one value is defined at runtime.

The `rtexprvalue` element defines whether an attribute's value is hard-coded at design time, as a constant string, or is the result of the evaluation of a Java expression, at runtime (`rtexprvalue` stands for "runtime expression value"). If it's dynamic, the value of `rtexprvalue` must be `true` or `yes`, and the value of the attribute must be calculated with a JSP expression. If the attribute is static, it must be `false` or `no`, and the value must be hard-coded at design time. The default value is `false`. Static attributes must be passed as strings.

The `type` element holds the Java type of the attribute, if it's dynamic.

Here's the syntax for the `attribute` subelements:

```
<!ELEMENT name     (#PCDATA) >

<!ELEMENT required    (#PCDATA) >

<!ELEMENT rtexprvalue (#PCDATA) >

<!ELEMENT type (#PCDATA) >
```

Listing 2.13 takes a number of attributes so that you can examine the various configurations made.

Listing 2.13   **Using Attributes**

```
<jspBook:defineHREmplRecord type="103" index="<%=emplBean.getIndex()%>"
deps="<%=emplBean.getDepsEnum()%>" />

<jspBook:defineHREmplRecord type="102" index="<%=emplBean.getIndex()%>" />
```

Listing 2.14 is a pertinent configuration file for the `defineHREmplRecord` tag.

Listing 2.14   **Attribute Declarations**

```
<attribute>
  <name>type</name>
  <required>true</required>
  <rtexprvalue>false</rtexprvalue>
</attribute>

<attribute>
  <name>index</name>
  <required>true</required>
  <rtexprvalue>true</rtexprvalue>
</attribute>

<attribute>
  <name>deps</name>
  <required>false</required>
  <rtexprvalue>true</rtexprvalue>
  <type>java.util.Enumeration</type>
</attribute>
```

The first attribute, `type`, is required, and its value must be provided in design time. The second, `index`, is also required, and its value is provided at runtime as a JSP expression that will be evaluated. The third attribute, `deps`, is not required but, if provided, must have its value calculated at runtime via a JSP expression also.

Putting It All Together

Now that you've seen all the elements present in a tag library descriptor file, you can see them declared together in a whole document. Listing 2.15 declares the HR tag library that will enable pretty printing of employee records in the HR pages.

Listing 2.15 **The TLD for the HR Tag Library**

```
<!ATTLIST taglib id ID #IMPLIED xmlns CDATA #FIXED
 "http://java.sun.com/dtd/web-jsptaglibrary_1_2.dtd">

<taglib>

  <tlib-version>1.1.0</tlib-version>
  <jsp-version>1.2</jsp-version>
  <short-name>hr</short-name>
  <uri>urn:jspBook.exampleTags</uri>
  <display-name>Human Resources Display Tags</display-name>
  <small-icon>/icons/hrs.gif</small-icon>
  <large-icon>/icons/hr.gif</large-icon>
  <description>
    this is the comprehensive TLD example
  </description>

  <validator>
   <validator-class>
     jsp.book.examples.HRValidator
   </validator-class>
  </validator>

  <listener>
    <listener-class>
      hr.HRStdTableSetListener
    </listener-class>
  </listener>

  <tag>

    <name>defineHREmplRecord</name>
    <tag-class>hr.defineHREmplRecord</tag-class>
    <body-content>empty</body-content>
    <variable>
      <name-from-attribute>empl</name-from-attribute>
      <variable-class>hr.HREmployee</variable-class>
      <scope>AT_BEGIN</scope>
    </variable>

    <attribute>
      <name>type</name>
      <required>true</required>
      <rtexprvalue>false</rtexprvalue>
    </attribute>

    <attribute>
      <name>index</name>
      <required>true</required>
      <rtexprvalue>true</rtexprvalue>
```

```
      </attribute>

      <attribute>
        <name>deps</name>
        <required>false</required>
        <rtexprvalue>true</rtexprvalue>
        <type>java.util.Enumeration</type>
      </attribute>

    </tag>

    <tag>

      <name>displayHREmplRecord</name>
      <tag-class>hr.displayHREmplRecord</tag-class>
      <body-content>empty</body-content>
      <variable>
        <name-from-attribute>empl</name-from-attribute>
        <variable-class>hr.HREmployee</variable-class>
        <scope>AT_BEGIN</scope>
      </variable>

      <attribute>
        <name>index</name>
        <required>true</required>
        <rtexprvalue>true</rtexprvalue>
      </attribute>

    </tag>

  </taglib>
```

Here you can see each element in a tag library context. The classes
`defineHREmplRecord` and `displayHREmplRecord` will be defined in the next chapter.

Commercial Support

As the industry momentum increases toward JavaServer Pages, it will also increase
toward tag libraries, which have been part of the JSP spec since JSP 1.1. Tag Library
Descriptor version 1.2 introduced several elements that will provide better integration
with GUI-based JSP composition tools and IDEs.

You have seen that the TLD now supports version and descriptive information at
both library and tag levels. Several vendors are already supporting tag libraries on their
tools. Examples are Borland's Jbuilder and Allaire's JrunStudio, just to mention a few.

Summary

The main concepts of tag development and tag library organization were presented in this chapter. You learned what a tag is and what it is not. You also learned that a tag has quite a flexible structure and can perform a number of roles, such as helping to fulfill some data structure, partition some complex process, and process raw data. Tags can optionally have a body.

Tag libraries are organized around the Tag Library Descriptor (TLD) file, where all components in a library, the tag classes, script variables, event listeners, and so on, are described, named, and parameterized, as needed. You learned about the relationship between the `taglib` directive in a JSP, the Web application deployment descriptor file, the web.xml file, and the TLD file. You also saw how one references the other until a complete description of a tag is reached during JSP translation time.

3

Writing Custom Tags

THIS CHAPTER PRESENTS THE INTERFACES AND CLASSES that constitute the JSP Tag Extension API 1.1, which are the building blocks that you will use to create your tag libraries.

Simple Tags

A tag is called a *simple tag* if it does not manipulate its body content. Either it has no body content at all, or it has content and the JSP container just evaluates and possibly includes it into the output stream, without making it available to the simple tag.

Simple tags implement the `Tag` interface. Optionally they can extend the `TagSupport` class, which provides a number of utility methods.

Tag Handlers

A tag handler is a Java class that implements the desired functionality of a custom action. It is essentially a Java bean that is instantiated with a zero-argument constructor instead of via `java.beans.Bean.instantiate`, and it implements either the `Tag`, `IterateTag`, or `BodyTag` interface.

It is important to separate the concepts of tag and tag handler. A tag represents a custom action textually in a JSP page. It is a textual specification to execute the

custom action in a precise order inside the JSP file. The tag handler, on the other
hand, is the Java class that the JSP container will load and execute, and it implements
that custom action.

The tag handler is a container-managed object. This means that the container will
maintain the necessary references to the tag. The tag designer must avoid maintaining
such references outside the tag handler context that comprise the first method called
(doStartTag) and the last one (either doEndTag or doFinally), depending on whether
the tag handler implements the TryCatchFinally interface or not. The container is
also responsible for initializing a tag handler and setting the predefined properties,
which are parent and pageContext, and all the properties exposed as attributes, which
are specified in the TLD.

A tag handler can access server-side objects. The Tag interface, which is the most
basic interface that a tag handler can implement in the Tag Extension API 1.1, provides the pageContext property, through which any object stored in any scope within
the application (the session defined by application requests, the application requests,
the application context and the page context) is available, and any resource in the
web application is available, too. Those can be accessed through the PageContext.
getContext method, which provides access to the ServletContext object that
represents the web application.

A tag handler can access the enclosing tags. The Tag interface also provides the tag
handler with a getParent method, through which a tag can access the reference to the
enclosing tag. Through introspection or explicit referencing, it can access the properties defined in the parent.

Listing 3.1 presents a first example of a tag handler. It implements the Tag interface
through extending the convenience class TagSupport, and it implements the more-
than-classic "Hello World!" example.

Listing 3.1   **The "Hello World!" Tag Handler Example**

```
package jspbook.example.tags;

import javax.servlet.jsp.*;
import javax.servlet.jsp.tagext.*;

public class HelloWorldTag extends TagSupport
{
    public int doStartTag() throws JspException
    {
        // gets the out stream from the page context
        // and writes Hello World! Then, since there's
        // no body evaluation, skips it.

        pageContext.getOut().println("Hello World!");
        return (SKIP_BODY);
    }
```

```
    public int doEndTag() throws JspException
    {

        return (EVAL_PAGE);
    }
}
```

A tag handler is a Java class. It implements an interface defining the expected methods that a tag handler must implement to effectively communicate with the JSP container. This tag handler implements the `Tag` interface. It presents two methods that make part of the `Tag` interface: `doStartTag` and `doEndTag`. In this tag handler, most of the processing occurs inside the `doStartTag` method. It prints the "Hello World!" message. The `HelloWorldTag` tag handler class will be represented in the JSP by a tag, defined by the following Tag Library Descriptor file (TLD file) fragment, shown in Listing 3.2.

Listing 3.2   **The TLD Declaration for the *hello* Tag, Representing the**
***HelloWorldTag* Tag Handler**

```
<tag>
  <name>hello</name>
  <tagclass>jspbook.example.tags.HelloTag</tagclass>
  <bodycontent>empty</bodycontent>
</tag>
```

The tag will be used in the JSP file with no attributes and no body content. To do that, it is necessary to compile and deploy the tag, either in a JAR archive file or directly in a directory on the classpath. Then it is necessary to provide the TLD file and register this TLD file in the web application deployment descriptor. After that, the tag will be ready for use. Refer to Chapter 2, "Introduction to Tag Libraries," to see a detailed description of the Tag Library Descriptor file and how to declare it with the web application deployment descriptor, the web.xml file. Listing 3.3 shows the JSP using the `hello` tag in a tag library called `example`.

Listing 3.3   **Using the *hello* Tag**

```
<%@ taglib uri="/WEB-INF/example.tld" prefix="example" %>
<html>
 <body>
  <center>
   <h1><example:hello/></h1>
  </center>
 </body>
</html>
```

This page will show the "Hello World!" message in the top of the page as an HTML heading type 1.

You will notice the use of a prefix attribute defined in the `taglib` directive and used in the `hello` tag, as `example:hello`. This is done to avoid a collision of names when two tag library designers define a tag with the same name. This situation was depicted in Chapter 2 in the section "Custom Tags and XML Namespaces."

The question here is, why is it defined locally instead of being defined once and for all in the TLD, for instance? The point is that defining it on the TLD or in the web application deployment descriptor (the web.xml file) would place the prefix outside the page designer vision, so it would make the work of remembering which prefixes were used for which libraries a lot more painful, to say the least. And the situation can arise in which a page designer must use a number of distinct prefixes to the same tag library in different pages. For instance, suppose that an application with a few hundred pages is using a number of distinct tag libraries, and you have to add another library to some of those pages. This new library will have to have a prefix that is different from any used. Potentially, it could end up using a distinct prefix in each page, which must be avoided by all means; this could occur specifically in a large organization with many page designers working under pressure.

How Tags Are Processed

The processing of a tag inside a JSP page follows the general processing of a JSP, which means that the page is parsed and translated into a servlet, and that servlet is then compiled into bytecode. Tags inside a JSP force the introduction of a protocol to call the needed methods in an orderly manner. This means that the method calls in the protocol must be inserted in the generated servlet by following the conventions for the tag interface (or subinterface) that a tag handler implements. The fragment in Listing 3.4 shows the processing of the `Bar` tag from the Jakarta Taglibs project, implementing the `Bar` tag presented in the section A.1.2 of the JSP specification, version 1.1. The code is an extract of the code generated for the intermediary servlet implementing the index.jsp page of the `jsp-specification` tag library from the Jakarta Taglibs project.

Listing 3.4 **Code Generated for the *Bar* Tag Invocation**

```
org.apache.taglibs.jspspec.BarTag _jspx_th_j_bar_0 = new
org.apache.taglibs.jspspec.BarTag();
                _jspx_th_j_bar_0.setPageContext(pageContext);
                _jspx_th_j_bar_0.setParent(null);
                _jspx_th_j_bar_0.setId("newbean");
                _jspx_th_j_bar_0.setAtt1("First attribute");
                _jspx_th_j_bar_0.setAtt2("Second");
                _jspx_th_j_bar_0.setAtt3("3rd");
                java.lang.String newbean = null;
                try {
                    int _jspx_eval_j_bar_0 = _jspx_th_j_bar_0.doStartTag();
                    newbean = (java.lang.String)
```

```
pageContext.findAttribute("newbean");
                    if (_jspx_eval_j_bar_0 == BodyTag.EVAL_BODY_BUFFERED)
                        throw new JspTagException("Since tag handler class
org.apache.taglibs.jspspec.BarTag does not implement BodyTag, it can't return
BodyTag.EVAL_BODY_TAG");
                    if (_jspx_eval_j_bar_0 != Tag.SKIP_BODY) {
                        do {
                            newbean = (java.lang.String)
pageContext.findAttribute("newbean");
                        // end
                        // begin
[file="D:\\tomcat40b3\\bin\\..\\webapps\\jspspec-
examples\\index.jsp";from=(16,0);to=(16,69)]
                        } while (_jspx_th_j_bar_0.doAfterBody() ==
BodyTag.EVAL_BODY_AGAIN);
                        newbean = (java.lang.String)
pageContext.findAttribute("newbean");
                    }
                    if (_jspx_th_j_bar_0.doEndTag() == Tag.SKIP_PAGE)
                        return;
                } finally {
                    _jspx_th_j_bar_0.release();
                }
```

Listing 3.4 presents the original code translated by Tomcat 4.0b3. You can see that the invocation sequence is exactly the same as that of an ordinary class. The invocation starts with the instantiation of the variable _jspx_th_j_bar_0, which will contain the instance for this tag.

Then follows the setter sequence, which is first the pageContext property and then the parent property. A detailed discussion of these properties follows in the section "The Tag Interface." Next is the invocation of each of the setter methods for the attributes identified in the tag as it is in the JSP source.

Then a try block encloses the calls to doStartTag. It prevents the return of a value not permitted if the BodyTag interface is not implemented. If there was any body in this tag, it is to be processed. Then the doEndTag method gets invoked to finish the processing of the tag. The last method to be executed in this translation is release, to free resources and refresh attributes.

The *Tag* Interface

The tag interface is the most basic interface a tag handler can implement. It provides the fundamental protocol for a tag handler to communicate with the JSP container. The structure of the Tag interface is shown in Table 3.1.

Table 3.1 **The Tag Interface**

Field or Method	Description
FIELDS	
EVAL_BODY_INCLUDE	A static final int that signals the JSP container that the tag has a body to be evaluated and included to the output stream. This value is to be returned as a result by the doStartTag method.
EVAL_PAGE	A static final int that signals the JSP container that the rest of the page is to be evaluated. This value is to be returned as a result by the doEndTag method.
SKIP_BODY	A static final int that signals the JSP container that the tag has no body or that the body is not to be evaluated due to internal results or conditions. This value is to be returned as a result by the doStartTag method.
SKIP_PAGE	A static final int that signals the JSP container that the rest of the page is not to be evaluated due to internal results or conditions. This value is to be returned as a result by the doEndTag method.
METHODS	
SetPageContext	Invoked by the container to instantiate the tag handler's pageContext.
SetParent	Invoked by the container to instantiate the tag handler's parent tag. The parent tag is the closest enclosing tag that this tag is in the body of.
GetParent	Retrieves the parent tag.
DoStartTag	Processes the starting tag for this instance of the tag handler. This method can return EVAL_BODY_INCLUDE, signaling that the body must be processed. It can also return SKIP_BODY, signaling that there is no body or that the body must not be processed.
doEndTag	Processes the ending tag for this instance of the tag handler. This method can return EVAL_PAGE, signaling that the rest of the JSP page must be processed, or it can return SKIP_PAGE, signaling that the rest of the JSP page must not be processed.
release	This must be used to clear the attribute values, restoring their default values, and long-term resources allocated. This is not intended to be used to reset the attributes between two calls to the tag.

The typical cycle of processing of a `Tag` tag handler is as follows:

1. The `Tag` tag handler enters the `doStartTag` method and executes the logic there, returning either `EVAL_BODY_INCLUDE` or `SKIP_BODY`.

2. The JSP container includes the body content in the out stream, if the value returned was `EVAL_BODY_INCLUDE`. In this case, tags and scriptlets in the body are processed.

3. If a `SKIP_BODY` was returned, no body evaluation takes place.

4. The `doEndTag` method is invoked, and the tag processing finalizes.

Preparing for Execution

As depicted in Chapter 2, the tag handler has a life cycle in which the first phase involves setting the implicit and explicit properties. Two methods are called by the JSP container before starting the processing of the tag: `setPageContext` and `setParent`.

After initializing the `pageContext` and the `parent` properties (remember, the parent property will receive a value only if such `parent` tag, a tag enclosing this one in its body, exists), the container determines which are the properties exposed as attributes and uses introspection to determine the respective setter methods to initialize each of them.

The *doStartTag* Method

The `doStartTag` method call corresponds to processing the opening part of a tag. This method assumes that the `setPageContext` and `setParent` methods have been previously called.

The `doStartTag` method is a very basic processing method in tag development. If the tag handler needs to execute some process before deciding whether the body should be evaluated, this must take place in the `doStartTag` method. Simple tags that have a body to be evaluated and possibly printed to the out stream fit in this category.

If a tag handler implements an `IterationTag`, the `doStartTag` method is responsible for setting up the iteration. If the tag processes its body, whatever processing needed to be set before body evaluation takes place in this method.

Under the `Tag` interface, the `doStartTag` method may return two possible values: `EVAL_BODY_INCLUDE` or `SKIP_BODY`.

The `EVAL_BODY_INCLUDE` return value signals to the JSP processor the body of this tag that should be evaluated and included to the output stream. The `SKIP_BODY` value signals that the body should not be evaluated or included to the output stream, but it should be discarded instead.

One tag design pattern that is centered on the `EVAL_BODY_INCLUDE` and `SKIP_BODY` values is the on/off design pattern. On/off tags are centered on the decision of whether to include their body contents to the output stream. Whatever processing occurs on the body is irrelevant to the logic that the tag implements; what is necessary is to decide whether to evaluate and include the body content.

Listing 3.5 shows such an on/off tag. If the user has been authenticated, it includes the contents of the body. If the user has not been authenticated, the body is skipped and the user never sees it. This tag is the first of the authorization tags, a tag library built around some functions useful to check the user credentials and authentication status.

Download Code

Not all methods of the tag interface were implemented in the code examples, to simplify reading and to make the points presented more evident. The code listings on the book's web site will be complete. Thus it is strongly recommended that you download the code instead of trying to type it in.

Listing 3.5   **The *checkLogon* On/Off Tag Handler**

```
package jspbook.example.authtags;

import javax.servlet.HttpServletRequest;
import javax.servlet.jsp.*;
import javax.servlet.jsp.tagext.*;

public class CheckLogonTag implements Tag
{
    public int doStartTag() throws JspException
    {
        // gets the request from the page context
        HttpServletRequest request = pageContext.getRequest();

        // if there is an authentication schema
        // performs the evaluation, if not skips the body
        if (request.getAuthType() != null)
        {
            // if the user was authenticated includes the
            // body, otherwise skips it.
            if (request.getUserPrincipal() != null)
                return (EVAL_BODY_INCLUDE);
            else return (SKIP_BODY);
        }

        // if it has not returned EVAL_BODY_INCLUDE yet
        // then the user has not been authenticated at all
        // so return SKIP_BODY

        return (SKIP_BODY);
    }

    public int doEndTag() throws JspException
    {
        return (EVAL_PAGE);
    }
}
```

The checkLogon tag has no attributes. It just decides whether the body will be included to the output stream given, depending on whether the user has been authenticated. Listing 3.5 assumes that container-managed security has been chosen.

Note that the doEndTag method plays no role at all in the processing of this tag, and it could be omitted. In most cases, when the doEndTag method is executed, the process of the on/off pattern tag has been completely exhausted. It could be that subsidiary processing is needed after the body is included. See the upcoming section "The doEndTag Method" for details.

The TLD specification for this tag is quite simple. Because it takes no attributes, the declaration resembles the declaration of the hello tag. Listing 3.6 presents the TLD declaration for the checkLogon tag.

Listing 3.6   **The TLD Declaration for the *checkLogon* Tag**

```
<tag>
  <name>checkLogon</name>
  <tagclass>
    jspbook.example.authtags.CheckLogonTag
  </tagclass>
  <bodycontent>JSP</bodycontent>
</tag>
```

The difference between the HelloWorld tag and the checkLogon tag is that checkLogon admits body contents but doesn't manipulate it. The JSP page presented in Listing 3.7 makes use of the checkLogon tag. It presents some data to the user, restricting the access of some portions of the page to authenticated users.

Listing 3.7   **The restrictedAccess.jsp Page**

```
<%@ taglib uri="/WEB-INF/example.tld" prefix="example"%>
<example:checkLogon>
<html>
<body>
<table width="100%">
  <tr>
    <td colspan="2" align="center">
      <h1> User 0001 Preferences </h1>
    </td>
  </tr>
  <tr>
    <td align="center"> Preferred Locale </td>
    <td><b>BR</b></td>
  </tr>
  <tr>
    <td align="center"> Preferred Language </td>
    <td><b>Portuguese</b></td>
  </tr>
  <tr>
```

continues

Listing 3.7   **Continued**

```
    <td align="center"> Timeframe </td>
    <td><b>+3</b></td>
  </tr>
  <tr>
    <td align="center"> Color Schema </td>
    <td><b>marine</b></td>
  </tr>
  <tr>
    <td align="center"> Font Face </td>
    <td><b>courier new</b></td>
  </tr>
</table>
</body>
</html>
</example:CheckLogon>
```

In this page, the simple fact that the checkLogon tag is present causes the page to display or not display. You will note that the tag is placed before the HTML template starts, and it comprises everything. The problem with this behavior is that if the user is not logged in, not even a message will display. This can be solved; for example, if checkLogon was a body tag, it would replace the entire body with an error message indicating that a login is necessary to access the page. Figure 3.1 shows the output of the restrictedAccess.jsp case with the user logged in. It shows the entire output of the page.

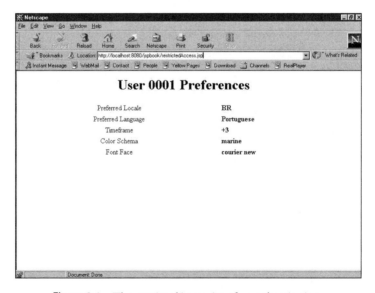

Figure 3.1   The restrictedAccess.jsp after authentication.

If the user has not been authenticated, or if an authentication schema has not been provided, nothing is shown. The output is a blank page. That's why a better approach would be provided by a body tag.

The *doEndTag* Method

The doEndTag method call corresponds to processing the closing part of a tag. This method assumes that all the processing of the tag to be executed has already taken place.

The doEndTag method is another basic processing method in tag development. If the tag handler needs to execute some process after the body has been evaluated, this must take place in the doEndTag method. Listing 3.8 presents a more complete example of the checkLogon tag; after access to the content has been granted, the name of the authenticated user is logged for security purposes.

Listing 3.8   **The *checkLogon* On/Off Tag Handler with Logging**

```
package jspbook.example.authtags;

import javax.servlet.HttpServletRequest;
import javax.servlet.jsp.*;
import javax.servlet.jsp.tagext.*;

public class CheckLogonWithLogginTag implements Tag
{
    public int doStartTag() throws JspException
    {
        // gets the request from the page context
        HttpServletRequest request = pageContext.getRequest();

        // if there is an authentication schema
        // performs the evaluation, if not skips the body
        if (request.getAuthType() != null)
        {
            // if the user was authenticated includes the
            // body, otherwise skips it.
            if (request.getUserPrincipal() != null)
                return (EVAL_BODY_INCLUDE);
            else return (SKIP_BODY);
        }

        // if it has not returned EVAL_BODY_INCLUDE yet
        // then the user has not been authenticated at all
        // so return SKIP_BODY

        return (SKIP_BODY);
    }

    public int doEndTag() throws JspException
```

continues

Listing 3.8 **Continued**

```
    {
        ServletContext ctx = pageContext.getServletContext();
        HttpServletRequest req = pageContext.getRequest();
        String msg = "invalid access attempt";
        if (req.getUserPrincipal() != null)          msg =
req.getUserPrincipal()+
                        "accessed restricted information";
        ctx.log(msg);
        return (EVAL_PAGE);
    }
}
```

Note that in Listing 3.8, the doEndTag method complements the crucial functionality of the tag, providing the most important part of it. Because it is always invoked after the processing of the body, it just logs the activity. The tag designer must keep this in mind. The designer can always distribute any behavior through the tag's methods, provided that the intended behavior doesn't conflict with the tag's life cycle. You will remember from Chapter 2's section on the life cycle of a simple tag that the doEndTag method always gets called after the processing of doStartTag. In the case of the CheckLogonWithLogginTag tag handler, this means that after the page has been included in the output stream, that access is logged. This action is the very reason for the tag, so, in the CheckLogonWithLogginTag tag handler, it is not the doStartTag method that plays the main role, but the doEndTag.

Listing 3.9 shows the TLD declaration for this tag.

Listing 3.9 **The TLD Declaration for the "Hello World" Tag**

```
    <tag>
      <name>checkLogonRec</name>
      <tagclass>
        jspbook.example.authtags.CheckLogonWithLoggingTag
      </tagclass>
      <bodycontent>JSP</bodycontent>
    </tag>
```

The JSP page presented in Listing 3.10 makes use of the checkLogonRec tag. As in Listing 3.7, this page presents some data to the user, restricting the access of some portions of the page to authenticated users. The difference is that each access is logged.

Listing 3.10 **The restrictedAccessRec.jsp Page**

```
<%@ taglib uri="/WEB-INF/example.tld" prefix="example"%>
<example:checkLogonRec>
<html>
<body>
<table width="100%">
  <tr>
```

```
      <td colspan="2" align="center">
        <h1> User 0001 Preferences </h1>
      </td>
    </tr>
    <tr>
      <td align="center"> Preferred Locale </td>
      <td><b>BR</b></td>
    </tr>
    <tr>
      <td align="center"> Preferred Language </td>
      <td><b>Portuguese</b></td>
    </tr>
    <tr>
      <td align="center"> Timeframe </td>
      <td><b>+3</b></td>
    </tr>
    <tr>
      <td align="center"> Color Schema </td>
      <td><b>marine</b></td>
    </tr>
    <tr>
      <td align="center"> Font Face </td>
      <td><b>courier new</b></td>
    </tr>
  </table>
  </body>
  </html>
</example:CheckLogonRec>
```

Listing 3.11 presents a fragment of the servlet.log file on Tomcat, showing the logged records generated by this tag. You can see the user's ID, which is wlsSilva, logged there.

Listing 3.11 **Log Records Generated by the *checkLogonRec* Tag**

```
2001-06-26 11:51:54 - path="/jspExample" : wlsSilva accessed restricted
information
2001-06-26 11:51:55 - path="/fpctd" :800
2001-06-26 11:51:55 - path="/fpctd" :LEVEL 3
2001-06-26 11:51:55 - path="/fpctd" :869
2001-06-26 11:51:55 - path="/fpctd" :LEVEL 2
```

Inheritance in Tag Handler Design

A tag handler is a Java class. As a result, it can inherit behavior from a superclass, or it can implement some necessary interface. (The term *ancestor* is avoided here to prevent confusion with the parent tag property and because enclosing tags will be referred to as ancestors later.) This is ultimately important to keep in mind because it will influence the way a tag library designer plans and implements tags.

Listing 3.12 is an example of such inheritance. Listing 3.13 presents a new version of the CheckLogonWithLoggingTag that extends the CheckLogonTag by inheritance.

Listing 3.12   **The *CheckLogonWithLoggingTag* Tag Handler Inherited**

```
package jspbook.example.authtags;

import javax.servlet.HttpServletRequest;
import javax.servlet.jsp.*;
import javax.servlet.jsp.tagext.*;

public class CheckLogonWithLogginTag extends CheckLogonTag
{

    public int doEndTag() throws JspException
    {

        ServletContext ctx = pageContext.getServletContext();
        HttpServletRequest req = pageContext.getRequest();
        String msg = req.getUserPrincipal()+
                    "accessed restricted information";
        ctx.log(msg);
        return (EVAL_PAGE);
    }

}
```

That's a dramatic change with no surprise at all. The functionality of the `doStartTag` method is provided by the superclass `CheckLogonTag`, while this tag provides just the additional functionality. This is the mechanism to use when a tag extends the behavior of some other tag. It is a common mistake of a newcomer to Java server-side programming to forget that all these classes—servlets, beans, tag handlers, and so on—are still Java classes with all object-oriented capabilities in place.

Sometimes a tag designer wants to provide a base that other tag designers will build tag libraries upon, or wants to define protocol tags designed to perform some process. For that, the best practice is to provide base classes and interfaces that the descendant tags will extend or implement. All the consecrated practices of good class design apply.

Attributes

Attributes are values that a tag maintains either to control or to feed the custom action that it represents. For instance, if a tag represents an object such as a database connection, the tag attributes will represent the properties needed to establish a connection; on the JDBC API, these are the JDBC driver class name, the database JDBC path, the username, and the password. If a tag represents a process, on the other hand, such as the JNDI lookup process, the attributes represent configuration values that will parameterize the process.

Attributes are implemented as properties of the tag handler that implement the tag. These properties become tag attributes when they are declared in the TLD file as such. It is important to note that tag attributes are not two-way arguments; they won't ever be used to output values from the tag handler. Listing 3.13 shows a variant of the

CheckLogonWithLoggingTag, where an attribute defines the name of the resource being accessed.

Listing 3.13   **The *CheckLogonWithNamedLoggingTag* Tag Handler Inherited**

```
package jspbook.example.authtags;

import javax.servlet.HttpServletRequest;
import javax.servlet.jsp.*;
import javax.servlet.jsp.tagext.*;

public class CheckLogonWithNamedLogginTag extends CheckLogonTag
{

    // attributes are implemented as properties
    protected String res = null;

    // such properties should have getter and setter methods
    public String getRes()
    {
        return this.res;
    }

    public void setRes(String value)
    {
        this.res = value;
    }

    public int doEndTag() throws JspException
    {
        ServletContext ctx = pageContext.getServletContext();
        HttpServletRequest req = pageContext.getRequest();
        String msg = req.getUserPrincipal()+
                        "accessed restricted information: "+res;
        ctx.log(msg);
        return (EVAL_PAGE);
    }
}
```

The res attribute is defined as a String property for the tag handler. Inside the tag, it is used normally because the setter for this property has already been invoked by the container. So, the property's value is available to the doEndTag method. As with a bean, the tag handler must have the property declaration, a setter method, and optionally a getter method. All tag handlers depicted in this book will contain both methods. Listing 3.14 shows the TLD fragment that describes this new tag. Note the attribute declaration.

Listing 3.14 *checkLogonWithNamedLogging* **Inherited**

```
<tag>
  <name>checkLogonWithNamedLogging</name>
  <tagclass>
    jspbook.example.authtags.CheckLogonWithNamedLoggingTag
  </tagclass>
  <bodycontent>JSP</bodycontent>
  <attribute>
    <name>resname</name>
    <required>true</required>
    <rtexprvalue>true</rtexprvalue>
  </attribute>
</tag>
```

The code fragment shown in Listing 3.15 shows the tag with the attribute valued. The fragment in Listing 3.16 shows the log after the execution of the doEndTag method.

Listing 3.15 **Using the *res* Attribute**

```
<%@ taglib uri="/WEB-INF/example.tld" prefix="example"%>
<example:checkLogonWithNamedLogging resname="Divisional Profile"/>
<html>
<body>
<table width="100%">
  <tr>
    <td colspan="2" align="center">
      <h1> Divisional Profile </h1>
    </td>
  </tr>
  <tr>
    <td align="center"> Division</td>
    <td><b>SalesBr</b></td>
  </tr>
  <tr>
    <td align="center"> Division Name </td>
    <td><b>Sales South America - Brazil</b></td>
  </tr>
  <tr>
    <td align="center"> Preferred Client </td>
    <td><b>Acme Indústria e Comércio Ltda</b></td>
  </tr>
  <tr>
    <td align="center"> Client Last Yr Movement (x1000) </td>
    <td><b>+120,000</b></td>
  </tr>
  <tr>
    <td align="center"> Client Last Movement (x1000) </td>
    <td><b>6,000</b></td>
  </tr>
  <tr>
```

```
      <td align="center"> General Account Manager </td>
      <td><b>Rob Bobberts</b></td>
  </tr>
  <tr>
      <td align="center"> Pref. Client Account Manager </td>
      <td><b>Johnny B. Good</b></td>
  </tr>
</table>
</body>
</html>
```

Listing 3.16   **Verifying the Log Entry Generated by the Tag**

```
2001-06-26 14:35:12 - path="/jspExample" : wlsSilva accessed restricted
information: Divisional Profile
2001-06-26 14:35:13 - path="/atmd" :init-profile
2001-06-26 14:35:13 - path="/atmd" :init-activity
```

Attribute Java Types, Runtime, and Static Values

Tag attributes can be of two forms regarding the way they are evaluated by the JSP container: They can be static, in which case the value will be a `String`, or they can be runtime expressions, which, by the current Tag Extension API specification, must be translated as a scriptlet expression. Note that a tag cannot take another tag's result directly as an attribute value. A very common mistake of a newcomer is to plan JSPs using tags as the entry for other tag's attributes, as in Listing 3.17.

Listing 3.17   **Wrong Way to Capture a Tag's Result**

```
...
<wrong:neverWorks attr="<wrong:noWay/>"/>
...
```

The result is either an exception or the use of the literal value of the tag specification—in this case, `<wrong:noWay/>`—used as a `String` type value for the other tag with unexpected results.

This is not allowed. There are two basic ways of dealing with such a situation. You can either turn the result of the `<wrong:noWay/>` tag into a bean to be stored in some scope in case you have control over the "wrong" tag library, or you can create a wrapper tag—in this case, a body tag—to capture the result of the `<wrong:noWay/>` tag and store it as a bean in some scope for the other tags to use. The first solution will be analyzed on the section on body tags. The second solution is described in the "`BodyTags`" section later in this chapter.

It is also important to note that tag return values *can be* used as values in plain HTML tags. Listing 3.18 is entirely correct.

Listing 3.18 **Correct way of Defining an HTML Attribute Value**

```
...
<a href='<fine:noProblems with="this"/>'>at all!</a>
...
```

Here the `<a>` HTML tag takes an `href` that is generated by the tag `<fine:noProblems.../>`. This is perfectly correct because the tag will be resolved at translation/request time in the server. After the page is generated, it is sent to the client's browser and then the `<a>` tag is interpreted. This takes place long after the `href` URL has been evaluated.

Request-time attributes are specified in the TLD by an `rtexprvalue` marker. These attributes receive a scriptlet as a value and can take any Java type or class, provided that the property in the tag handler is of the same type or is at least a superclass of the object being passed. Listing 3.19 presents a tag handler with a `java.util.Date` attribute. Listing 3.20 shows the way it is declared in the TLD, and Listing 3.21 shows how it can be entered in the JSP.

Listing 3.19 **The *WriteDateTag* Tag Handler**

```
package jspbook.example.authtags;

import javax.servlet.HttpServletRequest;
import java.util.Date;
import javax.servlet.jsp.*;
import javax.servlet.jsp.tagext.*;

public class WriteDateTag implements Tag
{
    Date date = null;

    public Date getDate()
    {
        return this.date;
    }

    public void setDate(Date value)
    {
        this.date = value;
    }

    public int doStartTag() throws JspException
    {
        pageContext.getOut().println(date.toString());
        return (EVAL_BODY_INCLUDE);
    }

}
```

Here you can see that the `date` property is declared as being of the class `java.util.Date`. `doStartTag` just writes it out. Listing 3.20 shows how this is reflected in the TLD.

Listing 3.20   **Declaring the *date* Attribute in the TLD**

```
<tag>
  <name>writeDate</name>
  <tagclass>
    jspbook.example.tags.WriteDateTag
  </tagclass>
  <bodycontent>JSP</bodycontent>
  <attribute>
    <name>date</name>
    <required>true</required>
    <rtexprvalue>true</rtexprvalue>
    <type>java.util.Date</type>
  </attribute>
</tag>
```

The `type` element of the previous attribute declaration defines the Java type of the runtime expression value that this attribute can be evaluated to. If additional validation is needed, a `TagExtraInfo` class (a TEI class) can be used. See Chapter 4, "Cooperating Tags and Validation," for more details on TEI classes. Listing 3.21 shows how this tag is used inside a JSP page.

Listing 3.21   **A *date* Attribute Being Passed**

```
...

<example:writeDate date="<%=(new java.util.Date())%>"/>'>
<example:writeDate date="<%=someObj.returnADate()%>"/>'>


...
```

The scriptlet in a runtime expression value can contain any valid Java expression returning the expected type. In Listing 3.21, there is the invocation of a constructor and some object call.

Translation-time attributes, on the other hand, cannot be of any Java type or class because they are specified as `String` constants. The value acceptable for a translation-time attribute is any value convertible to the target type by a valid `String`-to-type conversion in the Java language. In practical terms, it must be convertible by a `type.valueOf(String)` method into the `destination` property or must be from a corresponding primitive type. Listing 3.22 exemplifies such a case.

Listing 3.22 **The *WriteLongTag* Tag Handler**

```
package jspbook.example.authtags;

import javax.servlet.HttpServletRequest;
import javax.servlet.jsp.*;
import javax.servlet.jsp.tagext.*;

public class WriteLongTag implements Tag
{
    long value = null;

    public Long getValue()
    {
        return this.value;
    }

    public void setValue(long value)
    {
        this.value = value;
    }

    public int doStartTag() throws JspException
    {
        pageContext.getOut().println("value is "+ value);
        return (EVAL_BODY_INCLUDE);
    }

}
```

This time the value property is declared as being of type long. Listing 3.23 shows how this is reflected in the TLD.

Listing 3.23 **Declaring the *value* Attribute in the TLD**

```
<tag>
  <name>writeLong</name>
  <tagclass>
    jspbook.example.tags.WriteLongTag
  </tagclass>
  <bodycontent>JSP</bodycontent>
  <attribute>
    <name>value</name>
    <required>true</required>
    <rtexprvalue>false</rtexprvalue>
  </attribute>
</tag>
```

The value attribute has no type declaration because it is a translation-time attribute. Listing 3.24 shows how this tag is used inside a JSP page.

Listing 3.24   **A *long* Type Attribute Being Passed**

...

```
<example:writeLong value="3145678923456L"/>'>
```

...

Resetting State

The tag handler's `release` method is used to release resources and reset attribute values to their default values after processing has taken place. It is crucial for tags with attributes to call release after processing, to clean up all values assigned to attributes on tag invocation. This ensures that all attributes have their default values restored before the next tag invocation because the tag handler can be designed to depend on these default values. You cannot assign value to an attribute—only the JSP container can. The same reasoning applies to the tag's properties that are not attributes.

Mandatory versus Optional

Mandatory attributes represent a tag handler's properties whose values are crucial to the execution of its methods. The absence of these attributes will cause exceptions or produce invalid results. They must be made mandatory in the TLD by declaring the `<required>` element in the TLD with the value `true`, but it is important also to verify that these values are present and coherent before execution continues. Most often, this is done inside the `doStartTag` method and is a very early step. Listing 3.25 modifies the `WriteDataTag` tag handler to make the `date` attribute mandatory. The `<required>` element of tag declaration is fully discussed in Chapter 2.

Listing 3.25   **The *WriteDateTag* Tag Handler**

```
package jspbook.example.authtags;

import javax.servlet.HttpServletRequest;
import java.util.Date;
import javax.servlet.jsp.*;
import javax.servlet.jsp.tagext.*;

public class WriteDateTag implements Tag
{
    Date date = null;

    public Date getDate()
    {
        return this.date;
    }
```

continues

Listing 3.25 **Continued**

```java
    public void setDate(Date value)
    {
        this.date = value;
    }

    public int doStartTag() throws JspException
    {
        if (date == null)
            throw new JspException("the date attribute is mandatory");
        pageContext.getOut().println(date.toString());
        return (EVAL_BODY_INCLUDE);
    }

}
```

Attributes can be made optional by providing a default or alternative value and by making the <required> declaration in the TLD with a value of `false`. Listing 3.26 illustrates the code for a fully optional attribute.

Listing 3.26 **The *WriteDateTag* Tag Handler with Optional *date* Attribute**

```java
package jspbook.example.authtags;

import javax.servlet.HttpServletRequest;
import java.util.Date;
import javax.servlet.jsp.*;
import javax.servlet.jsp.tagext.*;

public class WriteDateTag implements Tag
{
    Date date = null;

    public Date getDate()
    {
        return this.date;
    }

    public void setDate(Date value)
    {
        this.date = value;
    }

    public int doStartTag() throws JspException
    {
        // if date is not provided use the current system date
        if (date == null)
            date = new Date();
```

```
pageContext.getOut().println(date.toString());
    return (EVAL_BODY_INCLUDE);
}

}
```

The if statement checks the date. If a date is not supplied, a new date attribute is instantiated with the current date and is used by default.

Patterns of Attribute Usage

Attributes have been used in a number of configurations that constitute a small number of design patterns repeated throughout a number of tag libraries and tags. These are the id-name, name-property-scope, name-value, and multiple attribute syntaxes.

The id-name Pattern

This pattern is reinforced even at the container level. Id attributes must have a unique value declaration. If two tags declare an id attribute with the same value in the same translation unit, the container will detect that as a translation error. You will remember that a translation unit comprises the JSP and all <%@ include %> directive defined includes.

It is useful to communicate values among tags. A tag cannot use another tags as input value for its attributes, so the only way to do this is to post the result of such tags as beans in some scope and then use those beans as input values for attributes.

This can be done either implicitly or explicitly. *Implicitly* means that the tag generating the value silently puts a bean in a scope—say, in its doStartTag method— and the tag consuming that bean accesses it silently in its doStartTag method. The evident problem in this approach is that it creates high coupling between those tags by introducing a heavy unsuspected dependence between them. If used separately, the dependent tag will fail without an apparent reason.

To avoid that, it is better for the generator tag to publish the beans that it defines with a public name and make the consuming tag use that public name. This is the *explicit* approach. Making the bean published clear and evident, the dependence becomes explicit also, and the page designer can plan in advance how to provide the bean needed. This reduces the dependence by allowing the page designer to think in alternative ways to provide the now explicitly needed value.

Two classic attribute names are used and reinforced throughout the Tag Extension API. The producing tag will use an id attribute to declare the name of a scope attribute that will store a bean that it produces. The consumer tag will retrieve that bean using a name attribute to get the name of the scope attribute where the bean was stored. This is the schema used by the standard JSP actions useBean and set/getProperty.

Listing 3.27 presents a tag handler that generates a bean representing the user properties, retrieved from an LDAP directory service using the JNDI API (check http://java.sun.com/products/jndi/index.html for more information on the JNDI API). It takes the username and defines a page scope attribute containing an instance of the javax.naming.directory.Attributes associated with that username.

Listing 3.27   **The *UserAttrTag* Tag Handler**

```
package jspbook.example.authtags;

import javax.servlet.HttpServletRequest;
import javax.naming.*;
import javax.naming.directory.*;
import javax.servlet.jsp.*;
import javax.servlet.jsp.tagext.*;

public class UserAttrTag implements Tag
{
    protected String id = null;
    protected String username = null;

    public String getId()
    {
        return this.id;
    }

    public void setId(String value)
    {
        this.id = value;
    }

    public String getUsername()
    {
        return this.username;
    }

    public void setUsername(String value)
    {
        this.username = value;
    }

    public int doStartTag() throws JspException
    {
        if (id == null)
            throw new JspException("the id attribute is mandatory");
        if (username == null)
            throw new JspException("the username attribute is mandatory");
        try
        {
            // parameterize the access to the Directory Service
```

```
        Hashtable param = new Hashtable();
        param.put(Context.INITIAL_CONTEXT_FACTORY,
                    "com.sun.jndi.ldap.LdapCtxFactory");
        param.put(Context.PROVIDER_URL,
                    "ldap://localhost:389/o=JSPExample");
        // access it
        DirContext ctx = new InitialDirContext(param);
        // retrieve the attributes needed
        Attributes attrs = ctx.getAttributes(
                        "cn="+username+", ou=People");

        // set the target attribute
        if (attrs.size() > 0)
           pageContext.setAttribute(id,attrs);
        else
           throw new JSPException("No information found");

        // everything went out smoothly
        return (EVAL_BODY_INCLUDE);
      }
      catch(NamingException e)
      {
        throw new JSPException("NamingException: "+
                              e.getMessage());
      }
      return SKIP_BODY;
   }


}
```

The first step in the doStartTag method is to certify that the id and username attributes were, in fact, provided. The rest of the job is plain JNDI access. For those unfamiliar with JNDI, the goal is to retrieve the attributes associated with a username. It is done after creating a LDAP directory context using the parameters passed in a java.util.Hashtable instance.

Then an Attributes instance is retrieved from the directory context with the getAttributes method. This method takes the organizational unit and the common name in an LDAP attribute list. The retrieved Attributes instance is stored as a page scope attribute with the id value as the name, if any attribute was returned. Listing 3.28 presents a fragment of the TLD file declaring the tag.

Listing 3.28 **Declaring the *usrAttr* Tag**

```
  <tag>
    <name>usrAttr</name>
    <tagclass>
      jspbook.example.authtags.UserAttrTag
    </tagclass>
```

continues

Listing 3.28 **Continued**

```
<bodycontent>empty</bodycontent>
<variable>
  <name-from-attribute>id</name-from-attribute>
  <variable-class>
    javax.naming.directory.Attributes
  </variable-class>
  <scope>AT_BEGIN</scope>
</variable>
<attribute>
  <name>id</name>
  <required>true</required>
  <rtexprvalue>false</rtexprvalue>
</attribute>
<attribute>
  <name>username</name>
  <required>true</required>
  <rtexprvalue>true</rtexprvalue>
</attribute>
</tag>
```

Here you can see the declaration of the variable id, which will be left for other tags in the auth package to use. The variable's name is defined by the id attribute. Both attributes, id and username, are required, and the username attribute takes a JSP expression as its value.

The consumer tag for the id attribute generated is presented in Listing 3.29. It takes a name attribute and retrieves the Attributes instance from the page scope. Then it writes out the desired attribute.

Listing 3.29 **The *WriteUserAttrTag* Tag Handler**

```
package jspbook.example.authtags;

import javax.servlet.HttpServletRequest;
import javax.naming.*;
import javax.naming.directory.*;
import javax.servlet.jsp.*;
import javax.servlet.jsp.tagext.*;

public class WriteUserAttrTag implements Tag
{
    protected String name = null;
    protected String attr = null;

    public String getName()
    {
        return this.name;
    }

    public void setName(String value)
```

```
{
    this.name = value;
}

public String getAttr()
{
    return this.attr;
}

public void setAttr(String value)
{
    this.attr = value;
}

public int doStartTag() throws JspException
{
    if (name == null)
       throw new JspException("the name attribute is mandatory");
    if (attr == null)
       throw new JspException("the attr attribute is mandatory");
    try
    {
      // retrieve the attributes needed from the page scope
      Attributes attrs = (Attributes)pageContext.getAttribute(name);

      // verify the attrs retrieved
      if (attrs == null)
         throw new JSPException("No information found");
      else if (attrs.size() == 0)
         throw new JSPException("No information found");

      String attrib = attrs.getAttribute(attr).get().toString();

      // everything went out smoothly
      pageContext.getOut().println(attrib);
      return (EVAL_BODY_INCLUDE);
    }
    catch(NamingException e)
    {
      throw new JSPException("NamingException: "+
                             e.getMessage());
    }
    return SKIP_BODY;
}

}
```

This tag puts out the value of a certain attribute retrieved from the LDAP directory service with the usrAttr tag. The TLD fragment declaring this tag is described in Listing 3.30.

Listing 3.30 **Declaring the *writeUsrTag***

```
<tag>
  <name>writeUserAttrTag</name>
  <tagclass>
    jspbook.example.authtags.WriteUserAttrTag
  </tagclass>
  <bodycontent>empty</bodycontent>
  <attribute>
    <name>name</name>
    <required>true</required>
    <rtexprvalue>false</rtexprvalue>
  </attribute>
  <attribute>
    <name>attr</name>
    <required>true</required>
    <rtexprvalue>true</rtexprvalue>
  </attribute>
</tag>
```

The JSP page example in Listing 3.31 presents an example using these two tags, usrAttr and writeUsrAttr. It shows a fancy page with the user profile.

Listing 3.31 **Using the User Attribute Tags**

```
<%@ taglib uri="/WEB-INF/example.tld" prefix="example"%>
<example:usrAttr id="usr" username="<%=request.getUserPrincipal()%>"/>
<html>
<body>
<table width="100%">
  <tr>
    <td colspan="2" align="center">
      <h1> User Preferences </h1>
    </td>
  </tr>
  <tr>
    <td align="center"> Preferred Locale </td>
    <td><b><example:writeUsrAttr name="usr" attr="locale"/></b></td>
  </tr>
  <tr>
    <td align="center"> Preferred Language </td>
    <td><b><example:writeUsrAttr name="usr" attr="language"/></b></td>
  </tr>
  <tr>
    <td align="center"> Timeframe </td>
    <td><b><example:writeUsrAttr name="usr" attr="timeframe"/></b></td>
  </tr>
  <tr>
    <td align="center"> Color Schema </td>
    <td><b><example:writeUsrAttr name="usr" attr="colorSchema"/></b></td>
  </tr>
```

```
  <tr>
    <td align="center"> Font Face </td>
    <td><b><example:writeUsrAttr name="usr" attr="fontFace"/></b></td>
  </tr>
</table>
</body>
</html>
```

The name-property-scope Pattern

The name-property-scope pattern is somehow linked with the previous pattern, in the sense that the property accessed is from a bean stored in some scope. The difference lies in the fact that accessing properties involves introspection of the bean structure to locate properties, which can be nested or indexed or both; the location of property editors; and the getter and setter methods. This can represent a big overhead to the tag designer if it is not part of the requirements for a serious number of tags. This pattern is quite useful when the data sources for your JSPs are mostly represented as beans or EJBs. In this case, it is crucial to be able to access bean properties, whatever scope the beans are stored in.

In the Struts framework, an Open Source framework for web application design, presented in detail in Chapters 6, "The Jakarta Struts Project"; 7, "Struts Tag Libraries"; and 8, "Anatomy of a Struts Application," a number of tags use the triplet name-property-scope to access beans stored in several scopes. These tags make use of a number of utilitarian classes: `RequestUtils`, `BeanUtils`, and `PropertyUtils`.

These three classes currently are being migrated to the Jakarta Commons framework. The `PropertyUtils` class provides a number of utility methods for generalized property getters and setters. In the Struts framework, an `ActionForm` bean can have indexed properties and nested properties. Indexed properties represent arrays, while nested properties represent beans that are properties of other beans, which are properties of the `ActionForm` bean. The `BeanUtils` class provides higher-level services to copy and filter out characters that cause problems with certain HTML interpreters, and it wraps up the calls to `PropertyUtils` methods. The `RequestUtils` class provides utility methods for request processing used by the controller servlet and other classes in the framework.

The name-value Pattern

The name-value pattern is often used to define comparison structures to tags dealing with logical operations or pattern matching. The name attribute defines the object that the tag will compare or match, and the value attribute defines a value that the object will be compared to or matched against.

The `MatchUserAttributeTag` tag handler shown in Listing 3.32 was designed to make use of the name-value pattern.

Listing 3.32 **The *MatchUserAttributeTag* Tag Handler**

```java
package jspbook.example.authtags;

import javax.servlet.HttpServletRequest;
import javax.naming.*;
import javax.naming.directory.*;
import javax.servlet.jsp.*;
import javax.servlet.jsp.tagext.*;

public class MatchUserAttributeTag implements Tag
{
    protected String name = null;
    protected String value = null;

    public String getName()
    {
        return this.name;
    }

    public void setName(String value)
    {
        this.name = value;
    }

    public String getValue()
    {
        return this.value;
    }

    public void setValue(String value)
    {
        this.value = value;
    }

    public int doStartTag() throws JspException
    {
        String valToCompare = "";
        if (name == null || value == null)
          throw new JspException("The name and the value attributes are
mandatory");
        try
        {
          // retrieve the attributes needed from the page scope
          Attributes attrs = (Attributes)pageContext.getAttribute(name);

          // verify the attrs retrieved
          if (attrs == null)
            throw new JSPException("No information found");
          else if (attrs.size() == 0)
            throw new JSPException("No information found");
```

```
        valToCompare = attrs.getAttribute(name).get().toString();
        if (valToCompare.equals(value))

        // everything went out smoothly
        return (EVAL_BODY_INCLUDE);
      }
      catch(NamingException e)
      {
        throw new JSPException("NamingException: "+
                               e.getMessage());
      }
      return SKIP_BODY;
    }

  }
```

The Multiple Attribute Syntaxes

Sometimes the API or the objects that a tag manipulates can have multiple configurations. For example, tags designed to manipulate JDBC API objects will have to support the driver-url-user-password method to connect a database and to support datasources, as defined in the JDBC 2.1 Extensions API. Many times these configurations are mutually exclusive: Using one makes the other redundant and is not allowed.

Unfortunately, there is no mechanism in the Tag Extension API so far to deal with this kind of situation. Attributes either are generally and independently required or are not. There is no way to define a set of attributes that is mutually exclusive. There is no way to define that a set of attributes replaces another set of attributes. It is the responsibility of the tag designer to reinforce these constraints within the code.

Listing 3.33 shows a variation of the writeUsrAttr tag; where the attribute is identified by name or by ordinal number. It is necessary to certify that at least one of attrName or attrNo is provided. To reinforce the fact that precisely one must be provided, the tag designer must check for the specific attribute combinations.

Listing 3.33   The *WriteUserAttr2Tag* Tag Handler

```
package jspbook.example.authtags;

import javax.servlet.HttpServletRequest;
import javax.naming.*;
import javax.naming.directory.*;
import javax.servlet.jsp.*;
import javax.servlet.jsp.tagext.*;

public class WriteUserAttr2Tag implements Tag
{
    protected String name = null;
    protected int num = -1;
```

continues

Listing 3.33 **Continued**

```
protected String attr = null;

public String getName()
{
    return this.name;
}

public void setName(String value)
{
    this.name = value;
}

public int getNum()
{
    return this.num;
}

public void setNum(int value)
{
    this.num = value;
}

public String getAttr()
{
    return this.attr;
}

public void setAttr(String value)
{
    this.attr = value;
}

public int doStartTag() throws JspException
{
    if ((name == null))
        throw new JspException("The name attribute is mandatory");
    if (attr == null && (num < 0))
        throw new JspException("Either the attr or the num attribute is
mandatory");
    try
    {
        // retrieve the attributes needed from the page scope
        Attributes attrs = (Attributes)pageContext.getAttribute(name);

        // verify the attrs retrieved
        if (attrs == null)
            throw new JSPException("No information found");
        else if (attrs.size() == 0)
            throw new JSPException("No information found");
```

```
      String attrib = null;

      if (name != null)
          attrib = attrs.getAttribute(attr).get().toString();

      else if (num >= 0)
          attrib = attrs.getAttribute(num).get().toString();

      // everything went out smoothly
      pageContext.getOut().println(attrib);
      return (EVAL_BODY_INCLUDE);
   }
   catch(NamingException e)
   {
     throw new JSPException("NamingException: "+
                            e.getMessage());
   }
   return SKIP_BODY;
  }

}
```

Listing 3.34 presents the TLD declaration for this tag. You will see that all the attributes in the possible configurations are declared not required.

Listing 3.34   **Declaring Alternative Attributes in the TLD**

```
<tag>
  <name>writeUsrAttr2</name>
  <tagclass>
    jspbook.example.authtags.WriteUserAttr2Tag
  </tagclass>
  <bodycontent>empty</bodycontent>
  <attribute>
    <name>name</name>
    <required>true</required>
    <rtexprvalue>false</rtexprvalue>
  </attribute>
  <attribute>
    <name>num</name>
    <required>false</required>
    <rtexprvalue>false</rtexprvalue>
  </attribute>
  <attribute>
    <name>attr</name>
    <required>false</required>
    <rtexprvalue>true</rtexprvalue>
  </attribute>
</tag>
```

You should note that even though having the attribute descriptor specifying it is a required attribute, the example tag handlers still check for the existence of the value. The WriteUsrAttr2Tag presents a case where checking its existence is crucial to avoid undesired behavior from the tag handler. This is because when attributes represent multiple configurations, all of them cannot be made to be required. Making one of them required will break the constraint. So, all the attributes in such configuration must be made not required, and it's the designer's responsibility to make sure that at least one of them is provided.

Tag Extra-Info classes, also called TEI classes, the subject of Chapter 4, provide part of the solution for the problem of controlling whether multiple attribute configurations can be accepted. The check of the presence of attributes can be made there with the isValid method. But if defaults are used to provide values omitted in an attribute configuration, the code in the TEI class must be complemented with further checking in the tag handler.

Another question that this pattern presents is whether it is better to provide a multiple attribute configuration or whether it is better to implement more than one tag. The general rule is: If the result produced by the tag remains the same through all the configurations, it is a multiple attribute case. If the result produced by the distinct configurations changes, it is best to implement more than one tag for each distinct configuration.

For instance, in the writeUsrAttr tag example, if, when given the name, the writeUsrAttr tag is supposed to produce an attribute's name, but, when given a number, it is supposed to produce a listing of that number's first attribute, it is better to split this functionality and have a second tag. One tag will produce a single attribute given its name, and the second tag will produce a list of the first n attributes, given n. This kind of iterative behavior is the subject of the next section.

Iteration Tags

Iteration tags re-evaluate their body contents as many times as some condition holds. This behavior is especially useful when generating content from collections that are based on some counter or logical condition. The IterationTag interface is an extension of the Tag interface, providing a doAfterBody method that will evaluate the context of the tag and decide whether another iteration is needed.

The *IterationTag* Interface

This interface was introduced in the Tag Extension API 1.1 and greatly simplified the creation of iterative processes in the JSP. This is because, before the introduction of this interface, it was necessary to create iterative tags using the BodyTag interface to be able to capture body evaluation results with the doAfterBody method, which was present only at that interface. The IterationTag interface brings the doAfterBody method closer to simple tags, making it simpler to implement iterative tags that do not need to manipulate their body content.

The point is that to iterate over, say, a collection, it is not always necessary to cope with body contents. Most often it is enough to have an entry point signaling that the body was again evaluated. The IterationTag interface acknowledges this fact by extending the Tag interface. Table 3.2 presents the structure of the IterationTag interface.

Table 3.2 **The *IterationTag* Interface Extends *Tag***

Field or Method	Description
FIELDS	
EVAL_BODY_INCLUDE	Inherited from Tag.
EVAL_PAGE	Inherited from Tag.
SKIP_BODY	Inherited from Tag.
SKIP_PAGE	Inherited from Tag.
EVAL_BODY_AGAIN	A static final int that signals the JSP container that the body of the tag should be evaluated again to fulfill the iterative process. This value is to be returned as a result by the doAfterBody method.
METHODS	
SetPageContext	Inherited from Tag.
SetParent	Inherited from Tag.
GetParent	Inherited from Tag.
DoStartTag	Inherited from Tag.
DoEndTag	Inherited from Tag.
Release	Inherited from Tag.
DoAfterBody	Executed after each evaluation of the body of the tag. It is an entry point in the iterative process where the tag designer can put logic that will check whether the process was fulfilled or whether it is necessary to perform another evaluation. If the process is fulfilled, this method must return SKIP_BODY. Otherwise, it must return EVAL_BODY_AGAIN. Then the body will be re-evaluated and the result will be included in the output stream. After that, this method is called again.

The typical cycle of processing of a IterationTag tag handler is as follows:

1. The doStartTag method is invoked and returns EVAL_BODY_INCLUDE.

2. The body content gets evaluated, and the doAfterBody method gets invoked to control the iteration process. Either a SKIP_BODY or EVAL_BODY_AGAIN are returned, signaling that the body won't be evaluated again or that it will be re-evaluated, respectively.

3. If a `EVAL_BODY_INCLUDE` was returned, the body content is re-evaluated and the `doAfterBody` method is called again, until it returns `SKIP_BODY`.

4. If a `SKIP_BODY` was returned, the `doEndTag` method is invoked and the tag processing finalizes.

The *doAfterBody* Method

The `doAfterBody` method is called after all initialization gets done, the `doStartTag` method is executed, and the body is evaluated for the first time. The body contents won't be available after this evaluation. This interface is aimed at processes in which the resulting body data is irrelevant to the iteration.

This is true most of the time. For instance, this is true when iterating over collections where the logic needed to decide for another iteration is based on whether the last element in the collection was reached. This is also true for counters in which the number of generated elements is important. And it is true in a limited number of `while` tags where a logic condition must be satisfied. In this last case, this interface is useful only if the logic in the `while` tag is external to the data—for instance, if an end-of-file (EOF) was reached or a structural condition on a Collection was exhausted. As was the case for attribute structure, a number of these cases of iteration repeat through tag libraries and tags, and they can be considered small design patterns for iterative tags.

The tags or scriptlets that are present in the body must be taken into account when deciding on another loop. This might be because they have changed the data in the loop criteria, or it might be because the configuration desired for the resulting body contents was reached. In any case, it is necessary to use the `BodyTag` interface instead of this one because the `BodyInterface` presents methods that enable you to capture what was generated by the body evaluation.

Iterating Through Collections

In tags that iterate over collections, the data that will serve as input for the content generation is represented by arrays or some collection, or enumeration, or map. On each loop, an item is retrieved by the `IterationTag` and is used by the tags in the body to generate content. This is mostly done using the id-name attribute pattern to pass the item in the collection to the body.

The simplest case is when the iteration occurs over a specific type of collection. The tags are designed for only that type, and they don't need to verify anything unless there are still items left in the collection to be used. This is the case in Listing 3.35, where the attributes of a user are retrieved all in a loop to build a table with.

Listing 3.35   **The *WriteUserAttrTableTag* Tag Handler**

```
package jspbook.example.authtags;

import javax.servlet.HttpServletRequest;
import javax.naming.*;
import javax.naming.directory.*;
import javax.servlet.jsp.*;
import javax.servlet.jsp.tagext.*;

public class WriteUserAttrTableTag implements IterationTag
{
    protected String id = null;
    protected String name = null;
    protected NamingEnumeration enum = null;

    public String getName()
    {
        return this.name;
    }

    public void setName(String value)
    {
        this.name = value;
    }

    public String getId()
    {
        return this.id;
    }

    public void setId(String value)
    {
        this.id = value;
    }


    // In an IterationTag the doStartTag method has an extra
    // responsibility. It starts the iteration.
    public int doStartTag() throws JspException
    {
        if ((name == null))
          throw new JspException("The name attribute is mandatory");
        try
        {
          // retrieve the attributes needed from the page scope
          Attributes attrs = (Attributes)pageContext.getAttribute(name);

          if (name != null)
            enum = attrs.getIds();
```

continues

Listing 3.35 **Continued**

```
          if (enum.hasMoreElements())
            Attribute attrib = attrs.get(enum.nextElement().toString());

          // everything went out smoothly
          pageContext.setAttribute(id,attrib);
          return (EVAL_BODY_INCLUDE);
        }
        catch(NamingException e)
        {
          throw new JSPException("NamingException: "+
                                 e.getMessage());
        }
        return SKIP_BODY;
      }

    // Here the iteration proceeds.
    public int doAfterBody() throws JspException
    {
      try
      {
        if (enum.hasMoreElements())
        {
          Attribute attrib = attrs.get(enum.nextElement().toString());

          // everything went out smoothly
          pageContext.setAttribute(id,attrib);
          return (EVAL_BODY_AGAIN);
        }
        else return SKIP_BODY;
      }
      catch(NamingException e)
      {
        throw new JSPException("NamingException: "+
                               e.getMessage());
      }
      return SKIP_BODY;
    }

    // Here the custom attributes are reset for another call
    public void release ()
    {
      id = null;
      name = null;
      enum = null;
    }

}
```

In this tag, the `Attributes` object posted into the page scope by `usrAttr` is used. An enumeration of the attribute `identifiers` is retrieved with the `getIds` method; the very first element of the enumeration is taken and posted in the page scope. All this happens in the `doStartTag` method. Listings 3.36 and 3.37 show two simple write attribute tags that retrieve the `Attribute` object and write its id and content to the output stream.

Listing 3.36 **The *SimpleWriteUserAttrIdTag* Tag Handler**

```
package jspbook.example.authtags;

import javax.servlet.HttpServletRequest;
import javax.naming.*;
import javax.naming.directory.*;
import javax.servlet.jsp.*;
import javax.servlet.jsp.tagext.*;

public class SimpleWriteUserAttrIdTag implements Tag
{
    protected String name = null;

    public String getName()
    {
        return this.name;
    }

    public void setName(String value)
    {
        this.name = value;
    }

    public int doStartTag() throws JspException
    {
        if (name == null)
          throw new JspException("the name attribute is mandatory");
        try
        {
          // retrieve the attributes needed from the page scope
          Attribute attr = (Attribute)pageContext.getAttribute(name);

          // verify the attrs retrieved
          if (attr == null)
             throw new JSPException("No information found");

          pageContext.getOut().println(attr.getId().toString());
        }
        catch(NamingException e)
        {
          throw new JSPException("NamingException: "+
                                 e.getMessage());
```

continues

Listing 3.36   **Continued**

```
    }
    return SKIP_BODY;
  }


}
```

The tag handler in Listing 3.37 writes the attribute value to the output stream.

Listing 3.37   **The *SimpleWriteUserAttrTag* Tag Handler**

```
package jspbook.example.authtags;

import javax.servlet.HttpServletRequest;
import javax.naming.*;
import javax.naming.directory.*;
import javax.servlet.jsp.*;
import javax.servlet.jsp.tagext.*;

public class SimpleWriteUserAttrTag implements Tag
{
    protected String name = null;

    public String getName()
    {
        return this.name;
    }

    public void setName(String value)
    {
        this.name = value;
    }

    public int doStartTag() throws JspException
    {
      if (name == null)
        throw new JspException("the name attribute is mandatory");
      try
      {
        // retrieve the attributes needed from the page scope
        Attribute attr = (Attribute)pageContext.getAttribute(name);

        // verify the attrs retrieved
        if (attr == null)
          throw new JSPException("No information found");

        pageContext.getOut().println(attr.get().toString());
      }
      catch(NamingException e)
      {
        throw new JSPException("NamingException: "+
```

```
                        e.getMessage());
        }
        return SKIP_BODY;
    }

}
```

The page in Listing 3.38 shows the JSP code using these tags to build a table with the user attributes retrieved. It is interesting to note that even though the `simpleWrite` tag is in the body of the `writeUsrAttrTable` tag, it is not manipulated by that tag. In fact, what is done with the JNDI `Attribute` object posted in the page scope is totally irrelevant to the `writeUsrAttrTable` tag.

Listing 3.38   **Using the User Attribute Iteration Tag**

```
<%@ taglib uri="/WEB-INF/example.tld" prefix="example"%>
<example:usrAttr id="usr" username="<%=request.getUserPrincipal()%>">
<html>
<body>
<table width="100%">
  <tr>
    <td colspan="2" align="center">
      <h1> User Preferences </h1>
    </td>
  </tr>
<example:writeUsrAttrTable id="attr" name="usr" />
  <tr>
    <td align="center"><example:simpleWriteUsrAttrId name="attr"/></td>
    <td><b><example:simpleWriteAttr name="attr"/></b></td>
  </tr>
</example:usrAttr>
</table>
</body>
</html>
```

Multitype collection looping is a kind of behavior in which the collection is generalized. For instance, it can be an array, a collection, a map, or a `Hashtable`. Generic looping tags are commonplace, and they can be found in several tag libraries. In the Struts framework, the `struts-logic` tag library offers the `iterate` tag, which can take a number of different collection types and iterate over them. In Listing 3.39, the `iterate` tag's `doStartTag` method is presented.

Listing 3.39   **Multicollection Iteration in the Struts Framework's *iterate* Tag**

```
// This source code is part of the Jakarta Struts project
// from the Apache Software Foundation. Refer to the full
// license terms in Appendix F.
    /**
```

continues

Listing 3.39 **Continued**

```
 * Construct an iterator for the specified collection, and begin
 * looping through the body once per element.
 *
 * @exception JspException if a JSP exception has occurred
 */
public int doStartTag() throws JspException {

    // Acquire the collection we are going to iterate over
       Object collection = this.collection;
    if (collection == null)
           collection =
               RequestUtils.lookup(pageContext, name, property, scope);
       if (collection == null) {
           JspException e = new JspException
               (messages.getMessage("iterate.collection"));
           RequestUtils.saveException(pageContext, e);
           throw e;
       }


    // Construct an iterator for this collection
    if (collection.getClass().isArray())
        collection = Arrays.asList((Object[]) collection);
    if (collection instanceof Collection)
        iterator = ((Collection) collection).iterator();
    else if (collection instanceof Iterator)
        iterator = (Iterator) collection;
    else if (collection instanceof Map)
        iterator = ((Map) collection).entrySet().iterator();
    else if (collection instanceof Enumeration)
        iterator = new IteratorAdapter((Enumeration)collection);
    else {
        JspException e = new JspException
           (messages.getMessage("iterate.iterator"));
        RequestUtils.saveException(pageContext, e);
        throw e;
    }

    // Calculate the starting offset
    if (offset == null)
        offsetValue = 0;
    else {
        try {
         offsetValue = Integer.parseInt(offset);
        } catch (NumberFormatException e) {
         Integer offsetObject =
           (Integer) pageContext.findAttribute(offset);
         if (offsetObject == null)
             offsetValue = 0;
         else
             offsetValue = offsetObject.intValue();
```

```
        }
    }
    if (offsetValue < 0)
        offsetValue = 0;

    // Calculate the rendering length
    if (length == null)
        lengthValue = 0;
    else {
        try {
         lengthValue = Integer.parseInt(length);
        } catch (NumberFormatException e) {
         Integer lengthObject =
           (Integer) pageContext.findAttribute(length);
         if (lengthObject == null)
             lengthValue = 0;
         else
             lengthValue = lengthObject.intValue();
        }
    }
    if (lengthValue < 0)
        lengthValue = 0;
    lengthCount = 0;

    // Skip the leading elements up to the starting offset
    for (int i = 0; i < offsetValue; i++) {
        if (iterator.hasNext()) {
            Object element = iterator.next();
        }
    }

    // Store the first value and evaluate, or skip the body if none
    if (iterator.hasNext()) {
        Object element = iterator.next();
            if (element == null)
                pageContext.removeAttribute(id);
            else
                pageContext.setAttribute(id, element);
        lengthCount++;
            started = true;
        return (EVAL_BODY_TAG);
    } else
            return (SKIP_BODY);

}
```

The core of the loop is the generic `Iterator` variable collection, which will receive the `collection` attribute. Then the method uses the `instanceof` operator to detect the class of this instance. The method ends by setting an offset and a top limit for the iteration. The source code for the `iterate` tag is fully discussed in Chapter 7.

Counters

Counters implement the flow structure `for`-loop. They can represent range looping when the counter delimits an offset and a top limit for the iteration. Then tags can retrieve the corresponding element from the collection, access the nth element in a JDBC resultset, and so on.

Implementing a generalized `for`-loop means implementing a generalized loop tag that, instead of looping through some collection, just posts an integer in a scripting variable, and that integer synchronizes the tags in the body. Listing 3.40 presents such a tag.

Listing 3.40   **The *SimpleForTag* Tag Handler**

```
package jspbook.example.authtags;

import javax.servlet.jsp.*;
import javax.servlet.jsp.tagext.*;

public class SimpleForTag implements Tag
{
    protected String id = null;
    protected int bottom = 0;
    protected int top = 0;
    protected int step = 0;
    protected int counter = 0;

    public String getId()
    {
        return this.id;
    }

    public void setId(String value)
    {
        this.id = value;
    }

    public int getBottom()
    {
        return this.bottom;
    }

    public void setBottom(int value)
    {
```

```
        this.bottom = value;
}

public int getTop()
{
    return this.top;
}

public void setTop(int value)
{
    this.top = value;
}

public int getStep()
{
    return this.step;
}

public void setStep(int value)
{
    this.step = value;
}

public int doStartTag() throws JspException
{
    if (id == null)
        throw new JspException("the id attribute is mandatory");

    if ((top > bottom && step > 0) ||
        (top < bottom && step < 0))
    {
        counter = bottom;
        pageContext.setAttribute(id,new Integer(counter));
        return EVAL_BODY_INCLUDE;
    }
    else if ((top > bottom && step < 0) ||
        (top < bottom && step > 0))
    {
        counter = top;
        pageContext.setAttribute(id,new Integer(counter));
        return EVAL_BODY_INCLUDE;
    }
    return SKIP_BODY;
}

public int doAfterBody() throws JspException
{

    if ((((top > bottom && step > 0) ||
        (top < bottom && step < 0)) && counter != top) ||
        (((top > bottom && step < 0) ||
```

continues

Listing 3.40   **Continued**

```
      (top < bottom && step > 0)) && counter != bottom ))
  {
      counter += step;
      pageContext.setAttribute(id,new Integer(counter));
      return EVAL_BODY_INCLUDE;
  }
  else return SKIP_BODY;
}


}
```

The doAfterBody method, which was presented in Listing 3.40, first checks whether the counter is consistent with the lower and upper bounds of the iteration and checks whether it still is in the admissible count interval. In the first case, the counting is progressive. If top is greater than bottom and step is positive, or if top is less than bottom and step is negative, it checks the counter page attribute, which represents the current count, against the top attribute. In the other case, the counting is retroactive.

If top is greater than bottom and step is negative, or if top is lesser than bottom and step is positive, it checks the counter page attribute against the bottom attribute. In either case, if the counter page attribute is consistent with the count interval, it is summed up to step and posted into the page scope attribute, and the EVAL_BODY_INCLUDE is returned, signaling that another iteration is needed. If the target value is reached, SKIP_BODY is returned and the doEndTag method gets invoked.

The example page for this tag, shown in Listing 3.41, uses a scriptlet expression and the writeAttribute tag to accept a numeric index for the attribute, which was shown in Listing 3.33, to loop through the attributes of a user.

Listing 3.41   **Using the *for* Iteration Tag**

```
<%@ taglib uri="/WEB-INF/example.tld" prefix="example"%>
<example:usrAttr id="usr" username="<%=request.getUserPrincipal()%>">
<html>
<body>
<table width="100%">
  <tr>
    <td align="center">
      <h1> User Preferences </h1>
    </td>
  </tr>
<example:simpleFor id="ctr" bottom="1" top="5" step="1" />
  <tr>
    <td align="center"><example:writeUsrAttr2 name="attr"
num="<%=((Integer)pageContext.getAttribute(ctr)).intValue()%>"/></td>
  </tr>
</example:simpleFor>
</table>
```

```
</body>
</html>
```

Figure 3.2 shows the result of processing this JSP.

Figure 3.2 The for tag in action.

while-like Tags

Implementing while-like loops is analogous to designing simple for tags. The constraint here is to know whether the control condition is external or internal to the body contents. *Internal conditions* mean that the body content tags will change the control variables and determine whether the loop stops. Internal conditions must be implemented with BodyTag tags.

External conditions are independent from the body contents and can be implemented with IterationTag tags. This kind of loop tag is interesting to use to express situations in which resource status is a factor in whether the body will be evaluated again. This is the case for the tag handler in Listing 3.42. It is a generic while loop that takes a boolean attribute to control the iteration.

Listing 3.42 **The *SimpleWhileTag* Tag Handler**

```
package jspbook.example.authtags;

import javax.servlet.jsp.*;
```

continues

Listing 3.42 **Continued**

```java
import javax.servlet.jsp.tagext.*;

public class SimpleWhileTag implements Tag
{
    protected boolean cond = false;

    public boolean getCond()
    {
        return this.cond;
    }

    public void setCond(boolean value)
    {
        this.cond = value;
    }


    public int doStartTag() throws JspException
    {
        if (cond == true) return EVAL_BODY_INCLUDE;
        else return SKIP_BODY;
    }

    public int doAfterBody() throws JspException
    {
        if (cond == true) return EVAL_BODY_AGAIN;
        else return SKIP_BODY;
    }


}
```

The page presented in Listing 3.43 makes use of this tag to run through a collection in a plain while loop behavior.

Listing 3.43 **Using the *while* Iteration Tag**

```jsp
<%@ taglib uri="/WEB-INF/example.tld" prefix="example"%>
<%
    Enumeration enum = System.getProperties().keys();
%>
<html>
<body>
<table width="100%">
  <tr>
    <td align="center">
      <h1> User Preferences </h1>
    </td>
  </tr>
<example:simpleWhile cond="<%=enum.hasMoreElements()%>" />
```

```
  <tr>
    <td><%=enum.nextElement().toString()%></td>
  </tr>
</example:simpleWhile>
</table>
</body>
</html>
```

The *TagSupport* Class

The TagSupport class (see Table 3.3) implements the IterationTag interface and provides a base class to develop both Tag and IterationTag tag handlers. It provides additional methods that simplify the access to attributes and the ancestor, meaning the enclosing tag.

Table 3.3   **The *TagSupport* Class That Implements the *IterationTag* Interface**

Field or Method	Description
FIELDS	
id	A String-type id attribute.
METHODS	
SetId	Setter method for the id attribute.
GetId	Getter method for the id attribute.
SetValue	Stores a key-value pair associated with this tag's instance.
GetValue	Gets a value, given a key.
GetValues	Returns an enumeration of the values in the key-value pairs collection.
removeValue	Removes a value from the key-value pairs collection, given the key.
findAncestorWithClass	Utilitarian method that uses getParent to find the instance of a given tag if it is enclosing this instance. This is a static method included to facilitate cooperation among tags.

The static method findAncestorWithClass is used to track the enclosing tags of interest to a certain tag. For instance, in the authorization tags tag library, presented so far, there are tags for writing the contents of a JNDI Attribute instance provided by the WriteUserAttrTableTag. If the designer wants to be sure that these tags are used only by a WriteUserAttrTableTag, he can use findAncestorWithClass more easily than getParent to ensure that the actual tag is enclosed by the correct one. Listing 3.44 shows a tag handler that will accept only attributes provided by the WriteUserAttrTableTag tag.

Listing 3.44   **The *SimpleWriteUserAttrTag* Tag Handler Constrained**

```
package jspbook.example.authtags;

import javax.servlet.HttpServletRequest;
import javax.naming.*;
import javax.naming.directory.*;
import javax.servlet.jsp.*;
import javax.servlet.jsp.tagext.*;

public class SimpleWriteUserAttrConstrTag extends TagSupport
{
    protected String name = null;

    public String getName()
    {
        return this.name;
    }

    public void setName(String value)
    {
        this.name = value;
    }

    public int doStartTag() throws JspException
    {

        if (TagSuport.findAncestorWithClass(this,
jspbook.example.authtags.WriteUserAttrTableTag.class) == null)
            throw new JspException("This tag must be enclosed by a
writeUserAttrTable tag");
        if (name == null)
            throw new JspException("The name attribute is
                                mandatory");
        try
        {
          // retrieve the attributes needed from the page scope
          Attribute attr = (Attribute)pageContext.getAttribute(name);

          // verify the attrs retrieved
          if (attr == null)
              throw new JSPException("No information found");

          pageContext.getOut().println(attr.get().toString());
        }
        catch(NamingException e)
        {
          throw new JSPException("NamingException: "+
                                e.getMessage());
        }
        return SKIP_BODY;
```

```
    }

}
```

Body Tags

Tags that need to manipulate their body content are called body tags. The most common example of a body tag is a tag whose body content consists of raw data. The BodyTag interface represents a tag that manipulates its body contents. A new field, EVAL_BODY_BUFFERED, is introduced, along with a new method, doInitBody.

The BodyContent class extends a JSPWriter, and it represents the content of the body in a body tag. It contains the result of the body evaluation; it won't contain any tags or JSP scriptlet code because these will get evaluated and the respective results will be generated. This result will be captured by the bodyContent attribute.

The *BodyTag* interface

The BodyTag interface is the interface that a tag that will manipulate its body content must implement (see Table 3.4). A tag handler implementing the BodyTag interface manipulates its body in the doInitBody and the doAfterBody methods. The body contents are retrieved by the container after evaluation by the setBodyContent method. The bodyContent property represents the captured content.

Table 3.4 **The *BodyTag* Interface That Extends the Iteration Tag**

Field or Method	Description
FIELDS	
EVAL_BODY_BUFFERED	A static final int that signals the JSP container that the tag has a body to be evaluated and captured in a BodyContent object. This value is to be returned as a result by the doStartTag method.
METHODS	
SetBodyContent	Invoked by the container to instantiate the tag handler's parent tag. The parent tag is the closest enclosing tag that this tag is in the body of.
DoInitBody	Processes the starting tag for this instance of the tag handler. This method can return EVAL_BODY_INCLUDE, signaling that the body must be processed, or SKIP_BODY, signaling that there is no body or that the body must not be processed.

The typical cycle of processing of a BodyTag tag handler is as follows:

1. The BodyTag tag handler returns EVAL_BODY_BUFFERED from its
   doStartTag method.

2. The setBodyContent method is invoked and the BodyContent object
   is initialized.

3. The doInitBody method is invoked to resynchronize variables and prepare
   for the evaluation of the body.

4. The body content is made available in the bodyContent property if the
   BodyTagSupport base class is used. It was captured by setBodyContent otherwise.
   On the doAfterBody method or doEndTag, if the body will be evaluated only
   once, the content can be inspected, copied, compared, or whatever.

5. The content is overwritten. New content is generated on the bodyContent
   object.

6. The new content is written to the output stream.

7. Either SKIP_BODY or EVAL_BODY_AGAIN is returned.

8. If SKIP_BODY is returned, the doEndTag method is invoked and the tag
   processing finalizes.

The BodyContent class extends a JSPWriter to provide methods to capture the
content in a String, for instance, or to replace the current content by one that the
tag generates. It doesn't make sense to talk about a BodyTag if it doesn't manipulate
a BodyContent object; it is so by definition. Otherwise, the tag handler would act as
a simple or iteration tag handler, and it would make more sense to design it as such.
Table 3.5 presents the structure of the BodyContent class.

Table 3.5   **The *BodyContent* Class That Extends JSPWriter**

Field, Constructor, or Method	Description
FIELDS	
autoFlush	Set to false. A BodyContent object cannot be in autoFlush mode because it cannot be flushed.
bufferSize	Specifies that the size of the buffer is unbounded.
DEFAULT_BUFFER, NO_BUFFER, UNBOUNDED_BUFFER	Inherited from JSPWriter.
CONSTRUCTORS	
bodyContent	The constructor of the BodyContent class.
METHODS	
getReader	Gets the value of the body content as a java.io.Reader.
clearBody	Clears the body of the tag.

flush	A BodyContent instance has no backing stream to write to. It depends on getting the stream of the tag that it was enclosed by or the page stream so that it cannot flush the buffer. The buffer is unbounded. This method was redefined in this class, so calling flush is illegal.
getEnclosingWriter	Gets the writer of the enclosing tag.
getString	Gets the body content represented by this class as a String.
writeOut	Writes the content of this BodyContent instance in the out stream, represented by the writer captured with getEnclosingWriter.

There is also a BodyTagSupport class, designed to provide a base for developing body tags (see Table 3.6). A body tag handler will implement BodyTag by extending the BodyTagSupport class and will make use of a BodyContent object, which the BodyTagSupport provides by default. This way, all that the tag designer must do is to create the methods necessary to implement the action.

Table 3.6 **The *BodyTagSupport* Class That Extends *TagSupport***

Field, Constructor, or Method	Description
FIELDS	
bodyContent	Is a bodyContent object that is available by default to the tag.
id, pageContext	Inherited from TagSupport.
EVAL_BODY_INCLUDE, EVAL_PAGE, SKIP_BODY, SKIP_PAGE	Inherited from Tag.
EVAL_BODY_AGAIN	Inherited from IterationTag.
CONSTRUCTORS	
BodyTagSupport	The default constructor.
METHODS	
getBodyContent	Gets the body content returning a BodyContent instance.
getPreviousOut	Gets the JSPWriter returned by the getEnclosingWriter method of the BodyContent object.

continues

Table 3.6　**Continued**

Field, Constructor, or Method	Description
SetBodyContent(BodyContent b)	Sets the bodyContent attribute with the current body content.
doStartTag	The doStartTag method on BodyTags can return also EVAL_BODY_BUFFERED.
doInitBody	Invoked by the container to prepare body evaluation.
doEndTag, release	Inherited from Tag.
findAncestorWithClass, getId, getParent, getValue, getValues, removeValue, setId, setPageContext, setParent, setValue	Inherited from TagSupport.

There are basically two courses of action for a BodyTag. It either sets its behavior driven by the body content, which means that the content will provide input for the action implemented, or it changes the body content and replaces it with something representing the actual content processed. This can be driven by either its current content or other variables. Both processes can be iterative.

Listing 3.45 is based on the following situation: You are using a third-party tag library in which you have no control whatsoever over the source code, and a tag of that code returns either an HTML table with user data or a String saying "user not found". The code in Listing 3.45 presents such a tag. The problem is that you need that result as an attribute of your own tag. You have seen that the situation depicted by Listing 3.17 is not admissible. A tag cannot have another tag as an attribute value. The same goes for standard actions. Neither useBean nor setProperty admits the tag as an attribute value.

Listing 3.45　**Third-Party Tag to Be Captured**

```
package jspbook.example.thirdpartytags;

import javax.servlet.HttpServletRequest;
import javax.naming.*;
import javax.naming.directory.*;
import javax.servlet.jsp.*;
import javax.servlet.jsp.tagext.*;
// Theoretically, this is unknown to the reader
public class ThirdPartyTag implements TagSupport
{
    protected String username = null;
```

```
public String getUsername()
{
    return this.username;
}

public void setUsername(String value)
{
    this.username = value;
}

public int doStartTag() throws JspException
{
    if (id == null)
        throw new JspException("the id attribute is mandatory");
    if (username == null)
        throw new JspException("the username attribute is mandatory");
    try
    {
        // parameterize the access to the Directory Service
        Hashtable param = new Hashtable();
        param.put(Context.INITIAL_CONTEXT_FACTORY,
                "com.sun.jndi.ldap.LdapCtxFactory");
        param.put(Context.PROVIDER_URL,
                "ldap://localhost:389/o=JSPExample");
        // access it
        DirContext ctx = new InitialDirContext(param);
        // retrieve the attributes needed
        Attributes attrs = ctx.getAttributes(
                            "cn="+username+", ou=People");

        // set the target attribute
        JspWriter out = pageContext.getOut();
        if (attrs.size() > 0)
        {
            out.println("<TABLE>");
            Enumeration enum = attrs.getAll();
            while (enum.hasMoreElements())
            {
                Attribute at = (Attribute)enum.nextElement();
                out.println("<TR><TD>");
                out.println(at.getId()+"</TD><TD>"+at.get());
                out.println("</TD></TR>");
            }
            out.println("</TABLE>");
        }
        else
            out.println("No information found");
    }
```

continues

Listing 3.45 **Continued**

```
    catch(NamingException e)
    {
      throw new JSPException("NamingException: "+
                             e.getMessage());
    }
    return SKIP_BODY;
  }

}
```

The solution in this case is to build a body tag that will wrap around the third-party tag and capture its output into a scripting variable. Of course, if any other content, such as raw content, a scriptlet, or any other tag, is inserted in the body of the wrapper tag, the result won't correspond to the result of the third-party tag, making the wrapper tag useless. This must be clearly pointed out to the page designer. The JSP fragment in Listing 3.46 shows this solution being used.

Listing 3.46 **Wrapping Around the Third-Party Tag**

```
. . . . .
<example:wrapper id="myVar">
  <thirdp:tpTag username="<%=request.getUserPrincipal()%>"/>
</example:wrapper>
. . . . .<%=myVar%> is ...
```

Listing 3.47 presents the wrapper body tag. It captures the body content, generated in this case only by the third-party tag, and places the String generated into a page-scope variable. This way the content of the third-party tag becomes available for your tags because it has an id property to publish it as a bean.

Listing 3.47 **The Wrapper *BodyTag***

```
package jspbook.example.tags;

import javax.servlet.jsp.*;
import javax.servlet.jsp.tagext.*;

public class WrapperTag extends BodyTagSupport
{

    public final int doEndTag() throws JspException {

      // All the wrapper class must do is to capture the String
      // written in the body. That, according to the
      // documentation of the third-party tag library, will
      // either represent an HTML table or a string

      // the captured body
```

```
    String wrapped = bodyContent.getString();

    if (wrapped != null)
    {
        pageContext.setAttribute(id,wrapped);
        return EVAL_PAGE;
    }

    return SKIP_PAGE;
}
```

Listings 3.45–3.47 illustrate the first scenario of usage for a `BodyTag`, which is a tag that captures its body but does not generate anything else. Instead, it just traps another tag or performs some side-effect process with the information provided by the tags in the body, but it does not generate new content.

In the next example, on the other hand, the goal is to capture the body and generate something to replace it. The tag captures the output of a data-generation object, which is a comma-delimited string list, and transforms it in an HTML table. The situation is that there is a `FeatureReader` class designed to cope with mapping shapes. This class just reads a proprietary shape format and converts it to a text like the fragment depicted in Listing 3.48.

Listing 3.48 **Sample Output for the** *FeatureReader* **Class**

```
BRA, 01, 02, 04, 05;
BRA, 09, 12, 14, 15;
BRA, 18, 22, 34, 37;

. . .
```

The `FeatureToTableTag` tag handler is described in Listing 3.49. It reads the feature list file and parses it, generating an HTML table equivalent to that. The feature list generated by the `FeatureReader` class provides a list of features separated by semicolons. Each feature constitutes a comma-separated string list.

Listing 3.49 **A Raw –Data–to–HTML Table Converter**

```
package jspbook.example.tags;

import javax.servlet.HttpServletRequest;
import javax.servlet.jsp.*;
import javax.servlet.jsp.tagext.*;

public class FeatureToTableTag extends BodyTagSupport
{

    protected String elSep  = ",";
    protected String linSep = ";";
```

continues

Listing 3.49   **Continued**

```
public String getElSep()
{
    return this.elSep;
}

public void setElSep(String value)
{
    this.elSep = value;
}

public String getLinSep()
{
    return this.linSep;
}

public void setLinSep(String value)
{
    this.linSep = value;
}

public int doEndTag() throws JspException
{
    String featureText = bodyContent.getString();
    StringBuffer outTable = new StringBuffer();
    StringTokenizer featTk = new
        StringTokenizer(featureText, linSep, false);

    // Scans the body content and generates a Table from it
    outTable.append("<TABLE>");
    while (featTk.hasMoreTokens())
    {
        String feat = (String)featTk.nextToken();
        StringTokenizer elTk = new StringTokenizer(feat, elSep, false);
        outTable.append("<TR>");
        while(elTk.hasMoreTokens())
        {
            outTable.append("<TD>");
            outTable.append((String)elTk.nextToken());
            outTable.append("</TD>");
        }
        outTable.append("</TR>");
    }
    outTable.append("</TABLE>");

    // Writes the new content out
    bodyContent.println(outTable.toString());
    bodyContent.writeOut(bodycontent.getEnclosingWriter());
```

```
        return EVAL_PAGE;
    }

    public void release()
    {
        // put the default values back
        elSep = ",";
        linSep = ";";
    }

}
```

The first part of the doEndTag just double-parses the feature text identifying each element. The first StringTokenizer parses the lines, separated by semicolons. The second parses the elements, separated by commas. Each line parsed causes the inclusion of a new <TR> HTML table row tag, and each feature element results in a new <TD> cell.

After the table is written in the StringBuffer, it is printed in the bodyContent. Because that object is a JSPWriter, the enclosing Writer (the page level JSPWriter, in this case) is taken and the new content is written. The usage of this tag is shown in Listing 3.50.

Listing 3.50   **Using the Raw Data–to–HTML Table Converter**

```
<%@ taglib uri="/WEB-INF/example.tld" prefix="example"%>
<%
    Enumeration enum = System.getProperties().keys();
%>
<html>
<body>
<H1> Raw Data </H1>
<example:rawToTable elSep="," linSep=";">
BRA, 01, 02, 04, 05;BRA, 09, 12, 14, 15;BRA, 18, 22, 34, 37;
BRA, 01, 02, 04, 05;BRA, 09, 12, 14, 15;BRA, 18, 22, 34, 37;
BRA, 01, 02, 04, 05;BRA, 09, 12, 14, 15;BRA, 18, 22, 34, 37;
BRA, 01, 02, 04, 05;BRA, 09, 12, 14, 15;BRA, 18, 22, 34, 37;
BRA, 01, 02, 04, 05;BRA, 09, 12, 14, 15;BRA, 18, 22, 34, 37;
BRA, 01, 02, 04, 05;BRA, 09, 12, 14, 15;BRA, 18, 22, 34, 37;
BRA, 01, 02, 04, 05;BRA, 09, 12, 14, 15;BRA, 18, 22, 34, 37;
BRA, 01, 02, 04, 05;BRA, 09, 12, 14, 15;BRA, 18, 22, 34, 37;
BRA, 01, 02, 04, 05;BRA, 09, 12, 14, 15;BRA, 18, 22, 34, 37;
</example:rawToTable>
</table>
</body>
</html>
```

This page will output the content as an HTML table with 27×5 cells.

It is important to note that the tag designer must be crystal clear about the type of content that the BodyTag will accept. This is so because what will be put in the body content will be totally decided by the page designer. For instance, if the BodyTag expects a certain result from another tag and that tag is wrongfully replaced, the BodyTag will get the wrong input in the body.

Another case to watch for is the body containing some misspelled value, such as a misspelled database URL in a JDBC connection tag. The best approach is to be defensive, to test all values captured by the bodyContent attribute, to implement the TryCatchFinally interface discussed in the next section, and to provide clear exception messages to drive the page designer to the right way.

The *TryCatchFinally* Interface

Sometimes a tag handler depends on resources that can be exhausted, such as database connections or file handlers, and these resources must be returned to their original state after the action has run its course, to avoid exhaustion and deadlocking. The problem is that when an exception is thrown, the execution is suspended. Therefore, any resources leased by this tag handler are locked or lost.

This can't be avoided by using a try-catch statement because body actions can throw exceptions outside the current tag's methods, cutting off the possibility of releasing such resources properly. For instance, the situation described by the example in Listing 3.51 is that an enclosing tag logs activities registered by enclosing the tags in a properties file. But the properties file is loaded in the doStartTag method to mark exact timing, the handler is maintained as a protected property, and doEndTag performs the bookkeeping and saves the file.

Listing 3.51 **The Relaxed Logger Tag**

```
package jspbook.example.tags;

import java.util.*;
import java.io.*;
import javax.servlet.jsp.*;
import javax.servlet.jsp.tagext.*;

public class LoggerTag extends TagSupport
{
    protected Properties log = new Properties();

public int doStartTag() throws JspException
    {

        if (getParent() != null)
          throw new JspException("The logger tag cannot be enclosed");

        try
        {
          // retrieve the current log
          log.load(new FileInputStream(
pageContext.getApplication().getRealpath("/access.log")));
          log.put("last update",new Date());
```

```
      }
      catch(Exception e)
      {
        throw new JSPException("Cannot access the log file");
      }
      return EVAL_BODY_INCLUDE;
    }


    public int doEndTag() throws JspException
    {

      try
      {
        // retrieve the operations and log them
        // this illustrates also the usage of the values
        // property of the TagSupport class
        Enumeration enum = values.keys();
        while (enum.hasMoreElements())
        {
            String aKey = keys.nextElement().toString();
            log.put(aKey,values.get(aKey).toString());
        }

        // retrieve the current log
        log.save(new
FileOutputStream(pageContext.getApplication().getRealpath("access.log")),"");
      }
      catch(Exception e)
      {
        throw new JSPException("Cannot access the log file");
      }
      return EVAL_PAGE;
    }


}
```

Now suppose that this tag is used to log the activities of the writeUsrAttr tag presented earlier. It must be revamped to log its activity to the logger. Listing 3.52 shows that.

Listing 3.52   **Logging the Activities with the Logger Values**

```
package jspbook.example.authtags;

import javax.servlet.HttpServletRequest;
import javax.naming.*;
import javax.naming.directory.*;
import javax.servlet.jsp.*;
import javax.servlet.jsp.tagext.*;
```

continues

Listing 3.52 **Continued**

```
public class writeUsrAttrRevampTag extends SimpleWriteUserAttrConstr
{
    public int doEndTag() throws JspException
    {

        LoggerTag logger = TagSuport.findAncestorWithClass(this,
jspbook.example.tags.LoggerTag.class);
        if (logger == null)
            throw new JspException("This tag must be enclosed by the logger tag");

logger.setValue(this.getClass().getName(),String.valueOf(System.currentTimeMillis(
)))
        return EVAL_PAGE;
    }

}
```

The situation of the access.log file is menaced by the writeUsrAttrRevamp tag
because introducing a user that is not registered with the LDAP server will cause a
JspException to be thrown. If this occurs, the processing of the logger tag is aborted,
and the file handler for the access.log properties file is held locked by the container
application.

To ensure that resources are released and that the flow of processing can continue
after an exception, the Tag Extension API 1.1 provides the TryCatchFinally interface.
All tag handlers that deal with exhaustible resources must preferably implement this
interface. The TryCatchFinally interface is described in Table 3.7.

Table 3.7 **The *TryCatchFinally* Interface**

Methods	Description
DoCatch	Processes the ending tag for this instance of the tag handler. This method can return EVAL_PAGE, signaling that the rest of the JSP page must be processed, or SKIP_PAGE, signaling that the rest of the JSP page must not be processed.
DoFinally	Clears the attribute values, restoring their default values. This is used to reset the attributes between two calls to the tag.

The typical cycle of processing of a TryCatchFinally tag handler is as follows:

1. The tag is processed normally by the JSP container, and a Throwable is thrown
    in that processing.
2. The doCatch method is invoked. It performs logging or recovery processing, or
    raises some Throwable to translate the error condition into clearer terms.

3. After the doCatch method gets invoked, the doFinally method is invoked. It releases allocated resources, unlocks locks placed, and so forth, to avoid exhausting critical resources.

4. If a throwable was raised by the doCatch method, it is propagated to the enclosing tag, which treats it, or the JSP container, which returns an error page and interrupts the evaluation of the page.

When a tag handler implements the TryCatchFinally interface, its life cycle changes. It is instantiated and initialized as with the other interfaces, but the tag evaluation process, starting with doStartTag and ending with doEndTag, is enclosed in a try block. Any exception thrown during the evaluation of that block, which includes the evaluation, re-evaluation, or body content treatment, will be captured. The catch block calls the doCatch method of that tag, and the finally block calls the doFinally method.

The doCatch method has an argument, which is the throwable that caused it to be executed. If no throwable was thrown, this method is ignored. Code must be put inside doCatch to recover from the exception situation. If an exception is thrown inside this method, the doFinally method gets invoked and the exception is chained up to the enclosing tags. For instance, suppose that you have a TryCatchFinally tag enclosed by another TryCatchFinally tag, and the enclosed tag gets an exception (a Throwable is enough, in fact). This doCatch method treats the original exception and raises another with a particular message. That exception will be captured by the enclosing tag and the exception raised by that one by its enclosing tag, and so forth.

The doFinally method is called in the finally block of that invocation and must be used to release resources, reinitialize attributes, and free the tag handler to end. The doFinally method should not throw any exceptions. Neither doCatch nor doFinally gets invoked if the exception occurs during the invocation of attribute setter methods.

Listing 3.53 shows up the logger tag revamped. It implements the TryCatchFinally interface.

Listing 3.53 **The Logger Tag Implementing** *TryCatchFinally*

```
package jspbook.example.tags;

import java.util.*;
import java.io.*;
import javax.servlet.jsp.*;
import javax.servlet.jsp.tagext.*;

public class LoggerTag extends TagSupport implements TryCatchFinally
{
    protected Properties log = new Properties();

    public int doStartTag() throws JspException
    {
```

continues

Listing 3.53 **Continued**

```
          if (getParent() != null)
             throw new JspException("The logger tag cannot be enclosed");

          try
          {
            // retrieve the current log
            log.load(new FileInputStream(
pageContext.getApplication().getRealpath("/access.log")));
            log.put("last update",new Date());
          }
          catch(Exception e)
          {
            throw new JSPException("Cannot access the log file");
          }
          return EVAL_BODY_INCLUDE;
       }

     public int doEndTag() throws JspException
     {

        try
        {
          // retrieve the operations and log them
          // this illustrates also the usage of the values
          // property of the TagSupport class
          Enumeration enum = values.keys();
          while (enum.hasMoreElements())
          {
              String aKey = keys.nextElement().toString();
              log.put(aKey,values.get(aKey).toString());
          }

          // retrieve the current log
          log.save(new
FileOutputStream(pageContext.getApplication().getRealpath("access.log")),"");
       }
       catch(Exception e)
       {
          throw new JSPException("Cannot access the log file");
       }
       return EVAL_PAGE;
     }

     public void doCatch(Throwable t) throws Throwable
     {
        log.put("Exception "+t.getMessage(),new Date());
     }

     public void doFinally
```

```
    {
        try
        {
            log.save(new
FileOutputStream(pageContext.getApplication().getRealpath("access.log")),"");
        }
        catch(Exception e)
        {
            application.log("Error closing the log file",e);
        }
    }

}
```

In Listing 3.53, the doCatch method tries to log the exception on the access file because the doFinally method will be invoked afterward to properly save and close the properties file. If an exception is thrown during its execution, doFinally tries to close the file. If it is not possible to do it, the exception raised is logged in the context log, and the file is lost.

Summary

This chapter presented the building blocks of the Tag Library Extension API. The most important piece of the API is the Tag interface, which defines a basic protocol for a tag to communicate with the JSP container. This is done through the insertion of a standard invocation sequence inside the servlet where the JSP is compiled.

The base of the protocol is the setter sequence, which initializes PageContext, the detected parent tag, if such parent exists—that is, if the tag is enclosed by any other (or possibly other instances of the same) tag.

Then doStartTag is invoked to process the heading part of a tag. The doStartTag method is used to process information that will be necessary to the tags enclosed by this tag, even if the body doesn't get processed or iterated. It sets up variables, prepares connections with J2EE data or application servers, and possibly starts iteration cycles.

doEndTag is invoked to provide termination of the action. It is the preferred method of providing finalization, but it is not the opposite of the doStartTag. Depending on how the action is organized, doEndTag can end up being the processing method in the tag.

State is reset by the release method. Its responsibility is to reset properties and properties published as attributes to their default value.

The IterationTag interface provides the base for iterative actions. Iterative actions have their body re-evaluated until a certain state is reached. This is the case when it is necessary to process elements in a collection or to control logical or counter-based iteration.

The doStartTag method settles the iterative process by setting offsets and top limit values, and by extracting the first element to process in collections; it is the method invoked before any evaluation of the body. The doAfterBody method is responsible for maintaining the iterative process, re-evaluating the stop conditions, and deciding whether the body should be re-evaluated.

Tags that need to manipulate the result of the evaluation of their body contents implement the BodyTag interface. This interface introduces a flag value intended to finalize the container. To do this, the body content must be captured and made available to the tag handler. A special class called BodyContent holds this data. It is passed to BodyTag via the setBodyContent method. doInitBody prepares for tag execution. The body content can be manipulated in any of the methods available: doStartTag, doEndTag, doAfterBody, and so on.

To provide a better platform for tag development, two auxiliary base classes are provided. The TagSupport class provides a base class for the development of Tag and IterationTag implementor tag handlers. The BodyTagSupport class provides for the development of BodyTags.

Tag handlers manipulate exhaustible resources such as JDBC connections or file handlers, and they must implement the TryCatchFinally interface. This interface provides two methods that are called in case of exceptions. The doCatch method is meant to recover from error situations, and the doFinally method is meant to provide a safe way of releasing resources allocated by the tag handler.

4

Cooperating Tags
and Validation

THIS CHAPTER PRESENTS THE MECHANISMS BY WHICH tags can cooperate to perform complex actions and the mechanisms to perform tag attribute validation. While the first topic builds upon the last chapter's examples to create more complex actions, the second topic introduces `TagExtraInfo` classes and tells how they are used to reinforce complex attribute configurations.

Regarding cooperation, tags are presented in the context of the J2EE architecture, the Java API, a web application component, and a JSP container itself. The use of `pageContext` is explored as a cooperation mechanism and the execution stack, and the parent-tag relationship is discussed as a further mechanism. Then the basic patterns of tag cooperation are explored, to show how tags are used as complimentary processes and as complimentary data structures.

Tags as First-Class Components

The Tag Library Extension API is an integral part of the Java Servlet API and is part of the web layer description of the Java 2 Enterprise Edition Architecture. Tags implement the JavaBeans component model, with restrictions. Their life cycle is defined under the life cycle of the JSP component. Tags are managed by the JSP container and have access to all the resources of the web application, as a servlet or JSP.

Tags also have full access to the J2EE API. They can access and use any of the J2EE API objects and interfaces, such as JNDI NamingContexts or JDBC connections and ResultSets. Tags can use any of the Java API objects and interfaces, such as the java.util package, for instance.

The J2EE blueprints define custom tags as "the mechanism provided by JSP technology for defining customized, declarative, and modular functionality for use by JSP pages." So, tags are part of the JSP technology, which makes them a web-layer component. They deliver modular functionality, which means that a tag can be reused through many JSP pages the same way because it is configured in a declarative way through attributes.

The J2EE blueprints define a component that, despite having a life cycle fully defined within the JSP page life cycle, provides functionality that can be designed, created, and maintained independently from the pages that use them. This means that custom tags have a large degree of independence regarding the JSP pages where they are ultimately used.

Tags Have Access to the Full Java API

Tags can be seen as JavaBeans, which means that they have access to the full Java API. Of course, some APIs are meaningful in a server-side application, and other APIs are not. For instance, the Swing API has little value in a server-side application, while the JAXP API for XML parsing is of great importance. Other APIs can be used in a custom tag design but in less common circumstances. For instance, the AWT API objects can be used to create graphics to be encoded in GIF or JPEG image formats and then can be saved as files to be further retrieved in a HTML page; however, that is not the most common of the tag applications.

Listing 4.1 presents a body tag that formats a date written in the tag's body by a scriptlet. This example offers the idea that the full API is available to a tag. If a class is created in a certain API, using this API with a tag library works exactly like using a class in any other Java program.

Listing 4.1 **A Date-Formatting Tag**

```
package jspbook.example.tags;

import java.util.*;
import java.text.*;
import javax.servlet.jsp.*;
import javax.servlet.jsp.tagext.*;

public class DateFormatTag extends BodyTagSupport
{
    protected String format = "yyyy-MM-dd hh:mm:ss";

    public String getFormat()
```

```
    {
        return this.format;
    }

    public void setFormat(String value)
    {
        this.format = value;
    }

    public int doEndTag() throws JspException
    {
        Locale loc = pageContext.getRequest().getLocale();
        String dateField = bodyContent.getString();
        SimpleDateFormat formatter = new SimpleDateFormat(format,loc);
        formatter.applyLocalizedPattern("dd/mm/yy");
        Date dfieldParsed = formatter.parse(dateField,new ParsePosition(0));
        formatter.applyLocalizedPattern(format);
        String dateString = formatter.format(dfieldParsed);
        bodyContent.println(dateString);
        bodyContent.writeOut(bodyContent.getEnclosingWriter());
    }

    public void release()
    {
        format = "yyyy-MM-dd hh:mm:ss";
    }
}
```

Accessing Objects in Several Scopes

Tags have access to the same runtime environment that the host JSP accesses. This means that a tag has full access to the several namespaces defined for the JSP—namely, the context, the session, the request, and, as demonstrated in Chapter 3, "Writing Custom Tags," the page namespace. This is done through the `pageContext` implicit property, which is automatically bound by the JSP container in the tag-initialization process. The JSP container calls the `setPageContext` method as the very first action in the initialization process.

Accessing the several scopes is crucial to integrating a custom tag in the application architecture. When developing web applications with beans, JSP pages, and servlets, a web developer uses the following attributes:

- Session attributes to store persistent objects bound to the user
- Request attributes to store objects bound to the current application transaction
- Context attributes to store generic or referential objects that need to be accessible from all the application
- Page attributes to store information needed for page processing itself

For instance, in a web application, depending on how the application is structured, either a servlet or an application-startup event listener can initialize a number of referential objects or collections—for example, a vector with the names of the states, or the ISO codes representing the Latin American countries. A Hashtable can represent this collection, having, as name-value pairs, the ISO code for a name and the associated name of country for a value. These name-value pairs are used throughout the application pages in a tag that builds up a select element. This kind of collection is put in the context namespace, stored in a context scope attribute. Listing 4.2 presents an application-level event listener that implements the ServletContextListener interface, which initializes a Hashtable with ISO codes and names of countries and puts it in the context namespace as a context scope attribute.

Listing 4.2   **The Codes/Names Application Listener**

```
package jspbook.example.utils;

import java.sql.*;
import java.util.*;
import javax.naming.*;
import javax.servlet.*;

public final class ExampleCtxtListener implements ServletContextListener
{

    private ServletContext context = null;

    public void contextDestroyed(ServletContextEvent event)
    {
      this.context = null;
    }


    public void contextInitialized(ServletContextEvent event)
    {
      this.context = event.getServletContext();
      try
        {
          Hashtable env = new Hashtable();
          Hashtable results = new Hashtable();
          env.put(Context.INITIAL_CONTEXT_FACTORY,
          "com.sun.jndi.rmi.registry.RegistryContextFactory");
          env.put(Context.PROVIDER_URL, "rmi://localhost:1099");
          env.put("java.naming.rmi.security.manager", "1");
          Context ctx = new InitialContext(env);

          // Get a Connection
          DataSource ds = (DataSource) ctx.lookup("EXAMPLEDS");
          Connection con = null;
```

```
            try {

                con = ds.getConnection();
                Statement st = con.createStatement(ResultSet.TYPE_SCROLL_INSENSITIVE,
                                        ResultSet.CONCUR_READ_ONLY);
                ResultSet res = st.executeQuery("SELECT ISO2CODE, NAME FROM
ISO_NAMES_TABLE");
                while (!res.isLast()) {
                    res.next();
                    results.put(rs.getString(1));
                    results.put(rs.getString(2));
                }
                if (!results.isEmpty())
                    this.context.setAttribute("CTRY_ISO_NAMES");
            } catch (SQLException sqle) {
                context.log("filter",sqle);
            }
            finally {
                if (con != null) try { con.close(); } catch (SQLException sqle2) {}
            }

        }
        catch (Exception e)
        {
            return;
        }


    }
```

The `ExampleCtxtListener` implements the `ServletContextListener` interface introduced in the Servlet API 2.3. That interface provides two methods to treat a `ServletContextEvent`: `contextInitialized` and `contextDestroyed`. In the example, the `contextInitialized` method is used to create a `Hashtable` containing the data needed by the application and then store it as a context attribute. This way, after the context is loaded, this attribute will be available there for use by all components in the application.

The tag handler depicted in Listing 4.3 will create an HTML select element from a certain context scope attribute. It is part of the application, not a generic tag handler. If the application has a lot of referential data to be used, the tag in Listing 4.3 will present the data in a `select` statement easily.

Listing 4.3   **A *select* Formatter Tag**

```
package jspbook.example.tags;

import java.util.*;
import javax.servlet.jsp.*;
import javax.servlet.jsp.tagext.*;
```

continues

Listing 4.3   **Continued**

```java
public class SelectFormatterTag extends TagSupport
{
    protected String name = null;
    protected String size = "1";
    protected String multi = null;
    protected String onChange = null;

    public String getName()
    {
        return this.name;
    }

    public void setName(String value)
    {
        this.name = value;
    }

    public String getSize()
    {
        return this.size;
    }

    public void setSize(String value)
    {
        this.size = value;
    }

    public String getMulti()
    {
        return this.multi;
    }

    public void setMulti(String value)
    {
        this.multi = value;
    }

    public String getOnChange()
    {
        return this.onChange;
    }

    public void setOnChange(String value)
    {
        this.onChange = value;
    }

    public int doStartTag() throws JspException
```

```
    {
        if (name == null)
            throw JspException("The attribute name is required");
        return SKIP_BODY;
    }


    public int doEndTag() throws JspException
    {
        ServletContext context = pageContext.getContext();
        Hashtable values = (Hashtable)context.getAttribute(name);
        JspWriter out = pageContext.getOut();
        out.println("<Select "+
        (multi != null?"multiple ":" ")+
        (size != null?"size="+size+" ":" size='1' ")+
        (onChange != null?"onChange='"+onChange+"' ":"")+
         ">");
        Enumeration enum= values.keys();
        while(enum.hasMoreElements())
        {
            String key = keys.nextElement().toString();
            out.print("<option value="+key.trim()+" >");
            out.print(values.get(key).toString());
            out.println("</options>");
        }
        out.println("</select>");
        return EVAL_PAGE;
    }

    public void release()
    {
        name = null;
        size = "1";
        multi = null;
        onChange = null;
    }
}
```

The SelectFormatterTag in Listing 4.3 accesses the attribute as a Hashtable in the context scope attribute whose name is given by the name tag attribute. The size, multi, and onChange tag attributes provide a minimum of flexibility to this tag. Implementing other HTML/JavaScript attributes on this tag is a matter of adding more correspondent tag attributes.

The tag is coordinated to work with the web application components by providing the tag elements to recover the necessary objects from the scopes where those were stored. Figure 4.1 illustrates such a schema. A servlet, JSP, event listener, or filter will provide information in some format as objects stored in some scope or in a wrapped request instance. The tag accesses that information through the pageContext methods and performs its action on them, possibly setting objects on some scope to be used by other components as well.

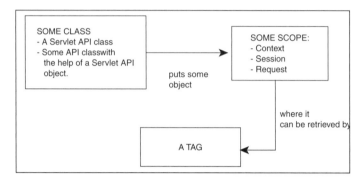

Figure 4.1   Cooperation in the web application.

To make such a tag generic means to abstract the collection upon which the tag is based. You could do this by explicitly accepting a type attribute or through introspection of the type of the collection retrieved and by providing it with the mechanisms to access the stored objects in any scope. One way to do this would be to explicitly provide it a scope attribute or use the `pageContext.findAttribute` method.

The `pageContext` property can be used to access the output writer or objects stored in several scopes, as was demonstrated in several examples (see the appropriate listings in Chapters 3 and 4). A tag handler can access resources inside the container, using the `ServletContext` to gain access to the resources. The `ServletContext` object can be used to access resources inside a web application and in other web applications inside the container. It can open HTTP connections and get remote resources as well.

Cooperation Among Tags

Most of the examples presented so far implemented simple processes, in which tags provided a simple action entirely contained by them or with the use of helper classes to abstract some functionality. The point is that tags can go much further than that when they work in cooperation. Complex actions can be implemented by a group of tags by either sharing some data representation schema or accessing the attributes of each other directly. These are the two big design patterns in tag cooperation.

Tags can share a set of common objects and can perform part of some complex action just by working with this common object. The basic mechanism to do so involves using the several namespaces available for a tag and defining script variables, which is all done through the `pageContext` property.

The second case of tag cooperation works through direct access to attributes in a tag by the tags in its body. This is done through the `TagSupport.findAncestor WithClass` or `getParent` methods.

Cooperating tags are generally oriented to provide some data structure or some subprocess of the action implementation. In the first pattern, some complex data structure must be built inside the page and then rendered out or used in some collateral effect. Examples of this include email tags, in which the several optional components of an email message are implemented as subtags that build the data structure that makes the email to be sent. The final action to be taken is to send the message itself and return an acknowledgement to the client.

In the second case, the several phases of a process are implemented as tags that can be assembled in a more complex action. The classical example is JDBC SQL querying, in which the several phases of the process—namely, finding a driver, getting a connection, creating a query, submitting it, and treating the results—are all treated by a number of tags working together. Where alternative configurations are seamlessly interchangeable, such as when using driver+path+user+password versus using data-sources+jndi lookup, multiple tags can be used in several arrangements.

Using the *pageContext* Property

The `pageContext` property provides access to the several scopes available to the host JSP and specifically to the page scope. This way, tags working in cooperation can communicate results with each other in a highly modular manner, more loosely coupled.

In this kind of cooperation mechanism, the nesting tag creates a layer of data or services for the nested tag, which by themselves create the next layer for the tags nested inside them, and so forth. So, in this scenario, the top parent tag creates some object and leaves it in some scope using `pageContext`. The nesting tags use it, and the object is released with the nesting tag.

The first example presented is a tag library that implements a small subset of the Java Messaging Service (JMS) API. The application needs to access a topical queue in a publish-subscribe schema and present the information in the queue to the user for an electronic election-control application. So, as soon as the votes of each region get computed for each candidate, they are published in that candidate's topical queue, in a `Hashtable` containing the region's codes and votes, proportional and absolute. Before coding this tag library, a brief comment on JMS may be needed.

JMS is the Java API for messaging. Messaging is a kind of middleware that provides communication between applications in a reliable, asynchronous way, making applications that need guaranteed delivery of messages easier to manage and write. A JMS application relies on a messaging service agent, which is a server-like application that controls the delivery of messages between the service client applications. A messaging service can be based on two models: pure queues or publisher-subscriber queues. In the pure queues model, the recipient client has a queue that the sender client posts a message to. This is a peer-to-peer model. In the publisher-subscriber model, the publishers write their messages to a topical queue, and the subscribers can be notified of that or can have immediate access, if they have subscribed for that specific queue. JMS supports both models.

In the application scenario depicted, the only information delivered is the current number of votes for a candidate and the percentage that the number represents from the total electorate. Of course, all the committees can access all the data to have a panoramic view of the position of their respective candidate. The application assumes that a publisher is defined and working, publishing the information on each adequate queue, so a web application tag library must be written to read the values from that queue and write them in a web page.

The tags are defined according to the structure of the objects on the JMS API:

- **topicConnection**—Represents a TopicConnection object. It uses a TopicConnectionFactory posted in a JNDI service or delivered as a bean in a scope.

- **topic**—Represents a Topic object. It also is considered to have been posted in some scope or in a JNDI service.

- **topicSession**—Is a TopicSession instance created under a topicConnection.

- **topicSubscriber**—Created under the connection and topic tags. Represents a TopicSubscriber instance.

- **message**—Is a message received from the message service and created under the topicSubscriber tag. It receives a message from Topic and writes it to the out stream. This message will be from the type ObjectMessage because it must deliver the absolute number of votes of a certain candidate X, the absolute percentage of the votes, and the relative percentage of the votes regarding the valid votes.

Because JMS requires the existence of a messaging service provider or messaging agent, in all examples it uses ObjectEvents, from ObjectCube, at http:// www.objectcube.com, an Open Source version of the commercial product ObjectEvents Pro.

Listing 4.4 presents the topicConnection tag handler. The doStartTag method tries to locate a TopicConnectionFactory instance from which it can create a TopicConnection object. This can be done by using a TopicConnectionFactory provided by the user, by accessing an attribute set in some scope passed through the name attribute/property, or by setting a JNDI name string that will be used to look up the correct instance. The TopicConnection object is then created and put into the page scope.

Listing 4.4   **The *TopicConnectionTag* Tag Handler**

```
package jspbook.example.tags;

import javax.jms.*;
import com.objectcube.objectevents.naming.*;
import javax.servlet.jsp.*;
import javax.servlet.jsp.tagext.*;

public class TopicConnectionTag extends TagSupport implements TryCatchFinally
{
    private TopicConnection tc = null;
```

```
protected TopicConnectionFactory tcf = null;
protected String name = null;
protected String JNDIName = null;

public String getTcf()
{
    return this.tcf;
}

public void setTcf(TopicConnectionFactory value)
{
    this.tcf = value;
}

public String getName()
{
    return this.name;
}

public void setName(String value)
{
    this.name = value;
}

 public String getJNDIName()
{
    return this.JNDIName;
}

public void setJNDIName(String value)
{
    this.JNDIName = value;
}

public int doStartTag() throws JspException
{

  TopicConnectionFactory intTcf = null;

  if (tcf == null && name == null && JNDIName == null)
      throw new JspException("The TopicConnectionFactory cannot be located.");

  if (id == null)
      throw new JspException("The id attribute is mandatory.");
  try
  {
      // Locates a TopicConnectionFactory to create a TopicConnection
      if (tcf == null)
      {
          if (JNDIName == null)
```

continues

Listing 4.4 **Continued**

```
                intTcf = (TopicConnectionFactory)pageContext.findAttribute(name);
            else
            {
                Context ctx = new InitialContext();
                intTcf = (TopicConnectionFactory)context.lookup(JNDIName);
            }
        }
        else intTcf = tcf;

        tc = intTcf.createTopicConnection();
        pageContext.setAttribute(id, tc);
        return EVAL_BODY_INCLUDE;

    }
    catch(JMSException e)
    {
        throw new JSPException("JMS Exception: "+ e.getMessage());
    }
    return SKIP_BODY;
}

public void doFinally()
{
    tc.close();
}

public void release()
{
    tc = null;
    tcf = null;
    name = null;
    JNDIName = null;
}

}
```

Note that an `intTcf` object is declared in the `doStartTag` method. This is because the properties declared as attributes cannot be attributed values but must be set via the setter methods. So, the `intTcf` object either receives a `Tcf` directly, as passed in the `tcf` attribute or receives it from some location. The `id` attribute is not declared because the tag handler extends `TagSupport`, which declares this attribute implicitly.

Also, because connections are quite sensitive objects to manage, the tag handler implements the `TryCatchFinally` interface and releases the connection in the very last `doFinally` method. This way, the concept that this tag implements works as follows:

1. A `topicConnection` tag establishes the connection.
2. Consumer tags are placed in the `topicConnection`'s body and can use that connection.

3. The doFinally method finalizes the connection on the tag closure.

Listing 4.5 displays the Topic tag handler, implementing a Topic in the server. It is very similar to the topicConnection tag handler; the same design solutions used in the topicConnection tag handler apply to this one.

Listing 4.5   **The *TopicTag* Tag Handler**

```
package jspbook.example.tags;

import javax.jms.*;
import com.objectcube.objectevents.naming.*;
import javax.servlet.jsp.*;
import javax.servlet.jsp.tagext.*;

public class TopicTag extends TagSupport implements TryCatchFinally
{
    private Topic topic = null;

    protected Topic tp = null;
    protected String name = null;
    protected String JNDIName = null;


    public Topic getTp()
    {
        return this.tp;
    }

    public void setTp(Topic value)
    {
        this.tp = value;
    }

    public String getName()
    {
        return this.name;
    }

    public void setName(String value)
    {
        this.name = value;
    }

     public String getJNDIName()
    {
        return this.JNDIName;
    }
```

continues

Listing 4.5 **Continued**

```java
public void setJNDIName(String value)
{
    this.JNDIName = value;
}

public int doStartTag() throws JspException
{

  if (tp == null && name == null && JNDIName == null)
      throw new JspException("The Topic cannot be located.");

  if (id == null)
       throw new JspException("The id attribute is mandatory.");
  try
  {
     // Locates a Topic
     if (tp == null)
     {
        if (JNDIName == null)
           topic = (Topic)pageContext.findAttribute(name);
        else
        {
           Context ctx = new InitialContext();
           topic = (Topic)context.lookup(JNDIName);
        }
     }
     else topic = tp;

     pageContext.setAttribute(id, topic);
  }
  catch(JMSException e)
  {
     throw new JSPException("JMS Exception: "+ e.getMessage());
  }
  return SKIP_BODY;
}

public void doFinally()
{
    tc.close();
}

public void release()
{
    topic = null;
    tp = null;
    name = null;
```

```
            JNDIName = null;
    }



}
```

Note that the `Topic` tag does not include any body action. The reason for that will be apparent in the example JSP using this tag library. The next tag handler, presented in Listing 4.6, implements the `topicSession` object.

Listing 4.6   **The *TopicSessionTag* Tag Handler**

```
package jspbook.example.tags;

import javax.jms.*;
import com.objectcube.objectevents.naming.*;
import javax.servlet.jsp.*;
import javax.servlet.jsp.tagext.*;

public class TopicSessionTag extends TagSupport implements TryCatchFinally
{
    private TopicSession session = null;

    protected String name = null;

    public String getName()
    {
        return this.name;
    }

    public void setName(String value)
    {
        this.name = value;
    }


    public int doStartTag() throws JspException
    {

      if (name == null)
          throw new JspException("Impossible establish a session.");

      if (id == null)
          throw new JspException("The id attribute is mandatory.");
      try
      {
          // Retrieves a TopicConnection from the page scope
          // and creates a session from it
          TopicConnection tc = (TopicConnection)pageContext.getAttribute(name);
```

continues

Listing 4.6 **Continued**

```
        session = tc.createTopicSession(false,AUTO_ACKNOWLEDGE);
        pageContext.setAttribute(id, session);
        return EVAL_BODY_INCLUDE;

    }
    catch(JMSException e)
    {
        throw new JSPException("JMS Exception: "+ e.getMessage());
    }
    return SKIP_BODY;
}

public void doFinally()
{
    session.close();
}

public void release()
{
    session = null;
    name = null;
}


}
```

The topicSubscriber tag, presented in Listing 4.7, is the real reason for all this trouble. It defines the element that actually accesses a topic, the repository for the messages that this class is registering to receive messages from.

Listing 4.7 **The *TopicSubscriberTag* Tag Handler**

```
package jspbook.example.tags;

import javax.jms.*;
import com.objectcube.objectevents.naming.*;
import javax.servlet.jsp.*;
import javax.servlet.jsp.tagext.*;

public class TopicSubscriberTag extends TagSupport implements TryCatchFinally
{
    private TopicSubscriber subs = null;

    protected String name = null;
    protected String topic = null;

    public String getName()
    {
```

```
        return this.name;
}

public void setName(String value)
{
    this.name = value;
}

public String getTopic()
{
    return this.topic;
}

public void setTopic(String value)
{
    this.topic = value;
}


public int doStartTag() throws JspException
{

  if (name == null || topic == null)
      throw new JspException("Impossible to access the server.");

  if (id == null)
      throw new JspException("The id attribute is mandatory.");
  try
  {
     // Retrieves a TopicSession and a Topic from the page scope
     // and creates a subscriber from them
     TopicSession ts = (TopicSession)pageContext.getAttribute(name);
     Topic tp = (Topic)pageContext.getAttribute(topic);
     subs = ts.createSubscriber(tp);
     pageContext.setAttribute(id, subs);
     return EVAL_BODY_INCLUDE;

  }
  catch(JMSException e)
  {
     throw new JSPException("JMS Exception: "+ e.getMessage());
  }
  return SKIP_BODY;
}

public void doFinally()
{
    subs.close();
}

public void release()
```

continues

Listing 4.7   **Continued**

```
    {
        subs = null;
        name = null;
        topic = null;
    }


}
```

The GetMapMessageTag, presented in Listing 4.8, gets a MapMessage from the server with all the candidate's data.

Listing 4.8   **The *GetMapMessageTag* Tag Handler**

```
package jspbook.example.tags;

import javax.jms.*;
import com.objectcube.objectevents.naming.*;
import javax.servlet.jsp.*;
import javax.servlet.jsp.tagext.*;

public class GetMapMessageTag extends TagSupport implements TryCatchFinally
{
    private MapMessage mmessage = null;

    protected String name = null;

    public String getName()
    {
        return this.name;
    }

    public void setName(String value)
    {
        this.name = value;
    }

    public int doStartTag() throws JspException
    {

      if (name == null)
         throw new JspException("Impossible to access the server.");

      if (id == null)
          throw new JspException("The id attribute is mandatory.");
      try
      {
         // Retrieves a TopicSession and a Topic from the page scope
         // and creates a subscriber from them
```

```
            TopicSubscriber ts = (TopicSubscriber)pageContext.getAttribute(name);
            mmessage = ts.receiveNoWait();
            pageContext.setAttribute(id, mmessage);
            return EVAL_BODY_INCLUDE;

        }
        catch(JMSException e)
        {
            throw new JSPException("JMS Exception: "+ e.getMessage());
        }
        return SKIP_BODY;
    }

    public void release()
    {
        name = null;
    }

}
```

The `GetMapMessageTag` tag handler puts on the page scope a map with a certain candidate's data. At this point, a tag is needed to scan the resulting `Hashtable` and write the values inside the message. The `WriteOutTag` tag handler, in Listing 4.9, does that.

Listing 4.9   **Writing the Information**

```
package jspbook.example.tags;

import java.util.*;
import javax.servlet.jsp.*;
import javax.servlet.jsp.tagext.*;

public class WriteOutTag extends TagSupport
{

    protected String name = null;
    protected String key = null;

    public String getName()
    {
        return this.name;
    }

    public void setName(String value)
    {
        this.name = value;
    }

    public String getKey()
    {
```

continues

Listing 4.9 **Continued**

```
        return this.key;
    }

    public void setKey(String value)
    {
        this.key = value;
    }

    public int doEndTag() throws JspException
    {

      if (name == null || key == null)
          throw new JspException("Impossible to access the server.");

      try
      {
         Hashtable hash = pageContext.getAttribute(name);
         pageContext.getOut().println(hash.get(key).toString());

      }
      catch(NullPointerException e)
      {
          throw new JSPException("n/a");
      }
      return EVAL_PAGE;
    }

    public void release()
    {
        name = null;
        key = null;
    }


}
```

So, how will these tags be used together? The mechanism of collaboration is quite
evident: Each tag leaves some object needed by the tags in the body on the page scope
and then reclaims that object on its closure. Listing 4.10 presents a JSP that uses the
JMS Topic tags to show the state of the election.

Listing 4.10 **Using the Messaging Tags**

```
<%@ taglib uri="/WEB-INF/example.tld" prefix="example" %>
<example:topic id="candA" JNDIName="Party=p1 Cand=A"/>
<example:topic id="candB" JNDIName="Party=p2 Cand=B"/>
<example:topic id="candC" JNDIName="Party=p3 Cand=C"/>
<html>
<body>
<table width="100%">
```

```
<tr>
  <th>Candidate</th>
  <th>region A abs</th>
  <th>region A rel</th>
  <th>region B abs</th>
  <th>region B rel</th>
  <th>region C abs</th>
  <th>region C rel</th>
  <th>total abs</th>
  <th>total rel</th>
</tr>
 <example:connection id="con1" JNDIName="TCFactory">
   <example:session id="session1" name="con1">
     <example:subscriber id="subsCandA" name="session1" topic="candA">
       <example:getMapMessage id="msg1" name="subsCandA">
         <tr>
           <td><example:writeOut msg="msg1" name="subs1" key="cand.name"/></td>
           <td><example:writeOut msg="msg1" name="subs1" key="abs.a"/></td>
           <td><example:writeOut msg="msg1" name="subs1" key="rel.a"/></td>
           <td><example:writeOut msg="msg1" name="subs1" key="abs.b"/></td>
           <td><example:writeOut msg="msg1" name="subs1" key="rel.b"/></td>
           <td><example:writeOut msg="msg1" name="subs1" key="abs.c"/></td>
           <td><example:writeOut msg="msg1" name="subs1" key="rel.c"/></td>
           <td><example:writeOut msg="msg1" name="subs1" key="total.abs"/></td>
           <td><example:writeOut msg="msg1" name="subs1" key="total.rel"/></td>
         </tr>
       </example:getMapMessage>
     </example:subscriber>
     <example:subscriber id="subsCandB" name="session1" topic="candB">
       <example:getMapMessage id="msg2" name="subsCandB">
         <tr>
           <td><example:writeOut msg="msg2" name="subs1" key="cand.name"/></td>
           <td><example:writeOut msg="msg2" name="subs1" key="abs.a"/></td>
           <td><example:writeOut msg="msg2" name="subs1" key="rel.a"/></td>
           <td><example:writeOut msg="msg2" name="subs1" key="abs.b"/></td>
           <td><example:writeOut msg="msg2" name="subs1" key="rel.b"/></td>
           <td><example:writeOut msg="msg2" name="subs1" key="abs.c"/></td>
           <td><example:writeOut msg="msg2" name="subs1" key="rel.c"/></td>
           <td><example:writeOut msg="msg2" name="subs1" key="total.abs"/></td>
           <td><example:writeOut msg="msg2" name="subs1" key="total.rel"/></td>
         </tr>
       </example:getMapMessage>
     </example:subscriber>
     <example:subscriber id="subsCandC" name="session1" topic="candC">
       <example:getMapMessage id="msg3" name="subsCandC">
         <tr>
           <td><example:writeOut msg="msg3" name="subs1" key="cand.name"/></td>
           <td><example:writeOut msg="msg3" name="subs1" key="abs.a"/></td>
           <td><example:writeOut msg="msg3" name="subs1" key="rel.a"/></td>
           <td><example:writeOut msg="msg3" name="subs1" key="abs.b"/></td>
           <td><example:writeOut msg="msg3" name="subs1" key="rel.b"/></td>
```

continues

Listing 4.10 **Continued**

```
            <td><example:writeOut msg="msg3" name="subs1" key="abs.c"/></td>
            <td><example:writeOut msg="msg3" name="subs1" key="rel.c"/></td>
            <td><example:writeOut msg="msg3" name="subs1" key="total.abs"/></td>
            <td><example:writeOut msg="msg3" name="subs1" key="total.rel"/></td>
          </tr>
        </example:getMapMessage>
      </example:subscriber>
    </example:session>
  </example:connection>
</table>
</body>
</html>
```

So, in Listing 4.10, the initial part creates three Topic objects from public Topic names on a JNDI server. Then a single connection and a single session are established with the messaging server. A subscriber scans the registered Topics, one at a time, grasping the most current message available and printing the results.

Defining Scripting Variables

Sometimes a portion of code is so particular to a situation that it really is not worth the effort to write and publish a tag for that. The obvious way is to write a small scriptlet that will do the job. The problem can be sharing values between tags and those small scriptlets.

To circumvent that, the Tag Library Extension API offers a mechanism for accessing and declaring scripting variables from and to a tag handler use.

A tag can declare a variable by specifying the variable characteristics in the TLD <variable> element seen in Chapter 2, "Introduction to Tag Libraries," or by using the TEI class to be introduced later in this chapter. Also, a variable in a tag is declared in a predefined scope: It can be limited for use inside the tag's body, it can be declared in the opening of the tag and can be used from that point on, or it can be declared at the closure of the tag and left for use by the remainder of the page.

A variable can be declared with the scope NESTED. When it is declared NESTED, the variable's definition is valid only inside a tag's body. So, scriptlet expressions inside the body are capable of referring to the variable. Both NESTED and AT_BEGIN variables must be instantiated by the doStartTag method. Listing 4.11 presents a variant of the GetMapMessageTag tag handler using a NESTED scope Hashtable variable with a constant name. Refer to Chapter 2 for more examples of TLD configuration for NESTED, AT-BEGIN, and AT-END variables.

Listing 4.11 **The *GetMapMessageTag* Tag Handler Using a *NESTED* Variable**

```
package jspbook.example.tags;

import javax.jms.*;
```

```
import com.objectcube.objectevents.naming.*;
import javax.servlet.jsp.*;
import javax.servlet.jsp.tagext.*;

public class GetMapMessageTag extends TagSupport implements TryCatchFinally
{
    private MapMessage mmessage = null;

    protected String name = null;

    public String getName()
    {
        return this.name;
    }

    public void setName(String value)
    {
        this.name = value;
    }

    public int doStartTag() throws JspException
    {

      if (name == null)
          throw new JspException("Impossible to access the server.");

      try
      {
        TopicSubscriber ts = (TopicSubscriber)pageContext.getAttribute(name);
        mmessage = ts.receiveNoWait();
        pageContext.setAttribute("varNested", mmessage);
        return EVAL_BODY_INCLUDE;

      }
      catch(JMSException e)
      {
          throw new JSPException("JMS Exception: "+ e.getMessage());
      }
      return SKIP_BODY;
    }

    public void release()
    {
        name = null;
    }

}
```

Listing 4.12 shows a fragment of the JSP used in the messaging example with this new configuration.

Listing 4.12   **Using a *NESTED* Variable**

```
The variable is still undefined here.

<example:getMapMessage name="subsCandC">
  <tr>
    <td><%= varNested.get("cand.name").toString()%></td>
    <td><%= varNested.get("abs.a").toString()%></td>
    <td><%= varNested.get("rel.a").toString()%></td>
    ...
  </tr>
</example:getMapMessage>

The variable does not exist here anymore.
```

The difference between the NESTED and AT_BEGIN variables is that the last ones remain valid after the tag has ended. This can be useful in a situation in which an inexhaustible resource, such as a data structure, needs to be generated by a set of tags and used by another set and scriptlets on another portion of the page, making nesting either impossible or the cause of a bad design.

In Listing 4.12, when using an AT_BEGIN variable, the variable still is used inside the getMessage body but also is available after the tag has been closed.

AT_END variables, on the other hand, are used after a tag is closed. This mostly is useful when a certain object is the result of a tag's action and will be used elsewhere in the page by tags and scriptlets. In Listing 4.12, when using an AT_END variable, it will not be defined inside the getMessage's body anymore but will be available after the tag has been closed.

Accessing the Runtime Stack

The other mechanism for cooperation among tags involves using the runtime stack to define the necessary objects in a tag and then accessing those objects using either the getParent or the TagSupport.findAncestorWithClass methods. The first is nice and plain—the necessary objects directly enclose the current tag. The second is useful when a reference object is defined in a tag that encloses a number of tags that will use it in different arrangements. It still uses the getParent method to find the ancestor requested, but it saves you the trouble of using recursion on the getParent to find the target tag.

This approach has the advantage of being more direct and uses less storage for the intermediate objects, but it introduces strong coupling between the tags.

Coupling and the Runtime Stack

Coupling gives you a measure of how dependent a certain piece of code is on another piece. For instance, a poorly designed object might expose an attribute type, and another poorly designed object might use this information to set or get values from that object. This creates a dependency between the two objects that is not always clearly visible to the application designer, and it leads to a number of problems when trying to use the dependent object outside the context of the first.

Two objects are said to have strong coupling when one of them is highly dependent on implementation details of the other. Of course, any change in that implementation will cause the dependent object to fail. This is why strong coupling is always undesirable and why coupling must be maintained minimally. The best situation is to have objects highly cohesive when one complements the functionality of the other and thus loosely coupled, with minimal dependency between them.

In tag libraries, using the runtime stack generated by enclosing and accessing information on the tag with the getParent method is something that must be carefully planned because it can lead to situations of strong coupling and can cause problems for the page designer trying to use the tag library.

Listings 4.13 and 4.14 present the `topicConnection` and `TopicSession` tag handlers, reshaped to use the `getParent` method directly instead of putting an object in some attribute at page scope.

Listing 4.13   **The** *TopicConnectionStackTag* **Tag Handler**

```
package jspbook.example.tags;

import javax.jms.*;
import com.objectcube.objectevents.naming.*;
import javax.servlet.jsp.*;
import javax.servlet.jsp.tagext.*;

public class TopicConnectionStackTag extends TagSupport implements TryCatchFinally
{
    private TopicConnection tc = null;

    protected TopicConnectionFactory tcf = null;
    protected String name = null;
    protected String JNDIName = null;

    public String getTcf()
    {
        return this.tcf;
    }

    public void setTcf(TopicConnectionFactory value)
    {
        this.tcf = value;
    }
```

continues

Listing 4.13   **Continued**

```
public String getName()
{
    return this.name;
}

public void setName(String value)
{
    this.name = value;
}

public String getJNDIName()
{
    return this.JNDIName;
}

public void setJNDIName(String value)
{
    this.JNDIName = value;
}

public String getTc()
{
    return this.tc;
}

public int doStartTag() throws JspException
{

  TopicConnectionFactory intTcf = null;

  if (tcf == null && name == null && JNDIName == null)
      throw new JspException("The TopicConnectionFactory cannot be located.");

  if (id == null)
      throw new JspException("The id attribute is mandatory.");
  try
  {
      // Locates a TopicConnectionFactory to create a TopicConnection
      if (tcf == null)
      {
          if (JNDIName == null)
              intTcf = (TopicConnectionFactory)pageContext.findAttribute(name);
          else
          {
              Context ctx = new InitialContext();
              intTcf = (TopicConnectionFactory)context.lookup(JNDIName);
          }
      }
      else intTcf = tcf;
```

```
            tc = intTcf.createTopicConnection();
            return EVAL_BODY_INCLUDE;

        }
        catch(JMSException e)
        {
            throw new JSPException("JMS Exception: "+ e.getMessage());
        }
        return SKIP_BODY;
    }

    public void doFinally()
    {
        tc.close();
    }

    public void release()
    {
        tc = null;
        tcf = null;
        name = null;
        JNDIName = null;
    }


}
```

Note that the connection object is no longer put in the page context. This tag implements the concept in this way:

1. A `topicConnection` tag establishes the connection.

2. Consumer tags are placed in the `topicConnection`'s body and can use that connection by accessing the tag and using `getTc` directly.

3. The `doFinally` method finalizes the connection upon tag closure.

The next tag handler, presented in Listing 4.14, implements the `topicSession` object accessing the parent tag instead of the `pageContext` object.

Listing 4.14   **The *TopicSessionStackTag* Tag Handler**

```
package jspbook.example.tags;

import javax.jms.*;
import com.objectcube.objectevents.naming.*;
import javax.servlet.jsp.*;
import javax.servlet.jsp.tagext.*;

public class TopicSessionStackTag extends TagSupport implements TryCatchFinally
{
```

continues

Listing 4.14 **Continued**

```java
    private TopicSession session = null;

    public String getSession()
    {
        return this.session;
    }

    public int doStartTag() throws JspException
    {

      try
      {
          // Retrieves a TopicConnection from the parent tag
          // and creates a session from it
          TopicConnectionStackTag tcst = (TopicConnectionStackTag)this.getParent();
          if (tcst == null)
             throw new JspException("No connection tag found.");
          TopicConnection tc = tcst.getTc();
          session = tc.createTopicSession(false,AUTO_ACKNOWLEDGE);
          pageContext.setAttribute(id, session);
          return EVAL_BODY_INCLUDE;

      }
      catch(JMSException e)
      {
          throw new JSPException("JMS Exception: "+ e.getMessage());
      }
      return SKIP_BODY;
    }

    public void doFinally()
    {
        session.close();
    }

    public void release()
    {
        session = null;
        name = null;
    }


  }
```

So, `TopicSessionStackTag` casts the result of the `getParent` to `TopicConnection`
`StackTag` and uses the `getTc` method in that tag to access the necessary `Topic`
`Connection`. It also publishes its session object to make it accessible in the same
manner by the other tags.

Listing 4.15 presents the electoral summary JSP using the JSM tags redesigned to
use the `getParent` method to access the other tag's methods.

Listing 4.15   **Using the Alternative Messaging Tags**

```
<%@ taglib uri="/WEB-INF/example.tld" prefix="example" %>
<example:topic id="candA" JNDIName="Party=p1 Cand=A"/>
<example:topic id="candB" JNDIName="Party=p2 Cand=B"/>
<example:topic id="candC" JNDIName="Party=p3 Cand=C"/>
<html>
<body>
<table width="100%">
<tr>
  <th>Candidate</th>
  <th>region A abs</th>
  <th>region A rel</th>
  <th>region B abs</th>
  <th>region B rel</th>
  <th>region C abs</th>
  <th>region C rel</th>
  <th>total abs</th>
  <th>total rel</th>
</tr>
 <example:connection JNDIName="TCFactory">
   <example:session>
     <example:subscriber topic="candA">
       <example:getMapMessage>
         <tr>
           <td><example:writeOut key="cand.name"/></td>
           <td><example:writeOut key="abs.a"/></td>
           <td><example:writeOut key="rel.a"/></td>
           <td><example:writeOut key="abs.b"/></td>
           <td><example:writeOut key="rel.b"/></td>
           <td><example:writeOut key="abs.c"/></td>
           <td><example:writeOut key="rel.c"/></td>
           <td><example:writeOut key="total.abs"/></td>
           <td><example:writeOut key="total.rel"/></td>
         </tr>
       </example:getMapMessage>
     </example:subscriber>
     <example:subscriber topic="candB">
       <example:getMapMessage>
         <tr>
           <td><example:writeOut key="cand.name"/></td>
           <td><example:writeOut key="abs.a"/></td>
           <td><example:writeOut key="rel.a"/></td>
           <td><example:writeOut key="abs.b"/></td>
           <td><example:writeOut key="rel.b"/></td>
           <td><example:writeOut key="abs.c"/></td>
           <td><example:writeOut key="rel.c"/></td>
           <td><example:writeOut key="total.abs"/></td>
           <td><example:writeOut key="total.rel"/></td>

         </tr>
```

continues

Listing 4.15   **Continued**

```
      </example:getMapMessage>
    </example:subscriber>
    <example:subscriber id="subsCandC" name="session1" topic="candC">
      <example:getMapMessage id="msg3" name="subsCandC">
        <tr>
          <td><example:writeOut key="cand.name"/></td>
          <td><example:writeOut key="abs.a"/></td>
          <td><example:writeOut key="rel.a"/></td>
          <td><example:writeOut key="abs.b"/></td>
          <td><example:writeOut key="rel.b"/></td>
          <td><example:writeOut key="abs.c"/></td>
          <td><example:writeOut key="rel.c"/></td>
          <td><example:writeOut key="total.abs"/></td>
          <td><example:writeOut key="total.rel"/></td>
        </tr>
      </example:getMapMessage>
    </example:subscriber>
  </example:session>
 </example:connection>
</table>
</body>
</html>
```

The notable element is that the tags look simpler to use than the previous ones. The problem with this approach is that these tags must be used with each other. For instance, it would be quite difficult to replace the `topicConnection` tag with another equivalent tag, taken from another tag library, because the session tag now requires the presence of a very specific parent tag.

Using Key-Values

A reverse situation occurs in tag cooperation when the enclosed tags generate objects to be used by the enclosing tag. In that case, the first model seen is reversed. The body tags define objects in the `pageContext` to be used by the enclosing tag. The second model still applies, and the body tags call setter methods on the parent tag instead of getter methods.

A third model, associated with the `getParent` method, can be used. It is especially useful if the tags generate lots of information to the parent, making it useless to post those objects in the page scope (or any other). This model uses the `Hashtable` property declared in the `TagSupport` class, which can be accessed via the `setValue`, `getValue`, and `getValues` methods in that class.

Suppose that a message-collector tag handler is implementing JMS durable subscriber access. This access instructs the messaging provider to retain all messages for the durable subscriber while it is inactive and then allows it to access all of them when it is connected. Listing 4.16 shows the `TopicDurableSubscriberTag` tag handler implementing this mechanism of cooperation. For simplification purposes, the message is of type `TextMessage`, and content is simple text.

Listing 4.16   **The** *TopicDurableSubscriberTag* **Tag Handler**

```
package jspbook.example.tags;

import javax.jms.*;
import com.objectcube.objectevents.naming.*;
import javax.servlet.jsp.*;
import javax.servlet.jsp.tagext.*;

public class TopicDurableSubscriberTag extends TagSupport implements
TryCatchFinally
{
    private TopicSubscriber subs = null;

    protected String name = null;
    protected String topic = null;

    public String getName()
    {
        return this.name;
    }

    public void setName(String value)
    {
        this.name = value;
    }

    public String getTopic()
    {
        return this.topic;
    }

    public void setTopic(String value)
    {
        this.topic = value;
    }


    public int doStartTag() throws JspException
    {

      if (name == null || topic == null)
          throw new JspException("Impossible to access the server.");

      if (id == null)
          throw new JspException("The id attribute is mandatory.");
      try
      {
         // Retrieves a TopicSession and a Topic from the page scope
         // and creates a subscriber from them
         TopicSession ts = (TopicSession)pageContext.getAttribute(name);
```

continues

Listing 4.16   **Continued**

```
            Topic tp = (Topic)pageContext.getAttribute(topic);
            subs =
ts.createDurableSubscriber(tp,tp.getTopicName()+System.currentTimeMillis);
            TextMessage mmessage = null;
            while((mmessage = subs.receiveNoWait()) != null)
                this.setValue(mmessage.getJMSMessageId(),mmessage);
            if (!values.empty()) return EVAL_BODY_INCLUDE;

        }
        catch(JMSException e)
        {
            throw new JSPException("JMS Exception: "+ e.getMessage());
        }
        return SKIP_BODY;
    }

    public void doFinally()
    {
        subs.close();
    }

    public void release()
    {
        subs = null;
        name = null;
        topic = null;
    }


}
```

The `TopicDurableSubscriberTag` tag handler described in Listing 4.16 retrieves all the messages available in that topic and puts them in the values `Hashtable`. What a "write out" tag does then is get to the `TopicDurableSubscriberTag` tag handler and call the `getValues` method to scan all the messages available and write them out. This is illustrated in Listing 4.17.

Listing 4.17   **The *WriteDurableOutTag* Tag Handler**

```
package jspbook.example.tags;

import java.util.*;
import javax.servlet.jsp.*;
import javax.servlet.jsp.tagext.*;

public class WriteDurableOutTag extends
{
    private Enumeration msgs = null;

    public int doStartTag() throws JspException
```

```
    {
      try
      {
          TopicDurableSubscriber subs = (TopicDurableSubscriberTag)
this.getParent();
          msgs = subs.getValues();
          if(msgs.hasMoreValues())
          {
            TextMessage aMessage = (TextMessage)msgs.nextElement();
            pageContext.getOut().println(aMessage.getText());
            return EVAL_BODY_INCLUDE;
          }
      }
      catch(Exception e)
      {
          throw new JSPException("JMS Exception: "+ e.getMessage());
      }
      return SKIP_BODY;
    }

    public int doAfterBody() throws JspException
    {

      try
      {
          if (msgs.hasMoreValues())
          {
            TextMessage aMessage = (TextMessage)msgs.nextElement();
            pageContext.getOut().println(aMessage.getText());
            return EVAL_BODY_AGAIN;
          }
      }
      catch(Exception e)
      {
          throw new JSPException("JMS Exception: "+ e.getMessage());
      }
      return SKIP_BODY;
    }

    public void release()
    {
        msgs = null;
    }

}
```

WriteDurableOutTag implements the IterationTag interface through the TagSupport class, which implements IterationTag, to write all the messages retrieved by the parent TopicDurableSubscriberTag tag handler.

In the examples seen so far, the goal of the tags in the body of the enclosing tags is to provide some action that somehow complements the action of the enclosing tags. Sessions complement connections, and subscribers complement sessions to get messages from a JMS `Topic`.

Treatment on the body is also distinct in `BodyTag` implementations. There, the tags in the body provide data that the enclosing tag uses to perform its action. This can be raw-data post in the body that afterward is captured in the `bodyContent` object and processed.

The focus of the cooperating tags changes in the next example, so the goal will be to modularly construct some complex, modular data structure to be used by the enclosing tag. That data structure may present multiple configurations, or it can be processed incomplete, possibly with diverse interpretations for the completed modules. It can also be the case that the data structure is too large to be created with a single set of attributes, which could make tag use too complicated. Listing 4.18 presents `CreateMessageTag` and the two type-based `CreateMessageBody` tags, which are the heart of the publisher part of the electoral example. This is done because the `Message` object in JMS is a modular data structure that is composed of an invariant header part and a variable body part that determines the type of message sent.

Listing 4.18   **The *CreateMessageTag* Tag Handler**

```
package jspbook.example.tags;

import javax.jms.*;
import com.objectcube.objectevents.naming.*;
import javax.servlet.jsp.*;
import javax.servlet.jsp.tagext.*;

public class CreateMessageTag extends TagSupport
{
    private TopicPublisher pub = null;
    private TopicSession session = null;

    protected String topic = null;
    protected String correlationId = null;

    public String getTopic()
    {
        return this.topic;
    }

    public void setTopic(String value)
    {
        this.topic = value;
    }

    public String getCorrelationId()
```

```
{
    return this.correlationId;
}

public void setCorrelationId (String value)
{
    this.correlationId = value;
}


public int doStartTag() throws JspException
{

  try
  {
     TopicPublisherTag tp = (TopicPublisherTag) getparent();
     pub = tp.getPublisher();
     session = tp.getSession();

     if (pub != null && session != null)
        return EVAL_BODY_INCLUDE;

  }
  catch(JMSException e)
  {
     throw new JSPException("JMS Exception: "+ e.getMessage());
  }
  return SKIP_BODY;
}

public int doEndTag() throws JspException
{

  try
  {
     if (getValue("MSG_TYPE").equals("TEXT"))
     {
        TextMessage msg = session.createTextMessage();
        if(correlationId != null)
          msg.setCorrelationId(correlationId);
        msg.setText(getValue("MSG_CONTENT"));
        pub.publish(topic,msg);
        return EVAL_PAGE;
     }
     if (getValue("MSG_TYPE").equals("MAP"))
     {
        MapMessage msg = session.createMapMessage();
        if(correlationId != null)
          msg.setCorrelationId(correlationId);
        Hashtable msgVals = (Hashtable)getValue("MSG_CONTENT");
        Enumeration enum = msgVals.keys();
```

continues

Listing 4.18   **Continued**

```
                while(enum.hasMoreValues)
                {
                    String key = enum.nextElement().toString();
                    Object val = msgVals.get(key);
                    msg.setObject(key,val);
                }
                pub.publish(topic,msg);
                return EVAL_PAGE;
            }
        }
        catch(JMSException e)
        {
            throw new JSPException("JMS Exception: "+ e.getMessage());
        }
        return SKIP_PAGE;
    }

    public void release()
    {
        pub = null;
        topic = null;
        correlationId = null;
    }
}
```

The doStartTag method in the CreateMessageTag tag handler checks the existence of TopicPublisher and TopicSession to create and send messages. If those objects are not present, the body is ignored and nothing happens. Listing 4.19 presents the CreateTextMessageTag. It won't create the Message object, but it will capture the text and define the values on the CreateMessage to be used by that tag to create and publish a message.

Listing 4.19   **The *CreateTextMessageTag* Tag Handler**

```
package jspbook.example.tags;

import javax.servlet.jsp.*;
import javax.servlet.jsp.tagext.*;

public class CreateTextMessageTag extends BodyTagSupport
{

    public int doEndTag() throws JspException
    {

      try
      {
          String msgText = bodyContent.getString();
          CreateMessageTag cmt = (CreateMessageTag) getParent();
```

```
        cmt.setValue("MSG_TYPE","TEXT");
        cmt.setValue("MSG_CONTENT",msgText);
        return EVAL_PAGE;

      }
      catch(JMSException e)
      {
        throw new JSPException("JMS Exception: "+ e.getMessage());
      }
      return SKIP_PAGE;
    }
  }
```

The CreateMapMessageTag tag handler differs from the CreateTextMessageTag tag handler in the way values are passed and in the deep data structure that will be passed upward to CreateMessageTag (see Listing 4.20). CreateTextMessageTag uses a String as a data structure because TextMessages content is made up of a block of text. MapMessages, on the other hand, use a set of name-value pairs as content. Different from ordinary Java Hashtables, the name-value pairs in MapMessages accept only Strings as names and accept only primitive data type values, such as int or char, as values.

Listing 4.20   **The *CreateMapMessageTag* Tag Handler**

```
package jspbook.example.tags;

import java.util.*;
import javax.servlet.jsp.*;
import javax.servlet.jsp.tagext.*;

public class CreateMapMessageTag extends TagSupport
{
    private Hashtable msgMap = new Hashtable();

    public void setMsgVal(String name, Object value)
    {
        this.msgMap.put(name,value);
    }

    public int doEndTag() throws JspException
    {

      try
      {
        CreateMessageTag cmt = (CreateMessageTag) getParent();
        if (!msgMap.isEmpty())
        {
           cmt.setValue("MSG_TYPE","MAP");
           cmt.setValue("MSG_CONTENT",msgMap);
```

continues

Listing 4.20 **Continued**

```
            return EVAL_PAGE;
        }
    }
    catch(JMSException e)
    {
        throw new JSPException("JMS Exception: "+ e.getMessage());
    }
    return SKIP_PAGE;
    }
}
```

To add the values that the CreateMapMessageTag tag handler uses to instantiate the MSG_CONTENT value on the CreateMessageTag tag handler, the AddValueTag tag handler comes in handy (see Listing 4.21). It takes an attribute and adds the attribute's value to the CreateMapMessageTag's Hashtable.

Listing 4.21 **The *AddValueTag* Tag Handler**

```
package jspbook.example.tags;

import javax.servlet.jsp.*;
import javax.servlet.jsp.tagext.*;

public class AddValueTag extends TagSupport
{
    protected String name = null;
    protected Object objValue = null;

    public String getName()
    {
        return this.name;
    }

    public void setName(String value)
    {
        this.name = value;
    }

    public Object getObjValue()
    {
        return this.objValue;
    }

    public void setObjValue(Object value)
    {
        this.objValue = value;
    }

    public int doEndTag() throws JspException
```

```
    {
      try
      {
        CreateMapMessageTag cmmt = (CreateMapMessageTag) getParent();
        if (name != null && objValue != null)
        {
          cmmt.setMsgVal(name,objValue);
        }
      }
      catch(Exception e)
      {
        throw new JSPException("JMS Exception: "+ e.getMessage());
      }
      return EVAL_PAGE;
    }
  }
```

So, for each key-value pair to be inserted in a `MapMessage`, there will be an `addValue` tag. The `addValue` tags will be enclosed by a `createMapMsg` tag, and that one will be enclosed by a `createMsg` tag. The JSP page fragment in Listing 4.22 shows the creation and posting of each of the two types of messages. The `createTextMessage` tag gets the text value directly from the body content, and the `createMapMessage` tag depends on `addValue` to populate its name-value pairs set.

Listing 4.22   **Adding Text and Name-Value Pairs Content to the**
createXXXMessage **Tags**

```
...

<example:createMsg>
  <example:createTxtMsg>
    This is the text to be sent by this message tag!
  </example:createTxtMsg>
</example:createMsg>

<example:createMsg>
  <example:createMapMsg>
    <addValue name="ex1" value="<%=new Integer(10)%>"/>
    <addValue name="ex2" value="<%=new Long(1231213312L)%>"/>
  </example:createMapMsg>
</example:createMsg>
...
```

Validation

Validation can be considered at two levels in the Tag Library Extension API: validation of a tag structure and validation of the use of a tag library on a page. To consubstantiate the validation mechanism, a number of translation-time classes are provided in the API. These represent the page data, the information available on the TLD, the variables defined or accessed by a tag, and so on. The core classes on the translation-time validation-oriented classes are the `TagExtraInfo` class and the `TagLibraryValidator` class.

Specifying Validation on the TLD

In Chapter 2, you saw that a number of elements in the TLD are connected to tag specification and other elements connected to validation of the specification provided. The first element to be specified, following the DTD order, is the `validator` element. It is an optional element composed of two subelements: `validator-class` and `init-params`.

The `validator-class` subelement specifies a fully qualified Java class name for an implementation of a `TagLibraryValidator` class that will be invoked when the page in which this tag library is used gets translated. To this class are passed a `PageData` object, an object with the XML representation of the page being translated, the TLD URI, the library prefix, and, through a call to `setInitParameters` method, a map with the values specified in the `init-parameter` subelements, if any.

The next element is the `TagExtraInfo` class specification. The `tei-class` element of each tag, if present, specifies the fully qualified Java class name for this class. The TEI will validate the tag structure and variables created or accessed by this tag.

Simple variables created or accessed by the tag can be specified by the variable subelement of each tag, if present. This element specifies the variable's name, type, and scope. More elaborated situations, such as conditional creation of variables, must be treated within a TEI class.

TEI Classes

A `TagExtraInfo` class is an abstract class that the tag library designer subclasses and has basically two main purposes: to declare scripting variables that the associated tag accesses or defines and to validate the tag usage. Within the Tag Library Extension API 1.2, the simpler cases of variable declaration can be done on the TLD only, making the use of TEI classes required only to validate the tag usage and necessary only when the declaration of such variables is really complex and subject to specific conditions.

A TEI class has two core methods: `isValid`, which states whether the tag usage is valid, and `getVariableInfo`, which returns a `VariableInfo` array with each variable's specification. The JSP container uses two additional methods to set up the `TagInfo` object for this TEI class: `setTagInfo` and `getTagInfo`. The `TagExtraInfo` is supposed to extend this object, providing additional information.

The `getVariableInfo` method takes a `TagData` object as an argument, representing the information that the JSP container has about this tag. It returns an array of `VariableInfo` objects, used to declare a variable back to the JSP container. The basic idea behind the `getVariableInfo` method is to use the TagData information to set up a `VariableInfo` instance for each variable set by this tag and then return the instances set in an array.

The `TagData` object provides access to the information that the JSP container has about the tag. It allows the `TagExtraInfo` object to access information about the attributes found in the tag, either individually or in an enumeration. It also gets and sets the values of attributes, and it offers a specific method to get the value of the id attribute.

Listing 4.23 presents a simple TEI class that declares a variable defined by the `TopicConnectionTag` tag handler. It extends the abstract `TagExtraInfo` class. It implements the `getVariableInfo` method and uses the `TagData` data argument to access the value of the id attribute and then create an instance of a `VariableInfo` class; it also declares these values in it. Then it inserts that instance in an array and returns it.

Listing 4.23   **The Simplest TEI Class**

```
public class TopicConnectionTEI extends TagExtraInfo {

  public final VariableInfo[] getVariableInfo(TagData data)
  {
    return new VariableInfo[]
    {
      new VariableInfo(
                   data.getId(),
                   "javax.jms.TopicConnection",
                   true,
                   VariableInfo.AT_END
                   )
    };
  }
}
```

More elaborate cases of the `getVariableInfo` method refer to creating multiple variables and the conditional creation of variables. If a certain configuration of attributes is found, a variable gets created. This is a more complicated situation and must be carefully evaluated to determine whether this is the best solution or whether creating an additional tag would work better. Chapter 5, "Design Considerations," suggests that this is a case for creating an additional tag. Listing 4.24 provides an example of creating multiple variables, each one in a distinct scope.

Listing 4.24   **Creating Multiple Variables**

```
public class MultipleExampleTEI extends TagExtraInfo {

  public final VariableInfo[] getVariableInfo(TagData data)
  {
    return new VariableInfo[]
    {
```

continues

Listing 4.24 **Continued**

```
        new VariableInfo(
                        data.getId(),
                        "java.lang.String",
                        true,
                        VariableInfo.AT_END
                        ),

        new VariableInfo(
                        data.getAttributeString("date"),
                        "java.util.Date",
                        true,
                        VariableInfo.NESTED
                        ),
        new VariableInfo(
                        data.getAttributeString("hash"),
                        "java.util.Hashtable",
                        true,
                        VariableInfo.AT_BEGIN
                        )
    };
  }
}
```

The isValid method is important when a tag must validate specific conditions occurring with the attributes (see Listing 4.25). Chapters 2 and 3 said that it is impossible to
impose a constraint in the TLD file stating that two attributes or sets of attributes were
mutually exclusive. This kind of constraint must be reinforced within the TEI class'
isValid method.

Listing 4.25 **Validating the *TopicConnectionTag* Attributes**

```
public class TopicConnectionTEI extends TagExtraInfo {

  public boolean isValid (TagData data)
  {
    boolean hasName = false;
    boolean hasTcf = false;
    boolean hasJNDIName = false;

    if (data.getAttribute("name") != null)
      hasName = true;

    if (data.getAttribute("tcf") != null)
      hasTcf = true;

    if (data.getAttribute("JNDIName") != null)
      hasJNDIName = true;
```

```
    // These check the attribute presence conditions

    if (!hasTcf && !hasName && !hasJNDIName)
    {
      return false;
    }

    if (hasTcf && hasName && hasJNDIName)
    {
      return false;
    }

    if (hasTcf && hasName || hasTcf && hasJNDIName ||
        hasJNDIName && hasName)
    {
      return false;
    }

    return true;
  }
}
```

The name, tcf, and JNDIName attributes in the TopicConnectionTag tag handler must be mutually exclusive, but at least one of them must be provided. The last three if statements check the following:

- The first checks to see if none of the three attributes was provided.
- The second checks to see if all the attributes were simultaneously provided.
- The last looks to see if any pairs of two of these attributes were provided.

If any of these situations is the case, the corresponding if causes the method to return false; the tag is considered invalid by the JSP container, and a JSPException is raised. If none of these is the case, the tag is valid and can be evaluated; the method returns true.

TagLibraryValidator Classes

The second mechanism of validation is the TagLibraryValidator class. Contrary to the TEI class, this validator acts upon the XML representation of the page and the URI of the TLD declared in the taglib directive, and the tag library used prefix, the prefix declared in the taglib directive, to validate the tag information against an XML schema.

Summary

This chapter examined the basic mechanisms of collaboration among tags in a tag library. You have learned the following key points:

1. A tag is a first-class web application component that can be integrated with components of the Servlet API other than a JSP page. The chapter illustrated coordination between an application filter and a tag.

2. A tag can access any of the available scopes defined in the `PageContext` instance, so it has full access to the very same runtime environment of the host JSP. Objects stored in any scope and scripting variables are also accessible from a tag.

3. A tag can define objects on any scope and mostly can use `pageContext` to access the page scope to exchange objects used in the cooperation schema. This is the first schema for tag cooperation.

4. The second cooperation schema uses the `getParent` method or the `findAncestorWithClass` method to access information in any of the enclosing tags. In fact, this defines a sort of runtime stack of enclosing tags.

5. The `TagSupport` class defines an internal `values` property that can hold name-value pairs. These can be used to hold objects defined by enclosed tags, and they can be used as an auxiliary schema for tag cooperation.

6. Tags can cooperate to co-implement a complex action or to co-build a complex data structure. The example presented the JMS Message data structure and a number of tags used to build it modularly.

7. The validation process must be reinforced in the TLD and under certain circumstances via the `TagExtraInfo` and `TagLibraryValidator` classes.

8. The TLD offers a number of elements to define those classes and their initialization parameters and information.

9. The main methods in the `TagExtraInfo` class are `getVariableInfo` and `isValid`. The first is used to declare script variables that a tag accesses or defines, and the second is used to reinforce constraints in the tag attribute set.

Design Considerations

5

THIS CHAPTER PRESENTS A NUMBER OF RECOMMENDATIONS and practices for the tag library designer to understand when creating a tag library project. The software team manager who wants to grasp the development cycle of a tag library and possibly integrate that in his organization's software process can also find a good foundation here.

Making a Case for Tag Libraries

Having presented the structure of the Tag Library Extension API, it is important to understand how this technology fits into the portfolio of a web application designer or design team.

The first consideration is that tag libraries change the way the web application team is organized. It also changes the technical requirements for dynamic page developers. And it changes the way web applications are maintained and functionality is enriched.

From a technical perspective, tag libraries provide a better way to encapsulate and deploy custom or recurrent functionality inside web applications. This is very important because a dynamic page is much more complex than it seems to be at a first glance.

Developing Dynamic Pages

JSP is the key presentation technology for web applications under the J2EE perspective. Generating dynamic content requires the page designer to possess at least a fair knowledge of HTML, which is still the primary language for web content development, and JavaScript, the primary language for development of dynamic HTML and client-side programming. Of course, it demands a good amount of page composition layout skills and graphic design ability to create pages with the appeal required by the market.

The problem arises when the page accesses data sources to publish. Then it demands to use server-side resources. In addition, it must access JavaBeans with standard actions or use scriptlets, and both solutions depend heavily on the use of the Java programming language. If the data source is a database (which is the most common case), SQL will get into place to retrieve the data. You could easily end up with a single piece of software containing four or even five languages at the same time. Listing 5.1 shows a fairly complete page with the several sections pointed out.

Listing 5.1   **A Typical Dynamic Page**

```
<%-- This is the JSP directive section --%>
<%@ page import="java.sql.*"%>
<%@ page import="java.util.*"%>
<%@ page import="java.naming.*"%>
<%@ page session="true"%>

<%-- This is the JSP Java code --%>
<%

    // This is not only Java code, but JNDI code.
    Hashtable env = new Hashtable();
    Hashtable results = new Hashtable();
    env.put(Context.INITIAL_CONTEXT_FACTORY,
"com.sun.jndi.rmi.registry.RegistryContextFactory");
    env.put(Context.PROVIDER_URL, "rmi://localhost:1099");
    env.put("java.naming.rmi.security.manager", "1");
    Context ctx = new InitialContext(env);

    // And this is JDBC code
    DataSource ds = (DataSource) ctx.lookup("EXAMPLEDS");
    Connection con = null;

    try
    {
        con = ds.getConnection();
        Statement stm = con.createStatement();

        // Here comes SQL, the 3rd language so far
        Resultset rs = stm.executeQuery("Select ID, NAME, SURNAME, NATIONALITY from
AUTHOR");
```

```
%>
<%-- This is HTML template --%>
<html>
<header>

<%-- This is JavaScript code the 4th language so far --%>
<script language="JavaScript1.2">
function showArticles(auth)
{
    window.open("authArticles.jsp?AUTH="+auth,"Author Articles","");
}
</script>
</header>
<body>
<h1>This is a static template inside a dynamic program block</h1>
<table>
<tr>
    <td>ID</td>
    <td>NAME</td>
    <td>SURNAME</td>
    <td>NATIONALITY</td>
</tr>

<%-- Back to JDBC code --%>
<%
    while(rs.next())
    {
        String id = rs.getString(1);
        String name = rs.getString(2);
        String surname = rs.getString(3);
        String nationality = rs.getString(4);
%>
<%-- This is HTML again --%>
<tr>
    <td><a href="javascript:showArticles(<%=id%>);"><%=id%></a></td>
    <td><%=name%></td>
    <td><%=surname%></td>
    <td><%=nationality%></td>
</tr>
<%-- This is the JSP Java code --%>
<%
    }
    }
    catch (Exception e)
    {
        application.log("author report exception", e);
%>
<%-- Some nice error message --%>
    <tr><td colspan="4"><i>Error retrieving data</i></td></tr>
<%
    }
```

continues

Listing 5.1 **Continued**

```
finally
{
   if (con != null)
      try { con.close(); }
      catch (SQLException sqle2)
      {
          application.log("error on closure of connection",sql2);
      }
%>
<%-- Closing the HTML page --%>
</table>
</body>
</html>
<%
   }
%>
```

The page presented in Listing 5.1 is not the most complex of the JSP pages. Despite that fact, it requires either a fair knowledge of Java programming from the page designer and the usage of a number of Java APIs, or a fair knowledge of page composition from a Java programmer.

Still more complicated problems are occurring in that page. It was said in Chapter 2, "Introduction to Tag Libraries," that a recurrent problem in web application design is the separation of presentation from core business logic and control logic. In this page, the three are mixed again. Access to the core resources (the `Datasource` object stored in a JNDI context), business logic (the SQl accessing core database tables), and presentation logic (the HTML template and the JSP expressions to present the retrieved data) are all interleaved. Maintaining this page is very difficult both for a page designer who is not accustomed to Java programming (or even to JNDI or JDBC programming) and for a Java programmer who is not accustomed to JavaScript or HTML.

JavaBeans don't help much in this scenario because, despite the fact that JavaBeans can be accessed with standard actions, they still demand that the page designer understand properties, property types, and any function that is a bit trivial. For example, iterating through an indexed property requires the Java code.

So, when creating dynamic pages, there is an undefined role in the development team. Either the Java programmer creates ugly data-oriented pages with bad graphics and poor design, or the web designer creates poor Java scriptlets with less programming knowledge, making the page less maintainable. Figure 5.1 depicts this situation.

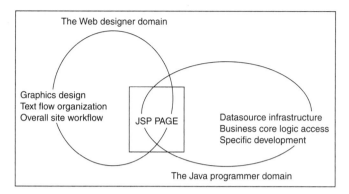

Figure 5.1   The roles of web designer and Java programmer
intersect in the creation of dynamic content.

Organizing a Page-Development Team

This scenario changes with the introduction of tag libraries to the web application
process. Tag libraries encapsulate complex functionality that provides the actions to
implement through tag handlers with an XML interface, and that makes it possible
to create dynamic content almost without the need for Java coding. The tag representation in a JSP page is quite familiar to someone accustomed to HTML composition.
The same reasoning applies to other protocols such as WML, XHTML, or even
XML itself.

The job of a web designer is greatly simplified because all that is needed is to learn
a few more tags with funny prefixes. Learning tag usage is a natural task for a web
designer. It's even more natural if the tags are well documented. The Java programmer,
on the other hand, will focus on providing the background infrastructure, in the form
of tag libraries, practically without worrying about HTML or JavaScript. Figure 5.2
shows the separation of the roles with the introduction of tag libraries.

Listing 5.2 shows the same page, but it uses tag libraries from the Jakarta Taglibs
project, from the Apache Software Foundation. The Jakarta Taglibs project is a repository for tag libraries developed under Open Source licensing. Chapter 9, "The Jakarta
Taglibs Project," explores those tag libraries in detail.

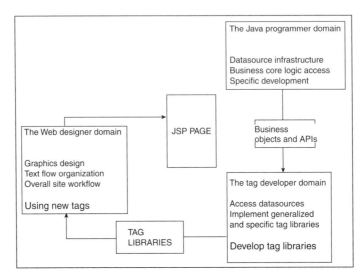

Figure 5.2 A new situation with tag libraries.

Listing 5.2 **Using Tag Libraries in the Page**

```
<%@ taglib uri="http://jakarta.apache.org/taglibs/dbtags" prefix="sql" %>

<sql:connection id="conn1">
  <sql:jndiName>EXAMPLEDS</sql:jndiName>
</sql:connection>

<html>
<header>
<script language="JavaScript1.2">
function showArticles(auth)
{
    window.open("authArticles.jsp?AUTH="+auth,"Author Articles","");
}
</script>
</header>
<body>
<h1>This is a static template inside a dynamic program block</h1>
<table>
<tr>
    <td>ID</td>
    <td>NAME</td>
    <td>SURNAME</td>
    <td>NATIONALITY</td>
</tr>

<sql:statement id="stmt1" conn="conn1">
```

```
<sql:query>
  Select ID, NAME, SURNAME, NATIONALITY from AUTHOR
</sql:query>
<sql:resultSet id="rset1">
  <tr>
    <td>
        <sql:getColumn position="1"/>
        <sql:wasNull>--</sql:wasNull>
    </td>
    <td>
        <sql:getColumn position="2"/>
        <sql:wasNull>[no description]</sql:wasNull>
    </td>
    <td>
        <sql:getColumn position="3"/>
        <sql:wasNull>[no description]</sql:wasNull>
    </td>
    <td>
        <sql:getColumn position="4"/>
        <sql:wasNull>--</sql:wasNull>
    </td>
  </tr>
</sql:resultSet>
</sql:statement>

</table>
</body>
</html>

<sql:closeConnection conn="conn1"/>
```

The page from Listing 5.2 shows a dramatic difference relative to the page from Listing 5.1. Code is made entirely of markup. The page is cleaner, and it is more evident to a web designer where to work with which technique. This page is also much simpler to maintain in absolute terms, which means that if the database access needs to be changed, it is evident where that is.

But that is not the most important aspect of maintainability. If the database infrastructure and the implementation objects change, the tag library will be updated, but this change is transparent to the web designer. It will be done by a tag library developer, and all that is needed to update the page generated from listing 5.2 is a redeployment of the tag library itself.

In Listing 5.1, the story is completely different. The Java code needs to be changed on each and every page using this approach when something regarding the data infrastructure changes. Furthermore, elements of the Java language, JavaScript, and HTML are mixed and are quite difficult to identify.

Tag Libraries in the Context of a Software Process

So, what is the role of a tag library in the context of a software process? To better answer that question, it is important to understand the life cycle of a tag itself. Then you must understand how that life cycle will fit the request cycle of a web application and what kind of solution will fit that life cycle.

When the JSP container finds a tag declaration, such as `<sql:getColumn position="3"/>`, it executes all the validation code and then inserts code in the translated servlet to call the tag-handler standard methods: to initialize the tag handler, `doStartTag` until `doEndTag` or `doFinally` is encountered. The result of those methods' execution is possibly included in the out stream. The overall result is returned to the client. From the client's point of view, the tag handler, which is executed during page generation, is simply invisible.

The best that the client can do is have visibility to a tag's results. Client-side objects are capable of invoking a tag to be processed, passing parameters to it only in the next request cycle after submitting a request to the server. This might seem trivial, but it is a recurrent problem for the newcomer. Despite the resemblance with XML, tags are a pure server-side technology.

Tag library development is not equivalent to JavaBeans development. Whereas beans can be developed to cover the full life cycle of an application, tag libraries must be hosted by a JSP and live in the translation cycle of the JSP only.

What kind of functionality can be packaged within a tag library and, more specifically, a tag? Almost any. But it is important to consider that the decision of whether to package a technology in a tag library is a decision that involves more than having the technology packaged.

Chapter 1, "Introduction to Servlets and JavaServer Pages," and Chapter 2 discussed application models that are currently used in web applications. The M-V-C application model is gaining the developer community's favor, but it is not mandatory. Applications are still being developed in a non–M-V-C manner, with business logic mixed with control logic and presentation logic all in the same page.

Whether or not the application is based on an M-V-C framework is a decision for the kind of structure permissible in the presentation layer. In well-constructed M-V-C applications, the presentation layer can contain only presentation logic and logic to access the data generated by the other layers. So, in the context of an M-V-C application, it doesn't make sense to have database connection or JDBC logic, for instance, even encapsulated in tag libraries. In non–M-V-C applications, on the other hand, any kind of logic can be implemented. Listing 5.2 is an example of such application.

Chapters 6–8 present the Struts framework. Struts is an example of an M-V-C framework that is strongly supported by tag libraries. The Struts JSP pages can still be used with any third-party tag library, but to generate data and access that data from the presentation JSPs, the framework offers four tag libraries to make it possible to render the objects generated by the framework's methods to the client. Chapter 9 presents the Jakarta Taglibs project, in which tag libraries offer additional functionality to any kind of application—even M-V-C applications, like Struts pages. For instance, the page in Listing 5.2 uses the DbTags tag library.

Focusing on the Business

The main idea to consider when developing or using tag libraries is that, as when developing or using component libraries, use must be focused on improving business performance and making the business more responsive. Flexibility in web application design and higher maintainability of production web applications reflect on the responsiveness of the business to the changes in the market structure or in the business orientation.

In the Internet age, web applications represent the business interface with the global market. Thus, if pages become simpler to develop and maintain, and offer richer and better-organized content as well as standardized views of the business objects that make the organization's business simpler to understand and to operate, then they are contributing to make a better business.

It is a task of the software-development manager to make sure that tag library development integrates with the company's existing technologies and methodologies. When using a M-V-C architecture, most of the business logic will be encapsulated in enterprise JavaBeans. A set of beans will provide the control logic and the rest of the business logic needed. By definition, tag libraries live in the presentation layer; they must be designed accordingly.

Designing a Tag Library

Like any software project, creating a tag library from scratch is a fairly complex task. First of all, this is because there are always alternative ways to do what the tag library is supposed to do. There are pitfalls to avoid, and there are trade-offs to consider— and there are always quite a number of them. Experience also pays back. Thus, we can fairly say that designing a tag library is not some exotic "webbie" process, but it requires the same kind of thinking that any serious piece of software requires from the designer team.

The concepts are all there: encapsulation, information hiding, cohesion, coupling, manageability, and maintainability. The design decisions will be equivalent. There still is the trade-off of old cohesion versus coupling. Maximizing tag cohesion means that the tags in a tag library will entirely cover the processes or objects that the tag library was designed to encapsulate, and each tag perfectly complements the others. However, this always tends to increase the number of tags. To avoid that, the granularity of the abstractions that each tag is implementing must be reduced; tags also get more generic, in terms of implementing more functions, and this tends to blur the boundaries between tags, generating dependencies and increasing coupling. Balancing the level of coupling and the level of cohesion is a delicate design decision. The goal still is to maximize cohesion and minimize coupling, but the best criteria is to keep them at a level that won't make the page designer suffer from the excess of tags or from heavy dependencies among tags that are strongly coupled.

The design cycle for a tag library is equivalent to that of a component library. A scenario analysis phase is involved in which the problem domain is considered. These are the three main types of scenarios that can take place:

- **A market opportunity can be identified.** A tag library can be designed to implement a certain API—for instance, the JNDI API—and it can be offered as a product to the market.

- **An intracompany opportunity can be identified.** The Human Resources department can create and publish some tag library to represent information about employees throughout the sites in the corporate intranet.

- **A specific issue can be addressed.** A tag library can be built to cope with the complexity of publishing information in a directory service for the security-management information systems.

Defining the scenario for a tag library also involves identifying the main abstractions that comprise the library's target domain. A library that implements the JNDI API will have to cope with a naming service, a directory service, service-stored objects and attributes, contexts, and so on. The question of whether there will be a tag for each abstraction or a couple of complex-action tags implementing the main operations in the API is another story.

The next phase is to design the tag library. Several aspects must be considered carefully in this phase. The first decision concerns what to implement. Which of the abstractions in the problem domain are relevant enough in the designer's approach, and how are these abstractions grouped? For instance, when implementing a JDBC-based tag library, is it important to implement a `ResultSet` interface as a tag? Is it a relevant abstraction for the tag designer? Jakarta Taglibs offers the DbTags tag library, where the `ResultSet` interface is a relevant abstraction for the tag designer and is implemented in the tag library. On the other hand, in the JRun tag library, to be seen in Chapter 10, "Commercial Tag Libraries," the `ResultSet` is not relevant, and a single SQL tag provides database access all at once.

Another decision must determine whether the library will implement processes or classes. A tag handler implements an action, and an action can represent an object's behavior or a process. Again, in the Jakarta Taglibs DbTags tag library, the interfaces that make the JDBC API were abstracted from the API and implemented as a set of tags. In the same project, but in the JNDI tag library instead, the tag library doesn't implement `Context` or `DirContext` interfaces, but the lookup or the search processes.

A point to consider at this phase is whether to implement these processes or classes in a single tag or as a cooperating group of actions, depending on how complex they are. A designer might choose to implement more tags in lower-granularity tags; another might choose to implement fewer tags with many attributes and several attribute configurations.

Scenario Analysis

Scenario analysis allows a designer to understand the nature of the problem domain and what the main abstractions in that problem domain are. Considering the potential of custom tags, a designer might encounter three possible basic scenarios:

- **Market-oriented domains**—These tag libraries implement generalized processes. They can be made available to the market and are not bound to specific application software. A company can implement a tag library to supply functionality to a category of applications, such as WAP or portal applications. It can supply tag implementations for an API, such as JNDI or JMS, or to APIs in vertical markets such as finance or seismology.

  Generalized libraries implement some generalized functionality that is interesting. A public API will fit in a JSP through a tag library in a modular way. For instance, if a certain API is used directly in scriptlets and some of its functions get deprecated, the scriptlets must be rewritten. On the other hand, a tag library will seamlessly overcome the changes through encapsulation.

  When implementing an API, it is important to have a model of usage for the API that corresponds to the most common usage model present in the market. Otherwise, the library won't reflect the market's needs. Examples of such tag libraries are the JNDI in Jakarta Taglibs, discussed in Chapter 9, and the EJB tag library in the Orion tags, covered in Chapter 10.

- **In-house specific libraries**—Web applications are making their way into intranets in much the same way as they are in the Internet. In this scenario, tag libraries can be built to supply functionality with a precise semantic in the company environment. A company can define an in-house tag library to implement the business services, such as printing an invoice or business objects—perhaps a customer profile that is used enterprise-wide. This has the advantage of encapsulating standardized views for standard data used in the many applications inside the company. For instance, a company might define a tag library to represent the standardized view of the Human Resources entities or to implement specific APIs used in the company's applications.

  The authentication tags presented in Chapter 3, "Writing Custom Tags," are an example of a hypothetical in-house tag library. Those tags implement functionality required by a security and authentication application that they support, even though they are all based on JNDI. In this case, the API is an accessory to the main function.

- **Complexity solving libraries**—A tag library can be built to solve web application design issues. For instance, it might encapsulate functions that are fairly complex to be implemented with scriptlets, such as mapping or authentication functions. In a mapping application, for instance, there are always many vectors or arrays representing shapes and lines. Setting up these data structures can be tricky for a newcomer, slowing the development of new applications and making maintenance of existent ones quite difficult.

Defining Actions

The first step to take when designing a tag library is to identify what candidate actions need to be implemented as tags. In a public API, such as JMS, the main abstractions and the critical functionality are all well defined. So, it is relatively easy to identify which are the candidate actions. Either they reflect the main objects in some API or they reflect the main functions present in the API.

The Jakarta Taglibs DbTags tag library implements the JDBC API. Examples of the tags in that library are listed here:

- **connection**—Encapsulates java.sql.Connection
- **statement**—Encapsulates java.sql.Statement
- **preparedStatement**—Encapsulates java.sql.PreparedStatement
- **resultSet**—Encapsulates java.sql.ResultSet

So, this library implements the main abstractions in the JDBC API, making the use of the tag library resemble the use of the JDBC API itself. This approach has the advantage of creating a certain familiarity with the tag library acquired previously with the JDBC API. The only problem with this approach is that general APIs usually present a fairly large number of abstractions, which means a fairly large number of tags to use. And some of the classes present in the API might be found meaningless in the context of a tag library and then would be discharged.

The JNDI tag library, on the other hand, does not implement the main abstractions present in the JNDI API, but it provides the main functions present there:

- **useContext**—Creates a context for use in a page
- **useDirContext**—Creates a directory context to be used
- **list**—Lists the elements in a certain context
- **lookup**—Looks for a particular object in a context and exports it
- **search**—Searches a directory context
- **getAttribute**—Can retrieve attributes from a Context, DirContext, Attributes, or an Attribute interface
- **forEachAttribute**—Allows iteration through the attributes from a DirContext, SearchResults, or Attributes interface

The approach taken in the JNDI tag library, of implementing processes instead of objects in the API, goes directly to the point. However, it can be more complex to design and maintain because, in most cases in any API, the main functions can be called only after a number of preparatory steps have been taken. And in most cases, these preparatory steps require parameterization, making the tag implementing the main function more complex to use. This then requires a large number of attributes, with many of them representing mutually exclusive configurations. For instance, the `useContext` tag takes 13 attributes, whereas `search` takes 14.

When that happens, the only solution is to break down that action into substeps. This means trouble because it introduces actions in the tag library that can have no meaning in terms of the API, making it incomprehensible to the web application programmer or designer.

Designing an in-house tag library can lead to very similar problems. A standard view to a certain entity can encapsulate quite complex behavior, and the resulting tag library might end up being huge and complex to use.

The golden rule here seems to be: Plan. Before starting to design a tag library, it is imperative to understand how the library will look to the end-user designer. It is important to think about whether it implements the abstractions that the end-user designer will be expecting and whether use is not restrained by an inadequate representation of the API's classes or an inadequate function set.

In Chapter 4, "Cooperating Tags and Validation," the example of the JMS API provides a good ground to analyze the proper process of selecting the candidates for tags. The scenario is an implementation of a publisher-subscriber JMS architecture. Like JDBC, JMS is based on connections, sessions, and message-processing objects.

Planning for Reuse

Tags can be thought of as reuse devices. A tag is designed to represent modular functions, but that doesn't make much sense if the tag is used on one page only—or even in one application only. Reusing a process or an abstraction, however, is not a simple task—far from it. Reuse is a characteristic that requires planning to understand which aspects of the action the tag represents as worth being reused, and to grasp the organization's attention and engagement.

If a certain aspect will require an independent attribute configuration to be correctly implemented, it must be considered that the overall complexity of the resulting tag will increase considerably. That extra complexity of use might prevent less skilled page designers from using the tag.

Identifying opportunities for reuse is also quite crucial to help in identifying opportunities for building tag libraries. The first candidates are recurrent scriptlets. If a scriptlet is used in a number of pages in a certain application and can potentially be present in a number of others, it is a strong candidate for becoming a tag. If a certain JSP or fragment is included in many pages, it is a candidate for becoming a tag. If a structure repeats itself in a number of pages, not identically, but in general terms, it is a candidate for becoming a tag. Listing 5.3 shows the `for` scriptlet being used a number of times in a page.

Listing 5.3   **A Menu That Shows the *for* Scriptlet Used Repeatedly**

```
<%

Vector v1 = (Vector)session.getAttribute("RGB_COLORS");
Vector v2 = (Vector)session.getAttribute("CMYK_COLORS");
Vector v3 = (Vector)session.getAttribute("RAINBOW_COLORS");

%>
<html>
<body>
<h1>Basic Colors and their Representations</h1>

<table>
<tr>
    <td>RGB COLORS</td>
</tr>
<%

for (int i=0; i<v1.size();i++)
{
    String color = (String)v1.elementAt(i);
%>
<tr>
    <td><%=color%></td>
</tr>
<%
}
%>
</table>

<table>
<tr>
    <td>CMYK COLORS</td>
</tr>
<%

for (int i=0; i<v2.size();i++)
{
    String color = (String)v2.elementAt(i);
%>
<tr>
    <td><%=color%></td>
</tr>
<%
}
%>
</table>

<table>
<tr>
```

```
      <td>RAINBOW COLORS</td>
   </tr>
   <%

   for (int i=0; i<v3.size();i++)
   {
      String color = (String)v3.elementAt(i);
   %>
   <tr>
      <td><%=color%></td>
   </tr>
   <%
   }
   %>
   </table>

   </body>
   </html>
```

The iteration shown constitutes a quite common structure in JSP programming and is present in countless pages. So, it can be chosen as a candidate for becoming a tag—say, the forVector tag. But not all iterations in an application are performed over vectors. This candidate will have limited application. Sometimes the object to iterate over can be an enumeration or a HashMap, so the collection to iterate over can be generalized. This decision expands the reuse opportunities of the forVector tag. Note that the reasoning is quite similar to that of reusing common classes.

In the Struts framework, the iterate tag represents a generalized iteration over a collection. It takes a single attribute representing a collection of a number of types, shown in Table 5.1.

Table 5.1 **The *iterate* Tag Structure**

Tag	Description
iterate	Iterates over a collection generating contents from the items of the collection. The attributes of this tag are as follows:

- collection—A runtime expression that evaluates to a collection of one of these types:
  - **Arrays**—An array of Java objects (primitive data types not allowed)
  - **Collection**—A java.util.Collection, including ArrayList and Vector
  - **Enumeration**—A java.util.Enumeration
  - **Iterator**—A java.util.Iterator.
  - **Maps**—A java.util.Map, HashMap, Hashtable, or TreeMap
- id—The script variable that will expose the items retrieved from collection.

continues

Table 5.1 **Continued**

Tag	Description
	• `length`—The maximum number of iterations to perform. This attribute can express the value itself or the name of a bean that defines that value. If not specified, the collection will be exhausted.
	• `name`—The name of a bean containing the collection to iterate over.
	• `property`—The name of the property of the bean expressed by `name`, containing the collection to iterate over.
	• `scope`—The scope of the bean expressed by `name`.
	• `offset`—The zero-relative index of the element in the collection where the iteration will start. Zero is the default.
	• `type`—The fully qualified Java class name of the element retrieved from the collection.
	Chapter 6, "The Jakarta Struts Project," and Chapter 7, "Struts Tag Libraries," discuss Struts and the Struts tag library, respectively.

Besides a collection attribute, the Struts `iterate` tag can take a bean name, scope, and property containing a collection and then iterate over it. This alternative configuration might seem to complicate the tag use, but this is quite the contrary. On the Struts framework, beans play a central role in representing the application state. So, this alternative configuration is crucial and strategic to making the `iterate` tag reusable for Struts-based applications.

Other facets of the `iterate` tag are the range specification and the variable exposure. Attribute length and offset deal with range iteration, so, opportunities for reuse again are expanded. The `id` and `type` attributes represent the exposure of an item of the collection to the body of the tag. Listing 5.4 shows an example of usage of the `iterate` tag.

Listing 5.4 **Using the struts-logic *iterate* Tag**

```
<%@ taglib uri="/WEB-INF/struts-logic.tld" prefix="logic" %>

<%

Vector v1 = (Vector)session.getAttribute("RGB_COLORS");
Vector v2 = (Vector)session.getAttribute("CMYK_COLORS");
Vector v3 = (Vector)session.getAttribute("RAINBOW_COLORS");

%>
<html>
<body>
<h1>Basic Colors and their Representations</h1>

<table>
```

```
<tr>
   <td>RGB COLORS</td>
</tr>
<logic:iterate id="color" collection="<%=v1%>">
<tr>
   <td><%=color%></td>
</tr>
</logic:iterate>

</table>
<table>
<tr>
   <td>CMYK COLORS</td>
</tr>
<logic:iterate id="color" collection="<%=v2%>">
<tr>
   <td><%=color%></td>
</tr>
</logic:iterate>
</table>

<table>
<tr>
   <td>RAINBOW COLORS</td>
</tr>
<logic:iterate id="color" collection="<%=v3%>">
<tr>
   <td><%=color%></td>
</tr>
</logic:iterate>
 </table>
 </body>
 </html>
```

As Listing 5.4 shows, the iterate tag can cope with the collection and iterate over its elements seamlessly, regardless of how the collection is implemented, making it quite flexible. The iterate tag is examined in detail in Chapter 7.

Cohesive Tag Handlers

When designing tags, the goal is to fulfill some action. To achieve this, a tag can accomplish the following:

- Access any defined scope in the runtime environment of a JSP
- Cooperate with other tags to implement complex actions
- Communicate and interact with a number of objects to implement the action that it is supposed to implement

The challenge is to maximize the cohesion among the implementing classes: tags, utility classes, entity classes, and web server–based objects, while maintaining the lowest level of coupling.

Tags represent reusable modules of code performing inside the JSP life cycle. When designing a tag, to maximize cohesion, it is important to focus the tag on one conceptual task only. For instance, in Chapter 4, the JMS tags cooperate to perform complex messaging operations. Each tag in the JMS example fulfills a specific role within the solution domain in that example. That role must be clearly defined before any code is written.

As mentioned in the beginning of this section, when designing a tag library that implements an API to make it modularly usable within JSP pages without the use of scriptlets, the roles of the tags comprising the library probably already will be defined. They are either the roles of objects in the API or the roles of the main functions in the API. The roles fulfilled by the tags in the JMS example in Chapter 4 are depicted in Table 5.2.

Table 5.2   **Roles Identified in the JMS Example of Chapter 4**

Tag	Role
topicConnection	This tag implements a `TopicConnection`. It establishes a connection with a JMS service in publisher-subscriber mode.
topic	A `topic` tag identifies a certain topic, a queue where a topic publisher pushes messages that the topic subscribers will pull out.
topicSession	The `TopicSession` is a central role in the topic-subscriber JMS schema. The `TopicConnection` object creates the `TopicSession`. The `TopicSession` will create publishers and subscribers.
topicSubscriber	The `TopicSubscriber` pushes messages out of the `Topic`. It registers interest in a topic with a JMS service.
getMapMessage	`MapMessages` are messages in which the body is a set of name-value pairs. In the example extensively discussed in Chapter 4, messages in the candidate's queue contain several electoral numbers, representing the candidate's results in several regions.
writeOut	The `WriteOut` tag writes a single value to the out stream, based on the name provided.

It is somewhat clear that some objects in this library have a strict hierarchical relationship: Connections create sessions within a factory method pattern, sessions create subscribers in the same way, and subscribers retrieve messages. This hierarchical relationship must be preserved because it is an important relationship within the API. That indicates that the tags will operate in a hierarchy, which is achieved by enclosing the dependant tags within the provider tags. Listing 5.5 shows a draft of such relationship.

Listing 5.5 **Hierarchical Relationships Are Naturally Modeled by Enclosing**

```
<topicConnection>
  <topicSession>
    <topicSubscriber>
      <getMapMessage>
        <writeOut>
        <writeOut>
        . . .
      </getMapMessage>
    </topicSubscriber>
  </topicSession>
</topicConnection>
```

The starter object is the `topicConnection`. It can be used to establish a number of `topicSessions`. Each of the `topicSessions` can be used to create a number of `topicSubscribers`, which retrieve messages with `getMapMessage`, which are used to supply the name-value pairs to `writeOut` tags.

So, these tags will cooperate and will have a hierarchical relationship implemented with one tag enclosing the others dependent on it. The next decision involves the cooperation schema to make the hierarchic relationship meaningful. As you learned in Chapter 4, two basic schemas exist. The main problem when using `getParent` runtime stack to implement cooperation among tags is that it can potentially increase coupling.

One way to circumvent that issue is to avoid passing data used for control in an enclosing tag down to the tags in the body. For instance, if a tag performs iteration, it is valid to access the core data structure generated or the current item of the iteration within the body, but not the iteration control variable. If it is a counter-based tag, the counter must remain hidden.

Maximizing tag cohesion is difficult. It tends to increase the number of tags because it makes the actions more finely grained and orthogonal, and they do not interfere with each other. But it also makes the tag library more difficult to use because it requires many tags to implement even simpler operations in a page. The trade-off here is to maintain the number of tags at a manageable level—a number that won't make using the API directly in a scriptlet more comfortable than using the tag library. Otherwise, the library won't be used.

Overloading Actions

Overloading is the opposite characteristic in respect to cohesion. Overloading a tag means aggregating actions with similar purposes on a tag, with the objective of simplifying the use of a process by reducing the number of tags necessary to carry on that process. To differentiate one overloaded action from the other, some attribute configuration must be supplied.

For instance, suppose that the `topicConnection` tag, presented in Chapter 4, was implemented to establish a connection with a JMS service in either publisher-subscriber mode or pure queue mode. In that case, two alternatives remain to configure it: using reflection to infer which kind of connection will be created or providing a distinct set of attributes for each implemented interface. Listing 5.6 shows the first approach.

Listing 5.6   **The *JMSConnectionTag* Tag Handler with Reflection**

```
package jspbook.example.tags;

import javax.jms.*;
import com.objectcube.objectevents.naming.*;
import javax.servlet.jsp.*;
import javax.servlet.jsp.tagext.*;

public class JMSConnectionTag extends TagSupport implements TryCatchFinally
{
    private Connection con = null;

    protected Object conFact = null;
    protected String name = null;
    protected String JNDIName = null;

    public String getConFact()
    {
        return this.conFact;
    }

    public void setConFact(Object value)
    {
        this.conFact = value;
    }

    public String getName()
    {
        return this.name;
    }

    public void setName(String value)
    {
        this.name = value;
    }

    public String getJNDIName()
    {
        return this.JNDIName;
    }

    public void setJNDIName(String value)
    {
        this.JNDIName = value;
    }
```

```java
public int doStartTag() throws JspException
{

  Object intConFact = null;
  try
  {
     // Locates a TopicConnectionFactory to create a TopicConnection
     if (conFact == null)
     {
        if (JNDIName == null)
           intConFact = pageContext.findAttribute(name);
        else
        {
           Context ctx = new InitialContext();
           intConFact = context.lookup(JNDIName);
        }
     }
     else intConFact = conFact;

     if (intConFact instanceof TopicConnection)
        con = intConFact.createTopicConnection();
     else
        con = intConFact.createQueueConnection();

     pageContext.setAttribute(id, tc);
     return EVAL_BODY_INCLUDE;

  }
  catch(JMSException e)
  {
     throw new JSPException("JMS Exception: "+ e.getMessage());
  }
  return SKIP_BODY;
}

public void doFinally()
{
   tc.close();
}

public void release()
{
   con = null;
   conFact = null;
   name = null;
   JNDIName = null;
}

}
```

The problem with this approach is that it makes visible a type of variable that will have to be resolved in every enclosed tag below it. This can lead to ambiguous interpretation of what is being generated by the tag in a certain moment, so a page designer might end up trying to create a `topicSession` out of a `queuedConnection`.

On the other hand, implementing the `JMSConnection` tag with attribute configurations makes it clearer that the tag implements more than one case of `Connection`. So, the coherent objects must be supplied to configure it, and the coherent enclosed tags must be supplied to make it work properly.

The problem with overloading is that it tends to increase the complexity of using a tag and the overall complexity of the body. Tags in the body must cope with the overloading in the enclosing tag. Multiple configurations on the enclosing tag can end up being transferred to the body. For instance, in Listing 5.6, the tags in the body must test which of the `Connection` interfaces the connection tag is supplying. If a tag implements a multimode method, it is necessary to cope with all the method's modes.

The key to overloading is to implement many input configurations, providing a single output object—or at least a set of resulting objects wrapped in a single interface.

Deployment Considerations

When deploying a tag library, it is important to plan how the library will be packaged, what kind of constraints the external elements impose on the packaging, and what the deployment scenario is for the library. The following list shows the several elements to consider:

- **External entities**—Most of the time, the design goals of a tag library will be to provide a small, reusable, modular process to be used in a JSP page. To support some actions, it will be necessary to provide some autonomous data structure that represents the state of some of the action's variables.

  For instance, it can be a control bean, representing an entity that parameterizes the action. It can be a collection with parameters that the action needs. It can be an interface implemented by some tags, exposed to orient the tag designer when extending or adding tags to the library.

- **Configuration files**—Classes and tag handlers might need parameter files or resource bundles provided. If these are to be stored in predefined paths or are to be located automatically by some class in the library, this will influence where the library can be deployed. The resource files in the Struts framework are deployed with a predefined path and must be located in the classpath. This will drive the deployment routine.

Common Pitfalls

When writing a tag library, many decisions must be made, and each decision drives the overall project in a certain direction. Sometimes the tag library project is driven to a dead end that the tag designer must recognize and correct. Basically this stems from problems relating to cohesion and overloading, or problems of result generation, such as the following:

- **Too many tags**—How to achieve balance between cohesion and overloading is always a challenging design decision. The most common mistake for a newcomer is to implement actions at a level that is too low, such as requiring the implementation of many small actions to perform a task that could be implemented with less fine granularity but still perfectly understandable tags.

- **Too many attributes**—This is the opposite problem. Some tag might have too many attributes, making it difficult to use. If this happens because the tag implements some very complex action that needs a big amount of information to work, too few options are left.

  If the object the tag takes a variable number of attributes, it is worthwhile to consider whether passing the necessary parameters in a map would solve the problem. For instance, the link tag in Struts receives the HTTP parameters for the target link as a map because it is impossible to predict how many parameters an arbitrary link will have. The same goes for the search string in a lookup tag in the JNDI library from Jakarta Taglibs. The naming path is provided as a `String`.

- **Attribute configuration**—This is another problem of overloading. A tag aggregates a number of aspects of some action, demanding the usage of diverse attribute configurations to correctly address one of those aspects. This might complicate tag usage in the body. The solution is to break down the different action configurations into different tags.

Generating Markup

A tag performs some action to produce some result, which can be a collateral effect, such as redirecting processing to an external resource, fulfilling some data structure (as with the `getMapMessage` tag), or writing the information on the out stream (as with the `writeOut` tag). The main issue when designing tags that generate markup is that this constitutes a form of coupling. The tag becomes dependent on a certain markup structure to make sense or to be correctly interpreted in the client side. Of course, it is an application design decision to generate a certain kind of content.

The best solution, with minimum coupling, of course, is to generate raw data as much as possible. If there is a tag that must publish some complex data structure, it is always preferable to write a `publishPiece` tag that will publish a smaller, unstructured part of the whole data structure. The `getMapMessage/writeOut` tags are an example of this approach.

Sometimes, however, it is interesting to write a tag to generate some markup content. It will usually do the following:

- **Provide some additional HTML/WML "control"**—Tags can be written to encapsulate some HTML structure that otherwise would have to be provided in a JSP include.

- **Extend an HTML/WML control**—The Struts framework offers the struts-html tag library to provide HTML replacement controls, making it seamless to initialize HTML forms with values returned in the framework's beans. The JRun tag library provides a set of tags to make data validation easier.

- **Provide some XML operation**—The scrape, xsl, and xtags tag libraries from the Jakarta Taglibs project, detailed in Chapter 9, are examples of tags providing XML operations.

As an example of the first case, consider the page shown in Listing 5.7. The page includes the fragment page in Listing 5.8 to provide an HTML-based menu that is text-only and quite fast to download.

Listing 5.7 **Using a Menu HTML Fragment**

```
<%@ taglib uri='/WEB-INF/struts-template.tld' prefix='template' %>
<%@ taglib uri='/WEB-INF/struts-html.tld' prefix='html' %>
<%@ taglib uri='/WEB-INF/struts-bean.tld' prefix='bean' %>
<html:html>
<header>
 <html:base/>
</header>
<body>

<template:insert template="/headerTemplate.jsp">
  <template:put name="module" content="Main Menu" direct="true"/>
</template:insert>

<html:link page="/searchAuthor.jsp">
  <bean:message key="author.search"/>
</html:link>

<html:link page="/searchJournal.jsp">
  <bean:message key="journal.search"/>
</html:link>

<html:link page="/searchArticle.jsp">
  <bean:message key="article.search"/>
</html:link>

<template:insert template="/footerTemplate.jsp"/>
</body>
</html:html>
```

The menu fragment page can be encapsulated in a tag using a collection instead, making it parameterized through attributes.

Listing 5.8   **The Menu HTML Fragment**

```
<%@ taglib uri='/WEB-INF/struts-template.tld' prefix='template' %>
<%@ taglib uri='/WEB-INF/struts-html.tld' prefix='html' %>
<%@ taglib uri='/WEB-INF/struts-bean.tld' prefix='bean' %>
<html:html>
<header>
 <html:base/>
</header>
<body>

<template:insert template="/headerTemplate.jsp">
  <template:put name="module" content="Main Menu" direct="true"/>
</template:insert>

<html:link page="/searchAuthor.jsp">
  <bean:message key="author.search"/>
</html:link>

<html:link page="/searchJournal.jsp">
  <bean:message key="journal.search"/>
</html:link>

<html:link page="/searchArticle.jsp">
  <bean:message key="article.search"/>
</html:link>

<template:insert template="/footerTemplate.jsp"/>
</body>
</html:html>
```

A tag can be written to reuse the menu JSP supported by beans representing the menu items. The MenuNodeBean shown in Listing 5.9 provides the infrastructure necessary to build the menu correctly and make it reusable.

Listing 5.9   **The *MenuNodeBean* Bean**

```
package jspbook.example.utils;

public class MenuNodeBean extends Object
{
    private String code;
    private String desc;
    private String url;
    private String[] permissions;

    public String getCode()
```

continues

Listing 5.9 **Continued**

```java
{
   return this.code;
}
public void setCode(String value)
{
   this.code = value;
}

public String getDesc()
{
   return this.desc;
}
public void setDesc(String value)
{
   this.desc = value;
}

public String getUrl()
{
   return this.url;
}
public void setUrl(String value)
{
   this.url = value;
}

public String[] getPermissions()
{
   return this.permissions;
}
public void setPermissions(String[] value)
{
   this.permissions = value;
}

}
```

The tag implementing this menu will cope with HTML. It encapsulates the functionality created by the JSP, which must be included to a JSP implementing a menu, in Listing 5.8. This is presented in Listing 5.10.

Listing 5.10 **The *MenuTag* Tag Handler**

```java
package jspbook.example.tags

import java.util.Vector;
import java.io.IOException;
import javax.servlet.jsp.*;
import javax.servlet.jsp.tagext.*;
```

```java
public class MenuTag extends TagSupport
{
    protected Vector vec = null;
    protected String code = null;

    public void setVec(Vector values)
    {
        this.vec= values;
    }

    public void setCode(String value)
    {
        this.code = value;
    }

    public int doStartTag() throws JspException
    {
        StringBuffer menu = new StringBuffer();

        try
        {
            for(int i=0;i<vec.size();i++)
            {
                LinearMenu lm = (LinearMenu)vec.elementAt(i);

                if (code != null && lm.getCode().equals(code))
                {
                    if(menu.length() == 0)
                    {
                        menu.append("<font
color=red>"+lm.getDescr().toUpperCase()+"</font>");
                    }
                    else
                    {
                        menu.append(" | <font
color=red>"+lm.getDescr().toUpperCase()+"</font>");
                    }
                }
                else
                {
                    if(menu.length() == 0)
                    {
                        menu.append("<a
href=\""+lm.getUrl()+"\">"+lm.getDescr()+"</a>");
                    }
                    else
                    {
                        menu.append(" | <a
href=\""+lm.getUrl()+"\">"+lm.getDescr()+"</a>");
                    }
```

continues

Listing 5.10   **Continued**

```
                }
            }

            pageContext.getOut().println(menu.toString());
        }
        catch (Exception e)
        {
            pageContext.getServletContext().log("doStartTag",e);
            throw new JspException(e.getMessage());
        }

        return SKIP_BODY;
    }

    public void release()
    {
        vec = null;
        code = null;
    }
}
```

The MenuNode bean contains the menu items and is presented in Listing 5.11.

Listing 5.11   **The *MenuNode* Bean**

```
package jspbook.example.tags;

import java.io.Serializable;
import java.util.*;

public class MenuNode extends Object implements Serializable
{
    private String code;
    private String descr;
    private String url;

    public LinearMenu(String code, String descr, String url, Vector sec)
    {
        this.code = code;
        this.descr = descr;
        this.url = url;
    }

    public String getDescr()
    {
        return this.descr;
    }
    public String getCode()
    {
        return this.code;
```

```
    }
    public String getUrl()
    {
        return this.url;
    }

    public void setCode(String value)
    {
        this.code = value;
    }
    public void setDescr(String value)
    {
        this.descr = value;
    }
    public void setUrl(String value)
    {
        this.url = value;
    }
}
```

Now it is possible to replace the JSP include in the JSP page with the tag, which is presented in Listing 5.12. Note that the menu tag encapsulates a standard piece of HTML.

Listing 5.12 **Using a Menu HTML Fragment**

```
<%@ page import="java.util.Vector"%>
<%@ page import="jspbook.example.tags.MenuNode"%>
<%@ taglib URI="/WEB-INF/jspbook.tld" prefix="example"%>
<%
Vector menu = new Vector();
menu.addElement("1","foo","http://foo.com");
menu.addElement("1","bar","http://bar.com");
menu.addElement("1","uoo","http://uoo.com");
<html>
<body>
here is the menu: <example:menu vec="<%=menu%>"/>
</body>
</html>
```

The HTML menu can be added modularly to any JSP and can be reused at will.

When generating markup, it is important to remember that markup is a language. HTML, XHTML, XML, WML, and so on constitute languages and dialects that will establish dependencies, increasing coupling. So, if it is necessary to generate markup, a whole markup entity, preferably, must be generated. You should generate a whole HTML table, a whole XML element, and so forth.

Avoid fixing style and JavaScript information. Leave it open to the page designer to stuff style information in, if possible, the same way it would be done with the original piece of markup. In the struts-html tag library, all tags provide event-handler attributes for the same event handlers of the replaced controls. Style attributes allow a page designer to assign style classes for the replacement controls.

The Standard Tag Library

The JSP Standard Tag Library (JSPTL) is an effort of the Java community to provide a tag library that will be available in any JSP API–compliant container, offering a rich, cross-platform functionality to page designers. It is the subject of the JSR052 community process at Sun Microsystems. More detail about the Standard Tag Library is available at `http://www.jcp.org/jsr/detail/52.jsp`.

An early version release of the JSPTL is available at the Jakarta Taglibs Project site, `http://jakarta.apache.org/taglibs/doc/jsptl-doc/intro.html`. The release provides the JSP developer community with information and gathers feedback about this effort. It is not a standard at this point, and it is subject to change in the future, but it states the directions of the efforts of the JSR052 community process.

The importance of having a Standard Tag Library is that its functionality would be available in any compliant container, without the need for installing third-party products or depending on platform-specific tag libraries for the functionality that the JSPTL implements. This is in accordance with the Java principle of "write once, run anywhere."

The functionality offered in the early access release of the JSPTL covers an expression language provided to allow page developers to design JSPs free of scriptlets. The expression language offered contains tags to perform:

- **Configuration of the language**—The `context` and `expressionLanguage` tags configure the expression language to use, making it interchangeable.

- **Variable declaration and expression evaluation**—The `declare` tag facilitates declaring a scripting variable. The `expr` and `set` tags perform expression evaluation. The first includes the result in the out stream, as in the `<%=exp %>` scriptlet expression, and the second places the result in a scoped attribute.

- **Iteration tags**—Two iterative tags exist: `forEach`, which is collection-oriented, and `forTokens`, which iterates over tokens separated by a delimiter. The tag library also offers two interfaces and a convenient class that tag developers can use to develop iterator tags: `IteratorTag`, which is used to implement basic iterator functionality, and `IteratorTagStatus`, which is used to track the status of an iteration, such as the current index if the current iteration is the first. The `IteratorTagSupport` class offers convenient methods for building up iterative tags in the same manner that `TagSupport` uses for tags in the Tag Library Extension API.

- **Conditional processing tags**—There is an `if` tag for simple conditional processing; `choose-when-otherwise` tags, similar to `switch-case` processing; and a convenient `ConditionalTagSupport` class.

- **Validators**—Two tag library validators are provided to ensure that JSP pages meet specific criteria when using the JSPTL: `JsptlCoreTLV` ensures the page uses the core JSPTL tags correctly, and `ScriptFreeTLV` ensures that no scriptlets are present in the page.

The JSPTL is available for testing and gathering feedback. To offer your feedback to the JSR052 community process, refer to `jsr052-comments@sun.com`.

Summary

This chapter presented a number of design considerations to help the web application design team better organize its roles in the application/content pipeline, to aid the tag designer in the decisions that should be made when developing a tag library, and to provide examples of such decisions when they have been made.

II

The Struts Framework

6

The Jakarta
Struts Project

So far, you've considered what a tag library is, learned how to design one, and seen how this design influences the overall architecture of applications. Now it is time to review the Apache Jakarta Struts Project, its structure, its components, and its tag libraries. This chapter provides a complete case study and background on using this application's design framework.

Introducing Struts

The Struts project started at Apache Software Foundation's Jakarta Project as an implementation for the Model 2 architecture for web applications. It's an Open Source framework that provides the infrastructure upon which you can develop a full-powered web application.

Goals and Motivation

Discussion of the Model 2 architecture started soon after the release of the Servlet 2.1 and JSP 0.92 APIs. It was pretty clear that those technologies were competitors, to some extent, and a great deal of confusion was in the air regarding what was the best approach. Articles championing one or the other popped up everywhere.

Some articles called attention to a not-quite-new approach that seemed to be the answer for those questions. The idea was that none was the best approach. Servlets and JSP could work together, and the MVC design pattern could definitely help with that. The next section, "The MVC Design Pattern," explores the MVC design pattern in more detail.

That was not the position defended by Sun in the first versions of the J2EE Blueprints. There the privileged technology was JavaServer Pages. The J2EE Blueprints document explicitly defines JSP as a preferred solution where both apply. But then there came a reaction from the market. The first version of the J2EE Blueprints document offered an example that provided the first insight on the use of MVC on J2EE. That example defined a model called the Pet-Shop model, which received a number of criticisms because of the exclusive use of JSP.

That early Pet-Shop example implemented the Control role of the MVC design pattern with a mute JSP, which is a JSP that generates no output to the browser. The market was complaining that maybe a mute JSP was not the best fit for the Control role on the MVC schema. The next section explores the MVC design pattern in more detail.

Struts was created by Craig R. McClanahan, staff engineer at Sun and one of Tomcat's project leaders, in May 2000. It was donated to the Jakarta Project to become an Open Source initiative, a standard framework implementing the Model 2 design pattern for web application development. Struts is different from the Pet-Shop model in that it proposes a servlet in the role of Control and uses a sophisticated set of auxiliary classes in the request-processing pipeline.

The goal of Struts is to provide a standard framework for web application development. Where generality is concerned, Struts doesn't make any inference regarding the type of business or application objects it will be dealing with. Application data can be gathered directly from a database, from CORBA objects, from EJBs, from XML trees, or from ordinary beans. Requests are associated with specific actions via an XML configuration file.

To provide flexibility, the framework makes intensive use of tag libraries, which can be plugged in or not, mixed with custom tag libraries, and even used independently from the MVC core. View components are implemented as JSP pages that make use of Struts tags to present the information in a productive way.

Before describing Struts in more detail, it is important to understand the ideas behind the MVC design pattern.

The MVC Design Pattern

The SmallTalk community introduced the MVC design pattern as a way to deal with the complexities of user interface design in a clear object-oriented way. One of the problems developers experienced most at the time was how to deal with user interface design in complex GUI environments. The common approach was to build all-in-one interface classes that dealt with presentation, processing, and response to the user's inputs. That was always a big source of complexity and maintenance problems.

This is clearly characteristic of the early web applications based on servlets or in JSPs, the so-called Model 1 architecture. The problem with Model 1 systems is intensive language mixing. Servlet-based systems must generate HTML as output, and these systems suffer from long chains of `println` method calls. JSP-based systems must generate data, and they suffer from endless scriptlets. Data generation, control, and presentation are again mixed in an all-in-one object. This causes two facets of the same problem: One facet is to mix HTML and client-level presentation logic with data abstraction in a component with a programmatic nature, such as a servlet. The other facet is mixing the control logic, which is essentially programmatic, with data abstraction and presentation logic in a component that is essentially declarative in nature. The problem is always the same: Control logic, data abstraction, and presentation logic are mixed in some component.

Listing 6.1 and Listing 6.2 present these problematic Model 1 components. They show how complicated such components can grow and why an alternative approach was urgently needed. The goal is the same in both—even the auxiliary code needed is identical. The goal is to generate a report with a title and number of pages for the articles in the Article DB.

Listing 6.1 **An Example Model 1 JSP**

```
<%@ page import="java.sql.*" %>
<%@ page import="com.codestudio.util.*" %>

<table>
   <tr>
    <td>Article</td>
    <td>Title</td>
    <td>No. Of Pages</td>
   </tr>

<%

try {
        Class.forName("com.codestudio.sql.PoolMan").newInstance();
} catch (Exception e) {
        application.log("Could Not Find the PoolMan Driver.");
}

Connection con = DriverManager.getConnection("jdbc:poolman");
try {
    Statement stm = con.createStatement();
    ResultSet rs = stm.executeQuery("select ARTICLE_ID, TITLE, PAGES FROM
ARTICLES");
    while (rs.next()) {
%>
```

continues

Listing 6.1 **Continued**

```
  <tr>
   <td><%=rs.getString(1)%></td>
   <td><%=rs.getString(2)%></td>
   <td><%=rs.getString(3)%></td>
  </tr>
<%
    }
}
catch (SQLException sqle) {}
finally {
  con.close();
}

%>
</table>
```

Listing 6.2 **An Example Model 1 Servlet**

```
import java.sql.*;
import java.io.*;
import javax.Servlet.*;
import javax.Servlet.http.*;
import com.codestudio.util.*;

public class Model_1_Servlet extends HttpServlet
{

  public void service (HttpServletRequest request, HttpServletResponse response)
  throws ServletException, IOException
  {

PrintWriter out = response.getWriter();
out.println("<table>");
  out.println("<tr>");
   out.println("<td>Article</td>");
   out.println("<td>Title</td>");
   out.println("<td>No. Of Pages</td>");
  out.println("</tr>");


try {
        Class.forName("com.codestudio.sql.PoolMan").newInstance();
} catch (Exception e) {
        application.log("Could Not Find the PoolMan Driver.");
}

Connection con = DriverManager.getConnection("jdbc:poolman");
try {
    Statement stm = con.createStatement();
```

```
    ResultSet rs = stm.executeQuery("select ARTICLE_ID, TITLE, PAGES FROM
ARTICLES");
    while (rs.next()) {
%>
  out.println("<tr>");
  out.println("<td>"+rs.getString(1)+"</td>");
  out.println("<td>"+rs.getString(2)+"</td>");
  out.println("<td>"+rs.getString(3)+"</td>");
  out.println("</tr>");
<%
    }
}
catch (SQLException sqle) {}
finally {
  con.close();
}
out.println("</table>");

  }

}
```

In Listing 6.1, you can see a typical Model 1 JSP with a scriptlet that retrieves data with JDBC. You can see how mixed the JDBC code and the JSP template are. This is a text page that the page designer will have to maintain, and it is clear that he won't be able to maintain it without a solid skill in Java programming. Although this might seem like a crude example, it is just equivalent to the usage of Beans either to abstract the database operations or to abstract the results of those operations, which are the most common approaches. Either way, the control logic will still be out of place, and this problem is better addressed by the MVC pattern.

The situation is symmetrical regarding the servlet in Listing 6.2. Here the Java code is perfectly in place, but the servlet programmer will have to maintain the HTML output code also, and he won't be able to generate quality results without a solid skill in web page design. Clearly, in these two examples, interface code is mixed with data maintenance/access code. Presentation, flow-of-control, and core data are mixed in an all-in-one class. The same old problem is back. It must be concluded that no Model 1 approach will ever solve this kind of problem.

The MVC solves that by promoting a strong separation of roles in interface design. It introduces three clearly distinct roles for the interface classes:

- **Model**—The Model represents the application abstraction, the object that implements the data that the application must maintain. Of course, it is the most important component of all.

- **View**—The View represents some translation of the Model state into a user interface schema. It can be a report, a screen presentation window, a spreadsheet, and a graphic. It represents any way to translate the Model data into user-readable language.

- **Control**—In the classic MVC design pattern, the Control is responsible for processing user inputs, initiating some change in the Model state. This is sufficient for a GUI environment but not for the web arena.

This arrangement works because it is supported by a subscribe/notify schema. GUI interfaces often implement this kind of schema as a message/event mechanism. Each action conducted by the user fires an event in the GUI environment that the components can catch and then it fires updating events for the next components in the arrangement. The Control components intercept user-input events and trigger Model refresh events. Model objects trigger View refresh events. The View is updated, and the data reaches the user. This is the most commonly used approach in GUI-based RAD systems.

This schema won't work in the web environment, however, because there is no such event mechanism. In the web, the controller takes the responsibility for the flow of control also. It is responsible for maintaining the core processing flow, and it must refer to some subscription or command-definition schema to decide which Model or request processor component to transfer control to when a user request arrives. After that, it gets the output generated by a Model component and redirects the flow of control to some View object (see Figure 6.1).

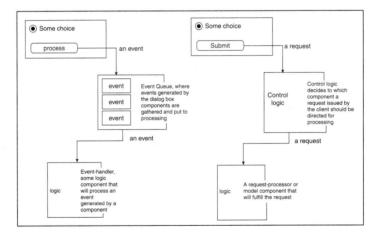

Figure 6.1 Comparing the MVC design pattern used by conventional GUI-based applications with its web application counterpart.

Because the objects in the Model are often of a more abstract and general nature, such as business objects implemented in EJBs or some other mechanism, sometimes it is necessary to translate user request data into something that the Model can use. For example, perhaps the same system must take into account Model objects distinct in nature—part of them might be implemented as CORBA objects and part might be implemented as EJB.

To avoid overloading the Control with those Model-specific details, some auxiliary classes are used to help in this translation. The Control delegates the request processing to these classes that will translate the request data in some format adequate to the target Model object and then call it. So, these new parties are included in the Control role as request processors.

The developers discussing Model 2 decided to place a servlet in the role of the Control, served by auxiliary request-processing classes. They then placed a JSP in the role of the View, the natural fit for it, and let the Model be implemented as needed, provided that request processors could address them when necessary.

Struts MVC Model

The Struts framework implements the MVC design pattern by placing a servlet, called `ActionServlet`, in the role of the controller. In fact, its Control mechanism is based on three main classes: The `ActionServlet` class receives the user request and dispatches it to an `Action` class instance, based on a action mapping defined in a XML configuration file and encapsulated by an `ActionMapping` class instance.

The `Action` objects, which are mapped to actions in the action-mapping file, translate requests into some call to the core business objects, if any.

It is not desirable for the `Action` class to resolve the request directly because it is part of the Control logic. The Action class's role is to translate the request variables into core Model class variables, to make it possible to invoke the Model class's methods and resolve the request, and to enable the results obtained from the request processing to reach the presentation JSP for that results in an adequate format. In Struts, this means in some `ActionForm` instance. Another responsibility of the `Action` class is to provide for transaction error control, making sure that a request is not resubmitted accidentally and that any error condition detected gets treated by the error-treatment mechanism. Although it's considered bad design, the request can end up being resolved by an `Action` class.

Depending on what is signalled by the `Action` object, the `ActionServlet` redirects the request to a target JSP that will find the needed `ActionForm` object (or any other object specifically designed for the application). `ActionServlet` then displays the data back to the user, possibly making use of the Struts tag library to optimize this job.

The tags in Struts tag library will access the `ActionForm` bean automatically; those tags retrieve the `ActionForm` properties and act upon them. The `ActionForm` bean makes it possible to retain information regarding the user input, validation results, and errors detected. This is so that, if such errors are detected, control will be redirected back to the originating form, and the form state to be restored to enable the user to correct whatever was wrong.

Download, Configuration, and Installation

As with any framework, using Struts requires a great deal of configuration. There are application resources to define, actions to define, and control flow paths to route.

The first step is obviously to get Struts. It can be downloaded from the project page at the Jakarta site: `http://jakarta.apache.org/jakarta-struts/release/v1.0`. You can download either a binary version or a source version. Source downloads are meant for Struts developers who want to have a deep understanding of it or who want to customize the framework. Customizing the framework's classes is not a good approach because the custom changes introduced can end up conflicting with the changes made in the framework's classes by the development community. At any rate, any changes introduced, conflicting or not with further versions of the framework, will have to be reapplied to newer releases of the customized classes. Otherwise, the custom version and the standard version of the framework will diverge until it becomes impossible to identify the standard classes again. If your goal is to develop a Struts-based application, download the binary distribution.

You will need to install an XML parser compatible with JAXP version 1.0.1 and make sure that it is on the classpath. You can try JAXP reference implementation from Sun at `http://java.sun.com/xml`, or Xerces, Apache's Open Source XML parser, at `http://xml.apache.org`.

You will also need JDBC 2.0 Optional Package Binary (jdbc2_0-stdext.jar, provided with the Struts distribution) in your classpath.

After unzipping the distribution and configuring the required packages, you are ready to develop your application. Developing a Struts application typically involves the following activities:

- Writing the Model-level objects, if these don't exist.
- Writing an `Action` class for each action identified. In the worst case, this will contain the logic for the request processing. It usually contains code to invoke methods in the target Model-level business objects.
- Possibly writing `ActionMapping` classes for custom mapping situations.
- Writing the presentation JSP, preferably with intensive use of the Struts tag library.
- Writing the `ActionForm` bean for each form in the system. This will preserve the user data for validation and correction.
- Writing the action information in the action-configuration file, while each action is defined and stuffed with the correlated components.
- Adding resources to the resource-configuration file.

When you have these components in place, it is time to deploy them to a server for testing or production purposes. Deploying Struts on a server will require some specific procedures, depending on the server.

Struts Main Components

As you have seen, Struts implements the MVC design pattern, putting a servlet in the role of the Control. That servlet decides which actions to invoke, based on the action-mapping definitions; it redispatches control from the action to some target, possibly on the View layer. The same action component activates some Model class to act upon the application's data. This section covers the components that make Struts and their responsibilities in an application.

The *ActionServlet* as the Controller Component

The core component in the whole Control mechanism in Struts is the `ActionServlet` class. It manages the application flow of control from the action-mapping configuration file, application and Struts internal message resources, and the application-defined data sources.

On initialization, the `ActionServlet` does the following:

- Clears the action-mapping cache.

- Loads the internal message resources-configuration file and caches the Struts-defined messages.

- Initializes the debug level from the debug `init` parameter.

- Loads the application message resources-configuration file and caches the application-defined messages. This uses the application `init` parameter.

- Initializes the action-mapping cache with `init` parameters. Then loads the action-configuration file and passes it to the `Digester` utilitarian class. `Digester` takes a number of predefined rules and parses an XML file, retrieving the values that trigger the corresponding rules; then it executes some process in response. `Digester` parses the action-mapping configuration file and caches all mapping information within the `ActionForward`, `ActionMapping`, and `FormBean`, along with the data sources and general caches.

- Initializes upload parameters, such as maximum file size, temporary directory, and so on.

- Initializes application-defined data sources.

- Initializes other configuration parameters, such as locale or content, and publishes the control caches as context-level attributes.

- Initializes the servlet-mapping information.

When it's initialized, the `ActionServlet` will accept user requests. For each request arriving, it does the following:

1. Identifies the action to invoke from the request query string.

2. Calls that action's `perform` method, if the action requested was already instantiated. If not, the proper `Action` class is loaded, and an instance is instantiated and cached.

3. Instantiates an `ActionForm` bean if this mapping specifies one invocation of the `perform` method. The `ActionForm` bean will be initialized with the submitted form's field values.

The `ActionServlet` executes these steps in response to either a `GET` or a `POST HTTP` command indifferently.

The *ActionMapping* Class

The `ActionMapping` class represents the information that the `ActionServlet` knows about an action mapping. Whenever a request arrives and is mapped to an action, an instance of this class is passed to it as an argument of the action's `perform` method.

This is the information that the predefined `ActionMapping` class holds:

- **attribute**—This contains the name of an attribute that stores the `ActionForm` bean associated with this client request. The attribute can be defined either in the request or in the session. The `scope` property defines where to find the attribute.

- **forward**—A request can be fulfilled by an action in three ways. It can be forwarded to a resource, the resource can be included in the response, or an `Action` class can be made responsible for it. Three properties on the `ActionMapping` class should be used for the respective situations: `forward`, `include`, or `type`. Only one can be specified at a time. The `forward` attribute contains the context-relative path of the resource that should serve this request (via a call to `RequestDispatcher.forward()`).

- **forwards**—A request can have more than one possible destination upon the fulfilment of a request by an `Action` class. The mapping defines each destination that is associated by the `ActionServlet` with an `ActionForward` instance. This property holds the set of such `ActionForwards`.

- **include**—See the previous `forward` explanation. This is the context-relative path of the resource that should serve this request (via a call to `RequestDispatcher.include()`).

- **input**—If the request being processed was generated by an input form, the `validate` property is true, and errors are encountered; then the control is returned to the form specified by this property. It contains a context-relative path of the input form to which control should be returned.

- **mappings**—This is the `ActionMappings` collection that the current `ActionMapping` being processed is part of.

- **name**—This is the name of the form bean, if any, that is associated with this action.

- **parameter**—This can be used to pass extra information to the `Action` instance. You can consider subclassing the `ActionMapping` class to add properties that a particular implementation of Struts might require. Just add the properties, their getter and setter methods.

- **path**—This requests the URI path used to select this mapping. If extension mapping is used for the controller servlet, the extension will be stripped before comparisons against this value are made.

- **prefix**—This is the prefix used to match request parameter names to form bean property names, if any.

- **scope**—This can be either `request` or `session`. It defines the scope where the attribute specified by the `attribute` property is found.

- **suffix**—Suffix used to match request parameter names when populating the properties of our `ActionForm` bean (if any).

- **type**—See the previous `forward` property explanation. This is the fully qualified Java class name of the `Action` implementation class used by this mapping.

- **unknown**—If set to `true`, this defines this action as the default for the application. There can be only one default action.

- **validate**—This is set to `true` if the `validate()` method of the form bean (if any) associated with this mapping should be called.

A number of properties also are currently deprecated and should not be used anymore. They were replaced by other properties in the previous list. They are maintained to preserve compatibility with previous versions of this class, however; they are as follows:

- **actionClass**—Replaced by `type`
- **formAttribute**—Replaced by `attribute`
- **formClass**—Replaced by `name`
- **formPrefix**—Replaced by `prefix`
- **formScope**—Replaced by `scope`
- **formSuffix**—Replaced by `suffix`
- **inputForm**—Replaced by `input`

Sometimes it might be necessary to subclass the `ActionMapping` to accommodate information that the action instance needs—perhaps to invoke the proper Model process or because it is required by the classes that implement the Model itself. For instance, some configuration parameter is needed to locate the proper EJB or CORBA object that will provide the core process being invoked.

The example application in Struts defines a class called `ApplicationMapping` with two default URI—one is to be used when validation on the `ActionForm` related to the mapping is successful, and the other is to be used for failure. You can check that class on the struts-example.war archive, under the webapps subdirectory.

Listing 6.3 presents the `SecSensitiveMapping` class, which added an authorization context and extra security information properties to the default mapping.

Listing 6.3   **Adding a Property to** *ActionMapping*

```
package jspbook.example.authcontrol;
import org.apache.struts.action.ActionMapping;

public final class SecSensitiveMapping extends ActionMapping
{

    private AuthContext authContext = null;
    private String secExtraInfo = null;


    public AuthContext getAuthContext()
    {
        if (this.authContext != null)
            return (this.authContext);
     else return new authContext();
    }

    public String getSecExtraInfo()
    {
        if(this.secExtraInfo != null)
        return (this.secExtraInfo);
        else return "no restrictions";
    }

    public void setAuthContext(AuthContext val)
    {

        this.authContext=val;
    }

    public void setSecExtraInfo(String val)
    {

        this.secExtraInfo = val;
    }


}
```

Refer to the example code on the companion web site for a description of the `AuthContext` class used in this example.

The *ActionForm* Class

The ActionForm class is an abstract class that provides a basic structure to build up ActionForm beans to be used in form data input on Struts. FormBeans is the name by which these beans were initially called in the early versions of Struts.

To develop the ActionForm beans that make your Struts application, you must derive them from ActionForm. For each form in the application, there will be a corresponding ActionForm subclass designed by you, the application developer, to cope with the data contained in that form. When a user submits the form, the request is processed by the ActionServlet that does the following:

- Detects which, if any, ActionForm subclass is associated with this mapping.
- Verifies whether an instance exists in any of the valid scopes. The valid scopes are the request or the session scopes.
- Instantiates it if no other instance is found.
- Populates it with the form data gathered from the request parameters.
- Calls the ActionForm subclass's validate method.
- Passes the ActionForm subclass instance to the Action class instance as an argument of the perform method, if validation was successful.

The most important method in the ActionForm class is the validate method. This method is called after the properties on the class have been filled in with the data passed in the request parameters but before the perform method on the action responsible for this request is called. The validation process is part of the ActionServlet process method and works as follows:

1. It checks whether the submit was cancelled. Struts offers an option to cancel a submit with a control implemented in the HTML tag library, which causes the data to turn to what it was before the editing has taken place. If this is the case, the validation process is silently aborted.

2. It checks whether the mapping specifies no validation. This means whether the validate attribute of the ActionMapping object instantiated for this request evaluates to false. If so, the validation process is silently aborted.

3. Data is validated by calling the ActionForm subclass's validate method. If the ActionErrors instance returned by the validate method is null or empty, it means that the validation process was successful and that the request processing can continue. If the ActionErrors instance is not null or empty, errors are present and something else must be done:

    - If the request has a multipart component (a file to upload, for instance), the multipart component is rolled back (all temporary files created are deleted).
    - The mapping is checked to see if it has the input form URI associated with it. It is the contents of the ActionMapping input property. It is the form that

will receive the data and the `ActionErrors` object and then show them to the user for resubmission or other corrective action. If that value is null, an `SC_INTERNAL_SERVER_ERROR` HTTP error is returned to the browser.

■ If the input property has a valid URI, the `ActionErrors` instance is placed in a standard request attribute, and control is returned to that form via a `RequestDispatcher` forward call.

4. If errors occurred, the `validate` process returns a Boolean `false`.

Listing 6.4 shows the code for a typical `ActionForm` subclass that will treat the data collected by the form shown in Listing 6.5.

Listing 6.4   **The *AuthorForm* Bean**

```
package jspbook.example.articledb;

import javax.servlet.http.HttpServletRequest;
import org.apache.struts.action.*;

public final class AuthorForm extends ActionForm
{

    private String name = null; //author's name...
    private String surname = null; // surname...
    private String nationality = null; // and nationality

    public String getName()
    {
      return (this.name);
    }

    public void setName(String value)
    {
        this.name = value;
    }

    public String getSurname()
    {
      return (this.surname);
    }

    public void setSurname(String value)
    {
        this.surname = value;
    }

    public String getNationality()
    {
      return (this.nationality);
```

```
    }

    public void setNationality(String value)
    {
        this.nationality = value;
    }

    public void reset(ActionMapping mapping, HttpServletRequest request)
    {
        this.name = null;
        this.surname = null;
        this.nationality = null;
    }

    public ActionErrors validate(ActionMapping mapping,
                                 HttpServletRequest request) {

        ActionErrors errors = new ActionErrors();
        if ((name == null) || (name.length() < 1))
            errors.add("authorname",
                       new ActionError("error.authorname.required"));
        if ((surname == null) || (surname.length() < 1))
            errors.add("authorsurname",
                       new ActionError("error.authorsurname.required"));
        if ((nationality == null) || (nationality.length() < 1))
            errors.add("nationality",                      new
ActionError("error.nationality.required"));
        return errors;
    }
}
```

The AuthorForm class in Listing 6.4 accepts the author's name, surname, and nationality, which are entered by the AuthorEdit.jsp input form page. It extends the ActionForm base class, and it checks the validate method. It imposes a non-null rule on all fields.

Listing 6.5 shows the page used to enter author data. As is usual in Struts applications, it makes heavy use of Struts tag libraries to deal with error treatment, internationalized messages and labels, and data-entry controls.

Listing 6.5 **The AuthorEdit.jsp Page**

```
<%@ page language="java" %>
<%@ taglib uri="/WEB-INF/struts-bean.tld" prefix="bean" %>
<%@ taglib uri="/WEB-INF/struts-html.tld" prefix="html" %>
<%@ taglib uri="/WEB-INF/struts-logic.tld" prefix="logic" %>

<html:html>
<head>
 <html:base/>
```

continues

Listing 6.5   **Continued**

```
</head>
<body bgcolor="white">

<html:errors/>

<html:form action="/authorEdit" focus="name">

<table border="0" width="100%">

  <tr>
    <th align="right">
      <bean:message key="prompt.authorName"/>
    </th>
    <td align="left">
      <html:text property="name" size="45"/>
    </td>
  </tr>

  <tr>
    <th align="right">
      <bean:message key="prompt.authorSurname"/>
    </th>
    <td align="left">
      <html:text property="surname" size="45"/>
    </td>
  </tr>

  <tr>
    <th align="right">
      <bean:message key="prompt.authorNationality"/>
    </th>
    <td align="left">
      <html:text property="nationality" size="2"/>
    </td>
  </tr>

  <tr>
    <td align="center">
        <html:submit>
          <bean:message key="button.save"/>
        </html:submit>
        <html:reset>
          <bean:message key="button.reset"/>
        </html:reset>
        <html:cancel>
          <bean:message key="button.cancel"/>
        </html:cancel>
    </td>
  </tr>
```

```
</table>

</html:form>

</body>
</html:html>
```

Listing 6.6 shows a fragment of the struts-config.xml file defining the edit author application functionality. It is implemented by the `AuthorEditAction` class. Check how the attributes of the `action` element match the properties on the `ActionMapping` class and put all the pieces together.

Listing 6.6 **The Action Mapping for the edit author Application Function**

```
<!-- Edit author -->
    <action path="/authorEdit"
            type=" jspbook.example.articledb.AuthorEditAction"
            name="AuthorForm"
            scope="request"
            validate="true">
        <forward name="success" path="/menu.jsp"/>
    </action>
```

As a remark, the `forward` element defined previously could have been omitted if there was a general `forward` for success defined in the struts-config.xml file leading any successful action to the menu.jsp page by default.

The *ActionErrors* and *ActionError* Classes

`ActionErrors` is a container for the errors captured in the validation process of form input data when a `validate` method of a form bean is executed. This is a standard class, in the sense that it is defined by the Struts framework to be used virtually unchanged in most of the cases. It stores the errors encountered in `validate` to be processed by the `errors` tag from the Struts HTML tag library.

`ActionError` represents an error condition detected during the execution of a `validate` method. It takes an error message from the application's resources and is stored on the `ActionErrors` container through the `add` method. Multiple errors detected will be added to the `ActionErrors` container that way. Then each error condition detected can be treated individually in an application.

On Struts, the standard way to treat errors is through the `errors` tag. For more on the `errors` tag, see the section on the Struts tag libraries, later in this chapter.

The *Action* Class

The Action class is the bridge between the web application HTTP request and the correlating core business logic to be invoked. Request parameters are processed inside the context of the Action class's perform method to start the business logic process required. The Action class also gets the results from the core logic components called; it also possibly prepares ActionForm components to receive results and determine which path to follow and then to which component in the system the control must be redirected to. It selects a target from the general forward actions available or the specific forward actions available on the forwards property of the mapping that this Action is part of.

This behavior can be summarized as shown in the following steps:

1. The perform method is called.

2. Request parameters available on an ActionForm instance are processed. The component is an argument of the perform method. It must be noted that these were already validated when the perform method was called. The goal here is to translate these parameters into the related core business logic components.

3. The core business logic entry point is called. It can be a method on a distributed object, an rpc call, or a SOAP call—whatever. This must invoke some process and return some result, even a signal of success or failure.

4. Based on the result returned by the core business logic process invoked, the Action class determines a destination where control must be redirected. It does this by wrapping up an ActionForward instance that will be the result that the perform method returns.

5. The ActionForward is returned to the ActionServlet as a result of the perform method. This way control is redirected to the destination that the ActionForward instance encodes.

The perform method is the main method (and, ideally, should be the sole method) in the Action implementation subclass. The idea behind this design is simple but powerful: The perform method constitutes a standard way for the ActionServlet to call variable behavior encapsulated behind the Action class.

As you have seen already, the behavior of the ActionServlet is mostly standard and not subject to change. The process method in the ActionServlet is responsible for the following:

- Wrapping up the proper ActionMapping for the incoming request
- Wrapping up ActionForm bean
- Eventually calling the validate method to check the submitted request parameters
- Calling the perform method of the action mapped to the request

- Getting the resulting `ActionForward` object returned by the action's `perform` method

- Redirecting control to the URI encapsulated by that `ActionForward`

Any kind of core business logic can and will be encapsulated this way, behind the `perform` method. So, different requests trigger distinct core logic processes, all though a standard call to this method.

It is also important to note that the `Action` class must be designed in a thread-safe manner. This is because there's only a single instance of an `Action` class per action element in the action-mapping configuration file. All requests that arrive mapped to some `Action` class are redirected to the same instance of that class. (This way, all serial resources accesses, such as shared data structures or files, must be synchronized). Instance variables must be avoided.

Listing 6.7 presents the code for the `GetArticleListAction` action class.

Listing 6.7 **The *GetArticleListAction* Class**

```
package jspbook.example.articledb;

import java.util.*;
import javax.servlet.*;
import java.io.IOException;
import org.apache.struts.action.*;
import org.apache.struts.util.*;
import java.lang.reflect.InvocationTargetException;

// Prepares a list of articles from the db

public final class GetArticleListAction extends Action {


  public ActionForward perform(ActionMapping mapping,
                      ActionForm acForm,
                      HttpServletRequest req,
                      HttpServletResponse resp)
    throws IOException, ServletException {

    Locale locale = getLocale(request);
    MessageResources messages = getResources();
    HttpSession session = request.getSession();


    //Model object implemented as a Bean
    Article art = new Article();
    ArticleListForm artList = new ArticleListForm();

    //Query the Article instance and set the response
    //in the ArticleListForm
```

continues

Listing 6.7   **Continued**

```
Hashtable lst = new Hashtable();
lst = art.getArticleList(request, Action.DATA_SOURCE_KEY);
artList.setList(lst);


  // Set the bean in the appropriate scope
  if (mapping.getScope().equals("request"))
    request.setAttribute(mapping.getAttribute(), artList);
  else
    session.setAttribute(mapping.getAttribute(), artList);

  // Forward control to the article List page
  return (mapping.findForward("articleList"));

}

}
```

When the process involves data entry, it is often necessary to coordinate data preparation and data update actions. It is also necessary to prevent double submission, which sometimes is quite tricky to detect at the database level. For instance, suppose that you are setting up a process to edit client orders. These orders can have an automatic sequence on the database to provide an order number. This can make it difficult to determine from the data submitted whether an incoming order is a duplicate or whether it is a new order that clones the precedent.

To avoid resubmission problems in Struts, the `Action` class uses a transaction token that synchronizes the data-preparation action with a single submission to the data-processing action. It is the programmer's responsibility to set this token on an action and reset or remove it when finished.

The basic script for these coordinating actions works like this:

1. On the data-preparation action:

   - Retrieve or set up the data. If it is an input action, this data can come from standard tables, lookups, and so on.

   - Wrap up an `ActionForm` bean to hold the data.

   - Save a transaction token on the session. This is done with a call to the `saveToken` method.

   - Forward control to the data-entry form.

2. On the data-processing action:

   - Verify whether this action was cancelled. If so, clean up the session and redirect control to the appropriate target.

- Validate the transaction token. If it is valid, remove it from the session with a call to the `resetToken` method. If not, set up an `ActionError` to hold an out-of-sequence error.

- Process the core business logic involved.

- If there were errors, set up a new transaction token and redirect control to the input form, represented by the `input` property on the current mapping.

- If no errors were detected, redirect control to the appropriate component (usually some kind of menu).

The *ActionForward* Class

This class encapsulates the URI that the `ActionServlet` must redirect control to, either by using a `RequestDispatcher forward` method or by using a response `sendRedirect` method. If the URI is to be redirected with a call to `forward`, it will be relative to the context root. If it is to be redirected with a call to `sendRedirect`, it will be an absolute address.

The `ActionForward` class presents three properties: `name`, `path`, and `redirect`. The `name` property is used to identify this instance when a mapping performs a lookup with its `findForward` method or when it returns the whole `forwards` names with `findForwards`. Path holds the URI that this `ActionForward` encapsulates. `redirect` is a Boolean value that holds true if the URI must be redirected with `sendRedirect`.

Listing 6.9 illustrates the use of `ActionForward` inside the `perform` method of an `Action` class.

Listing 6.9 **The *GetArticleListAction* Class**

```
    // Forward control to some page depending on the state of
    // the system

if (action.equals("EDIT_AUTHOR"))
    return (mapping.findForward("edAuth"));
else if (action.equals("EDIT_ARTICLE"))
    return (mapping.findForward("edArt"));
else if (action.equals("REGISTER_USER"))
{
    // Redirect to a central server with sendRedirect
    ActionForward ff = new
ActionForward("http://authserver:8080/authControl",true);
    return (ff);
}
```

In the first two options, the `ActionForward` is retrieved from the mapping information through the `ActionMapping findForward` method. In Listing 6.9, the application must redirect the request directly to an external application with `sendRedirect`, so it uses the `ActionForward(uri,redirect)` constructor to signal that the URI must be reached with a `sendRedirect` call.

Struts JSP Pages

A web application designed under the Struts framework is supposed to have the View component based on JSP pages that makes use of the rich Struts tag libraries. This way the application can benefit from the framework's facilities, such as internationalization, consistent labelling, and error treatment.

Although this is the preferred way, the framework does not mandate the use of tag libraries. Provided that the programmer supplies the code necessary to access the `ActionForm` beans and possibly also the `ActionError` instances for error treatment, standard JSP pages can be used with no harm.

The Action Mappings Configuration File

The main control file in the Struts framework is the struts-config.xml XML file, where action mappings are specified. This file's structure is described by the struts-config DTD file. The top-level element is struts-config. Basically, it consists of the following elements:

- **data-sources**—A set of data-source elements, describing parameters needed to instantiate JDBC 2.0 Standard Extension DataSource objects

- **form-beans**—A set of form-bean elements that describe the form beans that this application uses

- **global-forwards**—A set of forward elements describing general available forward URIs

- **action-mappings**—A set of action elements describing a request-to-action mapping

Each of the subelements listed is described in the next sections.

Data Sources and the *data-source* Element

A data-source element describes the parameters necessary to configure a JDBC 2.0 Standard Extension DataSource. These parameters are defined as attributes of the `data-source` element:

- **autoCommit**—The default auto-commit state to be set when creating a new connection to the database.

- **description**—A description for this data source.

- **driverClass**—The complete Java class name of the JDBC driver to be used. This is a required attribute.

- **key**—Once created, this DataSource will be stored under an attribute on the application servlet context. This attribute holds the name to be used for the context's attribute. The default attribute name is specified by the `Action.DATA_SOURCE_KEY` String.

- **loginTimeout**—The maximum number of seconds to wait for a connection to be created or returned.

- **maxCount**—The maximum number of connections to be created.

- **minCount**—The minimum number of connections to be created.

- **password**—The database password to use when connecting. This is a required attribute.

- **readOnly**—The default read-only state for newly created connections.

- **url**—The JDBC URL to use when connecting. This is a required attribute.

- **user**—The database username to use when connecting. This is a required attribute.

The code fragment in Listing 6.10 describes a data-sources element with two DataSources defined.

Listing 6.10 **Defining DataSources in the *data-sources* Element**

```
<data-sources>
  <data-source
     autoCommit="false"
    description="First Database Config"
    driverClass=" org.gjt.mm.mysql.Driver"
       maxCount="4"
       minCount="2"
       password="admin"
            url="jdbc:mysql://localhost/ARTICLEDB"
            user="admin"
  />
  <data-source
     autoCommit="false"
    description="Second Database Config"
    driverClass="oracle.jdbc.driver.OracleDriver"
            key="REFDB"
       maxCount="4"
       minCount="2"
       password="admin"
            url="jdbc:oracle:thin:@localhost:1521/AUTHORDB"
            user="admin"
  />
</data-sources>
```

The code fragment in Listing 6.10 shows a configuration with two databases: a MySQL-based ARTICLEDB database and an Oracle-based AUTHORDB database. The ARTICLEDB DataSource element is stored under the default key, the default attribute name defined by Action.DATA_SOURCE_KEY. The second database DataSource will be stored under the attribute named REFDB.

Form-Bean Elements

Each form-bean element defines an `ActionForm` subclass used by the application. It has two attributes:

- **name**—Name by which this form bean will be referenced in the configuration file
- **type**—The full Java class name for this bean

Listing 6.11 presents a fragment of a form-beans element for the ArticleDB application.

Listing 6.11   **Defining the Form Beans Used in ArticleDB**

```
<form-beans>

<!-- EditArticle form bean -->
<form-bean
    name="editArticleForm"
    type="jspbook.example.EditArticleForm"
/>

<!-- EditJournal form bean -->
<form-bean
    name="editJournalForm"
    type="jspbook.example.EditJournalForm"
/>

<!-- Edit Author form bean -->
<form-bean
    name="editAuthorForm"
    type="jspbook.example.EditAuthorForm"
/>

</form-beans>
```

Global-Forwards Elements

The global-forwards elements provide a way to have URIs that are called from many points in the application to be declared without redundancy. This includes a main menu, a login page, and so on.

The `forward` element represents a global forward. It uses two attributes: `name`, which identifies this global-forward for access by the action components on the application; and `path`, which holds the URI to be redirected to when this `forward` is processed.

A global-forward is retrieved by the `ActionMapping` `findForward` method. When the `findForward` method can't find a locally defined forward with the specified name, it searches the global-forwards available and returns the one it finds.

Listing 6.12 presents a fragment of a global-forwards element for the articledb application.

Listing 6.12   **Defining Global-Forwards**

```
<global-forwards>
  <forward  name="logoff"   path="/logoff"/>
  <forward  name="logon"    path="/logon.jsp"/>
  <forward  name="nonAuth"  path="/invalidUser"/>
  <forward  name="menu"     path="/menu.jsp"/>
</global-forwards>
```

Action-Mappings

The action-mappings section of the struts-config.xml file is by far the most important one because it is the one that defines the application's workflow: This determines which request is mapped to which `Action` subclass and, from there, which possible `forwards` can be invoked, adding the global-forwards to the list. It defines which are the input forms that generated data, whether the data entered should be validated, and whether the `ActionForm` bean representing that data will be found on the session or the request scope.

The `action` element has a number of attributes defining these parameters of the mapping, and the body of the `action` element contains the set of `forwards` that can be invoked from the related `Action` class and added to the global-forwards available, if any. It also contains property initialization information for custom `ActionMapping` classes, along with a number of presentation-oriented elements—`icon`, `display-name`, and `description`, meant to support development tools. The attributes on the `action` element are `id`, `attribute`, `className`, `forward`, `include`, `input`, `name`, `parameter`, `path`, `prefix`, `scope`, `suffix`, `type`, `unknown`, and `validate`. These are the properties defined in the `ActionMapping` class, with the exception of `className`, which is optional and defines a custom `ActionMapping` class to be used in this mapping, and `id`, which identifies this mapping.

The body of the `mapping` element contains the `forwards` that can be used by the `Action` class after processing. These are `forward` elements, the same kind as defined in the global-forwards element.

The `set-property` element is used when you subclass the `ActionMapping` class and add custom properties to it. Using `set-property` elements, you can still benefit from the way the struts-config.xml file gets loaded into `ActionMapping` instances by the Digester utility. With this element, you can specify initial values for the specific properties on your `ActionMapping` subclasses without having to alter the struts-config DTD for every `ActionMapping` customization implemented.

Listing 6.13 shows a fragment of a struts-config.xml action-mappings element, with several actions of the ArticleDB application configured. A complete example is provided in Chapter 8, "Anatomy of a Struts Application."

Listing 6.13   **Action-Mappings on the struts-config.xml File**

```
<action-mappings>

    <!-- The basic query in the application -->
    <action     path="/getArticleList"
type="jspbook.example.GetArticleListAction"
            name="articleListForm"
          scope="request"
       validate="false">
      <forward name="success" path="/articleList.jsp"/>
    </action>

    <!-- Detail info on a certain article -->
    <action     path="/getArticleDetail"
            type="jspbook.example.articleDB.GetArticleDetailAction"
            name="articleForm"
          scope="request"
       validate="false">
      <forward name="success" path="/articleDetail.jsp"/>
    </action>

    <!-- Centralized logon -->
    <action     path="/logon"
            type="jspbook.example.authcontrol.LogonAction"
            name="logonForm"
          scope="request"
          input="/logon.jsp"
        className="jspbook.example.authcontrol.SecSensitiveMapping"
       validate="true">
      <forward name="success" path="/menu.jsp"/>
      <set-property name="secExtraInfo" value="public level"/>
      <set-property name="authContext" value="articleDB"/>
    </action>

    ...

</action-mappings>
```

The first action in Listing 6.13 maps the /getArticleList request path with the GetArticleListAction class, which needs an ArticleListForm bean. In case of success, control will be redirected to the articleList.jsp page. This form bean won't be validated.

The second action shows more detailed information on a specific article. Again, there is the `ArticleForm` bean to hold information; it won't be validated, and, in case of success, articleDetail.jsp is called.

The third mapping presents a centralized logon facility, something that is pretty common in many organizations. Everything is different here. There is an outsider `LogonAction` class coming from the `authControl` package, together with `SecSensitiveMapping`, which has two extra attributes. These are initialized by `set-property` elements inside the action mapping. The `className` attribute declares the specific `ActionMapping` used in this example.

Internal or Administrative Actions

Besides the application's specific actions, Struts itself uses actions to execute some internal tasks, such as `AddMapping`, `AddForward`, and `RemoveFormBean`. These are not meant to be modified.

Resource Management

One strength of Struts is the possibility to have internationalization, error treatment, and standard labelling with centralized resource administration. There are two levels of resource bundles on Struts: system and application resources. Application resources are declared in a properties file named ApplicationResources.properties, which must be the WEB-INF directory of your application.

Struts Tag Libraries

Struts design is based on the premise that JavaBeans will represent the state of whatever application is built with it. The `ActionForm` beans constitute the standard way of representing that state. They capture information from an input form and make that information available to business process components inside the `Action` classes, and vice versa, making information resulting from the business components processing available to the presentation JSPs.

The Struts-Bean tag library provides facilities to create beans and `String` constants in a scope, access bean properties, copy beans and bean properties from scope to scope, render internationalized messages from the application resource bundles, output bean properties, access Struts internal objects, and access headers, parameters, and cookies.

The bean library won't provide a presentation infrastructure, however. The Struts-HTML tag library provides the form bean–aware HTML controls that render form beans and present it in text, as well as select check boxes, text areas, passwords, and other components. It also provides the `errors` tag that renders `ActionError` messages and is the key tag in the error-treatment mechanism.

Tags on the Struts-Logic tag library are of four different kinds:

- Comparison tags constitute a kind of expression language that allows you to compare bean properties, cookies, script variables, parameters and headers to a value.

- The `String`-matching tags allow you to match a substring with a given `String`.

- Tags redirect control to another resource either through `forward` or through `sendRedirect`.

- The `iterate` tag allows iteration over collections.

The Struts-Template tags make a JSP template mechanism created for sharing common structures with pages that share a common design. It provides a versatile alternative to the recurrent use of page includes.

Besides these four libraries, virtually any tag library can be used with Struts. A useful example is the Taglibs DBTags library. It allows access to JDBC objects from JSP tags and is detailed in Chapter 9, "The Jakarta Taglibs Project." Many tags also are being written to deal with disconnected Rowsets, `Hashmaps`, and so on.

The Struts tag libraries are detailed in Chapter 7, "Struts Tag Libraries."

Tools and Utilities

Apart from the intrinsic components that make Struts, there are tools and components designed as accessories to aid in the administrative tasks in the system. The most evident and, at the same time, least noted of these is Digester. It aids the `ActionServlet` in loading and processing the struts-config.xml and, by extension, serves as the real core of any Struts application.

Struts Digester Tool

Within the context of a Struts application, the Digester tool is responsible for parsing the struts-config.xml file and creating the several objects that the configuration file describes (actions, action-mappings, global-forwards, and data sources) to make them available to the `ActionServlet`. It is not a Struts-specific tool. It was designed to provide a generalized way to parse an XML file and generate both objects based on that file and a set of rules describing how the objects and the XML file are related. Digester is implemented by the `org.apache.struts.digester.Digester` class and can be used in a context outside Struts.

This approach resembles the approach of the Simple API for XML (SAX API), in which a set of events that Digester retrieves from the provided rules is triggered by the XML elements present in the file. You will find Digester very simple to use, mainly in the way XML elements are described in the rules.

To use Digester in an application, do the following:

1. Create a new instance of the `org.apache.struts.digester.Digester` class. Digester is not thread-safe, so it is important to have a new instance for each thread that you intend to use it.

2. Set the configuration properties. These drive the parsing process.

3. Load in the Digester stack the objects that will have properties initialized by the data parsed from the XML file.

4. Register the rules to be applied during the parsing. These rules will identify the desired information from the file.

5. Call the `parse` method.

More information on Digester can be found in the "Struts Digester User's Guide," which is part of the Struts documentation.

Summary

You learned in this chapter the basic structure of the Jakarta Struts framework, an MVC Model 2 framework for developing web applications.

You also saw the major components of Struts:

- **The `ActionServlet`**—This is the main controller in the Struts framework.

- **The `ActionMapping` class**—This class represents a mapping between an HTTP request and some action that processes that request. In the `ActionMapping` class, attributes are used to represent all the information available about a certain mapping. The `ActionMapping` can be subclassed when extra properties must be supplied. In that case, the subclass must implement the corresponding getter and setter methods for the additional properties. This subclass can be linked locally to a specific mapping with the `className` element, or it can be linked globally with the `type` attribute of the `ActionServlet` configuration information on your application's web.xml.

- **The `ActionForm` class**—This abstract class's subclasses represent the state of the web application. Data is moved from the presentation JSPs to the request processors and vice versa, preferably using `ActionForm` subclasses.

- **The `Action` class**—This abstract class's subclasses are the request processors of your application. They are the bridge between a specific request and the core business logic that the request is ultimately invoking.

- **The `ActionForward` class**—The `ActionForward` class encapsulates a URI to which control will be redirected by either a call to the `RequestDispatcher.forward` method or a call to the `HttpServletResponse.sendRedirect` method, respectively.

- **The ActionError class**—This class encapsulates a certain error message detected either during the validation process in the ActionForm bean or during the execution of the perform method of the Action class.

Apart from these components, the Struts framework counts a number of resources where the application is defined: application resources, the struts-config.xml file, and the Struts tag libraries. Another core part of the framework is the Digester utility, responsible for parsing the configuration file. Digester is an independent tool in Struts and can be used independently of the framework.

7

Struts Tag Libraries

This chapter presents the Struts tag libraries, which are part of the Jakarta Struts framework. These tag libraries provide a counterpart at the view side of the framework for the mechanisms of error treatment, internationalization, and state maintenance implemented with beans and classes in the control side of Struts. Some of the tags in these libraries will provide a good example of how a tag integrates with inner components and beans to create part of some mechanism in an application.

The Struts tag libraries provide the Struts application designer a flexible way to do the following:

- Access the application and framework objects under several scopes (session, context, request, or page)

- Render those objects to the output, handling errors detected during the validation and information-processing phases

- Use the internationalization capabilities that the framework was built with

- Create page templates to benefit from reusable design with minimum effort and avoid the use of scriptlets to keep the page as clean as possible

Using the Struts tag libraries is not mandatory. However, it renders the application pages cleaner because it is not necessary to provide any extra code to access the objects that Struts will use, such as `ActionForm` beans, the application resource bundles, and so on. It's not even necessary to provide code for the inner objects that represent the application's logic; there are tags for that as well. Of course, the application designer can decide to abandon the use of the standard `ActionForm` beans in benefit from another representation, such as CachedRowSets, and then it will be necessary to also provide support for the JSP pages to deal with that representation.

The idea behind the Struts tag libraries is that the fewer scriptlets you use on a JSP, the better. You learned about the reasons for this in Chapter 5, "Design Considerations." Using scriptlet code makes JSP much more difficult to understand, which harms the separation of roles, thus making the page designer go deep into Java programming. Sometimes this involves bringing code from other levels in the application into the presentation level, which further detracts from the maintainability of the page. Using tag libraries, this code remains hidden from the page designer and is encapsulated for standard use.

Four libraries exist in the Struts framework: struts-bean, struts-html, struts-logic, and struts-template. The struts-bean library contains tags related to access and exposure of beans and properties and other objects in the context of an application. The struts-html library contains tags for rendering the application's data into HTML controls either for input or for output. The struts-logic library provides tags that implement logic operations over the bean properties and script variables, redirection of page control, and an `iterate` tag. The struts-template tag library provides a template mechanism to allow the reuse of certain design decisions over the application JSPs.

To provide backward compatibility with the previous versions of the framework, the struts-form library is still packed in. As of version 1.0 beta versions, this library was deprecated in benefit of struts-html.

You will gain a deeper understanding of each of these libraries, as well as how some of these tags were built, as you read the next sections.

The Struts-Bean Tag Library

The Struts framework is based on the assumption that the state of the application is represented by a set of `ActionForm` beans. The struts-bean tag library was designed to provide access and expose the following:

- **The contents of beans stored in a given scope**—The `define` tag is used to perform a number of operations on beans and bean properties.
- **Cookies**—The `cookie` tag provides access to information stored in cookies.
- **HTTP request header**—Access to HTTP request header content is provided by the `header` tag.
- **Page-context information**—The `page` tag provides access to page-context information and attributes.
- **Request parameters**—The `parameter` tag provides access to the contents of request parameters.

- **Web-application resources**—The `include` tag provides access to resources from a URI.

- **Intra-application requests**—It is possible to capture the contents of a request to the application and make it available as a bean in a given scope with the `include` tag.

- **Information on collections and arrays**—The size of collections and arrays is given by the `size` tag.

- **Struts internal objects information**—The `struts` tag enables you to expose some of the Struts configuration objects.

The tags in the struts-bean tag library share attributes from a common set, either to define a bean or to access one that was previously defined either by the application logic or by the local page logic in an enclosing tag. These shared attributes are listed here:

- **id**—Names the scripting variable containing a bean to be created as a result of the processing of this tag. It also defines the key to look up the bean in a scope, defined by the `scope` attribute, under which the bean will be stored.

- **name**—Holds the lookup value used to access a bean created in a scope or as a script variable. If no scope is defined, the bean will be looked up in the standard order: page, request, session, and context.

- **property**—Names a property of a bean identified by name and possibly scope. As shown in Chapter 6, "The Jakarta Struts Project," bean properties under Struts may be nested or indexed, or any combination of the two. The `property` attribute is used to access these nested and indexed properties through the `PropertyUtils` class.

- **scope**—Defines the scope under which a bean will be stored or looked up.

These attributes are used in a number of ways. They are not exclusively used this way by struts-bean tags; tags in other struts libraries also can access beans this way. In fact, these patterns are an elaboration of the most basic `id/name` pattern that you saw in Chapter 3, "Writing Custom Tags." Listing 7.1 presents some of the common design patterns that these attributes form, and the discussion that follows clarifies them further.

Listing 7.1 **Design Patterns Defined by the Shared Attributes**

```
<bean:someTag id="key1">
  <bean:anotherTagA name="key1" property="prop1"/>
  <bean:anotherTagA name="key1" property="prop2"/>
  <bean:anotherTagB name="key1"/>
</bean:someTag>

<bean:someTag id="key1" scope="someScope">
```

continues

Listing 7.1 **Continued**

```
  <bean:anotherTagC name="key1" property="prop1" scope="someScope"/>
  <bean:anotherTagD name="key1" scope="someScope">
</bean:someTag>

<bean:someTag id="key1" scope="someScope"/>
...
<bean:anotherTagE name="key1" scope="someScope"/>

<jsp:useBean id="key2" type="some.package.SomeType"/>
...
<jsp:getProperty name="key2" property="someProp"/>
<bean:someTag name="key2"/>
```

In the first example set in Listing 7.1, a tag (`someTag`) in the struts-bean library will generate a bean with a key "`key1`". This is placed in the page context by default and is accessed by two tags: `anotherTagA` accesses properties in the bean, while the `anotherTagB` tag accesses the bean itself. This is a typical producer-consumer design, as you saw in Chapter 4, "Cooperating Tags and Validation."

In the second set, the bean is placed in a scope. Again, `anotherTagC` accesses a property of the stored bean, while `anotherTagD` accesses the bean itself. The third example presents the same pattern, but outside the producer tag's body.

In the fourth example, a standard tag needs to be used with the bean. In this case, for tags outside the Struts tag libraries, it is necessary to define the bean with the `jsp:useBean` tag before referring to the bean in those tags. The `define` tag is not a replacement for the `jsp:useBean` standard action after all.

To declare the struts-bean library in a page, you use the `taglib` directive. Because the deployment of a Struts application requires the deployment of the framework class files and configuration files, the TLD most often is available locally:

```
<%@ taglib uri="/WEB-INF/struts-bean.tld" prefix="bean" %>
```

Table 7.1 describes the tags in the struts-bean tag library.

Table 7.1 **The Struts–Bean Tag Library Tags**

Tag	Description
cookie	Accesses the value of a request cookie and exposes it in a script variable. If the `multiple` attribute contains a value, all matching values are retrieved as a `Cookie[]`. If the `multiple` attribute contains no value, the first value of the cookie is returned in a cookie. The attributes of this tag are as follows:

- **id**—The id attribute was defined previously in the discussion preceding Listing 7.1.

- **multiple**—Any value of this attribute is used to match the values of the selected cookie. The matching values are returned in a `Cookie[]`. If `multiple` is not specified, the first value of the selected cookie is returned.

- **name**—This attribute contains the name of the cookie to look up.

- **value**—If no cookie is found under the given name and `multiple`, this value is returned by default.

define   Acts as a key tag on the struts-bean tag library. It is used to create a bean reference to a bean in a scope, copy beans and bean properties, and define `String` constants. Beans created or referenced by this tag are completely interoperable with beans created or referenced by the `jsp:useBean` standard JSP action.

The `define` tag supports some features not present on the `jsp:useBean` action:

- Creates or replaces a bean under the given identifier unconditionally
- Creates a bean using a distinct bean's property getter as source.
- Creates a bean from a literal `String`.
- Doesn't support nested content that is executed only if the bean is created.

The attributes on the `define` tag are as follows:

- **id, name, property, and scope**—These attributes were defined previously in the discussion preceding Listing 7.1.
- **toScope**—This attribute specifies the scope where the bean created will be stored. If this is not specified, the bean will be created on the page scope.
- **type**—This attribute gives the fully qualified Java class name of the bean identified by the `id` attribute. When creating a `String` constant through the `value` attribute, the type is `java.lang.String` by default. Otherwise, it is `java.lang.Object`.
- **value**—This attribute gives the `String` value to use when creating a `String` constant.

header   Accesses the value of a request header and exposes it in a `String` script variable. If the `multiple` attribute contains a value, all matching values are retrieved as a `String[]`. The attributes of this tag are as follows:

- **id**—The id attribute was defined previously.
- **multiple**—Any value of this attribute is used to match the values of the selected header. The matching values are returned in a `String[]` through a call to `HttpServletRequest.getHeaders()`. If `multiple` is not specified, the first value of the selected header is returned.
- **name**—This attribute contains the name of the header to look up.
- **value**—If no header is found under the given name and `multiple`, this value is returned by default.

include   Is an equivalent to `jsp:include`. It takes a request URL and exposes the resulting response data available as a `String`. This tag has the following attributes:

- **id**—The id attribute was defined previously.
- **forward**—This attribute contains the name of an `ActionForward` to be looked up and which URI will be included.
- **page**—This gives the context-relative URI of a resource to include.
- **href**—This attribute specifies the absolute URL, including the protocol identifier, of the resource to be included.

continues

Table 7.1 **Continued**

Tag	Description
	▪ **anchor**—This is an HTML anchor to be added to the generated hyperlink.
	▪ **transaction**—If the current transaction token is to be included in the URL generated by this tag, set this attribute to true. This is quite useful when another transaction will complement the processing of this one and must be taken as part of the same application transaction, to avoid accidental resubmission of any data.
	Only one among the forward, page, or href tags can be specified.
	The deprecated name attribute has been replaced by the page attribute.
	In forward and page, if the resource is part of the session, the session identifier JSESSIONID will be attached.
	Because href can point to an external URL, the session identifier is not attached.
message	Acts as another key tag in the struts-bean tag library. The message tag renders an internationalized String from the application resource bundles to the out stream, given a lookup key. The String rendered can have up to five parametric replacements, numbered from 0 to 4. A parametric replacement is marked in the resource String like "{0}" for the first replacement, "{1}" for the second, and so on. The message tag has the following attributes:
	▪ **arg0**, **arg1**, **arg2**, **arg3**, and **arg4**—Contain Strings that will be used as parametric replacements inside the String rendered by the tag. These values can be static or can be evaluated at runtime, and all are optional.
	▪ **bundle**—Gives the name of a context scope bean with a MessageResources other than specified by the default Action.MESSAGES_KEY to be used.
	▪ **key**—Specifies the key to be used to look up the desired String.
	▪ **locale**—Is specified if a locale other than the default Action.LOCALE_KEY must be used.
page	Exposes a page-context property as a bean. This tag has two attributes:
	▪ **id**—The id attribute was defined previously.
	▪ **property**—This attribute gives the page-context property to expose. The valid properties for this tag to expose are application, config, request, response, and session.
parameter	Accesses the value of a request parameter and exposes it in a String script variable. If the multiple attribute contains a value, all matching values are retrieved as a String[]. The attributes of this tag are as follows:
	▪ **id**—The id attribute was defined previously.
	▪ **multiple**—Any value of this attribute is used to match the values of the selected parameter. The matching values are returned in a String[] through a call to HttpServletRequest.getParameterValues(). If multiple is not specified, the first value of the selected parameter is returned.
	▪ **name**—This attribute contains the name of the parameter to look up.

- **value**—If no such parameter is found under the given name and multiple, this value will be returned by default.

resource Retrieves a web-application resource and makes it available as either a String or an InputStream. The attributes of the resource tag are as follows:

- **id**—The id attribute was defined previously.

- **input**—If this attribute is specified, the resource will be available as an InputStream; if not, it will be available as a String.

- **name**—This is the context-relative name of the web application resource desired, including the /.

size Counts the elements available in any collection, map, or array, and returns the result as an integer. The following attributes are used to specify the collection, array, or map to count:

- **id**, **name**, **property**, and **scope**—These attributes were defined previously.

- **collection**—This is a JSP expression that evaluates to a collection that will be counted.

One of the following combinations can be used to specify the collection to count: using the collection attribute, referring to a bean with the name attribute, or referring to a bean property specified by the name and property attributes. If it's not in the default scope, the scope attribute tells where to look up the bean.

struts Exposes control objects of the framework. These attributes specify the control object to expose:

- **id**—The id attribute was defined previously.

- **formBean**—This attribute gives the name of an ActionForm bean to retrieve.

- **forward**—This attribute gives the name of an ActionForward instance to retrieve.

- **mapping**—This is the name of an ActionMapping instance to retrieve.

Only one of formBean, forward, or mapping can be specified.

write Renders a bean property to the out stream. If a property editor is associated with the bean, the property will be retrieved with the getAsText method. Otherwise, the toString method will be used. The attributes present in the write tag are as follows:

- **name**, **property**, and **scope**—These attributes were defined previously in the discussion, preceding Listing 7.1.

- **filter**—If true, the rendered String will be filtered to avoid outputting characters sensitive in HTML. The default is true.

- **ignore**—If true and the bean specified by name is not found, this outputs nothing. Otherwise, an exception is thrown. The default is false.

The JSP page code in Listing 7.2 shows the use of the struts-bean library. The page presents user data extracted from a user handler.

Listing 7.2 **Using the Struts-Bean Tag Library**

```
<%@ page import="jspbook.example.authcontrol.UserHandler" %>
<%@ taglib uri="/WEB-INF/struts-bean.tld" prefix="bean" %>

<html>
<body>
<h1> <bean:message key="user.profile.title"/></h1>

<table border="1" width="100%">
<tr>
 <td><bean:message key="user.idnumber"/></td>
 <td>
   <bean:write name="userhnd" scope="session" property="idNum"/>
 </td>
</tr>
<tr>
 <td><bean:message key="user.name"/></td>
 <td>
   <bean:write name="userhnd" scope="session" property="name"/>
 </td>
</tr>
<tr>
 <td><bean:message key="user.surname"/></td>
 <td>
   <bean:write name="userhnd" scope="session" property="surname"/>
 </td>
</tr>
<tr>
 <td><bean:message key="user.division"/></td>
 <td>
   <bean:write name="userhnd" scope="session" property="division"/>
 </td>
</tr>
<tr>
 <td><bean:message key="user.extension"/></td>
 <td>
   <bean:write name="userhnd" scope="session" property="extension"/>
 </td>
</tr>
</table>

</body>
</html>
```

Listing 7.2 uses the `bean:message` and `bean:write` tags to expose user information in a table.

Understanding the *message* Tag

The struts-bean `message` tag is responsible for rendering internationalized strings in the scope of a Struts application. To do it, the tag accesses the application resource bundles and retrieves the desired string based on a key, and possibly a bundle and locale specifications. Apart from accessing resource bundles, being the sole internationalization tag in the framework renders this tag worthy of having a closer look. Listing 7.3 shows the source code for the `message` tag.

Listing 7.3 **The *message* Tag Source Code**

```
package org.apache.struts.taglib.bean;


import java.io.IOException;
import java.util.Locale;
import javax.servlet.jsp.JspException;
import javax.servlet.jsp.JspWriter;
import javax.servlet.jsp.PageContext;
import javax.servlet.jsp.tagext.TagSupport;
import org.apache.struts.action.Action;
import org.apache.struts.util.MessageResources;
import org.apache.struts.util.RequestUtils;
import org.apache.struts.util.ResponseUtils;


/**
 * Custom tag that retrieves an internationalized messages string (with
 * optional parametric replacement) from the <code>ActionResources</code>
 * object stored as a context attribute by our associated
 * <code>ActionServlet</code> implementation.
 *
 * @author Craig R. McClanahan
 * @version $Revision: 1.4 $ $Date: 2001/02/20 01:48:45 $
 */

public class MessageTag extends TagSupport {


    // -------------------------------------------------------- Properties


    /**
     * The first optional argument.
     */
    protected String arg0 = null;

    public String getArg0() {
      return (this.arg0);
    }
```

continues

Listing 7.3 **Continued**

```java
  public void setArg0(String arg0) {
    this.arg0 = arg0;
  }


  /**
   * The second optional argument.
   */
  protected String arg1 = null;

  public String getArg1() {
    return (this.arg1);
  }

  public void setArg1(String arg1) {
    this.arg1 = arg1;
  }


  /**
   * The third optional argument.
   */
  protected String arg2 = null;

  public String getArg2() {
    return (this.arg2);
  }

  public void setArg2(String arg2) {
    this.arg2 = arg2;
  }


  /**
   * The fourth optional argument.
   */
  protected String arg3 = null;

  public String getArg3() {
    return (this.arg3);
  }

  public void setArg3(String arg3) {
    this.arg3 = arg3;
  }


  /**
```

```
 * The fifth optional argument.
 */
protected String arg4 = null;

public String getArg4() {
  return (this.arg4);
}

public void setArg4(String arg4) {
  this.arg4 = arg4;
}


/**
 * The servlet context attribute key for our resources.
 */
protected String bundle = Action.MESSAGES_KEY;

public String getBundle() {
  return (this.bundle);
}

public void setBundle(String bundle) {
  this.bundle = bundle;
}


/**
 * The default Locale for our server.
 */
protected static final Locale defaultLocale = Locale.getDefault();


/**
 * The message key of the message to be retrieved.
 */
protected String key = null;

public String getKey() {
  return (this.key);
}

public void setKey(String key) {
  this.key = key;
}


/**
 * The session scope key under which our Locale is stored.
 */
```

continues

Listing 7.3 **Continued**

```java
protected String localeKey = Action.LOCALE_KEY;

public String getLocale() {
  return (this.localeKey);
}

public void setLocale(String localeKey) {
  this.localeKey = localeKey;
}


/**
 * The message resources for this package.
 */
protected static MessageResources messages =
  MessageResources.getMessageResources
  ("org.apache.struts.taglib.bean.LocalStrings");


// -------------------------------------------------------- Public Methods


/**
 * Process the start tag.
 *
 * @exception JspException if a JSP exception has occurred
 */
public int doStartTag() throws JspException {

  // Construct the optional arguments array we will be using
  Object args[] = new Object[5];
  args[0] = arg0;
  args[1] = arg1;
  args[2] = arg2;
  args[3] = arg3;
  args[4] = arg4;

  // Retrieve the message string we are looking for
  String message = RequestUtils.message(pageContext, this.bundle,
                                         this.localeKey, this.key, args);
  if (message == null) {
      JspException e = new JspException
        (messages.getMessage("message.message", key));
        RequestUtils.saveException(pageContext, e);
        throw e;
    }

  // Print the retrieved message to our output writer
    ResponseUtils.write(pageContext, message);
```

```
            // Continue processing this page
            return (SKIP_BODY);

        }


        /**
         * Release any acquired resources.
         */
        public void release() {

            super.release();
            arg0 = null;
            arg1 = null;
            arg2 = null;
            arg3 = null;
            arg4 = null;
            bundle = Action.MESSAGES_KEY;
            key = null;
            localeKey = Action.LOCALE_KEY;

        }

    }
```

The first part of the code deals with the parametric replacement attributes `arg0` to `arg4`. The next is the resource bundle attribute. Note how it is initialized to the standard `Action.MESSAGES_KEY` by default. This way, if no bundle attribute is found, no call to `setBundle` is made; thus, the default `Action.MESSAGES_KEY` gets used and retrieved as needed by `getBundle`. The very same reasoning applies to the locale attribute and the `Action.LOCALE_KEY` standard key. The key property is mandatory and is initialized to null to avoid being left blank.

The last property being initialized is a protected `MessageResources` property, which contains error messages to be used by this tag's processing in case of errors.

The `doStartTag` method first initializes an array of objects with the parametric replacement arguments specified in the `argX` attributes. Then the method retrieves the message from the bundle specified by the bundle, locale, and key specified. The parametric replacement attribute array is passed, and substitution is made, returning the final string of the message. This is done by the `RequestUtils` utilitarian class `message` method.

After retrieving the message, it is written in the out stream by the `ResponseUtils` utilitarian class `write` method. The tag signals the body to be skipped, and the page evaluation continues.

The `release` method then reinitializes all the `argX` and key attributes to null, and it reinitializes the bundle and locale attributes to their default values. This way, the next message tag can be processed.

The Struts-Html Tag Library

The struts-html tag library is designed to allow the page designer to write HTML presentation pages that are aware of the bean infrastructure that makes the Struts framework. These tags also share a number of common attributes for dealing with Struts bean infrastructure, JavaScript event handlers, easy page navigation, and CSS style sheets.

The attributes related to the bean infrastructure are listed here:

- **name**—The name of the attribute containing the ActionForm bean whose property will render in this control's content. If not specified, the default bean defined by the html:form tag is used.

- **property**—The name of the request parameter that will hold this field's value when the form is submitted. This request parameter will be retrieved by the ActionServlet to fulfill the ActionForm bean that will be passed to the action mapped to the request, closing the cycle of processing for this field.

- **value**—Value of the label to be used with the control this field renders to—for instance, the label of a button. This value will be submitted as the value of the field. The default value is Click.

Apart from the name, property, and value attributes, and because the tags in the struts-html tag library will mostly render to HTML controls in the browser, a number of JavaScript event handlers also are implemented to allow the page designer to specify JavaScript event handlers to the generated HTML controls. These are onblur, onchange, onclick, ondblclick, onfocus, onkeydown, onkeypress, onkeyup, onmousedown, onmousemove, onmouseout, onmouseover, and onmouseup. The onreset and onsubmit event handlers are specific for the html:form tag. Check in the JavaScript documentation for a definition of these event handlers.

The HTML navigation attributes help to move the focus to the field:

- **accesskey**—This is a keyboard character used to move the focus immediately to the field.

- **tabindex**—This is the tab order for this field. This must be a positive integer and must be in ascending order.

- **disabled**—If this is true, the rendered button will show disabled.

The CSS-related attributes deal with presentation styles and style sheets:

- **style**—A CSS style to be applied to this field
- **styleClass**—A CSS style sheet class to be applied to this field
- **styleId**—An identifier to be assigned to this field

The tags available in this library are listed in Table 7.2.

Table 7.2 **The Struts-Html Tag Library Tags**

Tag	Description
base	Renders to an HTML BASE tag. The sole target attribute renders to the target window defined by the HTML BASE. This tag is used inside the page header and provides a base address to resolve relative addresses in links on the page.
button	To be used inside a `html:form` tag. This tag renders to an HTML `<input>` tag with type `button`.
cancel	To be used inside an `html:form` tag. This tag renders to an HTML `<input>` tag with type `submit`. This control causes the `ActionServlet` to bypass the validate method on the `ActionForm`. The attribute specific of this control is:
	▪ **property**—This attribute must be left to the default value; otherwise, the automatic cancel detection will fail and you will have to provide a mechanism to detect a cancel.
checkbox	To be used inside a `html:form` tag. This tag renders to an HTML `<input>` tag with type `checkbox`. This control must be linked to a Boolean property, and it must be set to `false` in the `ActionForm` `reset` method to be evaluated correctly.
errors	Renders the error messages encapsulated in `ActionError` objects. There must be a `MessageResources` bean representing the application resources; this must be stored under the default request attribute, and the `MessageResources` must contain `error.header` and `error.footer` keys. The attributes specific to this tag are as follows:
	▪ **bundle**—The resource bundle where you find the error messages corresponding to the error keys in the `ActionErrors`.
	▪ **locale**—The locale to be used when rendering the error messages.
	▪ **name**—The name of the request scope bean containing the error messages to render. The default value is `Action.ERRORS_KEY`.
	▪ **property**—Tag that can be attached to a single field to display field-per-field error messages. To accomplish that, the `ActionError.property` property must be set to the value matching this attribute.
file	To be used inside a `html:form` tag. This tag renders to an HTML `<input>` tag with type `file select`. This control is used in multipart uploads. The attributes specific of this control are as follows:
	▪ **accept**—Comma-separated list of the file extensions accepted
	▪ **maxlength**—Maximum number of characters admitted
form	Renders to an HTML `<form>` tag. It provides a context for the execution of the form-related tags by referring to the `ActionForm` bean to be used when rendering the fields in the form. The attributes specific of this control are as follows:
	▪ **action**—This attribute is analogous to the HTML action attribute in the HTML form tag. This URL will be mapped to an action by the `ActionServlet`.

continues

Table 7.2 **Continued**

Tag	Description
	Please note that if you are using extension mapping for selecting the controller servlet, this value should be equal to the path attribute of the corresponding `<action>` element—optionally followed by the correct extension suffix.
	If you are using path mapping to select the controller servlet, this value should be exactly equal to the path attribute of the corresponding `<action>` element.
	■ **method**—This attribute defines the HTTP method to use, if `GET` or `POST`. The default method is `POST`.
	■ **enctype**—If `POST` was selected, this holds the `enctype` of the request.
	■ **focus**—This is the field name to receive the focus when this form is displayed.
	■ **name**—This attribute gives the name of the `ActionForm` bean associated with this form. If this attribute is not specified, this value is calculated from the struts-config.xml information, using the input and formbean associated with the mapping.
	■ **type**—This specifies the fully qualified Java class name of the `ActionForm` bean to be created in the scope, if none is present there.
	■ **scope**—This specifies the scope where the `ActionForm` bean is to be found or created.
hidden	To be used inside an `html:form` tag. This tag renders to an HTML `<input>` tag with type `hidden`.
html	This tag renders to an HTML `<html>` tag with language attributes extracted from the current locale. This tag presents the following attributes:
	■ **locale**—If true, causes a locale to be recorded based on the accept-language request header.
	■ **xhtml**—If true, causes an `xml:lang` element to be rendered on the `html` tag.
image	To be used inside an `html:form` tag. This tag renders to an HTML `<input>` tag with type `image`. This control is used to render image-based buttons. The attributes specific of this control are as follows:
	■ **alt**—Alternate text for the control
	■ **altKey**—`MessageResources` key to look up the alternate text for the control
	■ **border**—Width of the image border in pixels
	■ **bundle**—The resource bundle to use
	■ **locale**—The locale to use
	■ **page**—Context-relative path to the image to be used
	■ **pageKey**—`MessageResources` key to look up the context-relative path string to the image to be used
	■ **source**—Source URL to the image to be used
	■ **sourceKey**—`MessageResources` key to look up the URL to the image to be used

img	Renders to an HTML `<img>` tag. The attributes specific of this control are as follows:

- **alt**—Alternate text for the control
- **altKey**—`MessageResources` key to look up the alternate text for the control
- **border**—Width of the image border in pixels
- **bundle**—The resource bundle to use
- **locale**—The locale to use
- **page**—Context-relative path to the image to be used
- **pageKey**—`MessageResources` key to look up the context-relative path string to the image to be used
- **source**—Source URL to the image to be used
- **sourceKey**—`MessageResources` key to look up the URL to the image to be used.

link	Renders an `<a>` HTML element. Check the Struts documentation for revised information on this tag.
multibox	To be used inside an `html:form` tag. This tag renders to an HTML `<input>` tag with type `checkbox`, whose checked value is based on whether the value attribute is found on an array of values. One attribute is specific to this control:

- **value**—The value sent when the control is checked or verified against a set of values to determine the checked status

option	To be used inside an `html:select` tag. This tag renders to an HTML `<option>` tag.
options	To be used inside an `html:select` tag. This tag renders to an HTML `<option>` tag whose values are based on a collection. The attributes specific to this tag are as follows:

- **collection**—A collection of beans, each to be rendered to an option. The value of each option will have to be represented by a property called `property`, and the display text must be represented by a property called `labelProperty` on each bean.
- **name**—The name of the bean containing a collection, with the characteristics of the collection described in the `collection` attribute.
- **property**—The name of the property of the `ActionForm` bean containing a collection, with the characteristics of the collection described in the `collection` attribute.

password	To be used inside an `html:form` tag. This tag renders to an HTML `<input>` tag with type `password`. The attributes specific to this control are as follows:

- **maxlength**—Maximum number of characters admitted
- **redisplay**—A Boolean indicating whether the value must be redisplayed, if it exists

continues

Table 7.2 **Continued**

Tag	Description
radio	To be used inside an html:form tag. This tag renders to an HTML \<input\> tag with type radio.
reset	To be used inside an html:form tag. This tag renders to an HTML \<input\> tag with type reset.
rewrite	Renders an \<a\> HTML element. Check the Struts documentation for revised information on this tag.
select	To be used inside an html:form tag. This tag renders to an HTML \<select\> tag. One attribute is specific to this control: <ul><li>**multiple**—If false, the property representing this control's value must have a single value. If true, the property must have an array of any supported datatype.</li></ul>
submit	To be used inside an html:form tag. This tag renders to an HTML \<input\> tag with type submit.
text	To be used inside an html:form tag. This tag renders to an HTML \<input\> tag with type text.
textarea	To be used inside an html:form tag. This tag renders to an HTML \<textarea\> tag. The attributes specific of this control are as follows: <ul><li>**cols**—Number of columns of the rendered text area</li><li>**rows**—Number of rows of the rendered text area</li></ul>

The JSP page code in Listing 7.4 shows the use of the struts-html library. The page presents the author entry data form, using text fields and a select with an options tag based on a collection of beans that each contains a country name and ISO code.

Listing 7.4 **Using the Struts-Html Tag Library**

```
<%@ taglib uri="/WEB-INF/struts-bean.tld" prefix="bean" %>
<%@ taglib uri="/WEB-INF/struts-html.tld" prefix="html" %>

<html:html locale="true">
<head>
<title><bean:message key="author_edit.title"/></title>
<html:base/>
</head>
<body>

<html:errors/>

<html:form action="/authorEdit" focus="name">
<table border="0" width="100%">

  <tr>
    <th align="right">
      <bean:message key="author_edit.name"/>
```

```
          </th>
          <td align="left">
            <html:text property="name" size="45" maxlength="45"/>
          </td>
        </tr>

        <tr>
          <th align="right">
            <bean:message key="author_edit.surname"/>
          </th>
          <td align="left">
            <html:text property="surname" size="45" maxlength="45"/>
          </td>
        </tr>

        <tr>
          <th align="right">
            <bean:message key="author_edit.nationality"/>
          </th>
          <td align="left">
            <html:select property="nationality" multiple="false" size="5">
              <html:options collection="<%=nationsISOCodesAndNames%>"/>
            </html:select>
          </td>
        </tr>

      <tr>
          <td align="right">
            <html:submit property="submit" value="Submit"/>
          </td>
          <td align="left">
            <html:reset/>
          </td>
        </tr>

  </table>

  </html:form>

</body>
</html:html>
```

Understanding the *errors* Tag

The errors tag in the struts-html tag library renders errors captured during the validation process of the data submitted or during the processing of the mapped action. This tag's importance resides in the fact that it is the last chain in the error-treatment process inside Struts, rendering the error messages to the user. Listing 7.5 shows the source code for the errors tag.

Listing 7.5   **The *errors* Tag Source Code**

```
package org.apache.struts.taglib.html;


import java.io.IOException;
import java.util.Iterator;
import java.util.Locale;
import javax.servlet.jsp.JspException;
import javax.servlet.jsp.JspWriter;
import javax.servlet.jsp.PageContext;
import javax.servlet.jsp.tagext.TagSupport;
import org.apache.struts.action.Action;
import org.apache.struts.action.ActionError;
import org.apache.struts.action.ActionErrors;
import org.apache.struts.util.BeanUtils;
import org.apache.struts.util.ErrorMessages;
import org.apache.struts.util.MessageResources;
import org.apache.struts.util.RequestUtils;
import org.apache.struts.util.ResponseUtils;


/**
 * Custom tag that renders error messages if an appropriate request attribute
 * has been created.  The tag looks for a request attribute with a reserved
 * key, and assumes that it is either a String, a String array, containing
 * message keys to be looked up in the application's MessageResources, or
 * an object of type <code>org.apache.struts.action.ActionErrors</code>.
 * <p>
 * The following optional message keys will be utilized if corresponding
 * messages exist for them in the application resources:
 * <ul>
 * <li><b>errors.header</b> - If present, the corresponding message will be
 *     rendered prior to the individual list of error messages.
 * <li><b>errors.footer</b> - If present, the corresponding message will be
 *     rendered following the individual list of error messages.
 * <li><b>
 * </ul>
 *
 * @author Craig R. McClanahan
 * @version $Revision: 1.8 $ $Date: 2001/04/18 23:32:34 $
 */

public class ErrorsTag extends TagSupport {


    // ---------------------------------------------------------- Properties


    /**
     * The servlet context attribute key for our resources.
```

```
 */
protected String bundle = Action.MESSAGES_KEY;

public String getBundle() {
    return (this.bundle);
}

public void setBundle(String bundle) {
    this.bundle = bundle;
}


/**
 * The default locale on our server.
 */
protected static Locale defaultLocale = Locale.getDefault();


/**
 * The session attribute key for our locale.
 */
protected String locale = Action.LOCALE_KEY;

public String getLocale() {
    return (this.locale);
}

public void setLocale(String locale) {
    this.locale = locale;
}


/**
 * The message resources for this package.
 */
protected static MessageResources messages =
 MessageResources.getMessageResources(Constants.Package + ".LocalStrings");


/**
 * The request attribute key for our error messages (if any).
 */
protected String name = Action.ERROR_KEY;

public String getName() {
  return (this.name);
}

public void setName(String name) {
  this.name = name;
}
```

continues

Listing 7.5 **Continued**

```java
/**
 * The name of the property for which error messages should be returned,
 * or <code>null</code> to return all errors.
 */
protected String property = null;

public String getProperty() {
    return (this.property);
}

public void setProperty(String property) {
    this.property = property;
}



// ---------------------------------------------------- Public Methods


/**
 * Render the specified error messages if there are any.
 *
 * @exception JspException if a JSP exception has occurred
 */
public int doStartTag() throws JspException {

  // Were any error messages specified?
  ActionErrors errors = new ActionErrors();
  try {
      Object value = pageContext.getAttribute
            (name, PageContext.REQUEST_SCOPE);
      if (value == null) {
          ;
      } else if (value instanceof String) {
        errors.add(ActionErrors.GLOBAL_ERROR,
                    new ActionError((String) value));
      } else if (value instanceof String[]) {
            String keys[] = (String[]) value;
            for (int i = 0; i < keys.length; i++)
                errors.add(ActionErrors.GLOBAL_ERROR,
                        new ActionError(keys[i]));
        } else if (value instanceof ErrorMessages) {
          String keys[] = ((ErrorMessages) value).getErrors();
            if (keys == null)
                keys = new String[0];
            for (int i = 0; i < keys.length; i++)
                errors.add(ActionErrors.GLOBAL_ERROR,
```

```
                              new ActionError(keys[i]));
        } else if (value instanceof ActionErrors) {
            errors = (ActionErrors) value;
        } else {
            JspException e = new JspException
                (messages.getMessage("errorsTag.errors",
                                     value.getClass().getName()));
            RequestUtils.saveException(pageContext, e);
            throw e;
        }
    } catch (Exception e) {
        ;
}

  if (errors.empty())
    return (EVAL_BODY_INCLUDE);

  // Check for presence of header and footer message keys
  boolean headerPresent =
      RequestUtils.present(pageContext, bundle, locale, "errors.header");
  boolean footerPresent =
      RequestUtils.present(pageContext, bundle, locale, "errors.footer");

  // Render the error messages appropriately
StringBuffer results = new StringBuffer();
  String message = null;
  if (headerPresent)
      message = RequestUtils.message(pageContext, bundle,
                                     locale, "errors.header");
if (message != null) {
    results.append(message);
    results.append("\r\n");
}
  Iterator reports = null;
  if (property == null)
      reports = errors.get();
  else
      reports = errors.get(property);
  while (reports.hasNext()) {
      ActionError report = (ActionError) reports.next();
      message = RequestUtils.message(pageContext, bundle,
                                     locale, report.getKey(),
                                     report.getValues());
    if (message != null) {
      results.append(message);
      results.append("\r\n");
    }
}
  message = null;
  if (footerPresent)
      message = RequestUtils.message(pageContext, bundle,
                                     locale, "errors.footer");
```

continues

Listing 7.5   **Continued**

```
        if (message != null) {
           results.append(message);
           results.append("\r\n");
        }

        // Print the results to our output writer
          ResponseUtils.write(pageContext, results.toString());

        // Continue processing this page
        return (EVAL_BODY_INCLUDE);

    }



    /**
     * Release any acquired resources.
     */
    public void release() {

      super.release();
        bundle = Action.MESSAGES_KEY;
        locale = Action.LOCALE_KEY;
      name = Action.ERROR_KEY;
        property = null;

    }



  }
```

The `bundle`, `locale`, and `messageResources` attributes are defined in the same way
as the attributes were on the `message` tag. The `name` attribute contains the key under
which the error messages can be found. By default, that will be `Action.ERROR_KEY`.
The `property` attribute is used when the tag will present a specific message or
messages related with a specific situation. In that case, the correspondent `ActionError`
must have the `property` property with a value matching this attribute's value.

The `doStartTag` method first initializes an empty `ActionErrors` container class.
It then scans the session for the errors possibly available for rendering.

If no errors are found, nothing is added to the container. If a `String` is found, it
is wrapped in an `ActionError` instance and is added to the container. If an array of
`Strings String[]` is found, each of its elements is wrapped and added to the container,
as done previously. If an `ErrorMessages` instance is found, its messages `String[]` is
extracted and wrapped/added, as done previously. If an `ActionErrors` is found, it is
taken as the container. If anything else is found, a JSP exception is raised.

It is verified if the container contains any `ActionError`. If so, the processing continues; otherwise, the remainder of the JSP is evaluated. Then it is verified if the error's

header and footer are available in the current bundle under the current locale. If not, a JSP exception is raised. It then appends the header to a `StringBuffer` that will hold the rendered text.

Then it iterates through the `ActionErrors` container, retrieving each `ActionError`. `RequestUtils.message` is used to retrieve the corresponding error message from the bundle. The retrieved message is appended to the StringBuffer. If the `property` property has a value, only the keys under that value are retrieved.

Then it appends the error's footer to the `StringBuffer`. The buffer is rendered to the out stream using the `ResponseUtils.write` method, and it signals the JSP processor to evaluate the remainder of the page. The `release` method clears the `property` attribute, setting the other attributes to their default values.

The Struts-Logic Tag Library

The struts-logic tag library provides a number of tags to perform conditional generation of content. This includes `String` matching, iterate over a collection and generate content from the elements of the collection, and redirecting the control to another resource. This also brings application flow control to the presentation-layer JSPs.

The conditional generation tags perform value comparisons and generate output according to whether the value comparison is successful. Each of these tags takes a value and compares that value with some comparison value. These tags share a common set of attributes:

- **name**—The name of the variable to be compared with the value
- **property**—The property to be used in the comparison, from a bean specified by name
- **scope**—The scope of the bean specified by name
- **header**—The name of the request header to be compared with the value
- **parameter**—The name of the request parameter to be compared with the value
- **cookie**—The name of the cookie to be compared with the value
- **value**—The value to compare with the other attributes

Only `cookie`, `header`, `parameter`, `name`, `name+property`, and `name+property+scope` can be used at a time.

The same set of attributes is found in the `String` matching tags, along with a `location` attribute that states the matching will be performed at some position of the `String`. If the `location` attribute holds `start`, the matching will be performed at the beginning of the string. If `location` holds `end`, the matching will be performed at the end of the `String`.

The tags in the struts-logic library are shown in Table 7.3.

Table 7.3 **The Struts–Logic Tag Library Tags**

Tag	Description
equal, notEqual, greaterEqual, lessEqual, greaterThan, lessThan	The logic comparison tags all evaluate their body content according to whether the comparison reflects the logic depicted by each tag's name. For instance, the greaterEqual tag generates the content, evaluating its body, if one of the attributes-to-compare specified from the list of common attributes is greater than or equal to the value designated by the value attribute. The same reasoning applies to all these tags.
match, notMatch	Analogous to the logic comparison tags, the matching tags evaluate and include their body content in the out stream, depending on the result of a comparison of a given value with some attribute among the possible attributes. Depending on the attribute selected, different objects will be matched. The match tag includes its body to the out stream if the comparison value matches the specified object property. For instance, the cookie attribute defines the name of the cookie to be compared with the comparison value. In the match tag, if the cookie's value matches the comparison value, the body of the tag is evaluated and included in the out stream. In the notMatch tag, on the other hand, the body is included only if there is *no* match.
forward	This tag forwards control to the URI encapsulated by the ActionForward designated in the name attribute, which is the sole attribute of this tag. It uses either PageControl.forward or HttpServletResponse.sendRedirect, depending on whether the redirect attribute of the ActionForward holds true. See Chapter 6 for a description of the ActionForward class.
redirect	This tag performs an HttpServletResponse.sendRedirect to the URL represented by its attributes: <ul><li>**forward**—The name of an ActionForward instance that holds the desired URL</li><li>**href**—The literal URL</li><li>**page**—Context-relative path that the resource control will be transferred to</li><li>**name**—The name of a JSP bean containing a map with the query parameters to be used with the request generated by this tag</li><li>**paramId**—The name of a request parameter to be added to the request generated by this tag</li><li>**paramName**—The name of a String JSP bean containing the value for the request parameter designated by paramId</li><li>**paramProperty**—The property of the bean designated by paramName</li><li>**paramScope**—The scope of the bean designated by paramName</li></ul>

- **property**—The property of the bean designated by name containing the map containing the parameters to be used with the request generated by this tag

- **scope**—The scope of the bean designated by name

Note that exactly one of forward, href, page, or name must be specified.

iterate
: This tag iterates over a collection generating contents from the items of the collection. The attributes of this tag are as follows:

- **collection**—A runtime expression that evaluates to a collection of one of these types:

  - **array**—An array of Java objects (primitive data types are not allowed)

  - **collection**—A java.util.Collection, including ArrayList and Vector

  - **enumeration**—A java.util.Enumeration

  - **iterator**—A java.util.Iterator

  - **map**—A java.util.Map, HashMap, Hashtable, or TreeMap

  Check the Struts documentation for the details of this attribute.

- **id**—The script variable that will expose the items retrieved from the collection

- **length**—The maximum number of iterations to perform; this attribute can express the value itself or the name of a bean that defines that value; if not specified, the collection will be exhausted

- **name**—The name of a bean containing the collection to iterate over

- **property**—The name of the property of the bean expressed by name, containing the collection to iterate over

- **scope**—The scope of the bean expressed by name

- **id**—The script variable that will expose the items retrieved from collection

- **offset**—The zero-relative index of the element in the collection where the iteration will start; zero is the default

- **type**—The fully qualified Java class name of the element retrieved from the collection

present
: This tag checks the existence of a number of objects in the current request:

- **cookie**—Names the cookie; the existence will be checked

- **header**—Names the header; the existence will be checked

- **parameter**—Names the parameter; the existence will be checked, even if it is a zero-length String

continues

Table 7.3 **Continued**

Tag	Description
	■ **role**—Checks if the authenticated user (if any) is in this role.
	■ **name**, **property**, **scope**—Names the existence of the bean/non-null bean property in the specified scope.
	■ **user**—Checks if the current user principal has this name.

Listing 7.6 shows an example page using the struts-logic tags. In the example, the page is allowed to proceed only if the user is in the editors group and if a specified parameter is present in the request. If so, the collection that the parameter represents is used to generate contents.

Listing 7.6 **Using the Struts-Logic Tag Library Tags**

```
<%@ taglib uri="/WEB-INF/struts-bean.tld" prefix="bean" %>
<%@ taglib uri="/WEB-INF/struts-logic.tld" prefix="logic" %>
<%@ taglib uri="/WEB-INF/struts-html.tld" prefix="html" %>

<logic:present role="EDITOR">
  <logic:present parameter="JOURNAL_TYPES">

    <html:html locale="true">
    <head>
     <title><bean:message key="jType_browse.title"/></title>
     <html:base/>
    </head>
    <body>
     <table width="100%">
     <tr><td>
       <bean:message key="jType_browse.type"/>
     </td><td>
       <bean:message key="jType_browse.name"/>
     </td></tr>
     <bean:parameter id="jTypes" name="JOURNAL_TYPES"/>
     <logic:iterate id="ajType" name="jTypes">
       <tr><td>
         <bean:write name="ajType" property="type">
       </td><td>
         <bean:write name="ajType" property="name">
       </td></tr>
     </logic:iterate>
     </table>
    </body>
    </html:html>
  </logic:present>
</logic:present>
```

The example in Listing 7.6 presents the three struts-libraries reviewed so far, working together to render a list of types available on the request scope in an HTML table. The corresponding parameter presence is verified, then made a bean in the page scope, and then iterated over.

The *iterate* Tag

The significance of the iterate tag makes it the sole candidate for a detailed analysis. It is quite flexible in terms of the number of collection types that it can iterate over; it can accept a number of sources for those types. Listing 7.7 shows the code for the iterate tag.

Listing 7.7 **The *iterate* Tag Source Code**

```
package org.apache.struts.taglib.logic;


import java.util.Arrays;
import java.util.Collection;
import java.util.Enumeration;
import java.util.Iterator;
import java.util.Map;
import javax.servlet.jsp.JspException;
import javax.servlet.jsp.JspWriter;
import javax.servlet.jsp.PageContext;
import javax.servlet.jsp.tagext.BodyTagSupport;

import org.apache.struts.util.IteratorAdapter;
import org.apache.struts.util.MessageResources;
import org.apache.struts.util.PropertyUtils;
import org.apache.struts.util.RequestUtils;
import org.apache.struts.util.ResponseUtils;


/**
 * Custom tag that iterates the elements of a collection, which can be
 * either an attribute or the property of an attribute.  The collection
 * can be any of the following:  an array of objects, an Enumeration,
 * an Iterator, a Collection (which includes Lists, Sets and Vectors),
 * or a Map (which includes Hashtables) whose elements will be iterated over.
 *
 * @author Craig R. McClanahan
 * @version $Revision: 1.11 $ $Date: 2001/04/29 01:26:19 $
 */

public class IterateTag extends BodyTagSupport {


    // -------------------------------------------------- Instance Variables
```

continues

Listing 7.7 **Continued**

```java
/**
 * Iterator of the elements of this collection, while we are actually
 * running.
 */
protected Iterator iterator = null;


/**
 * The number of elements we have already rendered.
 */
protected int lengthCount = 0;


/**
 * The actual length value (calculated in the start tag).
 */
protected int lengthValue = 0;


/**
 * The message resources for this package.
 */
protected static MessageResources messages =
  MessageResources.getMessageResources
  ("org.apache.struts.taglib.logic.LocalStrings");


/**
 * The actual offset value (calculated in the start tag).
 */
protected int offsetValue = 0;


/**
 * Has this tag instance been started?
 */
protected boolean started = false;


// ------------------------------------------------------------- Properties


/**
 * The collection over which we will be iterating.
 */
protected Object collection = null;
```

```
public Object getCollection() {
  return (this.collection);
}

public void setCollection(Object collection) {
  this.collection = collection;
}


/**
 * The name of the scripting variable to be exposed.
 */
protected String id = null;

public String getId() {
  return (this.id);
}

public void setId(String id) {
  this.id = id;
}


/**
 * <p>Return the zero-relative index of the current iteration through the
 * loop.  If you specify an <code>offset</code>, the first iteration
 * through the loop will have that value; otherwise, the first iteration
 * will return zero.</p>
 *
 * <p>This property is read-only, and gives nested custom tags access to
 * this information.  Therefore, it is <strong>only</strong> valid in
 * between calls to <code>doStartTag()</code> and <code>doEndTag()</code>.
 * </p>
 */
public int getIndex() {
    if (started)
        return (offsetValue + lengthCount - 1);
    else
        return (0);
}


/**
 * The length value or attribute name (<=0 means no limit).
 */
protected String length = null;

public String getLength() {
  return (this.length);
}
```

continues

Listing 7.7 **Continued**

```java
public void setLength(String length) {
  this.length = length;
}


/**
 * The name of the collection or owning bean.
 */
protected String name = null;

public String getName() {
    return (this.name);
}

public void setName(String name) {
  this.name = name;
}


/**
 * The starting offset (zero relative).
 */
protected String offset = null;

public String getOffset() {
  return (this.offset);
}

public void setOffset(String offset) {
  this.offset = offset;
}


/**
 * The property name containing the collection.
 */
protected String property = null;

public String getProperty() {
  return (this.property);
}

public void setProperty(String property) {
  this.property = property;
}


/**
```

```
 * The scope of the bean specified by the name property, if any.
 */
protected String scope = null;

public String getScope() {
    return (this.scope);
}

public void setScope(String scope) {
    this.scope = scope;
}


/**
 * The Java class of each exposed element of the collection.
 */
protected String type = null;

public String getType() {
    return (this.type);
}

public void setType(String type) {
    this.type = type;
}


// -------------------------------------------------------- Public Methods


/**
 * Construct an iterator for the specified collection, and begin
 * looping through the body once per element.
 *
 * @exception JspException if a JSP exception has occurred
 */
public int doStartTag() throws JspException {

  // Acquire the collection we are going to iterate over
    Object collection = this.collection;
  if (collection == null)
      collection =
          RequestUtils.lookup(pageContext, name, property, scope);
    if (collection == null) {
        JspException e = new JspException
            (messages.getMessage("iterate.collection"));
        RequestUtils.saveException(pageContext, e);
        throw e;
    }
```

continues

Listing 7.7 **Continued**

```
// Construct an iterator for this collection
if (collection.getClass().isArray())
    collection = Arrays.asList((Object[]) collection);
if (collection instanceof Collection)
    iterator = ((Collection) collection).iterator();
else if (collection instanceof Iterator)
    iterator = (Iterator) collection;
else if (collection instanceof Map)
    iterator = ((Map) collection).entrySet().iterator();
else if (collection instanceof Enumeration)
    iterator = new IteratorAdapter((Enumeration)collection);
else {
    JspException e = new JspException
        (messages.getMessage("iterate.iterator"));
    RequestUtils.saveException(pageContext, e);
    throw e;
  }

// Calculate the starting offset
if (offset == null)
    offsetValue = 0;
else {
    try {
        offsetValue = Integer.parseInt(offset);
    } catch (NumberFormatException e) {
        Integer offsetObject =
          (Integer) pageContext.findAttribute(offset);
        if (offsetObject == null)
            offsetValue = 0;
        else
            offsetValue = offsetObject.intValue();
    }
}
if (offsetValue < 0)
    offsetValue = 0;

// Calculate the rendering length
if (length == null)
    lengthValue = 0;
else {
    try {
        lengthValue = Integer.parseInt(length);
    } catch (NumberFormatException e) {
        Integer lengthObject =
          (Integer) pageContext.findAttribute(length);
        if (lengthObject == null)
            lengthValue = 0;
        else
            lengthValue = lengthObject.intValue();
```

```
        }
    }
    if (lengthValue < 0)
        lengthValue = 0;
    lengthCount = 0;

    // Skip the leading elements up to the starting offset
    for (int i = 0; i < offsetValue; i++) {
        if (iterator.hasNext()) {
            Object element = iterator.next();
        }
    }

    // Store the first value and evaluate, or skip the body if none
    if (iterator.hasNext()) {
        Object element = iterator.next();
          if (element == null)
              pageContext.removeAttribute(id);
          else
              pageContext.setAttribute(id, element);
        lengthCount++;
          started = true;
        return (EVAL_BODY_TAG);
    } else
          return (SKIP_BODY);

}


/**
 * Make the next collection element available and loop, or
 * finish the iterations if there are no more elements.
 *
 * @exception JspException if a JSP exception has occurred
 */
public int doAfterBody() throws JspException {

    // Render the output from this iteration to the output stream
    if (bodyContent != null) {
        ResponseUtils.writePrevious(pageContext, bodyContent.getString());
        bodyContent.clearBody();
    }

    // Decide whether to iterate or quit
    if ((lengthValue > 0) && (lengthCount >= lengthValue))
        return (SKIP_BODY);
    if (iterator.hasNext()) {
        Object element = iterator.next();
          if (element == null)
              pageContext.removeAttribute(id);
          else
```

continues

Listing 7.7 **Continued**

```
                pageContext.setAttribute(id, element);
        lengthCount++;
        return (EVAL_BODY_TAG);
    } else
        return (SKIP_BODY);

}


/**
 * Clean up after processing this enumeration.
 *
 * @exception JspException if a JSP exception has occurred
 */
public int doEndTag() throws JspException {

    // Clean up our started state
    started = false;

    // Continue processing this page
    return (EVAL_PAGE);

}


/**
 * Release all allocated resources.
 */
public void release() {

  super.release();

  iterator = null;
  lengthCount = 0;
  lengthValue = 0;
  offsetValue = 0;

    id = null;
    collection = null;
    length = null;
    name = null;
    offset = null;
    property = null;
    scope = null;
    started = false;

}

}
```

The `iterate` tag is a `BodyTag`, which is different from the `message` and the `errors` tags. It extends the `BodyTagSupport` class. The `iterate` tag first presents some instance variables that will control the iteration and hold the actual iterator that will be used by the tag. The message resources also are initialized, as was done in the `message` and `error` tags.

The first attribute declared is the `collection` attribute, a Java object representing the actual collection. Because the type of the collection cannot be defined beforehand, it is defined at the highest level possible. Then the tag declares the name of the scripting variable that will hold the current iteration's returned item.

A `getIndex` method is declared to cope with the index of the actual element in the collection and the other attributes.

The `doStartTag` method first checks to see whether the collection attribute is used. If it is null, it tries to find a collection using the triple name-property-scope. The `RequestUtils` object is responsible for that, and the method lookup is used to find the collection. If no collection to iterate is found, a JSP exception is raised.

The next step is to determine the class that this collection is instance of. It can be an instance of one of the following classes:

- `java.util.Arrays`
- `java.util.Collection`
- `java.util.ArrayList`
- `java.util.Vector`
- `java.util.Enumeration`
- `java.util.Iterator`
- `java.util.Map`
- `java.util.HashMap`
- `java.util.Hashtable`
- `java.util.TreeMap`

If the collection is not an instance of one of these, a JSP exception is raised.

When the collection is found and is properly identified, the iteration starts. The offset of the first element of the iteration is calculated, the length of the iteration is calculated, and the iterator is positioned in the offset element, skipping all leading elements before it. If the iterator is successful in returning a first element, it places that element as a `pageContext` attribute using the `PageContext.setAttribute` method with the `id` value. Then the EVAL_BODY_TAG is signaled, the body gets evaluated, and the iteration proceeds. Otherwise, the body is skipped and the tag finishes the iteration.

The `doAfterBody` method just continues the iteration process. It writes the body contents to the out stream and checks whether the last element in the iteration was reached. If the iteration was not reached, the `doAfterBody` method removes the former element from the `pageContext` and adds the current one, if there is one. Then it signals `EVAL_BODY_TAG`. If the last element was reached, it signals `SKIP_BODY`, and the iteration is finished.

The `doEndTag` method switches the started flag to `false`, finishing the iteration, and the `release` method just resets all the attributes and instance variables to their default values.

The Struts–Template Tag Library

The `template` tag library was a late addition to the framework. It was initially created by David Geary, and it was presented and fully discussed in an article in *JavaWorld*, "JSP Templates," in the September 2000 issue. Then the library was donated to Struts.

The struts-template library provides a way to preserve page designs that are shared among a number of pages, such as sections, headers, or footers, and it dynamically loads the parts that vary. It does that with three tags, which are described in Table 7.4.

Table 7.4 **The Struts-Template Tag Library Tags**

Tag	Description
insert	The `insert` tag is the main tag in the template system. It is the controller that will insert a certain template in a page. It takes a sole attribute—the `template` attribute, which holds the URI of the template. It provides the context to the `put` tag described next.
put	The `put` tag assigns a value to a template parameter. Template parameters are a way to provide values that will instantiate a template in a certain execution. For instance, there can be a title template that will hold the static design for a title banner to be reused through all the pages in an application or organization, but the text of the title itself changes from case to case. If the title banner has a `titleText` parameter, it could be generally used and instantiated at the moment of. The `put` tag is used to provide such parametric values. The attributes of the `put` tag are as follows:
	• **name**—The name of the content. The name of the parameter in the template that this value will instantiate.
	• **role**—Attribute that checks whether the user is in the role. If this attribute is specified, the content is inserted in the template only if the user is in the role. If the user is not, this `put` tag is ignored.
	• **content**—The content that will be put in the template.
	• **direct**—If `false`, the content is included (processed and then included as in a JSP include). This is the default. If `true`, the content is output to the out stream directly.
get	The `get` tag is the counterpart for the `put` tag inside the template. Whatever is put by the `put` tag is retrieved in the template by the `get` tag is and written to the out stream. This tag presents the following attributes:

- **name**—Specifies the name of the content placed by `put` and retrieved by this `get`.

    - **role**—Checks whether the user is in the role. If this attribute is specified, the content will be `get` only if the user is in the role. If the user is not, this `put` is ignored.

    - **flush**—Flushes the out buffer before including the contents. This attribute exists to correct problems that might occur in some containers.

Listing 7.8 presents a small template page that shows a header to be used in the application's pages.

Listing 7.8 **The articleDBHeader.jsp Template**

```
<%@ taglib uri='/WEB-INF/struts-template.tld' prefix='template' %>

<table>
<tr>
 <td colspan="3">
   <h1><template:get name="title"/></h1>
 </td>
</tr>
<tr>
<td>
   User: <template:get name="username"/>
 </td>
 <td>
   Division: <template:get name="division"/>
 </td>
 <td>
   Logged at: <template:get name="logTime"/>
 </td>
</tr>
</table>
```

In this template, you can see the parametric replacement `get` tags. When this template is inserted, there must be a `put` for each `get` providing a value to be used. Listing 7.9 shows such a page.

Listing 7.9 **Using the Template in an Edit Page**

```
<%@ taglib uri="/WEB-INF/struts-bean.tld" prefix="bean" %>
<%@ taglib uri="/WEB-INF/struts-html.tld" prefix="html" %>
<%@ taglib uri="/WEB-INF/struts-template.tld"
          prefix="template" %>

<html:html locale="true">
<head>
```

continues

Listing 7.9   **Continued**

```
<title><bean:message key="author_edit.title"/></title>
<html:base/>
</head>
<body>

<html:errors/>

<bean:parameter id="userHnd" name="USER_HANDLER"/>

<template:insert name="artDBHeader.jsp">
  <template:put name="title" content="Edit Author Data"/>
  <template:put name="username" content="<%=userHnd.getUserName()%>"/>
  <template:put name="division" content="<%=userHnd.getDivision()%>"/>
  <template:put name="logTime" content="userHnd.getLogTime()"/>
</template:insert>

<html:form action="/authorEdit" focus="name">
<table border="0" width="100%">

  <tr>
    <th align="right">
      <bean:message key="author_edit.name"/>
    </th>
    <td align="left">
      <html:text property="name" size="45" maxlength="45"/>
    </td>
  </tr>

  <tr>
    <th align="right">
      <bean:message key="author_edit.surname"/>
    </th>
    <td align="left">
      <html:text property="surname" size="45" maxlength="45"/>
    </td>
  </tr>

    <tr>
    <th align="right">
      <bean:message key="author_edit.nationality"/>
    </th>
    <td align="left">
      <html:select property="nationality" multiple="false" size="5">
        <html:options collection="<%=nationsISOCodesAndNames%>"/>
      </html:select>
    </td>
  </tr>

  <tr>
```

```
  <td align="right">
    <html:submit property="submit" value="Submit"/>
  </td>
  <td align="left">
    <html:reset/>

  </td>
</tr>

</table>

</html:form>

</body>
</html:html>
```

Listing 7.9 is Listing 7.4 revamped to use a template. The values to be used in the template are provided in this page in the put tag.

Summary

The Struts tag libraries provide the necessary complement to the presentation layer of the framework, integrating the JSP controls with the core objects over which the framework was built. If this were done manually, it would certainly require a huge amount of tedious and repetitive JSP coding.

The struts-bean library provides basic bean and auxiliary objects support, and the message tag provides internationalized labeling.

The struts-html library provides the error tag that complements the error-treatment cycle initiated in the ActionServlet and the HTML control tags, which directly access the ActionForm bean properties to ease coding of Struts application interfaces.

Conditional and iterative content generation is provided by the struts-logic tag library. This provides a number of logical comparison tags and the iterate tag, which iterates over a collection generating content using the collection's retrieved elements. The present tag checks the existence of request elements.

The struts-template tags are used to provide reuse of shared designs through the application's pages. It counts three tags for that, providing also parametric replacement of values in the templates.

8

Anatomy of a Struts Application

THIS CHAPTER DISSECTS THE ARTICLEDB STRUTS-BASED application, its core components, the JSPs and use of Struts tag libraries on them, as well as action mapping and control. This chapter also presents some insight on the use of heavyweight technologies such as Enterprise JavaBeans (EJBs) and Struts.

The ArticleDB Application Scenario Analysis

The application presented in this chapter makes use of the Struts framework to provide a web interface to an article database. You will be able to search the database and find articles by author or by journal, number, and volume. When you are searching the article by the author, you will be able to find an author by his identification code or surname. Articles, authors, and journals may be searched and retrieved or may be fully edited. This section illustrates how a Struts application is organized and built, and how it is further deployed to a servlet container.

The Basic Design

The basic UML design for the ArticleDB application is presented in Figure 8.1. This is quite a small application, made of three main classes: `Articles`, `Authors`, and `Journals`. `Articles` have a single main author who is responsible for the article. Then they are published in a Journal, which is a container for articles. A Journal can be a representation of a Journal, a Magazine, or a Newspaper. This is a simple design.

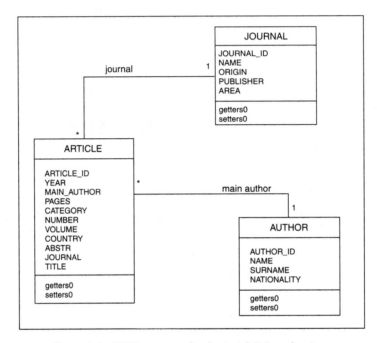

Figure 8.1   UML structure for the ArticleDB application.

The database for this application reflects its simplicity. It is made of three tables, ARTICLE, AUTHOR, and JOURNAL. The SQL script to create this database in a MySQL installation is shown in Listing 8.1.

Listing 8.1   **The ArticleDB SQL Schema**

```
###
### article
###

drop table if exists ARTICLE;

create table ARTICLE  (

ARTICLE_ID INTEGER PRIMARY KEY,
YEAR CHAR(4),
MAIN_AUTHOR CHAR(2),
PAGES INTEGER,
CATEGORY CHAR(1),
NUMBER INTEGER,
```

```
VOLUME INTEGER,
COUNTRY CHAR(2),
ABSTR VARCHAR(250),
JOURNAL CHAR(4),
TITLE VARCHAR(80)

);

###
###   author
###

drop table if exists AUTHOR;

create table AUTHOR   (

AUTHOR_ID CHAR(2),
NAME VARCHAR(45),
SURNAME VARCHAR(45),
NATIONALITY CHAR(2)

);

###
###   journal
###

drop table if exists JOURNAL;

create table JOURNAL   (

JOURNAL_ID CHAR(4),
NAME VARCHAR(45),
ORIGIN CHAR(2),
PUBLISHER VARCHAR(45),
AREA VARCHAR(20)

);
```

This database is available in a MySQL installation and is accessed through JDBC. The Struts connections manager will perform database connection management, using the MySql driver discussed in Appendix D, "MySQL."

Representing the Model with Helper Classes

In any application, a number of choices are always involved when you are designing the representation of the core application entities. You can use pure object-oriented design and provide a mapping between that design and a database layer that will provide for persistence. This has the overhead of dealing with the mapping configuration.

Another option is to rely on a fully featured distributed object architecture and framework, such as Enterprise Java Beans. This is a nice solution when the application is large enough (which is by no means a simple measure) and needs to have access to objects that are distributed and that implement core business processes to be used by a number of applications in the organization. Otherwise, as in this case, when the application is too small and can be centralized, EJBs (or any other distributed object framework) are always oversized.

Another option is to rely on simple beans. For this application, the main abstractions are encapsulated in helper classes, simple beans that will provide the SQL access to the database. Listing 8.2 shows the `AuthorHelper` class.

But representing the `Model` layer in Struts is not restricted to the use of JavaBeans only. Other options, such as XML or messaging, can be considered as well. The section "Variations on a Theme: EJBs, Messaging, and XML" provides more information on that.

Listing 8.2 **The *AuthorHelper* Class**

```
package jspbook.example.articledb;

import java.sql.*;
import javax.sql.*;
import javax.servlet.http.HttpServletRequest;
import org.apache.struts.action.*;

public final class AuthorHelper extends Object
{

    public Vector getAuthorList(HttpServletRequest request, String key)
    {
        Vector results = new Vector();
        HttpSession session = request.getSession(false);
        DataSource ds = (DataSource)session.getAttribute(key);
        Connection con = null;
        try
        {
            String id = request.getParameter("id");
            String surname = request.getParameter("surname");
            String criteria = "";

            if(id != null) criteria = " id = ?";
            else if(surname != null) criteria = " surname = ?";
            else return null;

            con = ds.getConnection();
            PrepareStatement stm = con.prepareStatement("Select id, name, surname,
nationality from author where "+criteria);
```

```
          if(id != null) stm.setString(1,id);
          else stm.setString(1,surname);

          ResultSet rs = stm.executeQuery();
          while(rs.next())
          {
              AuthorForm form = new AuthorForm();
              form.setId(rs.getString(1));
              form.setName(rs.getString(2));
              form.setSurname(rs.getString(3));
              form.setNationality(rs.getString(4));
              results.addElement(form);
          }
      }
      catch(Exception e) {con.close(); return null;}
      finally { con.close();}
      return results;
  }

  public ActionErrors insert(HttpServletRequest request, String key)
  {
      ActionErrors errors = new AuthorErrors();
      HttpSession session = request.getSession(false);
      DataSource ds = (DataSource)session.getAttribute(key);
      Connection con = null;
      try
      {
          AuthorForm form = request.getParameter("authorForm");

          if(form == null)
          {
              errors.add("nulldata",
                      new ActionError("error.data.required"));
              return errors;
          }

          con = ds.getConnection();
          PrepareStatement stm = con.prepareStatement("Insert into author values
(?,?,?,?)");

          stm.setString(1,form.getId());
          stm.setString(2,form.getName());
          stm.setString(3,form.getSurname());
          stm.setString(4,form.getNationality());

          stm.executeUpdate();
      }
      catch(Exception e)
      {
              errors.add("sqlerror",
                      new ActionError("error.sql.invalid"));
```

continues

Listing 8.2   **Continued**

```
                    return errors;
        }
        finally { con.close();}
        return errors;
    }

    public ActionErrors update(HttpServletRequest request, String key)
    {
        ActionErrors errors = new AuthorErrors();
        HttpSession session = request.getSession(false);
        DataSource ds = (DataSource)session.getAttribute(key);
        Connection con = null;
        try
        {
            AuthorForm form = request.getParameter("authorForm");

            if(form == null)
            {
                errors.add("nulldata",
                        new ActionError("error.data.required"));
                return errors;
            }

            con = ds.getConnection();
            PrepareStatement stm = con.prepareStatement("Update author set
name=?,surname=?,nationality=? where id=?");

            stm.setString(1,form.getName());
            stm.setString(2,form.getSurname());
            stm.setString(3,form.getNationality());
            stm.setString(4,form.getId());

            stm.executeUpdate();
        }
        catch(Exception e)
        {
                errors.add("sqlerror",
                        new ActionError("error.sql.invalid"));
                return errors;
        }
        finally { con.close();}
        return errors;
    }

    public ActionErrors delete(HttpServletRequest request, String key)
    {
        ActionErrors errors = new AuthorErrors();
        HttpSession session = request.getSession(false);
        DataSource ds = (DataSource)session.getAttribute(key);
```

```
        Connection con = null;
        try
        {
            AuthorForm form = request.getParameter("authorForm");

            if(form == null)
            {
                errors.add("nulldata",
                        new ActionError("error.data.required"));
                return errors;
            }

            con = ds.getConnection();
            PrepareStatement stm = con.prepareStatement("delete from author where
id=?");

            stm.setString(1,form.getId());

            stm.executeUpdate();
        }
        catch(Exception e)
        {
                errors.add("sqlerror",
                        new ActionError("error.sql.invalid"));
                return errors;
        }
        finally { con.close();}
        return errors;
    }

}
```

You will notice that this class basically wraps the SQL in an object interface. This is a better option than placing the SQL access directly into the perform method of Struts Action classes because, for instance, if the Model layer migrates into an EJB architecture, little needs be done on the application Action classes, and maintenance will be restricted to the helper classes layer.

Struts Core Components

As you saw in Chapter 6, "The Jakarta Struts Project," a Struts application is based on web components and core beans that represent the state of the application and JSP pages for the presentation. This section analyzes the core components for the ArticleDB application.

ArticleDB ActionForms

Listing 8.3 presents the `AuthorForm` class. It subclasses the standard `ActionForm` class and represents the abstraction of an author. This will provide the data for the data-entry and data-presentation pages.

Listing 8.3   **The AuthorForm Class**

```
package jspbook.example.articledb;

import javax.servlet.http.HttpServletRequest;
import org.apache.struts.action.*;

public final class AuthorForm extends ActionForm
{
    private String name = null; //author's name...
    private String surname = null; // surname...
    private String nationality = null; // and nationality

    public String getName()
    {
      return (this.name);
    }

    public void setName(String value)
    {
        this.name = value;
    }

    public String getSurname()
    {
      return (this.surname);
    }

    public void setSurname(String value)
    {
        this.surname = value;
    }

    public String getNationality()
    {
      return (this.nationality);
    }

    public void setNationality(String value)
    {
        this.nationality = value;
    }

    public void reset(ActionMapping mapping, HttpServletRequest request)
```

```
    {
        this.name = null;
        this.surname = null;
        this.nationality = null;
    }

    public ActionErrors validate(ActionMapping mapping,
                                 HttpServletRequest request) {

        ActionErrors errors = new ActionErrors();
        if ((name == null) || (name.length() < 1))
            errors.add("authorname",
                       new ActionError("error.authorname.required"));
        if ((surname == null) || (surname.length() < 1))
            errors.add("authorsurname",
                       new ActionError("error.authorsurname.required"));
        if ((nationality == null) || (nationality.length() < 1))
            errors.add("nationality",                     new
ActionError("error.nationality.required"));
        return errors;
    }
}
```

The reset method shown in Listing 8.3 just made all fields null, whereas the validate method checks to see if something was left blank. Listing 8.4 shows the JournalForm class. It also represents the full data structure of the Journal entity.

Listing 8.4   **The _JournalForm_ Class**

```
package jspbook.example.articledb;

import javax.servlet.http.HttpServletRequest;
import org.apache.struts.action.*;

public final class JournalForm extends ActionForm
{

    private String id = null; // id...
    private String name = null; //journal's name...
    private String origin = null; // country of origin...
    private String publisher = null; // publisher...
    private String area = null; // and area

    public String getId()
    {
      return (this.id);
    }

    public void setId(String value)
    {
```

continues

Listing 8.4 **Continued**

```
        this.id = value;
    }

    public String getName()
    {
      return (this.name);
    }

    public void setName(String value)
    {
        this.name = value;
    }

    public String getOrigin()
    {
      return (this.origin);
    }

    public void setOrigin(String value)
    {
        this.origin = value;
    }

    public String getPublisher()
    {
      return (this.publisher);
    }

    public void setPublisher(String value)
    {
        this.publisher = value;
    }

    public String getArea()
    {
      return (this.area);
    }

    public void setArea(String value)
    {
        this.area = value;
    }

    public void reset(ActionMapping mapping, HttpServletRequest request)
    {
        this.id = null;
        this.name = null;
        this.origin = null;
        this.publisher = null;
```

```
            this.area = null;
    }

    public ActionErrors validate(ActionMapping mapping,
                            HttpServletRequest request) {

        ActionErrors errors = new ActionErrors();
        if ((id == null) || (id.length() < 1))
            errors.add("journalid",
                    new ActionError("error.journalid.required"));
        if ((name == null) || (name.length() < 1))
            errors.add("journalname",
                    new ActionError("error.journalname.required"));
        if ((origin == null) || (origin.length() < 1))
            errors.add("journalorigin",
                    new ActionError("error.journalorigin.required"));
        if ((publisher == null) || (publisher.length() < 1))
            errors.add("journalpublisher",
                    new ActionError("error.journalpublisher.required"));
        if ((area == null) || (area.length() < 1))
            errors.add("journalarea",
                    new ActionError("error.journalarea.required"));
        return errors;
    }
}
```

Another thing to note is the use of `ActionError` and `ActionErrors` classes in the validation method. When a `validation` constraint fails, the Struts way is to collect an `ActionError` in an `ActionErrors` container and then return them. This way, the `ActionServlet` can detect the errors and act according to what is specified in the action mapping for the request in the struts–config.xml file.

Listing 8.5 shows the `ArticleForm` class. Its design follows the same structure as in the former ones.

Listing 8.5 **The ArticleForm Class**

```
package jspbook.example.articledb;

import javax.servlet.http.HttpServletRequest;
import org.apache.struts.action.*;

public final class ArticleForm extends ActionForm
{

    private String id = null; //article's id...
    private String year = null; //year...
    private String mainAuthor = null; //mainAuthor...
    private String pages = null; //pages...
    private String category = null; //category...
```

continues

Listing 8.5 **Continued**

```java
private String number = null; //number...
private String volume = null; //volume...
private String country = null; //country...
private String abstr = null; //abstract...
private String journal = null; //journal...
private String title = null; //and title

public String getId()
{
  return (this.id);
}

public void setId(String value)
{
    this.id = value;
}

public String getYear()
{
  return (this.year);
}

public void setYear(String value)
{
    this.Year = value;
}

public String getMainAuthor()
{
  return (this.mainAuthor);
}

public void setMainAuthor(String value)
{
    this.mainAuthor = value;
}

public String getPages()
{
  return (this.pages);
}

public void setPages(String value)
{
    this.pages = value;
}

public String getCategory()
{
```

```
    return (this.category);
}

public void setCategory(String value)
{
    this.category = value;
}

public String getNumber()
{
  return (this.number);
}

public void setNumber(String value)
{
    this.Number = value;
}

public String getVolume()
{
  return (this.volume);
}

public void setVolume(String value)
{
    this.volume = value;
}

public String getCountry()
{
  return (this.country);
}

public void setCountry(String value)
{
    this.country = value;
}

public String getAbstr()
{
  return (this.abstr);
}

public void setAbstr(String value)
{
    this.abstr = value;
}

public String getJournal()
{
  return (this.journal);
```

continues

Listing 8.5   **Continued**

```java
    }

    public void setJournal(String value)
    {
        this.journal = value;
    }

    public String getTitle()
    {
      return (this.title);
    }

    public void setTitle(String value)
    {
        this.title = value;
    }

    public void reset(ActionMapping mapping, HttpServletRequest request)
    {
        this.id = null;
        this.year = null;
        this.mainAuthor = null;
        this.pages = null;
        this.category = null;
        this.number = null;
        this.volume = null;
        this.country = null;
        this.abstr = null;
        this.journal = null;
        this.title = null;
    }

    public ActionErrors validate(ActionMapping mapping,
                                 HttpServletRequest request) {

        ActionErrors errors = new ActionErrors();
        if ((id == null) || (id.length() < 1))
            errors.add("articleid",
                    new ActionError("error.articleid.required"));
        if ((year == null) || (year.length() < 1))
            errors.add("articleyear",
                    new ActionError("error.articleyear.required"));
        if ((mainAuthor == null) || (mainAuthor.length() < 1))
            errors.add("articlemainauthor",
                    new ActionError("error.articlemainauthor.required"));
        if ((pages == null) || (pages.length() < 1))
            errors.add("articlepages",
                    new ActionError("error.articlepages.required"));
        if ((category == null) || (category.length() < 1))
```

```
                    errors.add("articlecategory",
                            new ActionError("error.articlecategory.required"));
        if ((number == null) || (number.length() < 1))
            errors.add("articlenumber",
                            new ActionError("error.articlenumber.required"));
        if ((volume == null) || (volume.length() < 1))
            errors.add("articlevolume",
                            new ActionError("error.articlevolume.required"));
        if ((country == null) || (country.length() < 1))
            errors.add("articlecountry",
                            new ActionError("error.articlecountry.required"));
        if ((abstr == null) || (abstr.length() < 1))
            errors.add("articleabstr",
                            new ActionError("error.articleabstr.required"));
        if ((journal == null) || (journal.length() < 1))
            errors.add("articlejournal",
                            new ActionError("error.articlejournal.required"));
        if ((title == null) || (title.length() < 1))
            errors.add("articletitle",
                            new ActionError("error.articletitle.required"));
        return errors;
    }
}
```

You will also note that there are many `ActionForm` classes. This is a characteristic of Struts. For more complex applications, in which forms tend to present views of data instead of data from single entities, the number of `ActionForm` classes can grow significantly.

The Actions

Actions represent what is to be done in the application. There is an action for each identified transaction or process. Even for a small application such as ArticleDB, the number of actions can grow excessively. This section presents the actions that relate to the operations over the author: `search`, `insert`, `update`, and `delete`. The `AuthorDataAction` class, which is shown in Listing 8.6, encapsulates the search process.

Listing 8.6   **The *AuthorDataAction* Class**

```
package jspbook.example.articledb;

import java.util.*;
import javax.servlet.*;
import java.io.IOException;
import org.apache.struts.action.*;
import org.apache.struts.util.*;
import java.lang.reflect.InvocationTargetException;

// Prepares a list of authors from the db
```

continues

Listing 8.6   **Continued**

```java
public final class AuthorDataAction extends Action {


    public ActionForward perform(ActionMapping mapping,
                                 ActionForm acForm,
                                 HttpServletRequest req,
                                 HttpServletResponse resp)
        throws IOException, ServletException {

        Locale locale = getLocale(request);
        MessageResources messages = getResources();
        HttpSession session = request.getSession();
        ActionErrors errors = new ActionErrors();

        String action = request.getParameter(ACTION);
        if (action == null || action.length() == 0)
            errors.add("noaction",
                           new ActionError("error.action.required"));


        //Model object implemented as a Bean
        AuthorHelper aut = new AuthorHelper();

        //Query the Article instance and set the response
        //in the ArticleListForm
        if (action.equals("search"))
        {
            AuthorForm[] lst = aut.getAuthorList(request, Action.DATA_SOURCE_KEY);

          // Set the bean in the appropriate scope
          request.setAttribute("results", lst);

          // Forward control to the article List page
          return (mapping.findForward("authorList"));
        }
        else if (action.equals("detail"))
        {
            AuthorForm form = new AuthorForm();
            form = aut.getAuthorDetail(request, Action.DATA_SOURCE_KEY);

          // Set the AuthorForm bean in the request scope
            request.setAttribute("detail", form);

          // Forward control to the article List page
          return (mapping.findForward("authorDetail"));
        }
```

```
    }

}
```
●

This class implements the `search author list` and the `search author details` processes. It does that by reading the `action` parameter and showing which process is being requested each time. Each link to an action in the application must specify the `action` parameter. This way the number of action classes can be reduced to a manageable level.

The problem with this approach is the question of which level the number of action classes can be reduced to. The answer to this question might seem trivial, but it is not. In this example, the criteria was to group all processes related to updating a certain entity. The search processes are also grouped in another class. This is because the update processes generate transaction tokens, while the search processes do not.

Listing 8.7   **The *AuthorEditAction* Class**

```java
package jspbook.example.articledb;

import java.util.*;
import javax.servlet.*;
import java.io.IOException;
import org.apache.struts.action.*;
import org.apache.struts.util.*;
import java.lang.reflect.InvocationTargetException;

// Prepares a list of authors from the db

public final class AuthorEditAction extends Action {


  public ActionForward perform(ActionMapping mapping,
                        ActionForm acForm,
                        HttpServletRequest req,
                        HttpServletResponse resp)
    throws IOException, ServletException {

    Locale locale = getLocale(request);
    MessageResources messages = getResources();
    HttpSession session = request.getSession();
    ActionErrors errors = new ActionErrors();

    String action = request.getParameter(ACTION);
    if (action == null || action.length() == 0)
      errors.add("noaction",
                    new ActionError("error.action.required"));
```

continues

Listing 8.7   **Continued**

```
//Model object implemented as a Bean
AuthorHelper aut = new AuthorHelper();          •

//Set an AuthorForm on the case of an update
//but nothing in case of an insert
if (action.equals("update"))
{
    AuthorForm aut = new ArticleForm();
    form = aut.getAuthorDetail(request, Action.DATA_SOURCE_KEY);

  // Set the AuthorForm bean in the pre-defined scope
    if (mapping.getScope().equals("request"))
        request.setAttribute(mapping.getAttribute(), form);
    else
        session.setAttribute(mapping.getAttribute(), form);
}

// Set a transaction control token
saveToken(request);

// Forward control to the author edit page
return (mapping.findForward("authorEdit"));
  }

}
```

This is another design that is mandatory in Struts: the use of the transaction token, which is used to avoid resubmission of a process. The `AuthorEditAction` class sets a transaction token with the `saveToken` method.

In Listing 8.8, you can see the `AuthorSubmitAction`, which will execute the transactions set by the previous class.

Listing 8.8   **The *AuthorSubmitAction* Class**

```
package jspbook.example.articledb;

import java.util.*;
import javax.servlet.*;
import java.io.IOException;
import org.apache.struts.action.*;
import org.apache.struts.util.*;
import java.lang.reflect.InvocationTargetException;

// Prepares a list of authors from the db

public final class AuthorSubmitAction extends Action {
```

```
public ActionForward perform(ActionMapping mapping,
                          ActionForm acForm,
                          HttpServletRequest req,
                          HttpServletResponse resp)
    throws IOException, ServletException {

    Locale locale = getLocale(request);
    MessageResources messages = getResources();
    HttpSession session = request.getSession();
    ActionErrors errors = new ActionErrors();

    String action = request.getParameter(ACTION);
    if (action == null || action.length() == 0)
        errors.add("noaction",
                          new ActionError("error.action.required"));


    // Was this transaction cancelled?
    if (isCancelled(request))
    {
      if (mapping.getAttribute() != null)
          session.removeAttribute(mapping.getAttribute());
          return (mapping.findForward("menu"));
    }

    //If the transaction token is not valid, there's an error
    if (!isTokenValid(request))
          errors.add(ActionErrors.GLOBAL_ERROR,
                          new ActionError("error.transaction.token"));

    //Either way, reset the token
    resetToken(request);

    //Model object implemented as a Bean
    AuthorHelper aut = new AuthorHelper();
    AuthorForm form = (AuthorForm) acForm;

    //Execute the data operations
    if (action.equals("insert"))
    {
        errors = aut.insertAuthor(form, Action.DATA_SOURCE_KEY))
        if (errors.empty())
      return (mapping.findForward("menu"));
    }
    else if (action.equals("update"))
    {
        errors = aut.updateAuthor(form, Action.DATA_SOURCE_KEY);
        if (errors.empty())
      return (mapping.findForward("menu"));
    }
    else if (action.equals("delete"))
```

continues

Listing 8.8   **Continued**

```
{
    errors = aut.deleteAuthor(form, Action.DATA_SOURCE_KEY);
    if (errors.empty())
  return (mapping.findForward("menu"));
}

//Report the errors detected
if (!errors.empty())
{
  saveErrors(request, errors);
    saveToken(request);
    return (new ActionForward(mapping.getInput()));
}
  }
}
```

The `AuthorSubmitAction.perform` method first verifies that the current transaction token is valid. If it is not, there has been an out-of-sequence error, and this transaction is being wrongfully submitted. In this case, an error is returned.

If the transaction token holds, it is reset because another submittal will cause problems. Then the classes needed are set and the proper core method is called in the helper class, according to the recalled action request parameter.

If any error was detected after process, then processing is redirected to the input form for correction. In that case, a new transaction token is generated.

The Application JSPs

As shown in Chapter 6 and Chapter 7, "Struts Tag Libraries," the JSPs play a central role in any Struts application because they complete the several standard processes built in the framework and provide the presentation layer. The next section analyzes the pages that make up part of the processes reviewed so far.

The Main Page and Templates

Because any application has shared static designs, such as logos or a particular organization of the pages, the struts-template library can be largely employed. In the ArticleDB application, there is a standard header template and a footer template. These are presented in Listings 8.9 and 8.10, respectively.

Listing 8.9   **The Header Template**

```
<%@ taglib uri="/WEB-INF/struts-template.tld" prefix="template" %>
<%@ taglib uri="/WEB-INF/struts-bean.tld" prefix="bean" %>
<p align="center">
  <h1><bean:message key="app.name" /></h1><br>
```

```
    <h4><template:get name="module"/></h4>
  </p>
  <hr width="100%" height="1">
```

The header template presents a centralized layout with a parametric replacement for the module name. That will be provided by the `module` parameter in all the application's pages. The footer template in Listing 8.10 doesn't use any parameters.

Listing 8.10   **The Footer Template**

```
<hr width="100%" height="1">
<p align="right">
  <font size="-2">ArticleDB App Example</font>
</p>
```

The main page in the application is the menu page (see Listing 8.11). There are no security constraints regarding this application, so there won't be a login schema. The page starts with a tag libraries declaration, the header template, and the links to the main processes in the application. These links use the struts-html library's `link` tag. Then the page closes with the footer template.

Listing 8.11   **The Menu Page**

```
<%@ taglib uri='/WEB-INF/struts-template.tld' prefix='template' %>
<%@ taglib uri='/WEB-INF/struts-html.tld' prefix='html' %>
<%@ taglib uri='/WEB-INF/struts-bean.tld' prefix='bean' %>
<html:html>
<header>
 <html:base/>
</header>
<body>

<template:insert template="/headerTemplate.jsp">
  <template:put name="module" content="Main Menu" direct="true"/>
</template:insert>

<html:link page="/searchAuthor.jsp">
  <bean:message key="author.search"/>
</html:link>

<html:link page="/searchJournal.jsp">
  <bean:message key="journal.search"/>
</html:link>

<html:link page="/searchArticle.jsp">
  <bean:message key="article.search"/>
</html:link>

<template:insert template="/footerTemplate.jsp"/>
```

continues

Listing 8.11   **Continued**

```
</body>
</html:html>
```

The Author Pages

The first page in the AuthorDB application is the searchAuthor.jsp page. It is presented in Listing 8.12. Again, there is the header template. This time, there is a form tag hat that points to the `AuthorDataAction` with an action of `search`. This triggers the `getAuthorList` method call.

Listing 8.12   **The searchAuthor.jsp Page**

```
<%@ taglib uri='/WEB-INF/struts-template.tld' prefix='template' %>
<%@ taglib uri='/WEB-INF/struts-html.tld' prefix='html' %>
<%@ taglib uri='/WEB-INF/struts-bean.tld' prefix='bean' %>
<html:html>
<header>
 <html:base/>
</header>
<body>

<template:insert template="/headerTemplate.jsp">
  <template:put name="module" content="Search Author" direct="true"/>
</template:insert>

<html:form action="/authorData">

<bean:message key="author.id"/><html:text name="id"/>
<bean:message key="author.surname"/><html:text name="surname"/>

<center><html:submit /><html:reset /></center>

</html:form>

<template:insert template="/footerTemplate.jsp"/>
</body>
</html:html>
```

The page presented in Listing 8.13 renders the vector of `AuthorForm` beans retrieved from the `AuthorDataAction/AuthorHelper` classes in a table. The `logic:iterate` tag will do the job.

Listing 8.13   **The Author Listing Page**

```
<%@ taglib uri='/WEB-INF/struts-template.tld' prefix='template' %>
<%@ taglib uri='/WEB-INF/struts-html.tld' prefix='html' %>
<%@ taglib uri='/WEB-INF/struts-bean.tld' prefix='bean' %>
```

```
<%@ taglib uri="/WEB-INF/struts-logic.tld" prefix="logic" %>

<html:html>
<header>
 <html:base/>
</header>
<body>

<template:insert template="/headerTemplate.jsp">
  <template:put name="module" content="Author Results" direct="true"/>
</template:insert>

     <table width="100%">
     <tr><td>
       <bean:message key="author.id"/>
     </td><td>
       <bean:message key="author.name"/>
     </td></tr>

     <bean:parameter id="results" name="results"/>
     <logic:iterate id="author" name="results">
       <tr><td>
         <html:link page="/authorData?action=detail">
            <bean:write name="author" property="id">
         </html:link>
       </td><td>
         <bean:write name="author" property="value">
       </td></tr>
     </logic:iterate>
     </table>

<template:insert template="/footerTemplate.jsp"/>
</body>
</html:html>
```

Listing 8.14 shows the author detail page. It is a read-only page that exposes the
AuthorForm, which is built with the bean:write tag.

Listing 8.14   **The Author Detail Template**

```
<%@ taglib uri='/WEB-INF/struts-template.tld' prefix='template' %>
<%@ taglib uri='/WEB-INF/struts-bean.tld' prefix='bean' %>
<%@ taglib uri="/WEB-INF/struts-logic.tld" prefix="logic" %>
<%@ taglib uri="/WEB-INF/struts-html.tld" prefix="html" %>

<html:html>
<header>
 <html:base/>
</header>
<body>
```

continues

Listing 8.14   **Continued**

```
<template:insert template="/headerTemplate.jsp">
  <template:put name="module" content="Author Detail" direct="true"/>
</template:insert>

<html:link page="/authorEdit?action=update&" paramId="id" paramName="detail"
paramproperty="id" paramScope="request"/>

<html:link page="/authorEdit?action=delete&" paramId="id" paramName="detail"
paramproperty="id" paramScope="request"/>

<bean:message key="author.id"/>:
<bean:write name="detail" property="id" scope="request"/>

<bean:message key="author.name"/>:
<bean:write name="detail" property="name" scope="request"/>

<bean:message key="author.surname"/>:
<bean:write name="detail" property="surname" scope="request"/>

<bean:message key="author.nationality"/>:
<bean:write name="detail" property="nationality" scope="request"/>

<template:insert template="/footerTemplate.jsp"/>
</body>
</html:html>
```

To provide an edit form, the author edit page uses the html library text tag in
conjunction with the `bean:message` tag. It is presented in Listing 8.15.

Listing 8.15   **The Author Entry Form**

```
<%@ taglib uri='/WEB-INF/struts-template.tld' prefix='template' %>
<%@ taglib uri='/WEB-INF/struts-html.tld' prefix='html' %>
<%@ taglib uri='/WEB-INF/struts-bean.tld' prefix='bean' %>
<%@ taglib uri="/WEB-INF/struts-logic.tld" prefix="logic" %>

<html:html>
<header>
 <html:base/>
</header>
<body>

<template:insert template="/headerTemplate.jsp">
  <template:put name="module" content="Author Results" direct="true"/>
</template:insert>

<html:form action="/authorSubmit">
<html:hidden name="action" value="<%=request.getParameter("action")%>"/>
```

```
<bean:message key="author.id"/><html:text name="id"/>
<bean:message key="author.name"/><html:text name="name"/>
<bean:message key="author.surname"/><html:text name="surname"/>
<bean:message key="author.nationality"/>
<html:select name="nationality" multiple="false"/>
 <html:options collection="<%=nationsISOCodesAndNames%>"/>
</html:select>

</html:form>

<template:insert template="/footerTemplate.jsp"/>
</body>
</html:html>
```

The nationality field is implemented through a collection-based `options` tag.

The ApplicationResources.properties File

The ApplicationResources.properties file is a Java properties file containing the set of key value pairs that create the several messages used throughout the Struts application. Listing 8.16 presents an extract of such a file.

Listing 8.16 **The ApplicationResources File**

```
error.sql.invalid=<li>The submitted SQL is invalid</li>
error.data.required=<li>The information requested is required</li>
error.authorname.required=<li>The AUTHOR NAME is required</li>
error.authorsurname.required=<li>The AUTHOR SURNAME is required</li>
error.authornationality.required=<li>The AUTHOR NATIONALITY is required</li>
```

This file must be on the classpath. Therefore, it is better placed in the WEB-INF/classes directory in the application. In a Struts example, you will see it declared and maintained in the entire classpath, which is as follows:

```
org.apache.struts.webapp.example.ApplicationResources.properties
```

The struts-config.xml File

The struts-config.xml file containing the configuration for the ArticleDB application is presented in Listing 8.17. Here you can see the three main sections:

- **Data sources**—Where the access to the MySQL database is configured for this application
- **form-beans**—Where the several `ActionForm` beans that constitute the application are declared
- **An extract of the actions section**—Where two of the actions discussed are declared

Listing 8.17 **An Extract of the struts-config.xml File**

```xml
<?xml version="1.0" encoding="ISO-8859-1" ?>

<!DOCTYPE struts-config PUBLIC
          "-//Apache Software Foundation//DTD Struts Configuration 1.0//EN"
          "http://jakarta.apache.org/struts/dtds/struts-config_1_0.dtd">

<struts-config>
  <data-sources>
    <data-source
      autoCommit="false"
      description="First Database Config"
      driverClass=" org.gjt.mm.mysql.Driver"
        maxCount="4"
        minCount="2"
        password="admin"
            url="jdbc:mysql://localhost/ARTICLEDB"
            user="admin"
    />
  </data-sources>

  <form-beans>
    <form-bean    name="authorForm"
                  type="jspbook.example.articledb.AuthorForm"/>

    <form-bean    name="journalForm"
                  type="jspbook.example.articledb.JournalForm"/>

    <form-bean    name="articleForm"
                  type="jspbook.example.articledb.ArticleForm"/>
  </form-beans>

  <action-mappings>
    <action    path="/authorEdit"
               type="jspbook.example.articledb.AuthorEditAction"
               name="authorForm"
              scope="request"
           validate="false">
      <forward name="authorEdit" path="/authorEdit.jsp"/>
    </action>

    <action    path="/searchAuthor"
               type="jspbook.example.articledb.AuthorDataAction"
               name="authorForm"
              scope="request"
           validate="false">
      <forward name="authorEdit" path="/searchAuthor.jsp"/>
    </action>
...
```

```
    </action-mappings>

  </struts-config>
```

The web.xml File

The web.xml web application deployment descriptor for this application follows the guidelines of the struts-example application. The only distinction is that, instead of using extension mapping, the ArticleDB application uses path mapping. Therefore, all action classes in the ArticleDB are accessed by the JSPs using a path specified in the struts-config.xml file, such as in /articleDB/searchAuthor.

Packaging Struts Applications

Deploying a Struts application involves the following:

- **Packaging the framework**—The struts.jar archive must be deployed in the /WEB-INF/lib directory of your application, whereas the four standard TLD files, one for each struts tag library, must be deployed under /WEB-INF itself.

- **Packaging the application files**—The ApplicationResources.properties file, along with all the resource bundles that make the resources for the application, must be on the classpath. It is better placed among the classes that constitute the application. The application class files can be deployed in the standard way, under the /WEB-INF/classes directory. All subsidiary components, including tag libraries, external libraries, and so on, must be deployed in the standard way.

Variations on a Theme: EJBs, Messaging, and XML

As mentioned in the previous section "Representing the Model with Helper Classes," all that Struts says about the `Model` layer of your web application is that it must be accessed through the application's `Action` classes. This section discusses three of the most popular alternatives to the helper classes presented in that section:

- **EJB technology**—This represents any distributed object platform.

- **Messaging**—The application has access to business logic through asynchronous messages. The Java API for Messaging is the Java Message Service API (JMS). Chapter 4, "Collaborating Tags and Validation," presented some examples using the JMS API.

- **XML data representation**—This is either when the application's main abstractions are designed as XML data objects or when it is generated from some business logic server in the form of XML documents.

Which of the three alternatives is better is not the point here, and it is also beyond the scope of this book. The fact under consideration is that all three are currently used to represent business logic, and the Struts framework is flexible enough to cope with them all.

Using EJB

The basic design of a Struts-EJB–based application follows the one outlined in Figure 8.2. The best practice to make EJBs and Struts `Action` classes work together is to isolate EJBs at the `Model` level and provide control and presentation of the web application solely through Struts and JSPs. In that design, instead of relying solely on a helper class to provide the `Model`, a business logic layer is encapsulated in entity/session beans.

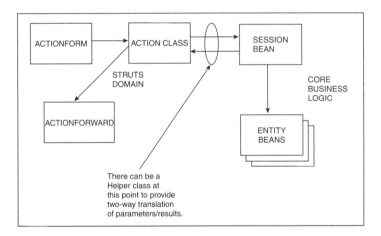

Figure 8.2   Using EJB with Struts.

The best approach is to use the session beans in a Facade or Command pattern, providing the translation of parametric data from the `ActionForm` beans either directly in the `Action` class or indirectly, through the use of a helper class.

The session bean that is called then can execute some logic, possibly interacting with a number of entity beans and then returning the process's results. The best approach for returning those results is to avoid passing object references because these can get broken; and because this won't be detected by Struts, leaving the Struts underlying error-treatment mechanism in the void.

Instead, it is recommended that you pass back objects only by value to the `Action` class. Either the session bean or the helper class interfacing with it can convert entity bean references into local beans and pass them back to the `Action` class.

Messaging

Sometimes the web application communicates with a remote application server in asynchronous mode to access business objects that implement the business logic that the web application requires. To provide that, the Java Messaging API (JMS API) can be used to communicate with asynchronous messaging middleware that will reliably deliver query messages and result messages back and forth. The Struts application communicates with the messaging service provider, such as SonicMQ or IBM's MQ Series, for instance.

The scenery is roughly the same as the previous one. You can use helper classes to encapsulate the messaging logic and provide a standard object-oriented interface to the messaging middleware. Or, you can stuff it all inside the `Action` classes. In publisher-subscriber applications, such as the one in Chapter 4, the helper classes will implement `TopicSubscriber` or `TopicPublisher` interfaces.

XML Data

The third alternative scenario presents XML as the `Model` object's representation schema. This can be generated by a standard document server in response to database queries, such as XML tree navigation. In this case, there are a number of alternatives to cope with XML data in Struts:

- **Use XML as content**—In this case, the `Action` class generates the response and dispatches it directly. To avoid problems with the `ActionServlet`, the `perform` method should return `null`. This sends a signal to the `ActionServlet` that the response will be generated by the `Action` class on its own.

- **Wrap and send**—Wrap the XML response in some container, such as a `StringBuffer` or Jakarta Element Construction Set element, a set of Java classes designed to programmatically generate markup content such as HTML or XML, and send this back to the presentation JSP inside an `ActionForm` property or inside a `request` attribute. On the JSP, you can use additional tag libraries to parse or transform that XML as if it were an XML data island. The Jakarta Taglibs project Xtags and XSP libraries can be used for that. See Chapter 9, "The Jakarta Taglibs Project," for more information on these libraries.

- **Digest it**—Use the `Digester` utility class and a set of rules that will read the XML objects and create beans representing them and then send the beans. IBM's Bean Scripting Framework (BSF) can be used in place of Digester also. This is useful when the business objects are commonly represented as EJB and the application must cope with an isolated XML server. Chapter 9 returns to the BSF.

- **Publish it**—Use some web-publishing framework, such as Apache Cocoon, to get your XML and publish it in as many output formats as you need. A standard or custom Cocoon producer can deal with it. As in the first item in this list, the perform method of the Action classes should return null. Or, in a mixed scenario, have it transferred to the JSP and some tag will treat it and get it sent to Cocoon. For more on Cocoon, check http://xml.apache.org.

In any scenario, XML will be treated as data. Using SOAP is equivalent to using any remote procedure call protocol (RPC protocol), such as RMI. The calls to remote objects will be better encapsulated in helper classes, and these will provide higher-level methods than the Struts Action classes will call.

Summary

In this chapter, you learned how a Struts application is built (class per class, JSP per JSP), how the Model layer can be designed for better flexibility, and several aspects that make the design of web application with Struts easier (such as error treatment, central management of ApplicationsResources, key-based labelling, and so on). You also learned how the several components in the application will interact—from application-specific Struts subclasses, such as the Action classes or ActionForm beans, and application-specific classes, such as helper classes and JSP pages.

The Jakarta Taglibs and Other Resources

9

The Jakarta
Taglibs Project

THIS CHAPTER DISCUSSES THE JAKARTA TAGLIBS PROJECT, an open source general-purpose tag library available at the Apache Software Foundation's Jakarta project at the Jakarta web site (`http://jakarta.apache.org`). This chapter presents the Taglibs project, its goals and perspectives, and the tag libraries that constitute the huge tag library already in the project's repository.

The Project

The project also offers a comprehensive tutorial on tag library development. The tutorial.html file is located under the /doc subdirectory of the directory where the Taglibs distributable was installed.

The Libraries Available and Under Development

The Taglibs project is considered to be a repository for a number of tag libraries under development, including the forthcoming Standard Tag Library. Table 9.1 is a list of the libraries present at the time of this writing.

Table 9.1   **Libraries Currently in the Taglibs Project**

Library	Purpose
Application	Access to `ServletContext`. This library contains tags that access the several attributes and parameters available on the `ServletContext`, the context of the web application that you saw in Chapter 1, "Introduction to Servlets and JavaServer Pages." The context is represented in a JSP by the application implicit object.
BSF	A test library that accesses objects scripted with the Bean Scripting Framework.
DateTime	Date and time utility tags.
Input	HTML form input elements. These can have a default value.
DBTags	Access to the JDBC API functionality. There are tags to access a database driver or DataSource object, submit queries, and present results.
JNDI	Access to the JNDI API functionality. There are tags to access a JNDI context, list, lookup and search functions, and many more.
JSP Spec Taglib	Example tags from the JSP specification, tags `foo` and `bar`.
Page	Access to `PageContext`. This library contains tags that access the several attributes and parameters available on `PageContext`, the local context set to the JSP page when it is loaded.
Regexp	Use of regular expressions. This tag library implements a number of Perl functions such as `match`, `split`, and `substitute`.
Request	Access to the `HTTPServletRequest` object and the several attributes and parameters available on the request object.
Response	Access to the attributes available on the `HTTPServletResponse` object.
Scrape	Library that extracts parts of other web pages for use in a page.
Session	Access to the session. This library contains tags that access the several attributes and parameters available on the session.
SQL Sample Taglib	Library that implements the SQL example tags present in the JSP specification. It is not supported anymore.
Utility	An example taglib. This library contains examples on how to code a tag and gives some of the techniques used, for illustration purposes.
XSL	Library that processes XML with style-sheet transformations.

In the following sections, each of these libraries will be presented with examples.

Using the Libraries of the Taglibs Project

To use the tag libraries available under the Taglibs project, you must download and unpack a binary distribution of the library or download, unpack, and build a source distribution. Both are available at the Jakarta web site, at `http://jakarta.apache.org/taglibs/binarydist.html`. Let's examine the steps in using the binary distribution.

After downloading the binary distribution archive and unpacking it, the several libraries that comprise the Taglibs project will appear—each on a separate subdirectory under the TAGLIB_HOME directory. For instance, there will be a TAGLIB_HOME/application directory containing the files for the application tag library.

Each subdirectory will contain four files, as follows:

- **A TLD**—Each library will contain a tag library descriptor that will be used by the developer.

- **The library resource file**—This is a JAR file containing the classes and resources that comprise the tag library itself. This must be deployed on the classpath for the web application. It is recommended that you deploy it under the /WEB-INF/lib subdirectory of the web application.

- **The doc web application**—This file will be named something like *–doc.war. The * is replaced by the name of the library. It is a web application archive file that contains documentation about the library relevant to the developer using it.

- **The examples web application**—This file will be named *-examples.war. The * is replaced by the name of the library. It is a web application archive file that contains examples of use of the library.

Remember that you have to declare each of the tag libraries used in your application inside a `<taglib>` element of your application's web application deployment descriptor file (web.xml), as you learned in Chapter 1 and Chapter 2, "Introduction to Tag Libraries." Also, each page using a tag library must have a `<@taglib>` directive describing a uri and a prefix for it. It is always highly recommended that you either stick with the most accepted names for that, to ease the identification of the libraries used, or use the library name as a prefix.

The default uri for Jakarta Taglibs libraries is `http://jakarta.apache.org/taglibs/{the name of the library}`. For instance, `http://jakarta.apache.org/taglibs/application`-1.0 is the uri for the application tag library.

Let's examine each of the libraries available in the Taglibs project in the next sections.

Application

The application tag library is designed to provide access to information available at the context, basically parameters and attributes. The context was discussed in Chapter 1. It is implemented as a `ServletContext` object and can contain parameters, attributes, and object methods that represent the environment of a web application from a servlet's perspective. The application tag library offers a number of tags for easily accessing those parameters and attributes from inside a page without needing to use scriptlets or the application object.

This tag library is compliant with the JSP Tag Library Extension API 1.1, which is part of the JSP API 1.2. It requires a servlet/JSP container compatible with JSP 1.2. At the time of this writing, the application library was at version 1.0. The short name of this library is application, which is recommended as a preferred prefix.

The tags available in the application library are listed in Table 9.2.

Table 9.2 **Application Library Tags**

Tag	Description
initparameter	The initparameter tag takes a required name attribute, which contains the name of the init parameter desired and retrieves its value on the out stream.
initparameters	The initparameters tag takes a required id attribute, which contains the name of a scripting variable defined in the body of the tag and loops through all the init parameters declared. The scripting variable represented by id can be used within getProperty standard actions to retrieve each init parameter's name and value.
existsinitparameter	The existsinitparameter tag takes two attributes:
	■ **name**—Holds the name of the desired init parameter.
	■ **value**—Holds true or false. If no value is defined, the default is true.
	If the value of the existsinitparameter tag matches the value attribute, its body is included in the output.
	For instance, if the value attribute is false and the desired init parameter is *not* found, the body of the tag will be included.
equalsinitparameter	The equalsinitparameter takes four attributes:
	■ **name**—Holds the name of the desired init parameter.
	■ **value**—Holds true or false. If no value is defined, the default is true. This attribute is optional.
	■ **match**—Holds the value to be matched with the value of the desired init parameter.
	■ **ignorecase**—Holds true or false. If no value is defined, the default is true. This attribute is optional.
	If value is true, the body of the tag will be included if the value of the init parameter matches the value of the match attribute. If value is false, the body will be included if the value of the init parameter does *not* match the value of the match attribute. If the ignorecase attribute holds true, the comparison will not be

case-sensitive. If it holds `false`, the comparison with the `match` attribute will be case-sensitive.

attribute	The `attribute` tag takes a required name, which contains the name of the desired attribute and retrieves its value on the out stream.
attributes	The `attributes` tag takes a required id, which contains the name of a scripting variable defined in the body of the tag and loops through all the attributes declared. The scripting variable represented by id can be used within getProperty standard actions to retrieve each attribute's name and value.
equalsattribute	The `equalsattribute` tag takes four attributes:

- **name**—Holds the name of the desired attribute.
- **value**—Holds `true` or `false`. If no value is defined, the default is `true`. This attribute is optional.
- **match**—Holds the value to be matched with the value of the desired `init` parameter.
- **ignorecase**—Holds `true` or `false`. If no value is defined, the default is `true`. This attribute is optional.

If `value` is `true`, the body of the tag will be included if the value of the attribute matches the value of `match`. If `value` is `false`, the body will be included if the value of the attribute does *not* match the value of `match`. If `ignorecase` is `true`, the comparison will not be case-sensitive. If it is `false`, the comparison with `match` will be case-sensitive.

existsattribute	The `existsattribute` tag takes two attributes:

- **name**—Holds the name of the desired attribute.
- **value**—Hold `true` or `false`. If no value is defined, the default is `true`.

If the value of the `existsattribute` tag matches `value`, its body is included in the output. For instance, if `value` is `false` and the desired attribute is *not* found, the body of the tag will be included.

setattribute	Takes the name of the attribute and sets its value to the content of the tag's body.
removeattribute	Takes the name of the attribute and removes it from the context namespace.

The application tag library in Listing 9.1 shows the use of the `attributes` and `initparameters` tags to retrieve a list of the `attributes` and `init` parameters declared in the current web application.

Listing 9.1   **Using the Application Tag Library**

```
<html>
<head>
   <title>JSP Book examples</title>
</head>
<body bgcolor="white">

<center>

<h1>Using the APPLICATION Taglib</h1></center>
<br>
<%@ taglib uri="http://jakarta.apache.org/taglibs/application-1.0" prefix="app" %>
<table>
<tr>
 <td colspan="2" align="center">Init Parameters detected</td>
</tr>
<tr>
 <td align="center">Name</td>
 <td align="center">Value</td>
</tr>
<app:initparameters id="ips">
 <tr>
  <td><jsp:getProperty name="ips" property="name"/></td>
  <td><jsp:getProperty name="ips" property="value"/></td>
 </tr>
</app:initparameters>
<tr>
 <td colspan="2" align="center">Attributes detected</td>
</tr>
<tr>
 <td align="center">Name</td>
 <td align="center">Value</td>
</tr>
<app:attributes id="ats">
 <tr>
  <td><jsp:getProperty name="ats" property="name"/></td>
  <td><jsp:getProperty name="ats" property="value"/></td>
 </tr>
</table>
</body>
</html>
```

First, the initparameters tag is used to loop through the init parameters, generating a table row per parameter. Then the attributes tag is used to expose the attributes in the context namespace in the same table.

These tags obey a model that will be used in other tag libraries in Jakarta Taglibs: Tag libraries that access attributes available on the context, session, request, or page provide a way to list the attributes, test for the existence of an attribute, and check and access their value. This is very useful for avoiding the exceptions thrown when trying to access an object that is supposed to be in an attribute but that is not found there. Listing 9.2 illustrates the use of `existsattribute` to check the availability of an object before using it.

Listing 9.2   **Fragment Showing the Use of** *existsattribute*

```
...
<application:existsattribute name="DATASOURCE_NAME">

<!-- this block will access the datasource name attribute -->

<%
    Context ct = new InitialContext();
    DataSource ds = (DataSource)
ct.lookup(application.getAttribute(DATASOURCE_NAME));
    ...

%>

</application:existsattribute>
...
```

In Listing 9.2, you can see the access to a JNDI context and the lookup of a JDBC DataSource object. This can be done directly because you have already tested for the attribute's existence with the `existsattribute`. This design is strongly encouraged because it makes it safe to access the attribute by certifying that the attribute is there. It simplifies the code by avoiding the scriptlet needed to test for null values, which is cleaner and clearer for the page designer. After examining other tag libraries in the Taglibs project, we will come back to this example and see what can be done about the scriptlet inside the `existsattribute` tag body.

BSF

The BSF tag library implements the Bean Scripting Framework project, which was originally developed on the IBM AlphaWorks site and has been moved (or graduated, according to the AlphaWorks terminology) under the IBM Open Source initiative at `http://oss.software.ibm.com/developerworks/projects/bsf`. The goal is to integrate scripting in languages other than Java in a JSP. If the respective BSF language processor is available, the selected language can be used to perform some specific operation. The tags available in the BSF library are listed in Table 9.3.

Table 9.3   **BSF Library Tags**

Tag	Description
Scriptlet	Takes a `language` attribute that indicates the BSF language that the script was written with. This happens only if the language processor is available when the script is executed; otherwise, it is ignored. It is analogous to JSP scriptlets.
Expression	Takes a `language` attribute that indicates the BSF language that the expression was written with. If the language processor is available, the expression is evaluated and the result is put on the out stream; otherwise, it is ignored. It is analogous to JSP expressions.

The example of using the application tag library, in Listing 9.3, shows a Perl expression inside a JSP with the BSF expression tag.

Listing 9.3   **Using the BSF Tags**[1]

```
<!--
// This source code is part of the Jakarta Taglibs project
// from the Apache Software Foundation. Refer to the full
// license terms in Appendix F.
-->
<html>
<%@ taglib uri="http://jakarta.apache.org/taglibs/bsf-2.0" prefix="bsf" %>
<head>
   <title>Temperature Table</title>
</head>
<body>
<h1>Temperature Table</h1>
<p>American tourists visiting Canada can use this handy temperature
table which converts from Fahrenheit to Celsius:
<br><br>

In TCL
<table BORDER COLS=2 WIDTH="20%" >
<tr BGCOLOR="#FFFF00">
<th>Fahrenheit</th>
<th>Celsius</th>
</tr>
<bsf:scriptlet language="tcl">
  package require java

  for {set i 60} {$i<=100} {incr i 10} {
    $out println "<tr ALIGN=RIGHT BGCOLOR=\"#CCCCCC\">"
    $out println "<td>$i</td>"
    $out println [concat "<td>" [format %4.2f [expr ($i - 32.0)*5/9]] "</td>"]
    $out println "</tr>"
```

1. This code is a fragment of a page in the Apache Taglibs project from the Apache Software Foundation (http://www.apache.org).

```
    }
</bsf:scriptlet>
</table>
<bsf:expression language="tcl">
    package require java ; java::new java.util.Date
</bsf:expression>


<hr>In Javascript
<table BORDER COLS=2 WIDTH="20%" >
<tr BGCOLOR="#FFFF00">
<th>Fahrenheit</th>
<th>Celsius</th>
</tr>
<bsf:scriptlet language="javascript">
  for (i=60; i<=100; i+=10) {
    out.println ("<tr ALIGN=RIGHT BGCOLOR=\"#CCCCCC\">")
    out.println ("<td>" +  i + "</td>")
    out.println ("<td>" + Math.round((i - 32)*5/9) + "</td>")
    out.println ("</tr>")
  }
</bsf:scriptlet>
</table>
<bsf:expression language="javascript"> new java.util.Date() </bsf:expression>


<hr>In Perl
<table BORDER COLS=2 WIDTH="20%" >
<tr BGCOLOR="#FFFF00">
<th>Fahrenheit</th>
<th>Celsius</th>
</tr>
<bsf:scriptlet language="perlscript">
  for ($i=60; $i<=100; $i+=10) {
    $out->println ("<tr ALIGN=RIGHT BGCOLOR=\"#CCCCCC\">");
    $out->println ("<td>$i</td>");
    $out->println ("<td>" . int(($i - 32)*5/9) . "</td>");
    $out->println ("</tr>");
  }
</bsf:scriptlet>
</table>
<bsf:expression language="perlscript"> CreateBean("java.util.Date")
</bsf:expression>


<hr>In JACL
<table BORDER COLS=2 WIDTH="20%" >
<tr BGCOLOR="#FFFF00">
<th>Fahrenheit</th>
<th>Celsius</th>
</tr>
<bsf:scriptlet language="jacl">
package require java
```

continues

Listing 9.3 **Continued**

```
for {set i 60} {$i<=100} {incr i 10} {
  $out println "<tr ALIGN=RIGHT BGCOLOR=\"#CCCCCC\">"
  $out println "<td>$i</td>"
  $out println [concat "<td>" [format %4.2f [expr ($i - 32.0)*5/9]] "</td>"]
  $out println "</tr>"
}
</bsf:scriptlet>
</table>


<hr>In JPython
<table BORDER COLS=2 WIDTH="20%" >
<tr BGCOLOR="#FFFF00">
<th>Fahrenheit</th>
<th>Celsius</th>
</tr>
<bsf:scriptlet language="jpython">
from java.util import Date;

for i in range(60,100,10):
  out.println ("<tr ALIGN=RIGHT BGCOLOR=\"#CCCCCC\">");
  out.println ("<td>%d</td>" % i);
  out.println ("<td>%4.2f</td>" % ((i - 32.0)*5/9));
  out.println ("</tr>");
</bsf:scriptlet>
</table>


<hr>In LotusScript
<table BORDER COLS=2 WIDTH="20%" >
<tr BGCOLOR="#FFFF00">
<th>Fahrenheit</th>
<th>Celsius</th>
</tr>
<bsf:scriptlet language="lotusscript">
for i = 60 to 100 step 10
    out.println "<tr ALIGN=RIGHT BGCOLOR=""#CCCCCC"">"
    out.println "<td>" &  i & "</td>"
    out.println "<td>" & format((i - 32)*5/9," 0.00") & "</td>"
    out.println "</tr>"
    next
</bsf:scriptlet>
</table>

<bsf:expression language="lotusscript"> CreateBean("java.util.Date")
</bsf:expression>

</body>
</html>
```

Listing 9.3 is an extract of the BSF example page temps.jsp, available in the BSF-examples application deployment file (bsf-examples.war). It was simplified regarding the original page. Here you can see the scriptlet tag being used three times, each generating the same results but coded with a distinct language. The first generates a Fahrenheit–Celsius table in Tcl, the second uses JavaScript, and the last uses Perlscript. After each table, a BSF expression creates a `java.util.Date` in the respective language.

Datetime

The datetime tag library offers a number of date and time utilitarian tags. These are related to the `locale` object and offer great help in dealing with date localization in JSP pages. The tags available in the datetime library are listed in Table 9.4.

Table 9.4 **Datetime Library Tags**

Tag	Description
ampms	Loops through the AM/PM designators placing the designator of the loop in the script variable defined by `id`.
currenttime	Gets the current time in milliseconds since January 1, 1970 GMT. This tag takes no attributes.
eras	Loops through the era designators placing the designator of the loop in the script variable defined by `id`.
format	Takes a date string and formats it with the format pattern provided. It takes three attributes:
	▪ **pattern**—This attribute represents the formatting string used to format this date.
	▪ **timezone**—This attribute holds the name of a Timezone script id variable.
	▪ **locale**—If this attribute is set to `true`, the user's locale is used to format the date.
	▪ **default**—This attribute contains the text to output if the body of this tag contains an invalid date.
	▪ **date**—This attribute holds a `java.util.Date` runtime variable (a scriptlet expression) that will be used in the formatting.
months	Loops through the months of the year, placing the month of the loop in the script variable defined by `id`.
parse	Parses a date string with the date pattern provided. It takes three attributes:
	▪ **pattern**—This attribute represents the formatting string used to format this date.

continues

Table 9.4   **Continued**

Tag	Description
	▪ `timezone`—This attribute holds the name of a Timezone script id variable.
	▪ `locale`—If this attribute is set to `true`, the user's locale is used to format the date.
timezone	Creates a script variable named after the `id` attribute with a new timezone.
timezones	Loops through the timezones available, placing the timezone details in a bean available in a scripting variable. It takes three attributes:
	▪ `id`—Holds the name for the scripting variable that will be made available by this tag. It is the only required attribute.
	▪ `locale`—Specifies the locale used to seek for the timezones available. If no locale is provided, the default Java locale is used instead.
	▪ `style`—Represents the name of a style of display for a timezone. It can be either `SHORT` or `LONG`.
weekdays	Loops through the weekdays, placing the day of the loop in the script variable defined by `id`.

The example of the datetime tag library, in Listing 9.4, shows a data entry page that displays and accepts a number of dates.

Listing 9.4   **Using the datetime Tags**

```
<html>
<%@ taglib uri="http://jakarta.apache.org/taglibs/datetime-1.0" prefix="dt" %>
<jsp:useBean id="vaccines" scope="session"/>
<head>
    <title>Vaccination Card</title>
</head>
<body>
<h1>Vaccination Card</h1>
<table border="1">
<tr>
 <td>name:</td>
 <td colspan="3">
  <jsp:getProperty name="vaccines" property="patient"/>
 </td>
</tr>
<%  for (int i=0;i<vaccines.getVaccines().size();i++) {
     Vaccine vacc = (Vaccine)vaccines.getVaccines().elementAt(i);
%>
<tr>
<td>vaccine:</td>
 <td><%=vacc.getVacc()%></td>
 <td>date:</td>
 <td>
     <dt:format pattern="YYYY-MM-DD">
```

```
        <%=vacc.getVaccDate()%>
      </dt:format>
  </td>
</tr>
<%  }  %>
</table>
</body>
</html>
```

The example displays the vaccination card of a certain patient. It shows the name and date of vaccination for each vaccine. The `vaccines` bean contains the data relevant to the page. Here, you can see the use of the format tag from the datetime tag library.

Input

This library has tags for HTML form input that accept default values. The tags available in the input library are listed in Table 9.5.

Table 9.5   **Input Library Tags**

Tag	Description
text	Provides an input tag with type `text`
textarea	Provides a `textarea` element
select	Provides a `select` element
radio	Provides an input tag with type `radio`
checkbox	Provides an input tag with type `checkbox`

Listing 9.5 presents a data-entry page that uses the input tag library.

Listing 9.5   **Using the input Tags for HTML Form Composition**

```
<html>
<%@ taglib uri="http://jakarta.apache.org/taglibs/input-0.90" prefix="input" %>
<head>
    <title>Vaccination Card</title>
</head>
<body>
<form action="vacc_data_entry.jsp">
<h1>Vaccination Card</h1>
<table border="1">
<tr>
 <td>name:</td>
 <td colspan="3">
  <input:text name="patient" default="pacient"/>
 </td>
</tr>
```

continues

Listing 9.5 **Continued**

```
<tr>
 <td>vaccine:</td>
 <td><input:text name="vacc" default="influenza"/></td>
 <td>date:</td>
 <td><input:text name="date" default="2001-03-20"/></td>
</tr>
<tr>
 <td>vaccine:</td>
 <td><input:text name="vacc" default="influenza"/></td>
 <td>date:</td>
 <td><input:text name="date" default="2001-03-20"/></td>
</tr>
<tr>
 <td>patient age group:</td>
 <td>
<% java.util.Hashtable o = new java.util.Hashtable(); %>
<% o.put("infant", "1"); %>
<% o.put("adult", "2"); %>
<% o.put("senior", "3"); %>
<input:select name="age_grp"
        default="1" options="<%= o %>" />

 </td>
 <td>sex:</td>
 <td>
<input:radio name="sex" value="M"/>Male
<input:radio name="sex" value="F"/>Female
 </td>
</tr>
</table>
</form>
</body>
</html>
```

Listing 9.5 shows the data entry form that will feed the vaccination card database. You can see a number of text entry fields with and without defaults. You also can see the select box that accepts a default value and a couple of radio boxes for the patient's gender.

jdbc

This tag library abstracts the objects and most relevant methods available in the Java Database Connectivity API. The tags available in the jdbc library are listed in Table 9.6.

Table 9.6　**jdbc Library Tags**

Tag	Description
connection	Encapsulates `java.sql.Connection`. It takes three attributes: - **id**—The id attribute defines a script variable with the name to reference this connection afterward. - **JndiName**—If there is a `DataSource` object available in a JNDI service, this holds the name of that and takes the connection from that `DataSource`. - **DataSource**—The `DataSource` object is not located in a JNDI service, but is in an attribute to be found by the `pageContext.findAttribute` method.
url	Encapsulates a JDBC URL. This tag will appear in the body of a connection tag to provide a database URL for the connection being established. When used, the `url` tag will be used in conjunction with a driver, a `userid` tag, and a `password` tag. This is obviously not a safe way because a database user ID and password will be left open in the page code.
driver	Encapsulates `java.sql.Driver`. It is used in the same way as the url tag and provides a driver name for the connection.
jndiName	Provides a JNDI name to a `DataSource` stored in a JNDI service, but is used in the body of a connection tag. It has an attribute with the name of an `init` parameter that can be used to hold the `DataSource` name.
userId	Provides a user ID to establish a connection to a database. This will also appear in the body of a connection tag.
password	Provides a password for the user ID declared with the `userid` tag.
closeConnection	Closes a connection opened by the `connection` tag. It takes a `conn` attribute, which holds the name declared by the `id` attribute in the `connection` tag.
statement	Represents a SQL statement.
escapeSql	SQL-escapes a `String` for use in a `query` tag body.
query	Holds the SQL text for the statement or `preparedStatement` tag.
execute	Executes a query in a statement or `preparedStatement` tags.
wasEmpty	If the result set returned is empty, includes its body contents in the out stream.
wasNotEmpty	If the result set returned is not empty, includes its body contents in the out stream.

continues

Table 9.6   **Continued**

Tag	Description
rowCount	Can be used inside a resultSet tag or after it. It must be used inside a Statement tag or a preparedStatement tag. If it is used inside a ResultSet tag, it prints the number of rows retrieved so far. If it is used after a ResultSet tag, it prints the total number of rows retrieved.
preparedStatement	Represents a PreparedStatement JDBC object. Use is the same as for statement.
setColumn	For use inside a preparedStatement tag. It sets a query parameter to a value.
resultSet	Represents a ResultSet returned as a result of a select in a statement. If the result set is not empty, this tag loops through the rows returned. Using a getColumn tag in the body of a resultSet retrieves a column.
wasNull	Includes its body if the last getColumn returned a null value.
wasNotNull	Includes its body if the last getColumn did not return a null value.
getColumn	Retrieves a column returned in a result set. It takes three attributes: • **position**—Specifies the position of the column to retrieve. • **to**—Holds the name of an attribute that will take the String value retrieved, instead of having it printed. • **Scope**—Changes the scope of the attribute. The default is page.
getNumber	Handles number retrieval. This tag offers more options for number formatting.
getTime	Handles time retrieval.
getDate	Handles date retrieval.
getTimestamp	Handles timestamp retrieval.

Listing 9.6 shows up an example of the jdbc tags. It accesses the article database that was introduced in Chapter 2, the MySQL database, through a URL and driver. It retrieves some articles from a user-defined topic. Assume that the topic has been chosen in another page and that this example will generate a response to that choice.

Listing 9.6   **Using the jdbc Tag Library**

```
<%
    String topic = request.getParameter("TOPIC");
    if (topic == null) topic="general";
%>
<html>
<%@ taglib uri="http://jakarta.apache.org/taglibs/jdbc" prefix="sql" %>
<head>
```

```
   <title>Article Database</title>
</head>
<sql:connection id="con">
 <sql:url>jdbc:mysql://localhost/ARTICLE_DB</sql:url>
 <sql:driver>org.gjt.mm.mysql.Driver</sql:driver>
</sql:connection>
<body>
<h1>Article Retrieval - Topic: <%=topic%></h1>
<table border="1">
<tr>
 <td>article</td>
 <td>author</td>
 <td>title</td>
</tr>
<sql:statement id="stmt" conn="con">
 <sql:query>
   select article_id, name, title from articles, authors
   where main_author=author_id and
   category='<sql:escapeSql><%=topic%></sql:escapeSql>'
   order by 1
 </sql:query>

 <%-- loop through the rows retrieved by the topic chosen --%>
 <sql:resultSet id="rs">
   <tr>
     <td><a href="detail.jsp?ART=<sql:getColumn position="1"/>"><sql:getColumn
position="1"/></td>
     <td><sql:getColumn position="2"/></td>
     <td><sql:getColumn position="3"/>
         <sql:wasNull>[no description]</sql:wasNull></td>
   </tr>
 </sql:resultSet>
</sql:statement>
<sql:closeConnection conn="con"/>
</table>
</body>
</html>
```

Listing 9.6 presents a complete example using the basic tags in the jdbc tag library. If you are familiar with the JDBC API, you will find almost the same mechanisms here. The difference lies in how comfortable it is to use these tags rather than hard-coding database access in Java. At first sight, you can see that the resultSet tag does almost the entire job of finding columns, converting them to Strings, and putting them out or putting them into an attribute. The connection tag also offers facilities to retrieve a DataSource object from a JNDI service. If you had a JNDI service available for the article database, you could code the connection tag simply as shown in Listing 9.7.

Listing 9.7   **Coding the *connection* Tag for the Article Database via a JNDI *DataSource***

```
...
<sql:connection jndiName="ARTICLE_DB_DS"/>
...
```

That will encapsulate the fragment used to access the JNDI service, as shown in Listing 9.8.

Listing 9.8   **Comparing the *connection* Tag with the Equivalent Java JNDI Scriptlet**

```
    Context ct = new InitialContext();
    DataSource ds = (DataSource)
ct.lookup(application.getAttribute(ARTICLE_DB_DS));
    ...
```

jndi

This library abstracts the Java Naming and Directories Interface API. The JDBC `DataSources` stored in JNDI services were used in Listings 9.2, 9.7, and 9.8. In Listing 9.8, you saw the basic pattern for accessing a directory service and retrieving an object stored there for sharing. The jndi tag library offers the main objects and methods available in the JNDI API for use in JSP coding. The tags available in the jndi library are listed in Table 9.7.

Table 9.7   **JNDI Tag Library Tags**

Tag	Description
useContext	Creates a context for use in a page. It has 13 attributes:
	■ **id**—This attribute specifies the name that this context will be referred by after this tag in a page.
	■ **envRef and env**—These provide environment information. Use envRef if the information is in an attribute. Otherwise, to provide that information with a `Hashtable`, use env.
	■ **url**, **providerUrl**, **or initialFactory**—One of these must be provided. The url attribute holds the value used to perform a lookup to the context created by the other attributes. The providerUrl attribute is equivalent to `Context.PROVIDER_URL`. The initialFactory attribute is equivalent to `Context.INITIAL_CONTEXT_FACTORY`.
	■ **dnsUrl**—This is equivalent to `Context.DNS_URL`.
	■ **authoritative**—This is equivalent to `Context.AUTHORITATIVE`.
	■ **batchSize**—This is equivalent to `Context.BATCHSIZE`.

- **objectFactories**—This is equivalent to
  Context.OBJECT_FACTORIES.

- **stateFactories**—This is equivalent to
  Context.STATE_FACTORIES.

- **urlPkgPrefixes**—This is equivalent to
  Context.URL_PKG_PREFIXES.

- **scope**—This gives the scope that the object represented by this
  context, named after the id attribute, will be exported to. By
  default, it is exported to the page scope.

list   Lists the elements in a context. It has 11 attributes:

- **contextRef and context**—Either contextRef or context must be
  provided. The first is a string that references a context. The second
  is a Context object.

- **name**—This attribute gives the name to perform the list against.

- **nameObj**—This is a Name object to be used in the list. If this and
  name are used and are both non-null, this will be taken.

- **bindings**—This is a Boolean stating whether bound objects
  are returned.

- **nameId**—This is the attribute name that the name listing will be
  exported to.

- **nameScope**—This attribute gives the scope of the attribute in
  nameId.

- **classId**—This gives the attribute name that the class name will be
  exported to.

- **classScope**—This gives the scope of the attribute in classId.

- **objId**—This specifies the attribute name that the bound object
  listing will be exported to.

- **objScope**—This gives the scope of the attribute in objectId.

lookup   Looks for a particular object and exports it. This tag has seven
attributes, as follows:

- **contextRef and context**—Either contextRef or context must be
  provided. The first is a string that references a context. The second
  is a Context object.

- **id**—This gives the attribute name for the object to be exported.

- **scope**—This is the scope for the attribute defined by id.

- **name**—This specifies the name to perform the lookup against.

- **nameObj**—This is a Name object to be used in the lookup. If this
  and name are used and are both non-null, this will be taken.

- **type**—This is the class to cast the returned object to.

continues

Table 9.7 **Continued**

Tag	Description
useDirContext	Equivalent to the useContext tag. The difference is that this tag generates DirContext objects instead.
search	Searches a useDirContext. This tag has 14 attributes:

- **name**—This is the name to perform the list against.
- **nameObj**—This is a Name object to be used in the list. If this and name are used and are both non-null, this will be taken.
- **contextRef and context**—Either contextRef or context must be provided. The first is a string that references a context. The second is a Context object.
- **id**—This is the attribute name for the object to be exported.
- **scope**—This specifies the scope for the attribute defined by id.
- **filter**—This is the LDAP-style filter to use.
- **countLimit**—This gives the maximum number of entries to return.
- **derefLink**—This attribute defines whether links will be dereferenced during the search.
- **attributes**—This is a comma-separated list of attributes to retrieve. Null means return all.
- **attributesSeparator**—This is an alternative separator to be used in the place of a comma.
- **bindings**—This is a Boolean stating whether bound objects are returned.
- **searchScope**—This attribute tells what scope the search is to be preformed against. One of subtree, subtree_scope, onelevel, onelevel_scope, object, or object_scope is used. (The variants are treated as the _scope variants).
- **timeLimit**—This attribute specifies the amount of time to wait before a timeout.

Tag	Description
getAttribute	Works as quite a rich tag. It can retrieve attributes from Context, DirContext, Attributes, or Attribute. For more information on this tag, refer to the jndi tag library documentation. This tag has six attributes:

- **id**—The attribute name for the object to be exported.
- **scope**—The scope for the attribute defined by id.
- **ref**—A pageContext attribute to perform the getAttribute upon.
- **object**—The actual object to perform the getAttribute upon.
- **attribute**—The name of the attribute to use against objects of types DirContext, SearchResults, or Attributes.

- **attribute**—A String. See the documentation.

forEachAttribute   Allows you to iterate through the attributes from DirContext, SearchResults, or Attributes. This tag takes four attributes, as follows:

- **id**—The attribute name for the object to be exported.

- **scope**—The scope that the attribute in the current iteration will be exported to.

- **ref**—A reference to a page scope attribute with an instance of either DirContext, SearchResults, or Attributes upon which JNDI attribute operations can be performed.

- **object**—The actual object to perform the getAttribute upon.

Listing 9.9 presents a fragment used to look up a DataSource object stored in a JNDI service.

Listing 9.9   **JNDI Tag Library Tags**

```
<%@ taglib uri="http://jakarta.apache.org/taglibs/jndi-1.0" prefix="jndi" %>

<jndi:useContext
    id='ctx'
    scope='page'
    initialFactory='com.sun.jndi.ldap.LdapCtxFactory'
    providerUrl='ldap://localhost:389/o=JSPBook'
/>

<jndi:lookup
  contextRef='ctx'
  name='<%= application.getAttribute(ARTICLE_DB_DS)%>'
  id="ds"
/>
...
```

jspspec

This library implements the foo and bar example tags shown in the JavaServer Pages API specification topics on tag libraries (see Chapter 10, "Commercial Tag Libraries").

page

The page tag library is used to access the attributes in the page namespace, available through the pageContext object. It is analogous to the application library that you saw earlier. The tags available in the page library are listed in Table 9.8.

Table 9.8   **The Page Tag Library Tags**

Tag	Description
Attribute	The `attribute` tag takes a required name that contains the name of the desired attribute and retrieves its value in the out stream.
Attributes	The `attributes` tag takes a required ID that contains the name of a scripting variable defined in the body of the tag and loops through all the attributes declared. The scripting variable represented by `id` can be used within `getProperty` standard actions to retrieve each attribute's name and value.
Equalsattribute	The `equalsattribute` tag takes four attributes: ■ **name**—Holds the name of the desired attribute. ■ **value**—Holds `true` or `false`. If no value is defined, the default is `true`. This attribute is optional. ■ **match**—Holds the value to be matched with the value of the desired `init` parameter. ■ **ignorecase**—Holds `true` or `false`. If no value is defined, the default is `true`. This attribute is optional. If `value` is `true`, the body of the tag will be included if the value of the attribute matches the value of `match`. If `value` is `false`, the body will be included if the value of the attribute does *not* match the value of `match`. If `ignorecase` is `true`, the comparison will not be case-sensitive. If it is `false`, the comparison with `match` will be case-sensitive.
existsattribute	The `existsattribute` tag takes two attributes: ■ **name**—Holds the name of the desired attribute. ■ **value**—Holds `true` or `false`. If no value is defined, the default is `true`. If the value of the `existsattribute` tag matches `value`, its body is included in the output. For instance, if `value` is `false` and the desired attribute is *not* found, the body of the tag will be included.
setattribute	This tag takes the name of the attribute and sets its value to the content of its body.
removeattribute	This tag takes the name of the attribute and removes it from the page namespace.

This library is used in the same way as the application library attribute tags.

regexp

The regexp tag library implements Perl-style regular expression processing. A regular expression (regexp) is a mechanism to search string patterns in text and then trigger some action on the occurrence of the pattern, such as change the text, print it, trigger some collateral effect (such as copying a file), and so on. The Perl regexp processor is recognized by its flexibility and ease of use. Perl expressions are powerful yet simple. The tags available in the regexp library are listed in Table 9.10.

The `regexp` tag creates a script variable containing the pattern to search in the text. This is done through `regexp` matching operations, metacharacters, and modifiers. The matching operations implemented by the regexp tag are listed here:

- **[m]/pattern/[i][m][s][x]**—Searches the pattern on the text using the designated modifiers.

- **s/pattern/replacement/[g][i][m][o][s][x]**—Searches the text for the pattern and replaces the pattern with the replacement when found using the designated modifiers.

- **split()**—Splits the text based on the pattern.

The modifiers applicable to a `regexp` operation in the context of the regexp tag library are as follows:

- **g**—Global match, to find all occurrences of the pattern

- **i**—Non–case-sensitive matching

- **m**—Multiline string

- **o**—Compilation of pattern only once

- **s**—Single-line string

- **x**—Use of extended regular expressions

Table 9.9 shows the control characters and contents of a pattern that can be used inside the `regexp` tag.

Table 9.9   **Metacharacters and Composition of the *regexp* Tag Patterns**

Metacharacter or Content	Meaning in the Pattern
text	This matches any text, such as apple or oranges.
.	The dot metacharacter matches a single character—any character.
?	The question metacharacter matches the character preceding it zero or one time only.
*	The star metacharacter matches the character preceding it zero times up to any number of times.
+	This works like the star metacharacter, but at least one occurrence is mandatory
\d	This matches a digit only.
\D	This is the nondigit metacharacter. It matches any character except a digit.
\w	This matches a letter, a digit, or an underscore only.

continues

Table 9.9　**Continued**

Metacharacter or Content	Meaning in the Pattern
\W	This matches any character except a digit, letter, or underscore.
\s	This matches only whitespace-like characters (space, tab, CR, and so on).
\S	This matches any character except a whitespace-like character.
\b	This is a word boundary match. It matches any word starting with the sequence that follows it. For example, \ban will match any, animal, and any other word starting with an.
\B	This is the opposite of \b.
{a}, {a,}, {a,b}	The curly braces match the character preceding them a minimum number of a times and a maximum number of b times. For example, aX{1,3}z will match aXz, aXXz, and aXXXz only. Using {a} will match the character exactly a times. Using {a,} will match the character at least a times.
[]	The brackets match any characters in the sequence inside it with the character in the position. For example, [nlm]otion will match notion, lotion, and motion. You can use ranges inside the brackets with a dash, as in a-zA-Z, meaning all letters, small caps or not, or 0-9A-F, meaning all digits and the letters A to F, as in hexadecimal numbers. To use the dash as a character, it must be the last character in the sequence. The caret (^) inverts the meaning of the brackets when it is the first character in the sequence. For instance, [^nlm]otion won't match notion, motion, or lotion, but it will match potion.
\	This is the escaping character. To use the ., ?, *, or + characters in a pattern, you must precede it by the backslash, as in \.txt to find .txt or *abb to find *abb.

You will find more information and examples on Perl regular expressions on the web. Some nice pages on the topic are maintained by the Humanities Computing Group at the University of Georgia, at http://www.english.uga.edu/humcomp/perl/regex2a.html, and the Perl site, at http://www.perl.com. A nice reference is "Mastering Regular Expressions," by Jeffrey E. Friedl.

Table 9.10　**The RegExp Tag Library Tags**

Tag	Description
regexp	Creates a regular expression script variable. The id attribute identifies the variable.
text	Creates a String script variable to hold the string to apply the regular expression for a match. The id attribute identifies it.

`existsmatch`	Tests for a match applying the regular expression defined by the attribute `regexp` with the `text` variable defined by the attribute text. If a match exists and the `value` attribute holds `true`, the body of the tag is included. If `value` holds `false`, the body will be included if a match does *not* exist. The value is `true` by default.
`substitute`	Implements the substitution operation on text by `regexp`.
`split`	Splits text on a `regexp`.
`match`	Loops through the matches found.
`group`	Takes a parenthesized group in a match.

Listing 9.10 shows an example of use for the regexp tags.

Listing 9.10 **Using the RegExp Tag Library**

```
<html>
<%@ taglib uri="http://jakarta.apache.org/taglibs/regexp-1.0" prefix="rx" %>
<head>
   <title>Jakarta REGEXP Taglib Example</title>
</head>
<body>
<h1>Jakarta REGEXP Taglib Example</h1>

<!-- match regexp "m/surname/mi" -->
<rx:regexp id="exp">m/surname/mi</rx:regexp>

<rx:text id="rawdata">
This is a text describing some person. This can be the result of a database query
processing, or some data transfer that is still not using XML. Here we can put a
lot of data, like a person's name, surname, address, date of birth, and so on.
</rx:text>

<rx:existsmatch regexp="exp" text="rawdata">
   A match was found!<br>
</rx:existsmatch>
<rx:existsmatch regexp="rx1" text="test" value="false">
   A match was not found!<br>
</rx:existsmatch>

</body>
</html>
```

Listing 9.10 shows the application of the `regexp` tag to define the regular expression to apply, the text tag to define the text to match against, and the `existsmatch` tag, which checks to see if there is a match with that regular expression.

request

The request tag library can be used to access the information available in the
`HttpServletRequest` object, the request implicit object in a JSP page. There are tags
to access request attributes, cookies, and so on. The tags available in the request library
are listed in Table 9.11.

Table 9.11   **The Request Tag Library Tags**

Tag	Description
cookie	Gets the value of the cookie defined by the `name` attribute.
cookies	Loops through the request cookies, placing the current cookie on the variable defined by `id`. If the `name` attribute is supplied, it gets the attributes of the corresponding cookie.
existscookie	Includes its body if the cookie defined by the `name` attribute exists and the `value` attribute holds `true`. If `value` holds `false`, it includes the body if the cookie is *not* found.
querystring	Gets the value of the query string parameter defined by the `name` attribute.
querystrings	Loops through the query string parameters, placing the current one in the variable defined by `id`.
existsquerystring	Includes its body if the query string parameter defined by the `name` attribute exists and the `value` attribute holds `true`. If `value` holds `false`, it includes the body if the query string parameter is *not* found.
header	Gets the value of the header defined by the `name` attribute.
headers	Loops through the headers, placing the current one in the variable defined by `id`.
headervalues	Loops through the multivalued header values, placing the current one in the variable defined by `id`.
existsheader	Includes its body if the header defined by the `name` attribute exists and the `value` attribute holds `true`. If `value` holds `false`, it includes the body if the header is *not* found.
issecure	Tests whether the connection was made through HTTPS. If `value` holds `false`, it tests whether the connection was *not* made through HTTPS.
issessionfromcookie	Tests whether the session was from a cookie. If `value` holds `false`, it tests whether the session was *not* from a cookie.
issessionfromurl	Tests whether the session was from URL encoding. If `value` holds `false`, it tests whether the session was *not* from URL encoding.
issessionvalid	Tests whether the session is valid. If `value` holds `false`, it tests whether the session was invalidated.

isuserinrole	Tests whether the remote user is in a role defined by the role attribute. If value holds false, it tests whether the user is *not* in the role.
parameter	Gets the value of the request parameter defined by the name attribute.
parameters	Loops through the request parameters, placing the current one in the variable defined by id.
parametervalues	Loops through the multivalued request parameter values, placing the current one in the variable defined by id.
existsparameter	Includes its body if the request parameter defined by the name attribute exists and the value attribute holds true. If value holds false, it includes the body if the request parameter is *not* found.
request	Places information about the request on the script variable defined by the id attribute.
attribute	Gets the value of the request attribute defined by name.
attributes	Loops through the request attributes, placing the current one in the variable defined by id.
existsattribute	Includes its body if the request attribute defined by name exists and value holds true. If value holds false, it includes the body if the request attribute is *not* found.
setattribute	Takes the name of the request attribute and sets its value to the content of its body.
removeattribute	Takes the name of the request attribute and removes it from the request namespace.

Listing 9.11 tests whether the connection is secure. If so, it loops through the request parameters, placing each on the out stream.

Listing 9.11 **Using the Request Tag Library**

```
<html>
<head>
   <title>Jakarta REQUEST Taglib Example</title>
</head>
<body bgcolor="white">

<center>
<h1>
Jakarta REQUEST Taglib Example</h1></center>
<br>
<%@ taglib uri="http://jakarta.apache.org/taglibs/request-1.0" prefix="req" %>

<req:issecure>

  <req:isuserinrole role="DEBUG">
```

continues

Listing 9.11　**Continued**

```
    <req:parameters id="param">
      <jsp:getProperty name="param" property="name"/> =
      <jsp:getProperty name="param" property="value"/>
    </req:parameters>

  </req:isuserinrole>

</req:issecure>

</body>
</html>
```

The `issecure` tag checks whether the connection was established over HTTPS. Then the `isuserinrole` tag is used to ensure that the user is in the `DEBUG` role. If so, the parameter list, created by the `parameters` tag, will be printed in the out stream.

response

The response tag library can be used to access the information available in the `HttpServletResponse` object, the less used response implicit object in a JSP page. The tags available in the response library are listed in Table 9.12.

Table 9.12　**The Response Tag Library Tags**

Tag	Description
addcookie	Adds a cookie to the response with the following information in the form of tag attributes: name, value, comment, domain, max age (attribute maxage), path, secure, and version.
value	Sets a cookie value. It is used in a cookie tag body.
comment	Gives the cookie's comment.
domain	Gives the cookie's domain.
maxage	Gives the cookie's max age.
path	Gives the cookie's path.
secure	Specifies whether the cookie requires secure transport (HTTPS).
version	Gives the cookie's version.
addheader	Adds the header identified by the name attribute with the value given by its body content.
addintheader	Adds an integer header.
adddateheader	Adds a date header.
setheader	Sets the value of a header with the value given by its body content.
setintheader	Sets the value of an integer header.

setdateheader	Sets the value of a date header.
containsheader	Checks whether the HTTP response contains the header identified by the `name` attribute. If the `value` attribute is `false`, it checks whether the HTTP response does *not* contain the header.
encodeurl	Encodes a URL with `JSESSIONID`. The URL is passed in this tag's body.
encoderedirecturl	Encodes a URL with `JSESSIONID` for use in a `sendredirect`.
senderror	Sends an HTTP error code. The `error` attribute holds the error code. The `reset` attribute holds `true` if the response information (headers, the response buffer, and so on) is to be reset.
setstatus	Sets a status code for the HTTP response. The code to return is passed via the `status` attribute.
sendredirect	Sends a redirect to the client's browser. The URL to redirect to is provided in the body content.
setcontenttype	Sets the content type for the response. The content type to set is provided in the body content.
flushbuffer	Flushes the out buffer.
iscommitted	Includes the body content if the response is already committed. If the `value` attribute is set to `false`, it includes the body content if the response is *not* committed.
skippage	Skips the remainder of the JSP.

The request and response libraries complement themselves quite naturally. Information such as cookies and headers can be gathered or tested in the request library and can be set in the response. In fact, you can see that the response library doesn't test anything; it adds or sets almost every parameter in the HTTP response. On the other hand, the request library can grasp, test, or check the existence of almost every parameter on the HTTP request. So, if you are generating a response to some request, you gather information with the request tags and set the adequate response with the response tags.

Listing 9.12 presents an example in which both libraries are used. If the user is in a certain role, a cookie is added to the page to broaden the information generated at client side.

Listing 9.12 **Using the Response Tag Library**

```
<html>
<head>
   <title>Jakarta REQUEST Taglib Example</title>
</head>
<body bgcolor="white">

<center>
<h1>
```

continues

Listing 9.12   **Continued**

```
Jakarta REQUEST Taglib Example</h1></center>
<br>
<%@ taglib uri="http://jakarta.apache.org/taglibs/request-1.0" prefix="req" %>

<%@ taglib uri="http://jakarta.apache.org/taglibs/response-1.0" prefix="res" %>

<req:issecure>

  <req:isuserinrole role="DEBUG">

    <res:addcookie name="LOG_LEVEL" value="DEBUG_VERBOSE" comment="debug logging
flag" maxage="-1" path="/JSPBook/" secure="true" version="1">

  </req:isuserinrole>

</req:issecure>

</body>
</html>
```

Here, if the transport is safe (HTTPS) and the user is debugging the application, then set a cookie that will require HTTPS and hold the log level to be used in the client-side code of that application.

scrape

The scrape library is used to extract parts of other web pages for use on this current page. This is especially useful in a number of situations. For instance, large companies or organizations tend to have a number of web development teams distributed and scoped by geographic area or by department. Or, these companies and organizations have been developing web pages and services for a long time now. Some information might be available in a table or div in a static page, or in a page of these applications developed remotely or a long ago; this information might be of interest inside a certain JSP in the application. The scrape tags are used to grasp this kind of information.

Another context involves deploying the core meaningful data present in a certain web site in a number of platforms that can't realize the rich graphics and exuberance present in feature-rich web pages, such as PDAs or wap cellphones. It can be convenient to extract (scrape) only the meaningful parts of such a page, assemble a specific page to accommodate that in an orderly manner (without having to regenerate all the information again), and then deploy that in a wap device or a PDA.

The tags available in the scrape library are listed in Table 9.13.

Table 9.13   **The Scrape Tag Library Tags**

Tag	Description
page	Sets the page that will be used in the scrape. This is the parent for the other scraping tags. This tag has two attributes: a URL for the desired page and the time to wait before accessing the page on url again. The url attribute is to be used if the page to scrap is static. If the page is dynamic, see the url tag entry.
scrape	Gives the definition of the scraping process for the page parent tag. It tells where to begin and end (the begin and end anchors), and it specifies an object to place the result in. The attributes are as follows:
	■ **id**—This attribute identifies the object to receive the results of the scrapping process.
	■ **begin**—This is the begin anchor.
	■ **end**—This is the end anchor.
	■ **strip**—If this is true, the result won't contain any tags; it will contain just raw data. The default is `false`.
	■ **anchors**—This attribute tells whether to include the anchors in the result. If it is `true`, the anchors will be included. The default value is `false`.
result	This retrieves the HTML extracted from a page in a scraping process.
url	This also does the scraping of the page in the page tag. This is to be used rather than the url attribute of the page tag if the page to scrap is dynamically generated.

Listing 9.13 presents a page from which you can access the vaccination dates table.

Listing 9.13   **The Page to Scrape Information From**

```
<html>
<body>
<H1> Vaccination dates </H1>
Here are the vaccination dates in the permanent vaccination calendar:
<table>
<tr>
<td>name</td>
<td>dose no.</td>
<td>date</td>
</tr>
<tr>
<td>influenza a</td>
<td>unique</td>
<td>sep-23</td>
</tr>
<tr>
<td>influenza f</td>
<td>1st</td>
```

continues

Listing 9.13 **Continued**

```
<td>jun-08</td>
</tr>
</table>
</body>
</html>
```

Listing 9.14 shows a JSP that needs to retrieve the table that Listing 9.13 points out. In Listing 9.14, we let the table tags appear just to use the scrape result as it is.

Listing 9.14 **Using the Scrape Tag Library**

```
<HTML>
<%@ taglib uri="http://kinetic.more.net/taglibs/scrape" prefix="scrp" %>

<HEAD>
 <TITLE>Example JSP using scrape taglib</TITLE>
</HEAD>

<BODY>

<scrp:page url="http://localhost:8080/jspbook/examples/vacc_dates.htm" time="11">
<scrp:scrape id="vacc" begin="<table>" end="</table>" anchors="true"/>

</scrp:page>

The table scraped from the vaccination dates page is placed here:
        <scrp:result scrape="vacc"/>

      </BODY>
</HTML>
```

session

As with the application, page, and request scopes, the session tag library enables you to access the attributes and methods from the HttpSession object, represented by the implicit session object in a JSP. The tags available in the session library are listed in Table 9.14.

Table 9.14 **The Session Tag Library Tags**

Tag	Description
attribute	Takes a required name, which contains the name of the desired attribute and retrieves its value on the out stream.
attributes	Takes a required id, which contains the name of a scripting variable defined in the body of the tag and loops through all

	the attributes declared. The scripting variable represented by id can be used within getProperty standard actions to retrieve each attribute's name and value.
existsattribute	Takes two attributes:
	■ **name**—Holds the name of the desired attribute.
	■ **value**—Holds `true` or `false`. If no value is defined, the default is `true`.
	If the value of the `existsattribute` tag matches `value`, its body is included in the output. For instance, if `value` is `false` and the desired attribute is *not* found, the body of the tag will be included.
setattribute	Takes the name of the attribute and sets its value to the content of the tag's body.
removeattribute	Takes the name of the attribute and removes it from the page namespace.
invalidate	Invalidates the current session.
isnew	Tests whether the session is new. It wraps around the `session.isNew` method.
session	Provides access to information about a session. The `id` attribute identifies a script variable to hold the session.
maxinactiveinterval	Sets the maximum interval that the session is kept while inactive.

Use of the session tag library is equivalent to use of the attribute tags of the other tag libraries that represent each namespace.

sql

This library implements the sql processing example tags shown in the JavaServer Pages API 1.1 specification, sections A.2.1 and A.2.2 (see Table 9.15). It is not considered a production-oriented tag library, and it is not maintained by the development group of the Taglibs project.

Table 9.15 **The Sql Tag Library Tags**

Tag	Description
Connection	Implements the JDBC `Connection` interface. Refer to the JSP 1.1 specification section A.2.1 for a description of this tag.
Userid	Enables you to specify the JDBC `Connection` userid attribute. Refer to the JSP 1.1 specification section A.2.1 for a description of this tag.
Password	Enables you to specify the JDBC `Connection` password attribute. Refer to the JSP 1.1 specification section A.2.1 for a description of this tag.

continues

Table 9.15 **Continued**

Tag	Description
Dburl	Enables you to specify the JDBC Connection database path attribute. Refer to the JSP 1.1 specification section A.2.1 for a description of this tag.
Driver	Enables you to specify the driver to use to establish the connection with the database. Refer to the JSP 1.1 specification section A.2.1 for a description of this tag.
Query	Implements a mix of the JDBC Statement/ResultSet interfaces. Refer to the JSP 1.1 specification section A.2.2 for a description of this tag.

utility

This tag library contains examples of tags. It provides a number of example tags designed to illustrate tag-development techniques, such as the implementation of iteration tags. It is not considered a production-oriented tag library, and it is not maintained by the development group of the Taglibs project (see Table 9.16).

Table 9.16 **The Utility Tag Library Tags**

Tag	Description
Hello	Prints the classical "Hello World" message.
Date	Takes no attributes and prints the current date.
MacroCopy	Takes no attributes and simply copies the body content to the out stream.
MacroPaste	"Pastes" the content represented by a Writer onto the out stream. It takes an attribute name, which takes the Writer to paste.
ShowSource	Prints the source of a specified JSP to the out stream. This tag takes an attribute jspFile, which holds the relative path and filename for the JSP to expose.
Include	Includes the output of the specified URL. Takes a single url attribute, which holds the URL to expose.
If	Is a simple conditional tag. It takes an attribute called predicate that evaluates to true when the content of the body is included in the out stream.

For	Is a simple iteration tag. It takes three attributes:

- **iterations**—Represents the number of iterations to perform.
- **begin**—Gives the offset of the first iteration.
- **varName**—Gives the name of a variable associated to the iteration.

UseBean	Is an equivalent to the `jsp:useBean` standard action. This tag associates a bean instance with an `id`. It takes six attributes, as follows:

- **id**—Contains the name of the scripting variable that will hold the bean instance.
- **scope**—Contains the scope where you can find the bean. Can be either `page`, `request`, `session`, or `application`.
- **className**—Contains the fully qualified Java class name of the bean.
- **type**—Declares the type of the scripting variable defined by `id`.
- **beanName**—Gives the name of the bean used in the java.beans.Beans.instantiate() method.
- **processRequest**—Used to maintain compatibility with JSP API version 0.92.

Validate	Generates JavaScript validation for required fields in a form. It takes three attributes:

- **name**—Holds the name of the form to validate. •
- **method**—Holds the name of the JavaScript method to generate.
- **reqdFields**—Holds a comma-separated list of the names of required fields in the form.

xsl

The xsl tag library is meant to produce XSL transformations from a number of input sources. The possible input sources are as follows:

- **A String object**—`String` object that contains the XML data to transform
- **A SAX API InputSource**—Defines a class to hold the source of XML data
- **An InputStream object**—A Java IO `InputStream`
- **A DOM API node**—A DOM API node of a DOM tree to transform
- **A Reader object**—A Java IO Reader
- **A XSLTInputSource object**—A XALAN class to input the XSL style sheet

The tags available in the xsl library are listed in Table 9.17.

Table 9.17 **The XSL Tag Library Tags**

Tag	Description
apply	Applies an XSL transformation on a XML input source. The attributes define which input sources to use:
	▪ **nameXML**—Shows the input source selected. It is a bean from one of the possible input sources.
	▪ **nameXsl**—Also is a bean from one of the possible input sources.
	▪ **propertyXml**—Defines a property in the bean identified in nameXml that will provide a valid input source.
	▪ **propertyXsl**—Defines a property in the bean identified in nameXsl that will provide a valid input source.
	▪ **xml**—Gives a context-relative path to a resource that contains the XML data.
	▪ **xsl**—Gives a context-relative path to a resource that contains the XSL data.
	Check the xsl tag library documentation for further information on the possible combination of these attributes.
export	Used to export the contents of a bean to the out stream. The bean is identified by the name attribute, and the scope is identified by the scope attribute. The default scope is page.
import	Imports the output of a servlet or JSP to a bean to be further processed by an apply tag. This tag has three attributes:
	▪ **id**—Identifies the bean to be created.
	▪ **page**—Gives the context-relative URI of the JSP or servlet to import.
	▪ **scope**—Gives the scope in which to create the bean.
include	Gives an alternative to jsp:include that will use the JSPWriter defined by this library. The page attribute contains a context-relative URI to the page to include.
showsource	Is a utility tag to return the source of a page specified by the jspFile attribute.

The xsl tag library is very useful in designing XML data islands. An XML data island takes an XML document containing data to be imported to the page and renders it with the dynamic output of the host page. The XML document can be static or dynamic. For instance, it can be generated by a transaction on a database.

Listing 9.15 presents an example of an XML data document that will serve as the basis for the data island.

Listing 9.15   **The XML Data to Transform**

```
<?xml version="1.0"?>
<order number="01">
<customer>001</customer>
<item>
<product>00101</product>
<qty>12</qty>
</item>
<item>
<product>01234</product>
<qty>8</qty>
</item>
<item>
<product>00101</product>
<qty>12</qty>
</item>
</order>
```

Listing 9.16 shows the XSL style sheet used to render the document.

Listing 9.16   **The XSL Style Sheet**

```
<?xml version="1.0"?>
<xsl:stylesheet version="1.0"
xmlns:xsl="http://www.w3.org/1999/XSL/Transform">

  <xsl:template match="/">
  <table width="100%">
     <tr><td colspan="2">Order Information</td></tr>
     <xsl:apply-templates/>
  </table>
</xsl:template>

<xsl:template match="order">
  <tr>
    <td colspan="2">Order: <xsl:value-of select="@number"/>
    </td>
  </tr>
     <xsl:apply-templates select="customer|item" > <xsl:sort
select="."/></xsl:apply-templates>
</xsl:template>

<xsl:template match="customer">
  <tr>
    <td colspan="2">Customer: <xsl:value-of select="."/>
    </td>
  </tr>
</xsl:template>
```

continues

```
<xsl:template match="item">
```

Listing 9.16   **Continued**

```
  <tr>
    <xsl:apply-templates select="product|qty"/>
  </tr>
</xsl:template>

<xsl:template match="product">
  <td> product: <xsl:value-of select="."/></td>
</xsl:template>

<xsl:template match="qty">
  <td> qty: <xsl:value-of select="."/></td>
</xsl:template>
```

The page using the XML data island made with the xsl tags is shown in Listing 9.17.

Listing 9.17   **Using an XML Data Island with the XSL Tag Library**

```
<html>
<%@taglib uri="http://jakarta.apache.org/taglibs/xsl-1.0" prefix="xsl" %>
<head>
<title>Jakarta XSL Example</title>
</head>
<body>

<H1>Order Description</H1>

<xsl:apply xml="/jspBook/orders.xml" xsl="/jspBook/orders.xsl"/>

</body>
</html>
```

Listing 9.17 uses the `apply` tag to render the orders.xml document, presented in Listing 9.15, with the style sheet in Listing 9.16. The result is a table describing the desired order.

Further Developments

The Jakarta Taglibs project is a very dynamic repository for tag libraries under development and released as Open Source products to the JSP application design community. During the time of this writing, a number of newer libraries were incorporated into the Taglibs:

- **Xtags**—This was originally developed under the SourceForge Open Source repository and then was moved into Jakarta. It is a tag library designed to provide XML processing capabilities going beyond.

- **Mailer**—This is a tag library designed to provide electronic mail capabilities, which means sending email, possibly with attachments.

- **I18N**—This is a tag library designed to help the page designer deal with the complexities of internationalization and the creation of internationalized pages.

The STL and Project Perspectives

The Jakarta Taglibs project is gaining acceptance from the developer community. New and powerful tag libraries will continue to be released under the Taglibs project. For instance, at the time of this writing, the jdbc tag library was released and is offering a much more powerful option for performing SQL database operations than the former test sql library. It is clear now that the role of the Taglibs project as a repository of quality Open Source tag libraries is widely recognized because many of the libraries discussed in this chapter were contributed or moved into the project at some point.

On the other hand, it is also clear that standardization is needed to provide at least a minimum set of tags that the developer can count on as having standard behavior available on any JSP API–compliant container. This need drove the creation of the Standard Tag Library specification request, which was approved in February 2000. You can find more information on the Standard Tag Library at `http://jcp.org/jsr/detail/052.jsp`.

Summary

This chapter introduced the Jakarta Taglibs project, hosted by the Apache Software Foundation. This project is meant to be a repository for quality Open Source tag libraries. At the time of this writing, it counts 16 tag libraries.

The libraries presently available are listed here:

- **application**—Representation of the application namespace
- **bsf**—An abstraction for the IBM Bean Scripting Framework
- **datetime**—Date and time utility tags
- **input**—HTML input tags with defaults
- **jdbc**—JDBC API–based tags for accessing and querying databases

- **jndi**—JNDI API–based tags for accessing, looking up, and querying name and directory services
- **jspspec, sql, and utility**—Example tag libraries
- **page**—Representation of the page namespace
- **regexp**—Perl-style regular expression utility tags
- **request**—Access to the request object information and namespace
- **response**—Access to the response object information
- **scrape**—Tags to extract fragments from a page for use on another page
- **session**—Access to the session information and namespace
- **xsl**—XSL transformation tags

10

Commercial Tag Libraries

THIS CHAPTER DISCUSSES THREE COMMERCIAL TAG LIBRARIES available in the market either as standalone products or as add-ons to some broader web development/production package. The three libraries considered are the JRun Tag Library, the Orion server tags, and the Bluestone taglib. These are discussed in this chapter, and a number of examples are presented with each.

JRun Tag Library

The JRun Tag Library is part of the Allaire's JRun application server (`http://allaire.com`). It is designed to provide the web developer easy access to several J2EE APIs, allowing development of highly sophisticated JavaServer Pages with less Java code. The JRun Tag Library covers three main areas:

- **J2EE tags**—These tags cover several J2EE APIs, such as JNDI, the names and directory service; JDBC, for database connectivity; JMS, for messaging; and JavaMail, for mail.

- **Client-side forms**—These tags supply some functions to create client HTML forms with JavaScript validation.

- **Flow control tags**—These tags enable you to control the flow of processing of the page. This includes a general loop for each tag, several conditional processing tags, and a scripting variable creation helper tag.

The next sections explore the JRun taglib in detail with a number of examples. The JRun application server is covered in more detail in Appendix B, "Allaire JRun."

J2EE Technologies Tags

J2EE technologies tags cover a number of J2EE technologies that are considered to be used more in server-side Java web applications. For instance, the J2EE makes intensive use of the JNDI API to access resources in resource repositories, and there's a tag for that. Table 10.1 correlates the J2EE technology with the corresponding tag in the JRun taglib.

Table 10.1   **J2EE Technologies Covered by the JRun Tag Library**

J2EE Technology	JRun Tags
Names and directory services (JNDI)	`jndi`
Database connectivity (JDBC)	`sql, sqlparam`
Messaging (JMS)	`sendmsg, msgparam, getmsg`
Transaction (JTA)	`transaction`
Mail (JavaMail)	`sendmail, mailparam, getmail`
Servlet (Servlet API)	`servlet, servletparam`
XML processing (JAXP)	`query2xml, xslt`

Table 10.2 provides a closer look at these tags.

Table 10.2   **J2EE JRun Tag Library Tags**

Tag	Description
`jndi`	Provides access to the services of a names and directory service through the JNDI API. This tag enables you to invoke lookup, list, search, and attribute services. The attributes define which server and service to invoke. There are seven attributes, which are as follows:

- **id**—Definition of the script variable to hold the results retrieved.
- **action**—A String stating the service to invoke. Valid values are `lookup`, `list`, `search`, and `attribute`.
- **name**—A String or a javax.naming.Name that states the name to look up or search for.
- **provider**—A String that represents the service provider class.
- **url**—The service provider URL.

- **scope**—Where to place the results. This must be one of the valid scopes, such as application, session, request, or page. The default is page.

- **attributes**—A set of attributes to search for in a search operation. This can be a java.util.Dictionary, a java.util.Map, or a javax.naming.Attributes.

sql Executes an SQL statement. It has a number of attributes that control the way the database connection will be established:

- **connection**—To be used if a java.sql.Connection object is provided.

- **id**—If the SQL statement returns a result set, defines a script variable to hold it.

- **scope**—Gives the scope where the variable will be stored. Valid values are `application`, `session`, `request`, and `page`. The default is `page`.

- **datasrc**—To be used if a javax.sql.DataSource object is provided.

- **driver, username, password, and url**—Establishes a connection to the database if no connection or datasource is provided.

sqlparam If the SQL statement is parameterized, can be used to specify a parameter. This tag is supposed to be used inside a `sql` tag. It has three attributes, which are as follows:

- **value**—Takes a java.lang.Object that represents the value of the parameter.

- **sqltype**—Gives the SQL type for the parameter. Check the JRun Tag Library Reference manual to get more information on the valid values.

- **scale**—Gives the number of digits after the decimal point if the SQL type is NUMERIC or DECIMAL.

sendmsg Sends an email message through the JMS API. This tag has seven attributes, which are as follows:

- **msgsrc**—An instance of javax.jms.QueueConnectionFactory or a String to be used to perform a JNDI lookup for a QueueConnection.

- **queue**—Attribute that takes a javax.jms.Queue or a String to be used to perform a JNDI lookup.

- **username**—The username used for MessageQueue authentication.

- **password**—Attribute used for authentication.

- **delivery**—Message delivery mode. Valid values are `PERSISTENT` and `NON_PERSISTENT`.

- **priority**—Message priority. This can be a String, int, or integer. The default is 4.

- **expire**—Time interval for the message to expire. Can be a String, long or Long, and is measured in milliseconds. By default, a message never expires.

continues

Table 10.2 **Continued**

Tag	Description
msgparam	Is used inside a sendmsg tag to specify the message properties. It takes two attributes: name, which is the parameter's name, and value.
getmsg	Retrieves messages from a queue using an SQL-like syntax. Results are placed in a descendant of allaire.taglib.Table called MessageTable. The attributes of this tag are as follows:

- **id**—Definition of the script variable to hold the results retrieved.

- **scope**—The scope where the variable will be stored. Valid values are application, session, request, and page. The default is page.

- **msgsrc**—An instance of javax.jms.QueueConnectionFactory or a String to be used to perform a JNDI lookup for a QueueConnection.

- **username**—The username used for MessageQueue authentication.

- **password**—Attribute also used for authentication.

| transaction | Defines a database or messaging-distributed transaction. You can wrap sql or messaging tags inside a transaction tag, and the statements covered by the transaction tag will be treated as being in a transaction. If one fails, then all will roll back. This tag has one attribute, timeout, which contains the time in seconds that this transaction must complete. |
| sendmail | Sends multipart mail messages, possibly with attachments. This tag has the following attributes: |

- **host**—A String with the URL of the mail server to be used.

- **port**—The port number that the server listens to. It can be a String, Integer, or int.

- **timeout**—Server timeout, in milliseconds. The default is 3000.

- **session**—If it is supplied, the JavaMail session is to be used instead of host/port combination. This can be a String to be used in a JNDI lookup for a JavaMail session.

- **sender**—Sender's email address. It can take a javax.mail.internet.InternetAddress.

- **recipient**—A list of recipients. It can be a comma-separated String, a String[], an Enumeration, an Iterator, a javax.mail.internet.InternetAddress, or a java.mail.internet.InternetAddress[] .

- **cc**—A list of copy recipients. It can be a comma-separated String, a String[], an Enumeration, an Iterator, a javax.mail.internet.InternetAddress, or a java.mail.internet.InternetAddress[].

- **bcc**—A list of blind-copy recipients. It can be a comma-separated String, a String[], an Enumeration, an Iterator, a javax.mail.internet.InternetAddress, or a java.mail.internet.InternetAddress[].

- **subject**—A String. The mail message subject.

This tag supports two modes with different syntaxes: the first syntax takes host, port, and timeout. The second syntax takes a JavaMail session with the session attribute instead. The remaining attributes are used in both.

Mailparam   Is used to easily attach files or messages to the body of a `sendmail` tag. This tag has three attributes:

- **attachurl**—This is a URL for a file to be attached to this email.

- **name and value**—These are to be used to include other email headers to this message.

getmail   Retrieves a set of mail messages from a mail server using an SQL-like syntax. Check the JRun Tag Library Reference manual to get more information on the valid search parameters.

This tag has the following attributes:

- **host**—The mail server to be used.

- **port**—The port that the server listens to.

- **timeout**—Server timeout, in milliseconds. The default is `3000`.

- **session**—If supplied, the JavaMail session to be used instead of host/port combination. Can be a String to be used in a JNDI lookup for a JavaMail session.

- **username**—Attribute to be used in user authentication.

- **password**—Attribute to be used in user authentication.

- **id**—The script variable that will contain the retrieved messages.

- **scope**—The scope where the result of this tag will be placed.

This tag has the same syntax modes of the `sendmail` tag.

servlet   Invokes a servlet. The only attribute is code, which contains the servlet name.

servletparam   Specifies servlet request attributes. It is to be used inside a `servlet` tag. The two attributes are name and value, respectively; these are the name and value of the request attribute.

query2xml   Converts tabular data into XML. The attributes of this tag are as follows:

- **query**—The data table. It can be an instance of ResultSet, RowSet, or allaire.taglib.Table. Or a String representing a pageContext attribute.

- **id**—If present, a reference to the XML document or reader created. If this is not present, the XML document will be included in the current JSP output.

- **type**—The type of XML object created. It can be DOM or TEXT. If it is DOM, then the object will be an instance of or.w3c.dom.Document. Otherwise, it will be a java.oi.BufferedReader.

continues

Table 10.2 **Continued**

Tag	Description
	▪ **scope**—Where to place the results. This must be one of the valid scopes: application, session, request, or page. The default is `page`.
	▪ **rootname**—Specification of the XML document root tag. The default is `table`.
	▪ **rowname**—Specification of the tag name for a row. The default is `row`.
`xslt`	Performs XSL transformations. This tag has four attributes:
	▪ **xsl**—The URL to a XSL template document.
	▪ **xml**—If present, the URL to an XML document. If it is omitted, the XML must be provided by a tag in this tag's body.
	▪ **id**—Definition of the script variable to hold the XSLT object.
	▪ **scope**—The scope where the variable will be stored. Valid values are `application`, `session`, `request`, and `page`. The default is `page`.

Client-Side Form-Processing Tags

The idea behind providing implementations for form-processing tags is to provide extra capabilities that will make the use of client-side forms easy for the developer. You have seen this approach used in Struts in Chapter 7, "Struts Tag Libraries." The form-processing tags in the JRun Tag Library are described in Table 10.3.

Table 10.3 **Client-Side Form-Processing JRun Tag Library Tags**

Tag	Purpose
`form`	Declares an HTML form and adds JavaScript validation. It has three attributes:
	▪ **name**—Specifies the HTML form name (and is mandatory).
	▪ **action**—Specifies the HTML action to submit this form.
	▪ **onSubmit**—Specifies a JavaScript function to be called when this form is submitted.
	The last two attributes are optional.
`input`	Declares an input element (text, radio, or checkboxes) with the corresponding JavaScript validation. This tag is supposed to be used within a jrun:form tag. It takes six attributes:
	▪ **name**—Mandatory attribute. This defines the HTML name of the input control.

- **type**—A String that controls which kind of validation will be carried against the field. Validation functions are defined in the form tag. Possible values are: text, checkbox, radio, password, creditcard, date, eurodate, float, integer, ssc, phone, time, and zipcode. The default value is text.

- **value**—A String that represents the field's initial value.

- **required**—A Boolean stating that the field must be entered.

- **onError**—The name of a JavaScript function to be called on validation failure.

- **onValidate**—The name of a JavaScript function that will perform custom validation.

Other HTML attributes are merely added to the generated input HTML tag.

select   Declares a select statement and adds the corresponding JavaScript validation. This tag has two modes of operation: It can be based on a database query or it can be based on a key-value pair collection. The first mode can take a java.sql.ResultSet, javax.sqlRowSet, Allaire's extensions allaire.taglib.Table, or a String that will hold the name of a page-level attribute with a query object. The second mode can take a subclass of java.util.Dictionary or java.util.Map.

The attributes in this tag determine the mode of operation. Providing the hashtable will put it on the second mode. The attributes are as follows:

- **name**—The only required attribute. It is the HTML name of the control.

- **size**—The HTML size attribute.

- **onError**—The name of a JavaScript function to be called on validation failure.

- **required**—A Boolean stating that the field must be entered.

- **selected**—A key that will be preselected in the drop-down box.

- **hashtable**—A key-value pair set that will be used to populate the select. The values are displayed, and the keys are the selectable values. If this is provided, the query attribute and related are not.

- **query**—Some SQL result set representation, as described previously. This triggers the query-based mode.

- **value**—The query field to be used as selectable value.

- **display**—The query field to be displayed in the drop-down box.

Flow-Control Tags

The flow-control tags provide programmatic control structures that are often built with scriptlets in JSP pages. Because the JRun Tag Library is compliant with JSP 1.1, it makes no use of the newer IterateTag interface in the implementation of the `foreach` generic loop. There is an `if` tag and a `switch`/`case` pair of tags, as described in Table 10.4.

Table 10.4   **Flow Control JRun Tag Library Tags**

Tag	Purpose
param	Defines an attribute in a scope. If the scope is the page scope, a script variable will be created. This tag must be at the top level and does not reset existing scrip variables. The attributes of the param tag are as follows: • **id**—The name of the attribute. • **scope**—A String, either page, session, request, or application. • **type**—The Java class of the attribute. • **default**—The default value of the attribute.
foreach	Loops through the items in an enumeration. It automatically detects the type of the enumeration, which can be a java.util.Enumeration, a javax.naming.NamingEnumeration, a java.sql.ResultSet, a javax.sql.RowSet, a java.util.Iterator, a allaire.taglib.Table, or a java.lang.Object[]. It has three attributes: • **item**—Defines the name of a script variable to host the item retrieved in a loop. This applies to Enumeration, NamingEnumeration, Iterator, and Object[]. • **type**—Gives the Java class of the attribute. • **group**—Gives the enumeration to iterate upon.
if	Implements an if conditional. Takes a single expr attribute, which holds an expression to be evaluated to a Boolean, a Boolean object, or a String containing `true`, `false`, `TRUE`, or `FALSE`, and then translated into `true` or `false`. If the expression is evaluated to `true`, the tag includes its body.
switch	Implements the switch clause for switch statements. It encloses a number of case tags in its body and has no attributes.
case	Implements the case clause for switch statements. It has the same single expr attribute as the `if` tag.

Orion Server Tags

The Orion server tags are not part of the Evermind's Orion server web and application container. They are offered free of charge and for redistribution at the Orion site, but they are meant to provide facilities to a developer working with the product. You can download these tag libraries at `http://www.orionserver.com`.

In fact, there are two libraries. One library, the EJB taglib, is designed to cover the intrinsics of the Enterprise JavaBeans API and to facilitate the use of EJBs in JavaServer pages. Another library, the generic Util taglib, is designed to provide a number of utilitarian tags for several purposes.

These two libraries are covered in the following sections.

EJB Tags

These tags offer a number of services to ease work with EJBs. The tags available in the EJB library are listed in Table 10.5.

Table 10.5 Orion Server EJB Tag Library Tags

Tag	Description
useHome	Looks up for an EJBHome interface and creates a script variable to hold it. This tag has three attributes:
	▪ **id**—Defines the script variable to hold the Home found.
	▪ **type**—Defines the Java type of the interface.
	▪ **location**—Tells where to look for the interface, as defined in the web application deployment descriptor.
useBean	Instantiates the EJB for use by the rest of the page. If the bean is not found, the body is evaluated.
	This tag also offers the context of use for the `createBean` tag, as you will see next. This tag has the following attributes:
	▪ **id**—Defines the script variable to hold the bean.
	▪ **type**—Defines the Java type of the EJB.
	▪ **value**—Gives the EJBObject instance to narrow.
	▪ **scope**—Gives one of the namespaces to place the bean in. The possible values are CONTEXT, SESSION, REQUEST, and PAGE. The default is PAGE.
createBean	Creates an instance of a bean based on the reference found by an `useBean` call. If used, this tag must be placed inside the body of a `useBean` tag.
	The only attribute is instance, and it defines a created EJBObject instance.
iterate	Iterates through the results of a Home. For instance, after a call on the findAllItems method, this tag iterates through the items on the enumeration returned. The attributes on the iterate tag are as follows:
	▪ **id**—Definition of the script variable that will hold the instance returned in a loop.
	▪ **type**—The Java class of the EJBs returned.
	▪ **collection**—The collection returned by the Home interface call.
	▪ **max**—An integer that expresses the maximum number of beans to iterate through.

Util Tags

Many vendors have already deemed it necessary to supply a number of basic tags to make the life of the JSP developer easier. These generally involve tags that control the flow of control in the page, authorization, or formatting. This is exactly the case with the util tags. They implement formatting of dates and currency, container-based authorization, iteration and a role-based conditional, and even a `sendMail` tag.

Hopefully, with the specification of the Standard Tag Library, the developer will soon be able to count on a set of actions available in every container by specification.

The tags available in the util library are listed in Table 10.6.

Table 10.6   **The Orion Server Util Tag Library Tags**

Tag	Description
displayCurrency	Formats a number of type double using the specified locale. Takes two attributes: ■ **amount**—Holds the number to format. ■ **locale**—Optionally specifies the Locale to use in the formatting.
displayDate	Formats a Date object with a given locale. Following the model of the previous tag, this one also has only two attributes: ■ **date**—A Date object that holds the date to format. ■ **locale**—A Locale to be used to format it.
displayNumber	Formats a number using a locale and a format. It takes three attributes: ■ **number and locale**—Are analogous to the ones in the first two tags. ■ **format**—Is the format to apply.
ifInRole	Tests whether the user is in a role. It has two attributes: the role to test against and a Boolean include attribute. If include is `true`, the tag will include the body if the user is in the role. If include is `false`, it will include the body if the user is *not* in the role. This test runs against the HttpServletRequest.isUserInRole method in a container-based authentication mode.
iterate	Iterates through the beans in a collection, evaluating the body contents in each iteration. It has four attributes, as follows: ■ **id**—Definition of the bean in the current loop to be used in the tag's body. ■ **type**—The class of the bean. ■ **collection**—The collection to iterate over. ■ **max**—The maximum number of iterations. This attribute is optional.
lastModified	Displays the last modified date of the JSP file. It has an optional locale attribute to format the date accordingly.

`sendMail`	Sends a mail message. The attributes define the information necessary to send the message. The message itself is defined in the body of the tag. The attributes are as follows:

- **from**—An optional String with the sender's email.

- **to**—An optional String of comma-separated recipient email addresses.

- **cc**—An optional String of comma separated copy recipient email addresses.

- **bcc**—An optional String of comma separated blind copy recipient email addresses.

- **subject**—The message's subject.

- **mimeType**—The mime type of the message. The default is text/plain.

- **session**—The mail session to use. It is a String with the JNDI name of the MailSession to use. The default MailSession will be used if this is not specified.

HP Bluestone Tag Library

The HP Bluestone Tag Library is available in all products from this vendor. The major areas covered by this tag library are related to J2EE technology and security.

The tags available in the HP Bluestone's library are listed in Table 10.7.

Table 10.7   **The Bluestone Tag Library Tags**

Tag	Description
`sql`	Is a database querying through SQL. It can access a JDBC datasource through JNDI lookup or using a driver name and JDBC URL. The attributes in this tag are as follows:

- **username and password**—Are used for database user authentication.

- **lookup**—Gives the JDBC datasource JNDI lookup String.

- **driverString and connectionUrl**—Are used to access the database via a driver class name and a JDBC URL. This is to be provided if lookup is absent.

- **dataLocation**—Tells where the data retrieved is stored.

- **noOutput**—If `true`, doesn't generate output; just retrieves the data silently.

- **successMsg and failureMsg**—Are messages to be included in the JSP output in either case.

continues

Table 10.7 **Continued**

Tag	Description
transaction	Specifies whether to enclose sql tags in a transaction. This tag has no attributes.
loop	Loops through the data retrieved by an sql tag. This tag has two attributes:
	▪ **dataLocation**—Used with the reference to the results retrieved by the sql tag.
	▪ **tableName**—Used by the SAP tag.
dataPlaceHolder	Represents a data element in a sql tag result object. It also has two attributes:
	▪ **col**—Gives the database column.
	▪ **structname**—Is used by the SAP tag.
email	Sends an email message. This tag has the following attributes:
	▪ **host**—The mail server address.
	▪ **port**—The mail server port.
	▪ **sender**—The email of the sender.
	▪ **recipient**—A comma-separated String of the email addresses of the mail recipients.
	▪ **cc**—A comma-separated String of the email addresses of the mail copy recipients.
	▪ **bcc**—A comma-separated String of the email addresses of the mail blind-copy recipients.
	▪ **subject**—The message subject.
	All the attributes are of String type.
taglibdoc	Documents a tag library based on a TLD file. Check for details on the Bluestone Tag Library Reference at http://gallery.bluestone.com.
xslTransform	Applies an XSL style sheet to an XML file or enclosed XML content. This tag contains two attributes:
	▪ **xsl**—Contains the URL to a XSL style sheet to be applied.
	▪ **xml**—If supplied, gives the URL to an XML document to be used in the XSL transform.
secureAccess	Checks whether the user is in a role defined by the Bluestone Security Console. The sole attribute is the required role. If so, the body content is included.
login	Takes a username and password as attributes, and tries to authenticate the user against the Bluestone server security controls.
logout	Performs a logout. It has no attributes.

`addUser`	Adds a user to a group or a role inside the context of the Bluestone Security Console. This tag has four attributes:

- **username**—The username to add.
- **groupPath**—A forward slash–separated path to the group that the username has to be added to. For instance, \readers\internet places a username in the subgroup internet of group readers.
- **securityManager**—The security manager to use in this operation. By default, the first security manager registered is used.
- **role**—The role to add the user to.

`userInfo`	Sets the context for the `getInfo` tag. It has two attributes: groupPath and securityManager, both working as in the previous tag.
`getInfo`	Is used to retrieve user attributes in the context defined by the `userInfo` tag. This tag has the sole attribute named attribute, which represents the user registration attribute to retrieve.
`jndi`	Performs a JNDI lookup operation and places the result in a scripting variable. This tag has two attributes:

- **lookup**—The String to look up.
- **varname**—The variable name where the result will be placed.

`ejbGetHome`	Looks up and retrieves a Home interface through a JNDI lookup service. This tag has four attributes:

- **homeId**—The name of a script variable to assign the Home retrieved.
- **scope**—The scope to place the variable.
- **type**—The Java class of the Home interface.
- **lookup**—The String used in a JNDI lookup to locate the Home interface.

`ejbCreate`	Invokes a create method on a Home interface. This tag has four attributes:

- **homeId**—The home on which the `create` method will be invoked. Possibly retrieved by a `ejbGetHome` tag.
- **returnId**—Definition of a script variable to hold the `EJBObject` created.
- **returnType**—The Java type of the `EJBObject` created.
- **scope**—The scope to place the variable.

`setParameter`	Is used to set the value of a parameter inside tags that implement the `ParameterizedTag` interface. An example of such is the ejbCreate, when the `create` method to be called is parameterized. The attributes on this tag are as follows:

- **type**—The Java type of the parameter.

continues

Table 10.7 **Continued**

Tag	Description
	▪ **name**—The name of the parameter.
	▪ **value**—The value to be assigned.
invokeMethod	Executes methods in Java objects. This tag needs `setParameter` for parameterized methods. The attributes in this tag are as follows:
	▪ **object**—The name of the instance to invoke the method of.
	▪ **method**—The method's name.
	▪ **returnType**—The Java type of the object returned.
	▪ **returnId**—Definition of a script variable to hold the returned object.
	▪ **scope**—Which scope to place the returned object.

This tag library also has tags dealing with Bluestone-specific technologies, such as the Dynamic Stylesheet Engine and the SIM/Cbs objects. Refer to the HP Bluestone Tag Library reference document, available at `http://gallery.bluestone.com`, for more details on those tags.

Understanding the Applicability of Such Tag Libraries

The tag libraries presented so far are designed for two purposes: to aid the page designer working in a specific server in dealing with the technologies that the server offers, and to ease the task of designing efficient JSPs.

In that sense, because all three servers presented are general J2EE application servers, EJB access is present in all three libraries. Two of them support JDBC database access, JNDI lookup, email support, distributed transactions, and XML/XSL processing. These are key technologies in the J2EE scenario.

The JRun Tag Library also offers support for messaging, which is critical to integrating web applications with messaging-based middleware. The Orion tags focus largely on data formatting and have a whole library dedicated to EJB access.

Supplied in a number of products, HP Bluestone's tag library also covers a number of proprietary technologies, including the Bluestone's Security Console.

Other Notable Libraries

Other vendors supply their respective tag libraries for general and specific purposes. For instance, portal vendors offer portal design tag libraries. Examples of such tag libraries are the InstantOnline tag library, from Gefion Software, available for purchase at `http://www.gefionsoftware.com`, and BEA Weblogic's Portal tags, from BEA at `http://www.bea.com`, used within the BEA Weblogic Server.

Summary

In this chapter, you have learned about the tag libraries provided as companions to three well-known commercial application servers: Allaire's JRun, Evermind's Orion server, and the whole line of HP Bluestone products, including the Total eServer.

These libraries offer support for a number of J2EE technologies:

- **EJB**—All offer extensive support for EJB.
- **JDBC database access and query**—This is supported by the JRun and Bluestone tags and is a notable omission in Orion's tags.
- **Mail messaging**—This feature is present in all three products.
- **Distributed transactions**—This feature is present in JRun and Bluestone products.
- **XML/XSL**—This feature is present in JRun and Bluestone products.
- **JMS messaging**—JRun Tag Library offers support for this as well.

11

Other Resources

THIS CHAPTER DEPICTS A NUMBER OF TAG LIBRARIES already on the Net, hosted by open source project repositories or by smaller open source project groups. Some projects are hosted by commercial companies that release them for free for non-commercial and non-governmental use. This chapter doesn't intend to exhaust the subject, but it provides an overview of some projects outside the scope of Sun and the Jakarta site. This chapter shows how this technology is evolving and attracting the minds of web application developers and the market.

First you will learn about some of the projects in SourceForge, one of the largest (if not the largest) open source software repositories on the Internet. A number of tag library projects currently are hosted there. The projects that have delivered some type of product at the time of this writing are presented there as well.

ColdJava.com (`http://coldjava.hypermart.net`) is the next library collection presented. It is described as one of the largest libraries on the Net, including more than a dozen tag sublibraries and a large number of miscellaneous tags. ColdJava has tag libraries to work with web applications, file and variable generation and control, and even WAP.

This chapter also presents other resources on the Internet for the various topics discussed, from servlet programming to tag library development.

Of course, other libraries are available. But the goal here is to provide a sampling of how this concept is being embraced by more developers and is becoming a major cornerstone in web applications and web content development.

Projects Hosted by SourceForge

SourceForge (`http://sourceforge.net`) is a well-known open source projects repository. SourceForge offers open source developers an opportunity to publish their materials for free—and possibly gather other developers into the effort and evolution of the final product.

A huge number of projects are hosted on SourceForge. Not all of them are related to web application development or are even written in Java. For example, many projects are written in C++, Perl, and PHP, just to mention a few.

At the time of this writing, there were five tag library projects: xtags, Jargus, Egavas tags, In16, and Dapact. Many of these libraries are still in alpha and beta stages. The possibility that they will evolve into a release-level product is always a matter of community involvement and acceptance, but these ongoing efforts show that tag libraries are getting attention from the market.

These libraries, which are being hosted at SourceForge, are open source software. Many of them are offered with the GNU LGPL license, but you should check the project page to see what kind of license is being applied to each specific library.

Jargus

Jargus is a tag library designed to help the page designer with parameter validation. It provides a server-side, uniform way to perform such validation and access the results of the validation process.

A validated form tag accepts validated tag-based controls such as `input` and `check` and submits a validation process. If the validation fails, the page is redisplayed so that proper action can be taken. The `message` tag shows error messages collected in the `JSPValidationHandler` class.

The Jargus library is available at the project page at `http://jargus.sourceforge.net`. Binaries are available, as are documentation and examples.

Egavas Tags

Egavas is a tag library designed to provide contextual information to applications as well as to access that context and its attributes, set those attributes with a `setProperty`-like tag, and display those attributes with a `getProperty`-like tag.

Egavas attaches the contextual info object to an application with the `AppContext` class. This class accesses the application logs, attributes, and configuration. An `AppContext` is associated to an application with the `egavas:new` tag. The `egavas:log` tag permits logging.

The Egavas tag library can be obtained from the project page at `http://sourceforge.net/projects/egavastags`. Binaries, documentation, and instructions to access the CVS repository can be obtained at the project site as well.

In16

This project counts a number of libraries. The html, form, and in16 libraries provide a number of form-processing tags with various levels of sophistication. For instance, the Deluxe tags, such as `DeluxeForm` and `DeluxeTextBox`, have validation capabilities.

The External tags provide access to directory, file, and the HTTP protocol. The `dir` tag manipulates directories, allowing creation, listing, deletion, and so forth. The `file` tag manipulates files. `http` and `httpparam` manipulate the HTTP protocol and parameters respectively. The File tags provide additional services to the external tags to manipulate file parameters such as date of the last update or size.

The Cache Manipulation tags `cache` and `cacheitem` allow caching of post-processed JSP content and further manipulation of it, including the capability to refresh it automatically. The Mail tags provide capabilities for sending email. The View tags allow manipulation of contents such as tag stripping or date and number formatting.

In16 can be obtained from the project summary page at `http://sourceforge.net/projects/jsptags`. Unfortunately, there's little documentation and few examples on the libraries.

DAPACT

Data Aware Processing and Control Tags (DAPACT) is a tag library designed to aid the JSP developer in creating pages based on live data, provided by a database or a data collection such as an array. In fact, this library has two components:

- A form-creation library, with tags such as `input`, `select`, and `simpletext`
- A library with data access, iteration, and logger tags

The `BaseIterator` tags are abstract classes used to derive specific data iterator tags used in real pages. General iterator tags also provide general access. The classes that will respond for data requests can be configured in a properties file.

The DAPACT library is available for download from the project summary page at `http://sourceforge.net/projects/dapact`. The package contains sources, binaries, and examples.

ColdJava.com

ColdJava.com is considered the largest tag library on the Net so far. It counts more than a dozen sublibraries and a number of nongrouped tags. Many of these tag libraries also support WAP/WML pages. These tags are all available at `http://coldjava.hypermart.net/`.

ColdJava is not open source software. These libraries can be used in non-commercial and non-governmental projects, but the vendor must be contacted for other uses.

Authorization

Authorization involves a basic set of tags to provide authorization control. There are tags to check authorized access, pop up a username/password dialog box to retrieve user identification, and set authorization levels.

Bar Charts

The bar charts tag library provides two tags to draw simple bar charts from a collection of data: hbar and vbar, for horizontal and vertical bar charts. Values and labels must be provided in comma-separated lists.

Conditional Tags

The conditional tags include the body contents on the occurrence of a condition on a request parameter. Three tags exist for that: IfParameterExists, IfParameterEquals, and IfParameterNotEquals. The first tag checks the existence of the parameter. The other two check the parameter existence and value against a provided value.

Cookie Tags

The Cookie tag library also provides three tags to add, get the value of, and check the existence of a cookie that is given a name.

The isCookie tag checks whether the given name represents a cookie. The cookie-manipulation tags are addCookie and getCookie. The values retrieved may be included in the output or made available in script variables.

DOM Tags

The DOM tag library provides DOM parsing of XML. It comes with six tags for that: domParse, domError, getDomError, getNodeText, getNodeAttribute, and getNodeCount.

The domParse tag allows parsing of XML documents stored in a file, either local or remote, or XML fragments held on a String script variable. If errors occur during the parsing process, the domError tag allows an alternate action to expose it. In the body of the domError tag, getDomError exposes the error detected by printing it to the output stream.

The next three tags are related to node processing:

- The getNodeCount tag counts the occurrences of a child node given by an XPath expression.

- The `getNodeText` tag includes the node content in the output.
- The `getNodeAttribute` includes the value of the given attribute in the output.

Escape

The Escape tag library is also useful for WAP/WML. This library is designed to allow conversion of HTML JSP content to WML for usage in WAP. It has two tags: `Escape` and `WMLEscape`. The `Escape` tag converts the enclosed tags into the escaped tags used in WAP. The `WMLEscape` does the same on the fly; it also allows you to split the resulting page in many WML card-compatible–size ones.

Files

The Files tag library enables you to manipulate files and directories on the server. It implements a series of simple operations: `moveFile`, `copyFile`, `deleteFile`, `writeFile`, `createDirectory`, `deleteDirectory`, `isFile`, and `isDirectory`.

LastModified

The LastModified library calculates and optionally prints the last modified date of the current page. It consists of one tag only.

POP

The POP library enables you to read messages and information from a mailbox in a POP server. It consists of four tags:

- The `POPReader` tag accesses the server, given a number of attributes such as the username, password, and host.
- The `size` tag gives the number of messages in the mailbox.
- The `delete` tag allows you to delete a message from the mailbox.
- The `letter` tag allows you to access the attributes of a given message.

Random

Random is another tag library that contains only one tag, the `randomValue` tag. This tag calculates a random integer in an interval, given the lower and upper limits.

Request

The Request tag library enables you to execute requests to other servers, including the result in the current page. The main tag is `HttpRequest`, which allows you to include either the whole contents returned or part of it, filtered by a template. The `getValue` tag enables you to get the result of the template filtering as a script variable.

WML Tags

The WML tag library consists of two tags that enable the creation of WML sections and HTML sections in the same document. The `WmlOn` tag defines a block of WML that will be processed if the page is requested by a WAP browser. The `WmlOff` tag defines the block that will be processed if the page was requested by an HTML browser.

Other Tags in the ColdJava Tag Library

Among the miscellaneous tags that you will find in the library is a `cache` tag to cache JSP-generated content, a `portal` tag to create portal-like interfaces, and a `unique id generator` tag, among others.

More Resources

So far, this chapter has presented the major concepts in web application development. A few links are presented in this section that might be useful to improve your understanding of topics just discussed.

What is the idea behind these links? It is simple: Open source software is a good source of knowledge. Openness is a nice concept for the beginner and a strong resource for the expert because it offers you deeply detailed access to solutions that were discussed, agreed upon, justified, and challenged by a large number of users— mainly volunteer contributors. The process goes like this: If you see something that you think you have a better solution to, submit your suggestion. If your suggestion is not feasible or is not the best solution for the problem, you will get a response justifying that. You will learn while you are engaged in that process, which is the best part.

In addition, these links contain lots of cool open source stuff on each of them— stuff to play with, read, and put your hands on.

Servlets and Servlet Programming

As you have seen, the Servlet API is the most basic API in the whole Java architecture for the web. It is the base for the JavaServer Pages API and, from that, to the Tag Extension API. It also defines the core objects that you have seen in all the examples. A page designer might work very well knowing only JSP syntax, but an application developer must have a broader vision. As you saw in Chapter 1, "Introduction to Servlets and JavaServer Pages," and in the discussion on Struts presented in Chapter 6, "The Jakarta Struts Project," these technologies are complimentary. Having servlets in your arsenal is quite strategic to understanding and designing strong web applications, content, and services.

CoolServlets, at `http://www.coolservlets.com`, is a site dedicated to promoting the servlet technology by offering free servlets (source included), among many other resources. It is the home of the servlet-based Jive Internet forum-management software as well.

JavaServer Pages Resources

The JavaServer Pages API is the base API for the Tag Extension API focused on in this book. If you are a tag designer, this is imperative to know completely because it will constitute the runtime environment for your tags. If you are a page designer or a content designer, having alternative points of view, example solutions in the technology, and success cases in your arsenal is always a good idea. Just remember that technical creativity comes mainly from experience and studying a good repertoire of solutions. It is important to note that although the focus of the discussion on these sites is JSP development, you also will find a lot of information and resources on tag libraries because they constitute an extension API. Three links of interest from third parties are presented here:

- **Java Zoom**—Java Zoom is the home of jChat, a very nice open source JSP-based chat application, at `http://www.javazoom.net`. Java Zoom is a site with a lot of free stuff and a forum section where you can post your questions about JSP programming. jChat itself is a good example of the use of servlets and JSPs.

- **JSP Insider**—At `http://www.jspinsider.com`, JSP Insider offers a vast amount of very interesting stuff, from links to a number of open source projects, even open source tag libraries, to a salaries survey. This is the home of the JSPBuzz newsletter.

- **JSP Resource Index**—The JSP Resource Index, at `http://www.jspin.com`, is a portal dedicated to JSP development. It also contains plenty of interesting material, including links to a large number of open source JSP and tag library projects.

Tag Libraries

The Tag Extension API is the newest of the technologies, but it already counts on a number of very interesting sites. Tags are one of the web components defined in Java2 Enterprise Edition.

The JSP Tags web site is a reference page to information related to JSP and tag libraries. At `http://jsptags.com/`, you will find an interesting and quite large list of tag library projects published on the Internet.

Struts

The Struts framework is being defined under the Jakarta Apache Project. At the time of this writing, it has more than 1200 users in its mailing list. Two links of interest from third parties are presented here:

- **Javacorporate Expresso Framework**—Javacorporate's Expresso is an open source web application development framework that is being integrated with Struts. You can improve your understanding of MVC and web application design in general by understanding the issues raised by the integration process, taking part in the discussion of the MVC design pattern, and looking over this site's nice example of how Struts influenced design decisions in Expresso, and vice versa. You will find Expresso at `http://www.jcorporate.com`.

- **Bluestone.com Struts Tutorial Pages**—HP Bluestone developer corner is a well-organized place where you will find Bluestone stuff and well-designed tutorials on Struts and tag libraries. It's worth checking out at `http://www.bluestone.com`.

General References

These are general Java knowledge links. Of course, the most important is Sun Microsystems, the home of all this technology. In the following sites, you will potentially find references to many of the technologies discussed. These sites are very important not only for JSP and tag library programming, but also to general Java programming:

- **Sun Microsystems and the Jakarta Project**—These are the pillars for web development, as you have seen throughout the book. Sun (`http://java.sun.com`) is the home of all Java technology, of course, and the Jakarta project (`http://jakarta.apache.org`) is the home of Tomcat, Struts, Taglibs, and a number of other interesting projects.

- **jGuru**—This is the jGuru super forum on Java technology. With a huge number of jGurus (the author's included), you will find articles and a huge Q&A section on an incredible number of topics. Check it out at `http://www.jguru.com`.

- **IBM DeveloperWorks**—DeveloperWorks is a resourceful site dealing with distributed computing, with emphasis in the Java language. It contains a large number of tutorials, vast documentation, technical articles, and so on for IBM products and general techniques as well. Have a look at it, at `http://www.ibm.com/developerworks`.

- **IBM AlphaWorks**—AlphaWorks is the IBM think tank for distributed computing mostly based on Java and XML. It is the home of alphabeans, which is a large collection of Java Beans designed to help application and web application development. It's worth having a look at, at `http://www.ibm.com/alphaworks`.

Summary

In this chapter you learned about a number of tag libraries that can be found on the Internet outside the scope of the Jakarta project. This is a brief sample of the interest that this technology is gathering from the developers in the market.

SourceForge is an open source repository that includes a number of tag library projects. This chapter presented five that have already produced some result: xtags, in16, DAPACT, Jargus, and Egavas tags.

The other good example is ColdJava.com. Although it's not an open source project, it offers a huge tag library to the market, with some interesting projects such as WAP-aware ones and its request library, among others.

This chapter also provided numerous references for additional material and access to a vast number of open source projects. Being involved in such projects offers an opportunity to enlarge your understanding of the technology and the processes behind technology evolution.

IV

Appendixes

Tomcat

THIS APPENDIX TELLS WHERE TO FIND TOMCAT, shows how to install it from the binary distributions available on the Internet, discusses its main features and capabilities, explains its structure, and tells how to deploy a web application to Tomcat.

At the time of this writing, Tomcat 4.0 was on development milestone five. Because it is the reference implementation of Servlet API 2.3 and JSP 1.2, we will stick with it.

Introducing Tomcat

Tomcat is the container offered by the Apache Software Foundation (ASF). It has been the reference implementation for the servlet and the JavaServer Pages APIs since the Servlet 2.2 and JSP 1.1 APIs. Originally, Tomcat was the code name for the Servlet API 2.2 reference container that Sun Microsystems was developing. At the 1999 ApacheCon Conference, however, Sun announced that its code was being handed out to the Apache Software Foundation along with the code base of Josper, the JSP processor that was renamed JASPER afterward, under an open source development project called Jakarta. Under the Jakarta Project, Tomcat enjoyed great acceptance from the market and was distributed as a first-production-quality release in version 3.1.

Tomcat is currently in the second-production-quality release at version 3.2.1; Tomcat 4.0 is in sight, and release 4.1 already is under discussion. Tomcat is being released under the terms of the Apache Open Source License.

Obtaining and Installing Tomcat

Tomcat is offered in two main distributions: a binary production-ready distribution and a source-code distribution meant mainly for the Tomcat development community. These distributions are available in Windows zip format file or UNIX tar.gz format file.

Tomcat binary distributions can be thought of as a complete out-of-the-box container that's compliant with servlet and JSP APIs. Its installation is pretty straightforward:

1. **Download.** Download the appropriate binary distribution from the Jakarta web site, `http://jakarta.apache.org/builds/jakarta-tomcat-4.0/release/`. The latest release at the time of this writing is 4.0b1, so you'll find a directory there with this name. If you use the Windows platform and a good archive manager, you can download either the tar.gz file or the zip file. It might be better to choose the tar.gz archive because it is smaller and can be easier to download over a modem connection. Keep in mind that Tomcat is full Java code, so no platform issues are involved.

2. **Unzip the distribution.** In the Windows platform, you have a number of choices for a good archive manager, such as WinZip or Winrar. On UNIX, you just use the traditional Gzip/Tar utilities, like this: `tar xvzf jakarta-tomcat-4.0-b1.tar.gz`.

3. **Make sure that you have an adequate JVM installed.** Tomcat is compliant with JDK 1.1; just make sure that you use 1.1.8, which is the latest. Tomcat is also compliant with the Java2 platform. At the time of this writing, some issues related to the Sun JDK 1.3 when installing Tomcat as an Windows NT service were already solved and will be available in a later release of the JDK. You can also use the Blackdown JDK on Linux or the IBM JDK for both platforms (Windows and Linux).

4. **Define two environment variables.** After downloading and exploding the compressed archives and making sure that an adequate JVM is available, define two environment variables:

   - `TOMCAT_HOME`. This variable must hold the complete path to the top-level directory where Tomcat was decompressed. If you unzipped Tomcat under `/usr/java` with the default folder names, the value of the `TOMCAT_HOME` variable will be `/usr/java/jakarta-tomcat`.

   - `JAVA_HOME`. This variable must hold the complete path to the top-level directory where the JDK was installed. If you installed the JVM 1.3 under `/usr/devel` with the default folder names, the value of the `JAVA_HOME` variable will be `/usr/devel/jdk1.3`.

Just make sure that you define and export (on UNIX) these variables. The Tomcat Minimalistic User Guide describes these steps in detail. You can find it in HTML format at the TOMCAT_HOME/docs/usg directory.

5. **Putting it on.** This depends on the platform you are using. On UNIX, you can use the startup.sh and shutdown.sh scripts found in TOMCAT_HOME/bin to manage Tomcat. These scripts are quite clever at setting the class path. On the Windows platform, if you are using a server environment such as Windows NT or Windows 2000, you have the option to start it in a user session, using the startup.bat and shutdown.bat scripts found at the same location, or you can install Tomcat as a service (see Figure A.1). In this case, additional steps are involved; you can find detailed information on that in the `TOMCAT_HOME/doc/NT_Service_HOW_TO` guide.

In client environments such as Windows 98, you must use the .bat files.

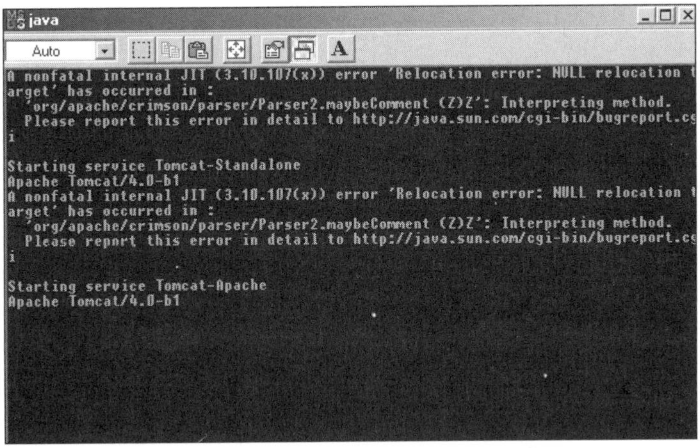

Figure A.1 Command prompt after starting Tomcat.

6. **Test Tomcat.** If everything was installed correctly, Tomcat will be alive and running. Just go to your web browser and type the location for Tomcat (let's say that you installed it on your own machine), followed by the default port number, 8080: `http://localhost:8080/`. Or, use the loopback address explicitly, like this: `http://127.0.0.1:8080/`. The Tomcat welcome page must show up, indicating that the installation was successful (see Figure A.2).

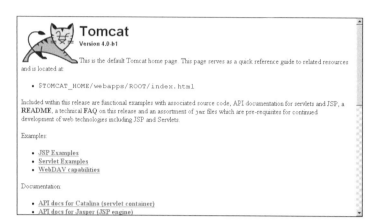

Figure A.2   Tomcat welcome page. If you get this, the installation was successful.

7. **Try some applications.** Tomcat comes with some example servlets and JSPs. You can try them to check whether the servlet and the JSP containers are working properly. Try `http://localhost:8080/examples`.

The Tomcat web container is quite flexible. For starters, it can be deployed as an embedded web server for use within an application that demands an internal web container. In this case, an alternative entry-point class, present in several distributions, can be used. The Tomcat web container can also be deployed on read-only media as a servlet container for an application running from a CD, such as demo apps or data CD–based apps. Tomcat can also run as your major web server, although this is not the most common case. In addition, it can have an instance running for each overdemanding web application on a server, or it can be attached to a popular web server, with many instances referenced.

   The Tomcat administrator can configure this functionality without much trouble via the configuration files present in the TOMCAT_HOME/conf directory.

Tomcat Configuration

After it's installed, Tomcat will run as a web container and as a web server on port 8080. Sometimes this is not convenient because there's another server using that port on the production environment or because you want Tomcat to be your default web server. Tomcat can be configured to perform in a number of situations. On the TOMCAT_HOME/conf directory, the main configuration file is an XML parameter file called server.xml. In this file, you can configure several parameters based on how Tomcat will be executed.

   Tomcat uses a component called TCPListener to listen to incoming HTTP requests. In the server.xml file, you can specify the port that the TCPListener will listen to. The default port is 8080. If you want use Tomcat as a default web server, change that to the default HTTP value, port 80, and restart Tomcat. After that, Tomcat will be listening to port 80, and the port number after Tomcat's addresses will be unnecessary. Try `http://localhost/` to get the welcome page again.

In the server.xml file, you will find a number of elements that you can configure to get better performance or a more diversified environment. For starters, you can change your logging options; Tomcat sends the master log to the console. You also can redirect that to a file; the logger component is responsible for that.

In addition, a developer can add a number of request/response controllers, called valves in Tomcat 4.0, that can be piped to provide sophisticated preprocessing schemas. The concept of a valve replaces the concept of a request interceptor present in Tomcat 3.X. Valves are small classes that extend the way Tomcat processes a request to generate a response. Among other uses, they can be used to ensure security and authorization and to provide better event tracking. Valves are more efficient and have a cleaner life cycle than request interceptors.

Listing A.1 shows an example server.xml file that accompanies the Tomcat binary distribution.

Listing A.1   **Example server.xml File**

```
<!-- Example Server Configuration File extracted from the default file -->

<Server port="8005" shutdown="SHUTDOWN" debug="0">
<Service name="Tomcat-Standalone">
<Connector className="org.apache.catalina.connector.http.HttpConnector"
port="8080" minProcessors="5" maxProcessors="75" acceptCount="10" debug="0" />
<Connector className="org.apache.catalina.connector.http.HttpConnector"
            port="8443" minProcessors="5" maxProcessors="75"
            acceptCount="10" debug="0" scheme="https" secure="true">
  <Factory className="org.apache.catalina.net.SSLServerSocketFactory"
            clientAuth="false" protocol="TLS"/>
</Connector>
<Connector className="org.apache.catalina.connector.test.HttpConnector"
            port="8081" minProcessors="5" maxProcessors="75"
            acceptCount="10" debug="0"/>
<!-- Define the top level container in our container hierarchy -->

<Engine name="Standalone" defaultHost="localhost" debug="0">
<Logger className="org.apache.catalina.logger.FileLogger" prefix="catalina_log."
suffix=".txt" timestamp="true" />
<Realm className="org.apache.catalina.realm.MemoryRealm" />

<!-- Define the default virtual host -->
<Host name="localhost" debug="0" appBase="webapps">

<Valve className="org.apache.catalina.valves.AccessLogValve" directory="logs"
prefix="localhost_access_log." suffix=".txt" pattern="common" />
```

continues

Listing A.1   **Continued**

```
<Logger className="org.apache.catalina.logger.FileLogger" directory="logs" Listing
prefix="localhost_log." suffix=".txt" timestamp="true" />

<Context path="" docBase="ROOT" debug="0"/>

</Host>
</Engine>
</Service>
</Server>
```

You can configure contexts as well. A context is a logical representation of a
web application for the container. You can set a number of parameters in a web
application, including the base directory (where the web application was deployed),
whether the application is reloadable (very useful during development but useless and
time/resource–consuming in a production environment), and which logger or collection of resources is to be used. Listing A.1 shows the declaration for the root context.

You will find the server.xml DTD in the TOMCAT_HOME/conf directory. This
DTD describes what is permitted in terms of configuration. The Tomcat Minimalistic
User Guide also describes how to configure Tomcat adequately.

Understanding Tomcat

At the time of this writing, the production-quality version of Tomcat is version 3.2.1,
but because we focus on the Servlet API 2.3 and JSP API version 1.2 here, we need
Tomcat 4.0. This is a major reformulation compared to the previous versions.

Tomcat 4.0 is based on two main components: the new Catalina Servlet API 2.3
container, and the JASPER JSP API 1.2–compliant container. Both are the reference
implementations for the respective APIs. Requests arriving through one of its listeners
(the TCPListener for TCP-based HTTP requests or AVJP for the Jserv/Tomcat Apj
protocol) are redirected to the Catalina servlet container.

Catalina represents the incorporation of a number of ideas for the next release of
Jserv, the Java Apache project servlet container, which lost momentum with the arrival
of Tomcat. Many features that were under discussion during that project were given to
Tomcat, including the new valve mechanism for request preprocessing, which replaced
the interceptor technology present in Tomcat 3.X.

JASPER is the JSP compiler and processor available in Tomcat. It was present in Tomcat 3.X and is evolving to fully support the new specs. One of the main goals of the developer team is to provide other web or J2EE containers and development tools that can use JASPER and Catalina independently. To accomplish that, the code bases for JASPER and Catalina were made completely independent, so they no longer have functional dependencies between them. JASPER runs under Tomcat as a servlet mapped to process ★.jsp file extensions.

To compile your JSP pages independently from a web container, Tomcat offers the jspc command-line utility. This can be extremely helpful with development tools or in read-only media-deployment scenarios.

Deploying Web Applications Under Tomcat

It is not particularly difficult to deploy a web application under Tomcat. If the application is deployed as a web application archive without further configuration issues, it is sufficient to deploy the web application archive under the TOMCAT_HOME/webapps directory and restart the server. On startup, Tomcat will detect the new web application archive file and will unzip it, creating all the dynamic structures needed to run it in a logical context.

In other cases, just copy the resources needed to a directory under TOMCAT_HOME/webapps named after the web application name. Upon restart, the process works in a manner similar to the one previously explained; just the detection is different. A new context is detected and logically created.

Applications that need to maintain an external base directory or that do not need to be reloadable must be declared in the server.xml file. Add a context entry for each, defining its attributes accordingly. Check out the Tomcat Minimalistic User Guide and the support documents for information on how to configure the several options for contexts.

For applications available to pass-through web servers, additional configuration is needed when Tomcat is attached as a servlet container to a server. The uriworkermap.properties file must hold the resource access pattern for the application. For instance, when deploying an application using JSPs, called jspBookEx, in a Tomcat-under-IIS installation, you must configure this:

```
/jspBookEx/*.jsp=apjv12
```

It's assumed, for the sake of simplicity, that apjv12 was configured to be the APJv12 listener for this Tomcat installation. Refer to the documentation for more detail on this process.

Tomcat on the Internet

The home page for Tomcat is the Jakarta Apache project page, at
`http://jakarta.apache.org`. Two main discussion lists exist for Tomcat: a developer
list, which discusses the further development for the product and the maintenance
of the current code base, and a user list, which discusses Tomcat applications, details
configuration pitfalls, and helps users with less experience in Tomcat. Because the
discussion at the developer list is always at a higher level than the discussion at the user
list, stick to the user list unless you are seriously thinking about joining the developer
group. This list has a very rich archive, so it's always a good idea to take few minutes
to check that before you post something to the list.

Tomcat is a voluntary effort. Bugs found in Tomcat can be reported to
`http://znutar.cortexity.com:8888/`. This will obviously help make the evolution
of this product faster and better.

B

Allaire JRun

THIS APPENDIX COVERS THE ALLAIRE JRUN application server from Allaire
(http://www.allaire.com). JRun has been around for quite a while, first providing
servlet engine capabilities and, since version 3.0, acting as a J2EE application server.
The current version, recently released, is version 3.1.

Introducing JRun

Originally, JRun was released as a servlet engine, the term used at the time to designate a program that provides servlets in a runtime environment. It was compliant with
the Servlet 2.0 and 2.1 API. JRun earned its creator, LiveSoftware, a solid reputation
for delivering a production-quality Servlet platform. LiveSoftware's policy of "no
charge for development version" gathered early sympathy of the then-flourishing
servlet development community. Before the release of JRun 3.0, Allaire, the creators
of ColdFusion, acquired LiveSoftware.

Currently, JRun is not a servlet container. Since version 3.0, JRun became a full
application server with support for the Java 2 Enterprise Edition API. It supports the
web-related Servlet and JSP APIs, but under JRun you can configure both web applications and EJBs.

As expected, JRun comes with lots of Allaire technology.

Obtaining and Installing JRun

JRun can be downloaded for development and evaluation, and it can be purchased from the Allaire web site at http://www.allaire.com/Products/JRun. You can choose to try it and download the time-limited, fully featured trial version. It comes as a self-extractable file. Follow these steps to install it under Windows NT/2000:

1. **Serial number**—A dialog screen appears requesting a serial number. What distinguishes a trial version, a production version, and a development version is the serial number. If you chose the trial version, a trial serial number will be sent to you so that you can unlock the server for a limited time. You then can use it in heavy load testing. If you purchased a license, a full-unlock serial number will be sent to you, and you will have the server fully available. If you don't enter a serial number, the server will install in developer version. This will unleash the full power of JRun, but it is limited to a maximum of five simultaneous connections.

2. **Location**—Choose where to install the server.

3. **Install option**—Choose whether to do a full install, a minimum install, or a custom install. The full install is recommended for development. The minimum install is recommended for production servers. The custom install shows another dialog box with additional options available. This is a usual install dialog box for Windows users.

4. **Folder name**—Select the folder name. This is another usual install dialog box.

5. **Installation on Windows NT/2000 as a service**—This is essential in a production server, but it is not recommended in a development installation, where there's a permanent need to restart the server.

6. **Runtime environment**—The install program locates the installed JVMs/JREs. You can either select one from the list or select Other and enter the location.

7. **Admin server port**—Enter the port number that you want the admin server to respond to. You'll learn more about the admin server in the following section, "Understanding JRun."

8. **Admin password**—Enter the password for the management console. You'll learn more about the management console in the following section, "Understanding JRun."

At this stage, if JRun is to be used in a standalone manner, as an autonomous web server, the installation is complete. That is not always the case, though. Production web servers such as Apache or Netscape servers are much more efficient in serving static content than most of the servlet containers. In that case, it might be better to have JRun attached to the production web server and let it serve only the servlets and JSPs needed.

This can be done using a connector module configured as a web server extension (for instance, ISAPI redirectors for IIS, or mod_* for Apache). The next few steps enable you to configure the connection with a hypothetical Apache server:

1. **Server to connect**—Which server will be connected to the external web server? You can select any of the servers defined on your JRun installation. You'll learn more about JRun servers in the following section, "Understanding JRun."

2. **External web server**—Specify the product and version of the web server that you want to connect to, as well as the platform on which it is installed. As of this writing, the supported web servers are the Apache Web Server, Netscape's Enterprise and Fastrack servers, Microsoft's Internet Information Server (IIS) and Personal Web Server (PWS), and Website Pro and Zeus Web Server. The web server must be stopped before you proceed because the connector wizard will change configuration settings on the server.

3. **JRun module address**—Specify the IP address and port that the JRun connector module will listen to.

4. **Location**—This step is specific to the web server that you want to connect. If you've chosen Apache, you must supply the location of the httpd.conf file. On the other hand, if you have chosen IIS, you must supply the location of IIS scripts directory and decide whether the ISAPI filter to be installed will be treated as a global filter.

5. **Completed installation**—Assuming that you chose Apache in Step 2, at this stage you have completed the installation. Restart both Apache, which is required, and JRun, just to give it a fresh start.

That's it. Requests to web applications residing on JRun that arrive on Apache will be routed to and served by the specific server in JRun.

Understanding JRun

JRun is not a single-server product. *Server* here can be understood as *container* was in Tomcat. Within a single installation of JRun, you can create multiple servers. Maybe you need to do it because of specific configurations that your web application requires, or maybe because you want an application running with its own JVM.

When installed, JRun offers you two servers preinstalled. One of them is the default server, where you can deploy web applications, EJB applications, and so on. It is the default servlet container.

The other is the admin server, which runs JRun Management Console (JMC) and other administrative applications. The JMC is a web application that controls all the configuration files in JRun and provides entry points to restart the several servers possibly running from a single console. (See Figure B.1.) From within it, you can manage web applications, EJBs, and J2EE applications.

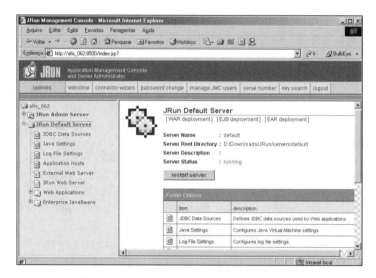

Figure B.1 The JRun Management Console.

Many features incorporated in the servlet technology were originally part of JRun, in some form. Many ideas were further developed into standard technologies—tag libraries are a good example. JRun has had a number of tag extensions—not custom tags, but proprietary technology—since early versions.

Deploying Web Applications Under JRun

To deploy a web application under JRun, you use the Management Console. You must follow these steps:

1. Open the JMC. Enter the JRun Management Console and select the server to which you will deploy the web application. On the left panel, choose the server name and then choose Web Applications. Don't expand the service tree further. On the panel that appears on the right (see Figure B.2), choose Deploy an Application.

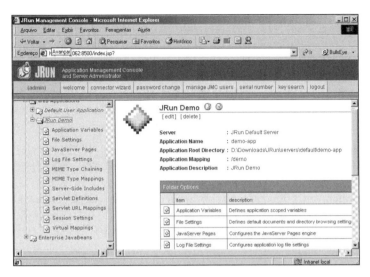

Figure B.2   The JMC server configuration.

2. Provide the parameters required on the panel (see Figure B.3):

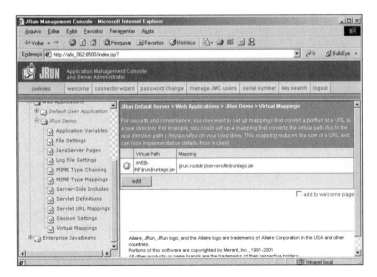

Figure B.3   Providing parameters via the JMC.

- **Servlet .war file or directory**—Give the complete path to the .war file that you want to deploy.

- **JRun server name**—Select the name of the server that you want to deploy the application to. The servers on the installation will appear in a list box.

- **Application name**—Enter a name for the application. This property will later be associated to a context in the servlet environment. There can't be two applications with the same name under the same server.

- **Application host**—If you are deploying this application in a multihost environment, select the host where the application will reside. If not, select All Hosts, which is the default option.

- **Application URL**—Give a forward slash–prefixed URL to which the application will be mapped and further accessed.

- **Application deploy directory**—Specify the root directory to deploy the application. This will also be the document root directory.

3. After providing the information required, press the Deploy button. The .war file is expanded according to your previous settings. Resources are put in place, and the web application main panel comes back. Then press the Refresh button on the browser, and you will see your application in the list at the right.

4. Restart the server under which the application was deployed.

5. Test access from another browser.

Further Information

Refer to the Allaire web site for further information on the product, beta releases, and service packs. Allaire maintains a forum to discuss common issues that JRun users find. The Allaire web site also offers a rich developer area where you can find technical articles on developing for and running JRun for performance, tips, code, links to external resources, and the developer exchange, where Java and Cold Fusion developers can publish their code to the JRun community.

C

Orion

THIS APPENDIX COVERS THE ORION APPLICATION SERVER and presents the product, shows how to install it, and discusses its main features and capabilities. At the time of this writing, Orion was at version 1.4.5.

Introducing Orion

The Orion application server is a commercial J2EE container offered by the Swedish company Evermind Data (http://www.orionserver.com). It implements the following technologies that make the J2EE architecture:

- **EJB**—This product is not only a web container, but it also offers a full EJB 1.1–compliant container with partial support for the EJB 2.0 draft.

- **Servlets and JSP**—Orion provides a full Servlet 2.2 and JSP 1.1–compliant container and partial support for the Servlet 2.3 draft.

- **JDBC**—Orion manages JDBC 2.0 connections and allows complete management and predefined configuration for a number of database products, including Oracle, PostgreSQL, HypersonicSQL, and others.

- **JNDI**—The server uses JNDI to query names and directory services using the JNDI 1.2 API.

- **JTA**—The server has resources to control JTA 1.0.1 transactions.
- **JMS**—Orion comes with the Orion JMS server, which is a JMS 1.0–compliant messaging server.
- **XML/XSL**—Orion has extensive resources to work with XML and related technologies. It comes with Apache products Xerces XML parser and Xalan XSL processor.
- **HTTP**—Orion comes with a production-level, HTTPS-capable web server that can be configured for clustering and load balancing. It also accepts SSI and comes with language processors for PHP, Perl, and the CGI protocol, among other resources.

The Orion application server also provides a comprehensive tag library available for the Orion developer. It comes with a distribution of the Java database HypersoniqSQL, which is an Open Source relational database distribution.

Obtaining and Installing Orion

The Orion server is available for download from the Orion home page at `<http://www.orionserver.com>` in two versions:

- As a freely downloadable fully featured developer version that can be used for development and in noncommercial installations
- As a commercial version that can be purchased online at the site

To have Orion installed, follow the next steps:

1. Download the latest package from the Orion server web site at `<http://www.orionserver.com>`. The package is distributed in a zip archive file called orionXXX.zip. The XXX represents the most current version. At the time of this writing, it was orion1_4_5.zip.

2. Unzip the orion zip file. The /orion directory will be created under the path that you used to unzip the distribution.

3. Copy the tools.jar file from your installation of the latest JDK to the /orion directory. This file can be found under the JDK's /lib directory.

4. Orion uses the default port 80. Make sure that you don't have another server using that port, or there will be conflict. Follow the documentation to change the port used. The documentation kit can be downloaded independently from the basic package at `<http://www.orionserver.com>`.

5. To start Orion, use this command:

   ```
   java -jar orion.jar
   ```

   The server then outputs a message stating that it has been initialized.

6. To test the server, access the server with a browser. For instance, if the server is running at the local machine, `http://localhost/` will show the Orion index page.

The critical steps in the installation routine are steps 3 and 4. Forgetting to have the tools.jar file copied into the /orion directory will hammer the installation because the compiling functions won't be present to the JSP container, for instance. And if another httpd service is leasing port 80, it will be unavailable to Orion, making it work as if the installation was unsuccessfull.

Orion Configuration

Orion can be configured via a number of XML documents used to parameterize the product and to declare web and generic J2EE applications.

The main file involved in the configuration is the Server.xml file. This file has a completely different meaning in Orion than it does in Tomcat. Here it is a global server-configuration file that points to the configuration files of a number of services offered by the server. The server-configuration file defines the following:

- Global application settings. The global application in an Orion server is the application considered as the default in the server environment. It is considered a parent application for the other ones.

- Application settings. These settings define application-specific information, such as parameterization and the location of application-deployment files.

- Logging, concurrency, clustering, and transaction settings. These settings define several server-specific parameters and control the overall server behavior, including the logging policy.

- Java compiler settings. These enable you to configure which Java compiler to use and to configure a path to the library that implements the compiler.

- J2EE support servers configuration settings. These setting define the path to a JDBC datasources description file, as well as the configuration of the JMS, JNDI, and mail servers.

The default-web-site.xml file describes a web site hosted in the web layer of the Orion application server. It describes where in a server or in a server cluster the web application is located, gives a path to it, assigns a web virtual hostname to it, tells whether it is secure (uses HTTPS and SSL), logging, and other parameters.

The principals.xml defines users and groups in the context of a server.

Other services are defined in auxiliary configuration files. The data-sources.xml file defines JDBC datasource settings. JMS.xml and RMI.xml contain parameters for the respective message and distributed object services. The load_balancer.xml file defines clustering parameters.

There are also Orion-specific deployment descriptor files for Orion applications deployment that can be generated automatically, as well as J2EE standard files. Check the documentation, which is available online and for download at the Orion server web site.

Other Features

It is important to note that Orion is not a servlet container, but a complete J2EE container implementation. The focus on Orion applications is on EJB components. However, it provides a complete web server implementation, including SSL support.

You can develop web components (servlets, JSP pages, and tag libraries) with Orion. A nice feature is the autocompilation of servlets. When this feature is enabled, it is enough to develop a servlet in a text editor and place it on the correct path. When it is requested for the first time, it will be compiled in a similar way to what is done with JSP pages.

For EJB development, Orion supports container-managed persistence quite nicely.

D

MySQL

THIS APPENDIX COVERS THE DATABASE SUPPORT that was presented in the examples in Chapters 2–10. This is a very short introduction to the components used, covering the database to the auxiliary classes. This is a basic three-level structure: a database, a number of support classes, and a JDBC 2.0–compliant driver.

MySQL Database

MySQL is a free open source database-management system from MySQL AB that is continuously gaining support from the market. It is attracting the developer community because of its easiness and lightness. In addition, it is being established as a de facto standard on the Internet, supporting web sites worldwide. Currently, MySQL is at version 3.23, the latest stable production version. MySQL is available for download at `http://mysql.com/downloads` in a vast number of platforms—specifically, a number of flavors of UNIX, with several distributions of Linux among them, and a version suitable for the Windows platform. Basically, MySQL is licensed under the terms of the GNU General Public License. For more information on MySQL licensing policies, check `http://www.mysql.com/documentation/mysql/bychapter/manual_Licensing_and_Support.html#Licensing_and_Support`.

MySQL is a competitive multithreaded and multiuser relational database-management system, with excellent performance and a number of tools and APIs available to the developer—both are part of the core project, such as the C API, and those that have been contributed by third parties, such as the excellent mm.jdbc Java JDBC API driver. MySQL is quite flexible, presenting a fair implementation of the ANSI SQL92 and the ODBC SQL standards with a number of extensions. Some remarkable absences, such as stored procedures, are already on the TODO list, so we can expect a very exciting development for this product in the foreseeable future.

In addition, a lot of literature about MySQL exists. As with any database-management product, productively working with MySQL requires a deep understanding of the product, whether for developing applications or for administering a database configuration. For an excellent reference to MySQL, check out the book MySQL, by Paul Dubois (New Riders Publishing), which is a complete reference on the subject.

MySQL and This Book

To get many of the examples in this book up and running, you will need the MySQL database. Refer to `http://mysql.com/documentation` for information on how to install the product for your preferred platform.

The MySQL product consists of a number of executables that constitute the MySQL server and administration utilities. To create the databases used in the examples, run the scripts provided on the book's web site (`www.newriders.com`) with the mySQL utility, as follows:

```
mysql JSPBOOK < jspBookExamples.sql
```

This creates the JSPBOOK database on the current mySQL installation and loads all the example data. Use `mySQLShow` to test the results:

```
mysqlshow JSPBOOK
```

This produces a list of the tables in the JSPBOOK database. After that, you are ready to run the example code.

The JDBC Driver

To run the example servlets and JSPs, you need an adequate MySql jdbc driver. The mm.jdbc MySql jdbc driver offers extensive support for JDBC 2.0 for most considered features. The mm.mysql JDBC driver is a free open source project hosted by sourceforge, at `http://mmmysql.sourceforge.net`. It can be downloaded directly from the project's page, and it is released under the terms of the GNU LGPL license. The driver is currently at version 2.0.4, which is considered a stable version. Performance data for the mm driver can be seen at `http://mmmysql.sourceforge.net/performance`.

To install the driver, just explode the compressed file on your local machine and deploy the mm.mysql-2.0.1-bin.jar archive file on your web application's class path.

In the case of the examples, you may deploy that file in the /WEB-INF/lib directory of the jspBook context under Tomcat.

The Poolman Object Pool

It is now a very standard technique to use connection pools to speed up JDBC connections on server-side Java web applications. Many products providing this functionality are on the market, including many freeware add-ons, many products embedded in application servers, and many products that are part of JDBC driver implementations. The Poolman is a free, open source Java object pool-management software that we used in the examples presented. It is now under the SourceForge open source initiative and can be obtained from `http://sourceforge.net/projects/poolman`.

At the time of this writing, Poolman is at version 1.4.1, which is considered a stable, production-ready version. It is not dedicated to JDBC connections, and it is not a database-connection pool; it is an object pool. This means that Poolman can pool any kind of Java object and provide many of these pools simultaneously. This is a very powerful resource. In some scenarios, you will really need these pools available—for instance, to implement a robust web application controller with strong performance when the number of requests delegated to request processors increases. (Request processors are the classes to which the controller will delegate the processing of a request.) In that case, the longer the request processors are kept loaded and ready to run, the better.

Downloading and Installing

Poolman can be downloaded from the project's page at sourceforge. To install it, unzip (or unzip/untar, if you are using UNIX) the distribution on your local machine. You will find a POOLMAN_HOME/lib directory with three files:

- The example poolman.props file
- The Poolman.jar archive file, which contains all the classes that make the product, and Sun's distribution for the JDBC 2.0 standard extensions
- The jdbc2_0-stdext.jar archive file

To use Poolman, you will have to put both jar files in the class path of your application. In the case of the book examples, deploy both of them, along with the poolmn.props file, on the /WEB-INF/lib directory of the jspBook web application context, under Tomcat.

Poolman and Databases

Poolman is also quite flexible for JDBC connection pooling. There are three main scenarios to follow in this case:

- **SQLUtil**—SQLUtil is a utility class that can perform SQL operations against a database, returning arrays of Hashtables as a result. Those results are cached by query and are refreshed at a configurable interval. The access parameters are obtained from the poolman.props file.

- **The Poolman driver**—The second scenario is to use the Poolman JDBC driver. It will refer to a database declared in the poolman.props file, and it is used as an ordinary JDBC driver.

- **The Poolman data source**—This is compliant with JDBC 2.0 data sources. A Poolman data source to a database can be put on a JNDI naming and directory service and can supply database connections on the fly.

The examples in the book all use the third scenario for the sake of simplicity and because it is the preferred way to access resources under the J2EE platform. Check out the jspBook_poolman.props file, which is available at the book resources web site, to get the configuration parameters for the examples in the book.

Mapping Servlet—
JSP Objects

THIS APPENDIX PROVIDES THE READER WHO is a novice to servlet/JSP Web application development with a reference mapping between the objects in the Servlet API 2.3 and their counterparts and references in the JSP page environment. Table E.1 presents this mapping.

Table E.1 **Mapping Servlet to JSP Objects**

Servlet Objects	JSP Objects
ServletConfig—To access the ServletContext inside a servlet, it is imperative to access the config information.	config—This is available at the page level. This variable is not frequently used.
ServletContext—This is available to servlet programmers via a function call: getServletContext() from the ServletConfig.	application—JSP designers can use this implicit object and access the context information directly.
ServletRequest	request
ServletResponse	response—This also is not frequently used.

continues

Table E.1 **Continued**

Servlet Objects	**JSP Objects**
`HttpSession`—This is available from the request object passed to the `Service` method, via the `getSession(boolean)` method call.	`session`
`HttpServletResponse.getWriter`—The `out` object implements a different class.	`out`—This JSPWriter instance provides the output streaming of the text generated by the JSP.
There is no counterpart. Servlet authors must refer to a number ofclasses that together provide part of theinformation that the `PageContext` classgathers. Such objects are the `ServletContext`, the `HttpSession`, the`HttpServletRequest` and `HttpServletResponse`, and the `output writer` objects. Even in that case, there is no counterpart for the page scope at the servlet. So, this concept and everything associated with it is void of meaning in the servlet world.	`pageContext`—This implicit variable is responsible for maintaining the execution context of a JSP page, such as initializing the other implicit variables, managing the page scope, accessing the page scope attributes, and so on.
There is no counterpart. Servlet authors must treat exceptions in the conventional Java way.	`exception`—This implicit object encapsulates the Throwable that was generated in the error condition. It is available in error pages.

The Apache Software License, Version 1.1

Copyright © 1999–2001 The Apache Software Foundation.
All rights reserved.

Redistribution and use in source and binary forms, with or without modification, are permitted provided that the following conditions are met:

1. Redistributions of source code must retain the above copyright notice, this list of conditions and the following disclaimer.

2. Redistributions in binary form must reproduce the above copyright notice, this list of conditions and the following disclaimer in the documentation and/or other materials provided with the distribution.

3. The end-user documentation included with the redistribution, if any, must include the following acknowledgement:

   "This product includes software developed by the Apache Software Foundation (http://www.apache.org/)." Alternately, this acknowledgement may appear in the software itself, if and wherever such third-party acknowledgements normally appear.

4. The names "The Jakarta Project", "Struts", and "Apache Software Foundation" must not be used to endorse or promote products derived from this software without prior written permission. For written permission, please contact apache@apache.org.

5. Products derived from this software may not be called "Apache" nor may "Apache" appear in their names without prior written permission of the Apache Group.

THIS SOFTWARE IS PROVIDED "AS IS" AND ANY EXPRESSED OR IMPLIED WARRANTIES, INCLUDING, BUT NOT LIMITED TO, THE IMPLIED WARRANTIES OF MERCHANTABILITY AND FITNESS FOR A PARTICULAR PURPOSE ARE DISCLAIMED. IN NO EVENT SHALL THE APACHE SOFTWARE FOUNDATION OR ITS CONTRIBUTORS BE LIABLE FOR ANY DIRECT, INDIRECT, INCIDENTAL, SPECIAL, EXEMPLARY, OR CONSEQUENTIAL DAMAGES (INCLUDING, BUT NOT LIMITED TO, PROCUREMENT OF SUBSTITUTE GOODS OR SERVICES; LOSS OF USE, DATA, OR PROFITS; OR BUSINESS INTERRUPTION) HOWEVER CAUSED AND ON ANY THEORY OF LIABILITY, WHETHER IN CONTRACT, STRICT LIABILITY, OR TORT (INCLUDING NEGLIGENCE OR OTHER-WISE) ARISING IN ANY WAY OUT OF THE USE OF THIS SOFTWARE, EVEN IF ADVISED OF THE POSSIBILITY OF SUCH DAMAGE.

==

This software consists of voluntary contributions made by many individuals on behalf of the Apache Software Foundation. For more information on the Apache Software Foundation, please see http://www.apache.org/.

Index

Symbols

A

F

G

H

I

K-L

Q-R

S

HOW TO CONTACT US

VISIT OUR WEB SITE

WWW.NEWRIDERS.COM

On our web site, you'll find information about our other books, authors, tables of contents, and book errata. You will also find information about book registration and how to purchase our books, both domestically and internationally.

EMAIL US

Contact us at: **nrfeedback@newriders.com**

- If you have comments or questions about this book
- To report errors that you have found in this book
- If you have a book proposal to submit or are interested in writing for New Riders
- If you are an expert in a computer topic or technology and are interested in being a technical editor who reviews manuscripts for technical accuracy

Contact us at: **nreducation@newriders.com**

- If you are an instructor from an educational institution who wants to preview New Riders books for classroom use. Email should include your name, title, school, department, address, phone number, office days/hours, text in use, and enrollment, along with your request for desk/examination copies and/or additional information.

Contact us at: **nrmedia@newriders.com**

- If you are a member of the media who is interested in reviewing copies of New Riders books. Send your name, mailing address, and email address, along with the name of the publication or web site you work for.

BULK PURCHASES/CORPORATE SALES

If you are interested in buying 10 or more copies of a title or want to set up an account for your company to purchase directly from the publisher at a substantial discount, contact us at 800-382-3419 or email your contact information to corpsales@pearsontechgroup.com. A sales representative will contact you with more information.

WRITE TO US

New Riders Publishing
201 W. 103rd St.
Indianapolis, IN 46290-1097

CALL/FAX US

Toll-free (800) 571-5840
If outside U.S. (317) 581-3500
Ask for New Riders
FAX: (317) 581-4663

VOICES THAT MATTER

RELATED NEW RIDERS TITLES

Inside XML

Steven Holzner

Inside XML is a foundation book that covers both the Microsoft and non-Microsoft approach to XML programming. It covers in detail the hot aspects of XML, such as DTD's vs. XML Schemas, CSS, XSL, XSLT, Xlinks, Xpointers, XHTML, RDF, CDF, parsing XML in Perl and Java, and much more.

ISBN: 0735710201
1100 pages
US$49.99

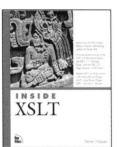

Inside XSLT

Steven Holzner

In order to work with XML fully you need to be up to speed with XSLT, and this is the book to get you there. Covering everything from creating Xpath expressions to transforming XML to HTML, *Inside XSLT* will have you heading straight down the road to programming efficiency.

ISBN: 0735711364
600 pages
US$49.99

ebXML: The New Global Standard for Doing Business Over the Internet

Alan Kotok, David R.R. Webber

To create an e-commerce initiative, managers need to understand that XML is the technology that will take them there. Companies understand that in order to achieve a successful Internet presence they need an e-commerce methodology implemented. Many department managers (the actual people who have to design, build, and execute the plan) don't know where to begin. *ebXML* will take them there.

ISBN: 0735711178
340 pages
US$34.99

XML, XSLT, Java, and JSP: A Case Study in Developing a Web Application

Westy Rockwell

A practical, hands-on experience in building web applications based on XML and Java technologies, this book is unique because it teaches the technologies by using them to build a web chat project throughout the book. The project is explained in great detail, after the reader is shown how to get and install the necessary tools to be able to customize this project and build other web applications.

ISBN: 0735710899
760 pages with CD-ROM
US$49.99

Perl for the Web

Chris Radcliff

Build quick-loading, high-performance, next-generation websites with the help of this book, which provides all the tools and techniques you need to work in Perl on the web.

ISBN: 0735711143
400 pages
U$44.99

C++ XML

Fabio Arciniegas

The demand for robust solutions is at an all-time high. Developers and programmers are asking the question, "How do I get the power performance found with C++ integrated into my web applications?" Fabio Arciniegas knows how. He has created the best way to bring C++ to the web through development with XML, and in this book, he shares the secrets developers and programmers worldwide are searching for.

ISBN: 073571052X
330 pages with CD-ROM
US$39.99

Solutions from experts you know and trust.

www.informit.com

New Riders has partnered with **InformIT.com** to bring technical information to your desktop. Drawing on New Riders authors and reviewers to provide additional information on topics you're interested in, **InformIT.com** has free, in-depth information you won't find anywhere else.

- **Master the skills you need, when you need them**

- **Call on resources from some of the best minds in the industry**

- **Get answers when you need them, using InformIT's comprehensive library or live experts online**

- **Go above and beyond what you find in New Riders books, extending your knowledge**

As an **InformIT** partner, **New Riders** has shared the wisdom and knowledge of our authors with you online. Visit **InformIT.com** to see what you're missing.

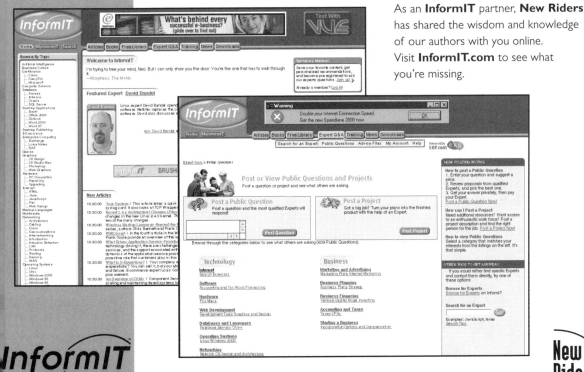

Publishing
the Voices
that Matter

OUR BOOKS

OUR AUTHORS

SUPPORT

web development | **graphics & design** | **server technology** | **certification**

NEWS/EVENTS

PRESS ROOM

EDUCATORS

ABOUT US

CONTACT US

WRITE/REVIEW

You already know that New Riders brings you the Voices that Matter.

But what does that mean? It means that New Riders brings you the

Voices that challenge your assumptions, take your talents to the next

level, or simply help you better understand the complex technical world

we're all navigating.

Visit **www.newriders.com** to find:

- ▶ Never before published chapters
- ▶ Sample chapters and excerpts
- ▶ Author bios
- ▶ Contests
- ▶ Up-to-date industry event information
- ▶ Book reviews
- ▶ Special offers
- ▶ Info on how to join our User Group program
- ▶ Inspirational galleries where you can submit your own masterpieces
- ▶ Ways to have your Voice heard

New Riders

WWW.NEWRIDERS.COM

Colophon

The image on the cover of this book, captured by photographer Sexto Sol of Mexico, is that of the Iguaçu Falls in Brazil and Argentina. The Iguaçu (reads like *Iguassu* with an accent on the *u*) Falls, along with the Victoria Falls in Zimbabwe and Niagara Falls in the United States and Canada, are called "sekai 3-dai taki," meaning the three largest falls in the world. This image was particularly chosen for this book because it is found at the home place of our author, Wellington L.S. da Silva.

In Iguaçu, the 275 individual cascades and waterfalls are more than 3km wide and 80m high, which makes them wider than Victoria Falls, higher than Niagara Falls, and more beautiful than either. The word *Iguaçu* means "great water" in local language, and the deepest part of the falls is called "Garganta do Diabo," or "Devil's Throat."

In addition to the great beauty of these falls is their thunderous roar that can be heard from miles away. As Vince Purcell, sound recordist for *The Greatest Places*, put it, "It's like white noise on a million televisions with the volume turned all the way up!"

This book was written and edited in Microsoft Word and was laid out in QuarkXpress. The fonts used in the body text are Bembo and MCPdigital. It was printed on 50# Husky Offset Smooth paper from R.R. Donnelley & Sons in Crawfordsville, Indiana. Prepress consisted of PostScript computer-to-plate technology (filmless process). The cover was printed at Moore Langen Printing in Terre Haute, Indiana, on 12pt, coated on one side.